O's Best Advice Ever!

Make Over Your Life with Oprah and Friends

Including Dr. Oz, Bob Greene, Suze Orman, Dr. Phil, Martha Beck, and more

From the Editors of **O, THE OPRAH MAGAZINE**

O's Best Advice Ever!

Make Over Your Life with Oprah and Friends

Including Dr. Oz, Bob Greene, Suze Orman, Dr. Phil, Martha Beck, and more

From the Editors of **O, THE OPRAH MAGAZINE**

Oxmoor House®

contents

Martha Beck

Valerie Monroe

HERE WE GO!

7 INTRODUCTION BY OPRAH

LIVING YOUR BEST LIFE

10 WHAT I KNOW FOR SURE

24 THE O INTERVIEWS

THE EXPERTS

94 LIVING A HEALTHY LIFE

136 LIVING INTELLIGENTLY

182 LIVING THOUGHTFULLY

242 LIVING BEAUTIFULLY

THE FAREWELL SEASON

300 25 YEARS OF *THE OPRAH WINFREY SHOW*

315 ABOUT THE CONTRIBUTORS   **316** PHOTOGRAPHY AND ART CREDITS   **317** INDEX

Bob Greene

Oprah Winfrey

Dr. Phil McGraw

Suze Orman

Nate Berkus

Dr. Mehmet Oz

Lisa Kogan

Adam Glassman

I FIRST MET DR. PHIL MCGRAW during one of the most challenging times in my life. I was on trial in 1998 after allegedly defaming the beef industry. Dr. Phil, who served as a consultant to my legal team, was as good at doling out the unvarnished truth as he was at delivering a clever line. I left Amarillo, Texas, not just with a victory for freedom of speech, but with something I couldn't wait to pass on to my viewers—Dr. Phil's tell-it-like-it-is advice.

Even now when I discover something great, I love to share it. That's why we've rounded up the very best wisdom and inspiration from my most trusted experts. Love a straight-talking friend as much as I do? Here, you'll find plenty of Dr. Phil at his finest, and that's just the beginning. In our big reunion in book form, I've invited everyone I've come to rely on—Suze Orman, Dr. Oz, Nate Berkus, Bob Greene, and Martha Beck, to name a few. Then we took the festivities up a notch by pulling together the best advice from the last decade from my friends at *O, The Oprah Magazine*—Adam Glassman's timeless fashion staples ("10 Items You Can Never Go Wrong With," page 257), Val Monroe's thoughts on turning 60 ("Hitting a Milestone?," page 280), and how Lisa Kogan discovers a handful of surprises in some pretty unexpected places ("Lisa Kogan Tells All," page 233).

One year when I was complaining about having to go back to a hectic work schedule after a relaxing summer vacation, comedian Jerry Seinfeld said something I've always remembered: "It's yours to design," he told me (read our full conversation on page 56). That's not just my privilege, but everyone's. We've each been given the extraordinary opportunity to sketch out the lives we most want to live. Jerry's comment came at just the right juncture for me—rather than running myself ragged that season, I actually built in some recovery time. Did that plan stick? Not every day. But what did stay with me was the message—creating your best life begins with making the best possible choices. I know that for sure.

After hosting my show for 25 seasons, it turns out that I've learned a few other things for sure—everything from tuning in to your gut instincts (page 304) to handling life's shake-ups, teensy and gigantic (page 307). So to celebrate the show's quarter-century run, we've assembled my greatest life lessons, each gleaned from my time on the air. Like this one on page 310: "It's more fun to give than to receive." Don't you think so? I still do, and I'm hoping this collection becomes your gift to yourself—one that you can read, savor, and return to in the years ahead.

LIVING

YOUR

O BEST LIFE

CHAPTER 1

What I Know for Sure

OPRAH | 10

CHAPTER 2

The O Interviews

OPRAH | 24

WHAT I KNOW FOR SURE: 2011

"Once you clarify your purpose
for doing something, the
way to do it becomes clear."

At first it was scary, the idea of moving on and undertaking a big new challenge. I wavered not over *Should I end the show?* (I knew it was time) but over *What to do next?* Sit back, relax, and rest on my laurels? Cruise the world? Garden and read for 12 months? Have lunch with friends every day? Or take what I've been blessed to build over 25 years and use it to keep building, reaching, and teaching?

I chose the latter because, as I have said before, it is my calling. (Though I confess that I hesitated briefly, in the midst of an especially exhausting week, and reconsidered becoming one of the ladies who lunch and lounge. All my friends said, "Don't do it. You'd be miserable without a mission." They were right.)

In July I read a *Vanity Fair* article about the making of Michael Jackson's album *Thriller.* The piece quoted some of Michael's friends saying that one of his biggest mistakes was never realizing that *Thriller*'s becoming the number-one-selling album in history was a once-in-a-lifetime phenomenon. And because he didn't realize that, he spent the rest of his life chasing that success.

Reading that was a big aha for me. The reason I had wavered was fear: I was afraid I wouldn't be able to duplicate what I've done. But as I thought about Michael Jackson, I began to see that not only can you not duplicate success, you're not supposed to. Every new endeavor is created out of the quality of the energy you bring to it and is meant to be its own thing.

So here I go. I'm in the countdown to the end of the great phenomenon of my life. Headed off to launch a network of shows intended to do what *The Oprah Winfrey Show* and *O, The Oprah Magazine* have done for years: inspire and entertain.

Everything you've ever done prepares you for all that you can do and be. So I move forward to start a new chapter with the lessons I've learned and the strength I've gained. OWN, the Oprah Winfrey Network, debuted January 1, 2011; in its kickoff year, we planned more than 600 hours of new programs. To fill the time 24/7/365, you need close to 9,000. We have a lot of work ahead.

You can see why I hesitated for a moment. Do I really want to take this on? But the launch was just the beginning of what will eventually be a channel filled with creative, meaningful, and mindful programming.

What I know for sure: Fear comes from uncertainty. Once you clarify your purpose for doing something, the way to do it becomes clear.

Let this be the year you release your fears about what you can achieve. Know for sure what you want and be willing to give yourself what you need to get it.

Cheers to new beginnings!

WHAT I KNOW FOR SURE: 2010

"Your life's journey is about becoming more of who you are."

My entire life is a miracle. And so is yours. That I know for sure.

No matter how you came to be—whether you were wanted or "an accident" (as I was labeled for many years)—your being here to read these words is awesome.

I say that not knowing the details of your life. What I do know is that every person carries her own story of hope and sorrow, victory and loss, redemption, joy, and light.

Everyone has had their share of life lessons. How well you learn from them is up to you.

When you choose to see the world as a classroom, you understand that all experiences are here to teach you something about yourself. And that your life's journey is about becoming more of who you are. Another miracle: We all get to share in the journey.

The hardest experiences are often the ones that teach us the most. I say this having just gotten off the phone with my lawyers discussing how to handle two pending lawsuits. The first question I asked them was, "What is this suit really about, and what am I supposed to learn from it?" Only when I can perceive what the real lesson is can I make the best decision—and grow from the experience.

After everything that's happened to me in 57 years on this Earth, what I'm most proud of is that I remain open to evolving. I know that every physical encounter has a metaphysical meaning. And I'm open to seeing it all.

I want to keep doing better and being better at who I am until I fulfill the promise of the miracle that is this life. **O**

"Having the best *things* is no substitute for having the best *life*."

The cover of my January 2009 magazine—the two versions of me standing side by side, one overweight, one not—stirred a lot of emotion. Thank you all for your avalanche of support and willingness to share your own truth. I had the confidence to do that cover because I knew I wasn't alone in feeling frustrated and embarrassed about my weight. An estimated 66 percent of American adults are either overweight or obese. And almost nobody's happy about it.

To those who say you've made peace with your size, I say good for you. For me, this is not about cosmetics. Or looking good in a pair of jeans. It's about optimal health, optimal living. A friend wrote me this e-mail after reading the issue: "Here's how I see your weight—it is your smoke detector. And we're all burning up the best part of our lives."

I'd never thought of it that way before, but it was an aha moment for me: The weight is an indicator warning, a flashing light blaring my disconnection from the center of myself. That's what out of balance really means: how far you've strayed, how distant you are from that which is sacred and holy.

What I know for sure now is that for me weight is a spiritual issue, not a food issue. Marianne Williamson struck a nerve when she sent this e-mail: "Your weight is really an invitation to your best life."

All these years of diets doomed to fail, I thought weight was the barrier.

Years ago I coauthored a book with Bob Greene called *Make the Connection.* The title was his idea. Even while writing my part, which involved sharing my frustrated journal entries about being fat (I was 237 pounds when Bob and I met), I would often say to him, "Remind me again; what's the connection?"

I did learn from him that my overeating wasn't about potato chips, that I needed to peel back the layers of my addiction to food and figure out what was eating me. Obviously, I didn't peel deeply enough.

Only now do I get, get, *get* it! The connection is loving, honoring, and protecting everything about yourself. Bob has often said to me, "Your weight is ultimately tied to your feelings of unworthiness." For 15 years, I vehemently disagreed, saying, "Listen, Bob Greene, I'm not one of those people who think they don't deserve what they have. I've worked hard for everything I own."

But as I move along the spiritual path to permanently resolving and managing the weight issue, I now see that a sense of unworthiness can come in many forms.

I've been an overachiever since I was 3 years old. Achieving to prove my worthiness.

Many times we insist on having all the best things because that's the only way we can ensure "quality of life" for ourselves. I can neglect myself in every other way, but if I have the best watch or pocketbook or car or square footage, I get to tell myself I'm the best and how much I deserve to have even more of the best.

What I know for sure: Having the best *things* is no substitute for having the best *life.*

Whatever your challenge—overeating, overindulging in any substance or activity, the loss of a relationship, money, position—let it be an open door to your holiest revelations about yourself, an invitation to your best life. **O**

With Bob Greene on the show in January 2009.

WHAT I KNOW FOR SURE: 2008

"If you can get paid for doing what you love, every paycheck is a bonus."

At the show's post-Oscar celebration in Hollywood, 2007.

I've always had a great relationship with money, even when I barely had any to relate to. I never feared not having it and never obsessed about what I had.

Like everyone else, I can remember every salary I ever made. I suppose we remember because a salary helps define the value of our service—and, unfortunately, for some people the value they place on themselves.

I first realized I was not my salary when I was 15 and making 50 cents an hour babysitting Mrs. Ashberry's rowdy kids and cleaning up after she pulled nearly every outfit from her closet every time she got dressed. Her bedroom always looked like the end-of-the-day, last-call sale at Macy's, with shoes and brightly colored necklaces and dresses everywhere. Just before flitting out the door (without leaving any info as to where she was going or how she could be reached in case of emergency), she'd say, "Oh, by the way, dear, would you mind tidying up things a bit?"

Well, yes, of course I did mind, and the first time I "tidied up," I did such a great job, I thought surely she'd pay me extra when she saw how I cleaned not only her room but the kids' rooms, too.

She never did. So I moved on and found a job that would pay me more—a job where I thought my efforts would be appreciated. There was a five-and-dime whose name I've forgotten not far from my father's store. I got hired there for $1.50 an hour. My job was to keep things straight, stock shelves, fold socks, etc. I wasn't allowed to work the cash register or speak to customers. I hated it. Two hours in, I found myself counting the hours to lunch. Then how much longer before I was off for the day.

At 15 I knew in my soul this was no way to live, or make money. I was bored beyond anything I've ever felt before or since. I wasn't *allowed* to go near the cash register or talk to customers. So after three days, I quit and went to work in my father's store for no salary.

I didn't like working there, either, but at least I could talk to people and not feel like my spirit was being drained by the hour. Still, I knew that no matter how much my father wanted it to be, that store would not be a part of my future life.

By the time I was 17, I was working in radio, making $100 a week. I would have done it for free. And that's when I made my peace with money. I decided that no matter what job I ever did, I wanted that same feeling I got when I first started in radio—the feeling of *I love this so much, even if you didn't pay me I'd show up every day, on time and happy to be here.* I recognized then what I know now for sure: If you can get paid for doing what you love, every paycheck is a bonus.

For me, money has always been about an energy exchange, following the law of cause and effect. I give my energy to the work and in exchange am rewarded with a different form of energy—money. This in turn lets me acquire, create, and build other forms of energy, from the necessities of food and shelter to material possessions that enhance the quality of life to endeavors that help others reach their fullest potential.

All these many years later, I still know I am not my income. I am not the *lifestyle* my income can afford me.

I let money serve its purpose. But I don't live to serve money. I think that's why we have such a beautiful relationship. **O**

"It makes no difference how many peaks you reach if there was no pleasure in the climb."

I just came in from a hike up the mountain in back of my house in Hawaii. Funny thing about a mountain: It always looks easier to climb when you're at the foot of it. My goal was to reach the top of the tree line—about 3,000 feet up from my house—in less than an hour. I started out strong, with good intentions, two bottles of water, sunscreen, my hat, and my golden retrievers, Luke and Layla.

A mountain, I realized more than ever today, is one of the great metaphors for life, reminding you that:

1. Challenges are often more difficult than they seem at the outset.

2. An ascent that at first looks smooth turns out to have unseen dips and ridges and valleys.

3. The higher you climb, the thicker the weeds.

4. You need a clear vision of where you're going if you want to avoid getting disoriented by the clouds that roll in and block your view.

5. You have to be determined to make it to the top. Otherwise every slip, stumble, and fall (all of which happened to me today, within that first hour) will give you an excuse to turn around and head home.

But I made a decision: I was going to make it to the eucalyptus grove at the top, no matter how long it took me. So I slowed down and stopped trying to meet a self-imposed timeline, forgot about how far the top was, and just focused on one foot in front of the other. Breathe in. Breathe out.

The result was that each step became its own accomplishment, and I took the time to look at the view from every level. *Wow*, I thought, *I need to do this more often in the daily meshugas of my life.*

I've been so focused on getting to the next level, I haven't enjoyed enough of the view from where I am. Years are a blur to me, and that's not just because I'm starting my 22nd season of the show this September and have talked to thousands of guests along the way.

It's because when you live life in the fast lane, as I have for most of my career, you end up speeding through, just moving to the next thing, doing more and more and filling your schedule until there's no time even to *think* about what you're doing. And as busy as I am, I often look in wonder at those of you who do all that you do *and* raise children and prepare meals every day and run a household.

I bow to your endurance.

As we're all blessed to witness another season here on planet Earth, I hope you're reading these words and thinking about your own life on adrenaline. And about how you, too, can manage with more attention to things that matter. Because with all that I know for sure, today I added this: It makes no difference how many peaks you reach if there was no pleasure in the climb.

I'm going to spend more time enjoying the view from here. **O**

Oprah, Luke, and Layla take a break from climbing, Hawaii, July 2007.

DAY #1: Gayle and Oprah kick off their road trip in Montecito, California.

"If you can survive 11 days in cramped quarters with a friend and come out laughing, your friendship is the real deal."

I thought I knew a lot about friendship until I spent 11 days traveling across the country in a Chevy Impala with my best friend, Gayle King. We've been close since she was 21 and I was 22, and have been through a lot together: my previous bad relationships, her divorce. We've vacationed together and worked together on the magazine.

On Memorial Day, we set out to "see the U.S.A. in a Chevrolet." Remember that commercial from years ago? Well, I always thought it was a charming idea.

When we pulled out of my driveway in California, we were singing the jingle loudly, with vibrato. Cracking ourselves up.

Three days in, around Holbrook, Arizona, we were mumbling the tune. And by Lamar, Colorado, five days in, we'd stopped singing altogether.

The trip was grueling. Every day, six, then eight, then ten hours with nothing but road stretched ahead.

When Gayle drove, she insisted on constant music: XM 23 the Heart. I wanted silence. "To be alone with my thoughts" became a running joke. As she sang along boisterously, I realized there wasn't a tune she didn't know. (She called almost every one her favorite.) This was as nerve-racking for me as the silence was for her when I was behind the wheel.

I learned patience. And when patience wore thin, I bought earplugs and headphones.

Every night, in a different hotel, we were exhausted but still able to laugh at ourselves. We laughed at my merging anxiety, interstate anxiety, and passing-another-vehicle anxiety. Oh, and crossing-a-bridge anxiety. Other than that, Gayle will tell you I'm a great driver.

She is indeed a masterly driver, taking the curves on the Pennsylvania Turnpike with ease and steadily leading us into New York. Only one glitch: Her contacts had been in too long and her eyes were tired. So we're approaching the George Washington Bridge, relieved to end the long run of eating Cheetos and pork rinds at gas stations. Dusk has fallen, and night is approaching fast. Gayle says, "I hate to tell you this, but I can't see."

"What do you mean, you can't see?" I try to ask calmly.

"All the headlights have halos. Do they look like they have halos to you?"

"Uhhhh, no, they do not. CAN YOU SEE THE LINES ON THE ROAD?" I'm shouting now, envisioning the headline: FRIENDS FINISH JOURNEY IN A CRASH ON GW BRIDGE.

There's nowhere to pull over, and cars are speeding by.

"I know this bridge very well," she says. "That's what's saving us. And I have a plan. When we get to the toll, I'm going to pull over and take out my contacts and get my glasses."

The toll is a long way ahead. "What can I do?" I say, near panic. "Do you need me to steer for you?"

"No," she says. "I'm going to hug the white lines. Can you take out my contacts and then put on my glasses?" she jokes.

At least I think she's joking.

"That would be dangerous and impossible," I say.

"Then turn up the air, I'm sweatin'."

We both sweated our way to the tollbooth. And safely pulled into New York.

The crew following us had T-shirts made: I SURVIVED THE ROAD TRIP.

What I know for sure is that if you can survive 11 days in cramped quarters with a friend and come out laughing, your friendship is the real deal. I know ours is. **O**

WHAT I KNOW FOR SURE: 2005

"As long as we play the 'us and them' game, we don't evolve as people, as a nation, as a planet."

Comforting a hurricane survivor in the Houston Astrodome, September 5, 2005.

I went down to Louisiana five days after Katrina hit to witness for myself the disastrous effects of the hurricane. Maya Angelou described it so profoundly, saying, "The land became water, and the water thought it was God." Sitting in the dry comfort of my Chicago apartment, I'd felt helpless, like many of you. I knew I had to do something. I went in part to assess how I could best serve. Telling the stories of anguish and abandonment, faith and courage was one way. Wrapping my arms around people still in shock that their lives had gone adrift and telling them to hold on to themselves and one another was even more important for me. I remember saying to one woman, "You can come up out of that storm and have a better life." And for a moment she smiled and said, "Maybe you're right."

I spent no more than ten minutes in the Superdome in New Orleans, where thousands of families had waited and waited for five days for help to come. Days afterward, I thought I could still smell the urine and feces, mixed with the pungency of decaying flesh. I imagine the nightmares the survivors must have. I said on the air, "I think we all—this country—owe these families an apology."

The next day, *O*'s editor at large, Gayle King, got a phone call from an irate reader canceling her subscription because "that Oprah has gotten too big for her britches, telling us the government needs to apologize to *those* people."

What I know for sure is that behind every catastrophe, there are great lessons to be learned. Among the many that we as a country need to get is that as long as we play the "us and them" game, we don't evolve as people, as a nation, as a planet. I see the Katrina travesty as an opportunity for the rest of us to live in the space of an open heart and to show our compassion. Of course there are a lot of big challenges, but therein lies an even greater chance for us to use our emotional response to this disaster in the most constructive way. Over the years, I've heard people lament about why God allows this or that. Babies starve and people suffer not because of what God does but because of what we don't do.

When I went to visit survivors in the Houston Astrodome, my whole body ached from hearing the stories of their agony. My heart was wrenched as I listened to mothers pleading with me to help them find their lost children. So much of what happened in the aftermath of Katrina was man-made. And as we've all seen, there's plenty of blame to go around. But I, too, choose to rise up out of that storm and see that in moments of desperation, fear, and helplessness, each of us can be a rainbow of hope, doing what we can to extend ourselves in kindness and grace to one another. And I know for sure that there is no *them*—there's only us. **O**

"How you spend your time defines who you are."

I am more aware of time now than I have ever been. Something about turning 50 does that to you, I guess. I feel an almost primal awareness in the core of myself that there's a finite amount of time left, and that feeling permeates everything I do and dictates how I react in every moment. I'm more conscious and appreciative of every experience, every awakening (gee, I'm still here; I get another chance today to get it right). I try to take them all in, even the negative ones, and see how they relate back to something I created: I believe nothing is happening out of order with yourself.

I take the time, even if it's only one minute in the morning, to breathe slowly and let myself feel the connection to all other breathing and vibrating energies in this world and beyond. I have found that recognizing your relationship to infinity makes the finite more palatable.

What I know for sure is that how you spend your time defines who you are. I try not to waste time—because I don't want to waste myself. I'm working on not letting people with dark energy consume any of my time. I've learned that the hard way, after giving up hours of myself and my time, which are synonymous when you think about it. I've learned from my experiences of getting sucked into other people's ego dysfunction that their darkness casts a shadow on the light you need to be for yourself and for others.

What I know for sure is that giving yourself time to just *be* and not *do* is essential to fulfilling your mission as a human *being*. I give myself Sundays. Sometimes I spend the whole day in my pajamas, sometimes I have church under the trees communing with nature…most times I just do nothing—piddling, I call it—and let my brain and body decompress from six days of nonstop mental bombardment. If I didn't do that, I would implode, literally, in a crazy psychic breakdown. And whenever I've slipped up and missed a Sunday, I've noticed a definite change in my disposition for the rest of the week. I know for sure that you cannot give and give and give to everybody else and not give back to yourself. You will end up empty, or at best less than what you can be for yourself and your family and your work. Replenish the well of yourself, *for* yourself first. And if you think there's no time to do that, what you're really saying is, "I have no life to give to or live for myself." And if you have no life to live for yourself, then why are you here?

I learned a big lesson about a decade ago. The phone was always ringing on Sundays, when I had set that aside as my time. I'd answer and feel agitated and irritable with the person who'd called. Stedman said to me on one of those occasions, "If you don't want to talk, why do you keep picking up the phone?" Aha moment: Just because the phone is ringing, that doesn't mean I have to respond. I control what I do with *my* time. We all do, even when it seems out of control. Protect your time. It *is* your life. 🄾

WHAT I KNOW FOR SURE: 2003

"Live so that at the end of each day, you can say, 'I did my very best.'"

There I am, sitting in Mr. Hooper's fifth-period algebra class, dreading the test we're about to take, when an announcement over the intercom tells us to go to the auditorium for a special guest speaker. *Hooray, I've been saved!* I say to myself, figuring that'll be the end of algebra for today. My escape's the only thing on my mind as my classmates and I enter the room, single file. I position myself in my seat and prepare to be bored to sleep in yet another assembly. But when the speaker is introduced as the Reverend Jesse Jackson, a civil rights leader who was with Dr. King the day he was shot, I sit up a little straighter. What I don't yet know is that I'm about to hear the speech of a lifetime.

The year was 1969. Because I was an A to B student, I thought I already understood the importance of doing my best. But that day, Reverend Jackson lit a fire in me that changed the way I see life. His speech was about the personal sacrifices that had been made for all of us, regardless of how our ancestors came to be here. He talked about those who'd gone before us, who'd paved the way for us to be sitting in an integrated high school in Nashville. He told us that what we owed ourselves was excellence. "Excellence is the best deterrent to racism," he said. "Therefore, be excellent."

I took him at his word. That evening I went home and made a poster bearing his challenge. I taped that poster to my mirror, where it stayed through my college years. Over time I added my own maxims: "If you want to be successful, be excellent." "If you want the best the world has to offer, offer the world your best."

Those words have helped me over many a hurdle, even when less than my best was evident. To this day, excellence is my intention. To be excellent in giving. In graciousness. In effort. In struggle and in strife. For me being excellent means always doing my personal best. In Don Miguel Ruiz's book *The Four Agreements,* the final agreement is just that: Always do your best. I know for sure that this is the most fulfilling path to personal freedom. Your best varies from day to day, Ruiz says, depending on how you're feeling. No matter. Give your best in every circumstance so that you have no reason to judge yourself and create guilt and shame. Live so that at the end of each day, you can say, "I did my very best." That's what it means to excel at the great game of living your best life. **O**

"Right now you are one choice away from a new beginning."

I've never been a white-water-raftin', bungee-jumpin' kind of girl—that's not how I define adventure for myself. What I know for sure is this: The most important journey of our lives doesn't necessarily involve climbing the highest peak or trekking around the world. The biggest adventure you can ever take is to live the life of your dreams.

Maybe you're like so many women I've talked to over the years who have suspended their deepest desires in order to accommodate everything and everyone else. You ignore the nudge—that whisper that often comes in the form of emptiness or restlessness—to finally get on with what you know you should be doing. I understand how easy it is to rationalize: Your mate and your children need you; the job you admit makes you miserable demands so much of your time. But what happens to your spirit when you work hard at something unfulfilling? It completely drains you. It robs you of your life force. You end up depleted, depressed, and angry.

Don't waste another day on that road. Right now you are one choice away from a new beginning—one that leads you toward becoming the fullest human being you can be. Starting over begins with looking inward. It means ridding yourself of distractions and paying attention to that inkling you've been ignoring. There are times when, with three different people pulling me in five different directions at Harpo, I literally walk into my closet with all my shoes, sit on the floor, and go still as a stone. When I walk out, I am centered on what's most important and can make decisions based on what's right for me—not on what everyone else wants or needs. I've learned that the more stressful and chaotic things are on the outside, the calmer you need to get on the inside. It's the only way you can connect with where your spirit is leading you.

Be prepared—when you finally summon the courage to cast a vote for yourself, you can expect obstacles. The whole world will rise up to tell you who you cannot become and what you cannot do. Those around you will be threatened as you exceed the limited expectations they've always had for you. And in moments of weakness, your fear and self-doubt may cause you to falter. Remember that you can't get rid of the fear or doubt; you just learn to live with it, to ride its wave. As someone wise once said, cowards behave because of fear—but the courageous behave in spite of fear.

One of my favorite gospel songs is by Donnie McClurkin, and it has a refrain that gives me strength: *We fall down, but we get up.* The true measure of your courage is not whether you reach your goal—it's whether you decide to get back on your feet no matter how many times you've failed. Having the courage to stand up and pursue your dreams will give you life's greatest reward and life's greatest adventure. **O**

Oprah on safari in Botswana, December 2000.

"Ultimately, you have nothing to prove to anyone but yourself."

How can I realize my potential more fully? That's a question I still ask myself, especially when contemplating what's next in my life. In every job I've taken and in every city I've lived, I have known that it's time to move on when I've grown as much as I can grow. When I left Baltimore in 1983, almost everyone around me doubted whether I had the stuff to handle a talk show in a tough market like Chicago, where Phil Donahue was king—but I took the step anyway. I knew I had to if I didn't want to become stagnant.

What that move and many others since have taught me is that the true meaning of courage is to be afraid, and then, with your knees knocking and your heart racing, to step out anyway—even when that step makes sense to nobody but you. I know that's not easy. But making a bold move is the only way to truly advance toward the grandest vision the universe has for you. If you allow it to, fear will completely immobilize you. And once it has you in its grip, it will fight to keep you from ever becoming your best self.

What I know for sure is this: Whatever you fear most has no power—it is your *fear* that has the power. The thing itself cannot touch you. But if you allow your fear to seep into your mind and overtake your thoughts, it will rob you of your life. Each time you give in to your panic, you will actually lose strength, while whatever you're afraid of will gain that strength. That's why the only real cure for fear is courage. You must decide that no matter how difficult the path ahead seems, you will push past your anxiety and keep on stepping.

A few years ago, I wrote this question in my journal every day: "What am I afraid of?" Over time I realized that I had often seemed so brave on the outside but had lived much of my inner life in bondage. I was afraid that others wouldn't like me. I felt that no matter how hard I tried to become a good girl, I would always secretly believe I was a promiscuous teenager who had allowed men to sexually abuse me. I was terrified that if I said no to people, they would reject me. Everything I did, thought, felt, said, or even ate was connected to the fear I carried around with me—and I allowed it to block me from ever knowing who I really was.

As my friend Phil McGraw often says, you can't change what you don't acknowledge. Before I could challenge my fear and begin changing what I believed about myself, I had to admit that, yes, I had always been afraid—and that my fear was a form of slavery. As author Neale Donald Walsch says, "So long as you're still worried about what others think of you, you are owned by them. Only when you require no approval from outside yourself can you own yourself."

It's true that when you dare to step out, speak up, change yourself, or even simply do something outside of what others call the norm, the results may not always be pleasant. You'll fall down. Others will call you nutty. You'll be so exhausted that you'll want to quit. And as I've learned, people *won't* like you all the time. But the alternatives are even scarier: You might find yourself stuck in a miserable rut for years at a time. Or you could spend too many days languishing in regret, always wondering, What would my life have been like if I hadn't cared so much about what people thought?

And what if you decided right now that you will stop letting fear block you? You might discover the joy of tuning out what everybody wants for you and finally pay attention to what you need. And you'll learn that, ultimately, you have nothing to prove to anyone but yourself. That is what it truly means to live without fear—and to keep reaching for your fullest potential. ❶

"Happiness is never something you get from other people. The happiness you feel is in direct proportion to the love you give."

In the third grade, I learned the Golden Rule: Do unto others as you would have them do unto you. I loved those words. I wrote them on everything and carried them around in my book satchel.

I was a good-deed doer. At one point, I even thought I was going to be a missionary. Every Sunday, I would go to church, sit second pew to the right, take out a notepad, and write down everything the minister said. At school the next day, I would recite the sermon on the playground. I called it Monday-morning devotion. My classmates would see me coming and say, "Here comes that preacher." I was 8 years old at the time.

When the Progressive Missionary Baptist Church was trying to raise money for the poor children of Costa Rica, I started a campaign. I was going to collect more money than anyone else. I gave up my lunch money and convinced the other kids on the playground to do the same. It was all part of the principle of "Do unto others" that I lived by.

In the fifth grade, I ran into some problems. There was a girl in my class who didn't like me, so I went around school talking about her. One of my friends pointed out that if I believed in doing unto others and was talking about this girl, chances are she was talking about me, too. "I don't care," I replied, "because I don't like her, anyway."

For a long time, whenever I would say or do something that went against my better self, I would try to justify it that way. What I didn't understand is that all of your actions, both good and bad, come back to you and most often not from the people you are acting toward.

Now I know that you receive from the world what you give to the world. I understand it from physics as the third law of motion: For every action, there's an equal and opposite reaction. It is the essence of what Eastern philosophers call karma. In *The Color Purple,* the character Celie explained it to Mister: "Everything you try to do to me, already done to you."

Your actions revolve around you as surely as the Earth revolves around the sun. The more conscious I became of this, the more quickly my actions came back.

Today I try to do well and be well with everyone I reach or encounter. I make sure to use my life for that which can be of goodwill. Yes, this has brought me great wealth. More important, it has fortified me spiritually and emotionally.

When people say they are looking for happiness, I ask, "What are you giving to the world?" I'll never forget this couple who appeared on my show. The wife couldn't understand why their relationship had broken down. She kept saying, "He used to make me so happy. He doesn't make me happy anymore." What she couldn't see was that she was the cause of her own effect. Happiness is never something you get from other people. The happiness you feel is in direct proportion to the love you are able to give.

If you think something is missing in your life or you're not getting what you deserve, remember that there's no Yellow Brick Road. You lead life; it doesn't lead you.

See what comes into your life when you spend extra time with your children. Let go of your anger with your boss or co-worker and see what gets returned. Be loving to yourself and others and see that love reciprocated. This rule works every time, whether or not you are aware of it. It occurs in little things, big things, and the biggest things.

I have an advantage because I work in a profession in which everything I do generates an immediate response in overnight ratings, e-mails, and phone calls. Every day of your life, you are performing your own show, and the returns may come in more slowly or be less obvious. But everything is being returned. What you're thinking, what you're saying, what you're doing is having an impact on you and the people around you right now. I know it for sure.

Oprah

Oprah Talks to You!

Ten *O* readers—women of all ages, from all over the country—ask Oprah the tough questions (and a few fun ones, too).

After more than three decades as an interviewer, I've asked questions of everyone from rock 'n' roll singers to politicians, movie stars to convicted felons. But as *O's* tenth anniversary approached, the editors had a brainstorm: Wouldn't it be interesting to turn the tables and have someone interview me for a change? "Sure," I said. "Who do you have in mind?" And that's when I had *my* brainstorm: It should be a group of readers.

Which is how, during a snowy week in February 2010, ten women from across the country found themselves flying to Chicago to join me for a taping of the show and some lively conversation in my Harpo office. Ranging in age from 25 to 54, the women included a professor, a writer, a psychiatry resident, and a research analyst. They came from as far as Kirkland, Washington, and as close as Urbana, Illinois, and along with their suitcases, they brought a long list of questions—everything from whether I'm planning to write an autobiography to who's on my iPod to how I know whether I've had a good day.

The morning of the interview had been filled to overflowing. I'd already taped the show and done an hour-long radio program with Gayle King. So by the time Gayle and I—and my cocker spaniel, Sadie!—joined the women in my office, I couldn't have been more ready to kick off my shoes, let down my hair, and dish.

Oprah: This is so exciting—I'm glad you're all here, especially since it usually feels like there are only about five people left in the world who I haven't already chatted with. You can ask anything—it's impossible to embarrass me, and there's no wrong question. So who wants to start us off?

Ellyn: I'll start, if I can go back to what you just said. After interviewing so many people, are there any who got away, and who are the ones you still want to talk to?

Oprah: Who got away was Elvis Presley. When I was a kid, I always wanted to talk to Elvis. Another was Jackie Onassis. I had the pleasure and honor of meeting her—I actually ate her clam chowder at my friend Maria Shriver's wedding shower. There's a picture from the shower where I'm wearing one of those appliquéd sweaters and Jackie is wearing a cashmere sweater and an Hermès scarf—classic, classic, classic. I look like 1985, and she looks like Jackie O. Later, because she was a book editor, she called and asked if I would write a book. As much as I loved Jackie O, I said no, I was not ready to do a book. But I said, "If *you* ever want to do an interview…" and she said, "I probably will never do an interview." So that was another one who got away. As far as who I'd still like to talk to, I really want to interview O.J. Simpson's daughter, Sydney Simpson. And Susan Smith, the South Carolina woman who drowned her children by buckling them into her car and letting it roll into a lake. Not because of the horrific-ness of what she did, but because she changed the way we look at parents in this country. When somebody comes forward and says, "My child is missing," we now suspect the parents first. She changed the paradigm.

Barbara: When you're interviewing someone like Susan Smith, how are you able to remain objective?

Oprah: I approach every interview by asking, *What is my intention? What do I really want to accomplish?* You can't accomplish anything if you're judging. I believe that all pain is the same, that all of us have had difficulties and challenges, and that our pain is in inverse proportion to how much we were loved as a child. If you didn't receive love, then you have a lot of dysfunction that you're forever trying to work out. For me, it shows up as eating and food. For somebody else it might show up as drugs. But for some women it might be more like, *Well, I don't know how to handle my life, so I'm going to put my child in the freezer.* That seems extreme, but I really do believe we're all on a spectrum. And knowing that, I can talk to anybody.

Kelli: Most people don't have that gift of being nonjudgmental.

Oprah: Well, I'm nonjudgmental in an interview. Out of an interview, there's a whole other side of me!

Kelli: But the world is always watching and judging *you*. How has the public scrutiny you've had to endure affected your life?

Oprah: Years ago, it made me cry a lot because I'm such a pleaser. I would say that's my single greatest character flaw: the importance I put on wanting to be liked. That comes from having been abused as a child—being beaten and not even being able to be angry or to have any emotions about it. I was trained to believe that other people's feelings were more important than my own, and that only through pleasing somebody could I be loved. It took me 56 years to overcome that. And by the way, in all those 56 years I never once called my parents to share anything with them. Not "I got a job," "I met a guy," "I made a million dollars"—not once, ever. I'm in awe of people who felt their parents' love every day of their lives. They start out in the world with a full cup. The rest of us go through life trying to fill ours.

Keisha: Have you reconsidered writing an autobiography?

Oprah: It just so happens that there's a new biography, which I did not approve, and I hear that 850 people were interviewed for it. I don't *know* 850 people! My circle is tight, tight, tight. If there are 850 people talking about you, it can't all be good. But to answer your question, yes, I did consider writing my own story, back in 1993. At the time, I had a lawyer-agent-manager who said, "You know, you're turning 40 next year—I think you should do an autobiography." I said, "Really. Forty—okay." Because,

MEET THE INTERVIEW CREW

We couldn't fit *all* our readers into Oprah's office for a Q&A session, but these ten great conversationalists were happy to stand in.

Ellyn Shull, 46
Kirkland, Washington
Writer

Kelli Coleman, 25
New York City
Marketing professional

Kristy Nicholas, 33
Houston
Communications directo

you know, 40 used to be a big deal. Now it's 50 is the new 40 and 40 is the new 30, but back then….

Anyway, I got led into doing this book. And I worked on it for a year, and then when it came time to release it, I didn't want to. I brought my little cabinet together—Stedman, Gayle, a couple of other friends—and Stedman was really opposed to it, though not because of anything I was saying about him. He thought I shouldn't speak of my family as candidly as I did. He also kept saying, "It's not going to help anybody just to tell the story." He thought the story of my life should be an example to other people, rather than just "I did this, I did this, I did this." I listened to that. I was in the middle of a huge learning curve at that time. I was learning that your life really just begins at 40. You shouldn't be trying to write your life story then! But calling the publisher to say I wasn't going to do the book was the hardest thing I'd ever done. They'd had a big Oprah-is-going-to-write-a-book party, and all I could remember was the shrimp they'd served—how big those shrimp were. I was thinking, *Oh my God, they must have spent so much money on those shrimp!*

Several years ago, Nelson Mandela told me I should do my autobiography, just for the record. I don't feel compelled to do that. And I don't know how I could write it all down. Or what I would write. I remember when I opened my school, I said to Maya Angelou, who is like a mother to me, "This will be my legacy—this school." And Maya, in her Maya-like way, said, "You have no idea what your legacy will be."

Michelle: I've heard you say that you thought you'd grow up to be a teacher. Is that why you set up the school in South Africa—because school was so important to you?
Oprah: I started the school because I'd been searching for how I could best be used. My hope for the show and the magazine has always been that they will have meaning, that they will be worthy of people's time. In the elevator before I go out to do a show, my prayer is that I am used for something greater than myself. That it's not just chatter. I don't get up every morning to come here and just have a little chatty talk. I have always been searching for how I can best be used. And education was my solace growing up. It was my bright and shining moment, my savior. I wanted to give that to other girls. I wanted to do for the girls in South Africa what my teachers had done for me. I wanted them to be able to go to school for free and thrive there.

Vanessa: But sometimes when we try to help others, we fail. I'm a psychiatry resident in the Bronx, and I have patients who can't make it to their appointment because they're in the process of getting evicted—or they make it to the appointment, but then their kids don't make it to school. It's frustrating. How do you not become cynical?
Oprah: There's no room for cynicism in the world. I'm not cynical because I know that if one person isn't ready to be reached, somebody else is. But I have learned that I'm not good with children who are delinquents. I tried working with kids like that, and then I said, "I'm going to get arrested for popping somebody upside the head." What I'm really good at is, "If you want the opportunity, I'll provide it."

Kate: My favorite Oprah-ism is that the universe talks to you first in a whisper, and then gets louder and louder until you get the message. Can you share a time when you experienced that?
Oprah: It happens every day. Not like Moses and the burning bush, but the universe is speaking to us all the time. Just recently somebody called me, wanting me to help them out. I don't loan money, but if you need something and I decide that you're not going to keep coming back to ask for more, I'll just give it to you. This person was about to lose their house. And I said, "Okay, maybe."

Barbara Raymond, 54
Middletown, New York
Call center supervisor

Lisa Torain, 42
Riverview, Florida
Research analyst

Vanessa Greenberg, 28
Bronx, New York
Psychiatry resident

Kate O'Halloran, 34
Lexington, Massachusetts
Human resources associate

Kate: A stranger?

Oprah: No, somebody who'd worked here a long time ago and who'd fallen on hard times. And then, in the middle of a conversation yesterday, that person's name came up in some other context—and that person's name hadn't come up in 15 years. That was the universe saying, "Go back to that thought and see what you can do."

Lisa: Is there anything you can't do? Anything that's not attainable for you?

Oprah: I would like to have a little more balance. In the makeup room before coming out here, I was saying to Gayle that I think I've lost sight of my best life. The other day when I was cleaning out a drawer, I found an old gratitude journal and started looking through it, and at some point I just stopped and said, "God, I was so happy then." I was happy over little things: mango sorbet, and running, and the way my feet felt touching the ground when I ran. Back then, I didn't appreciate the time I got to spend with myself. Now I do—it's why I'm bringing the show to a close. My obligations have become my life.

Lisa: Would you ever consider paring way down? If you had to pare down to nothing, would it be okay?

Oprah: You mean give up my worldly possessions? I'm not crazy! No, no, no. But there are obligations I would pare back. I love everything that I do. I love it. But I keep saying yes to everything, and managing it all gets to be overwhelming. A typical day for me starts here with a 6:30 workout; by 7:30 I'm in the makeup chair. And then I don't usually get in the car to leave until 9, 10 o'clock at night. Get home just in time to breathe, get the damn puppy thing done—I don't know what I was thinking, getting a puppy—then go to bed, get up, and start the whole process all over again. It's too much. Today is lovely; I get to sit and talk with you guys. This is a restful day. I had only one show to do today. Yesterday I did three. The day before, I did three. In between doing three, I'm trying to talk to South Africa, because the girls are taking their PSATs. So I'm doing school. I'm on the phone about the magazine. I'm doing a full-hour radio show. I'm doing everything that goes with starting a new television network. So it really was time to end the show.

Violet: Are you going to act again?

Oprah: You know, I'm thinking about it. There's a part of me that says, *Don't take on another thing.* But I love acting, because it's a vacation from myself. I get to suspend being myself and become somebody else.

Barbara: Speaking of different roles, with all the focus that the show and the maga-zine have had on marriage and motherhood, how do you feel about never having experienced either?

Oprah: I used to get that question all the time: Why haven't you married Stedman? Actually, Stedman asked me to marry him, and at first I said "*Yes!*" but it turned out that I wanted to be asked to be married more than I wanted to be married. Had it not been for big-mouth Gayle King over there, it wouldn't have become the big public thing that it became. Gayle was there when he asked me, and then she went on TV—she was anchoring the news back then—and told everybody. And it became this big hoo-da-ha-da thing.

Gayle: I was so excited!

Barbara: How long ago was that?

Oprah: 1993. My friends were going to give me a party. Remember that, Gayle? Everybody was going to give me a—what do you call those?

Gayle: An engagement party. A shower.

Oprah: It was a shower. And I was saying, "I don't want this, I don't want this." And Gayle says, "Oh, everybody gets cold feet." And I say, "I don't have cold feet—my feet are stuck in a cement block surrounded by ice!" It just felt like the wrong thing for me. This was at the same time that I was supposed to have the book coming out. We were in Miami, in the back of a limousine, coming back from the party with the big shrimp, and Stedman asks, "So when is the book coming out?" The book was coming out September 14 or something, and our wedding had been scheduled for September 8. We had a date and everything. So Stedman says, "Well, I don't want to have my wedding in competition with your book." And I remember thinking, *Yes! Really? Okay, great!* I ended up canceling both, and we have not discussed it since that day.

Barbara: But you're still together.

Oprah: Still together. And what we *have* discussed is the fact that had we gotten married, we would definitely not

Violet Harris, 54
Urbana, Illinois
Professor and associate dean

Keisha Sutton-James, 37
New York City
Radio broadcasting company VP

Michelle Hankey, 4
Cape Coral, Florida
Teacher

still be together. Because instinctively, I understood that to do what I do every day is so nontraditional that it would have been difficult to try to conform to a traditional way of being. And Stedman's a pretty traditional man. You know, the show became my life. It became my children. And I knew I was not the kind of woman who could get home and make sure dinner was on the table. I do that when I feel like it, and if I don't feel like it, there's some Raisin Bran in there, get yourself a banana, and that's it.

Barbara: How do you feel about not having children?

Oprah: Really good. No regrets whatsoever. Gayle grew up writing the names of her would-be children, making little hearts and putting children's names in them. Never occurred to me to do that. I never had a desire. And I don't think I could have this life *and* have children. One of the lessons I've learned from doing the show is just how much sacrifice and attention is required to do the job of mothering well. Nothing in my background prepared or trained me to do that. So I don't have any regrets about it at all. And I do feel like I am a mother in a broader sense—to a generation of viewers who've grown up with me.

Kristy: You are.

Oprah: I have deep, deep love and affection for the people who've grown up watching. And when the show ends, it will not just be about my ending. I feel like it will almost be

the end of an era for people who were 10 years old when the show started and are now 35—the kids who used to come home from school and watch with their mothers. We've been on longer than *Bonanza* was! It's a relationship.

Kristy: What will you do the morning after your last show?

Oprah: Sleep in. Because that is going to be a really big party.

Lisa: Looking back over the years, was there ever a show where you felt, *I shouldn't have done that*?

Oprah: There was certainly some bad hair and bad choices. The '80s were tough on everybody! But yes, there were some things I did that, today, I'm embarrassed to say I did. Years ago I did a show about women whose husbands had cheated on them. At the time we thought, *What a great booking—you've got the mistress, you've got the wife, you've got the husband—they all agreed to come on.* But at one point, one of the husbands said to his wife—and this was live television—that his girlfriend was pregnant. And I saw the pain in his wife's face, and thought, *I'm responsible for that.* I didn't know her husband was going to say it, but I was responsible. I thought, *That is not what this platform is supposed to be for. You're not supposed to do that to anybody, ever.* The whole audience did what you all just did—everybody went "Oooh!" And the wife did what she could to hold on to herself. But in her eyes I saw the humiliation. There's nothing worse than being humiliated.

There's nothing worse that you can do to a person than to make them feel worthless.

The flip side is, the greatest thing you can do is to make somebody feel that they matter. So that is my secret to interviewing: How do I find the common denominator that allows a person to know that I hear them, and that what they say means something to me? If you can do that in all your relationships, whether it's with your children, your boss, your girlfriends, or your spouse—if you can be present enough to really emit that energy, that's all anybody is looking for.

Violet: *That's the book you should write.*

Oprah: It would take too much time to write, though. That's a lot of time.

Keisha: **After you pare down?**

Oprah: After my party.

Keisha: **Yes! Okay, next question: I think most would agree that you've transcended race. How do you balance your identity as a black woman with your need to reach a broader audience? Do you ever feel a conflict of conscience?**

Oprah: Being a black woman has never been an issue for me. It's just always been what is. This is who I am. I have never given it a moment's thought, because it's so integrated into who I am. I am, first, a child born of God. I really do believe that of myself. I am spirit in a body, and I have incarnated as a female who is black in the United States of America. No better place to be born in the world. Earlier this year when the movie *Precious* got all its Oscar nominations, Gabby Sidibe, who was nominated—she'd never acted before in her life, was raised in Harlem—her name was called in the same breath as Meryl Streep's. Only in America can that happen. On the other hand, I understand that I carry the energy of every single person who came before me and didn't have the opportunity to do what I do. I think about that. I carry that with me. It's not like I'm sitting there with Tom Cruise thinking, *The ancestors are here*—

Gayle: **Come on, Harriet!**

Oprah: Exactly. Harriet Tubman, Sojourner Truth—come on, everybody, come meet Tom Cruise! No, I'm not thinking that. But I am aware of the people who came before.

Ellyn: **Is there anything else you want to say about your relationship with God?**

Oprah: Is there anything more you want to ask me? We can talk all day about my relationship with God. That's the big one. My favorite Bible verse is Psalms 37:4. "Delight thyself in the Lord and He will give you the desires of your heart." To me, the Lord is all that is good, all that is great, all that is love, all that is timeless, all that is peace. Delight thyself in all those things, and you will

You Asked, Oprah Answered

As our interview wrapped, Oprah had time for a lightning round of your most frequently asked questions:

What dead person would you most like to meet or get advice from?
Jesus.

What's your all-time most memorable meal?
Cornbread and black-eyed peas.

What's the one thing you can't do because you're famous?
Have a pootie in a public restroom.

What makes you laugh?
Talking to Gayle King on the phone at night.

Where have you visited that you'd like to return?
My house in Hawaii.

In the movie of your life, who would play you?
Kimberly Elise.

If you could change places with someone—
Wouldn't.

What's the best material gift you've ever received?
A convertible Bentley from Tyler Perry, who also makes me laugh out loud.

Who was your most difficult interview?
Can't say. They're still around.

Do you still dream big?
I'm dreaming really big for my new network, OWN.

After ten years of writing "What I Know for Sure" in *O,* **do you know anything else for sure?**
Maya Angelou warned me I shouldn't do that column because it was going to be a pain to come up with something new every month. I know for sure: She was right!

have the desires of your heart. And what I've realized is that all my issues—my health problems, weight problems, all that—are deeply related to my getting so consumed with my schedule. For years I told people to keep a gratitude journal, but the last few years I've been too busy to keep one myself. I'd be so tired when I got home that it was like, *Okay, I'm grateful for…*

Ellyn: **This bed!**

Oprah: Right. When I was a kid, my grandmother said, "Pray on your knees." And that's how I always prayed. But the last few years it's been like, *I'm too tired. Can I just pray lying down? Okay, God, thank you.* So I've been crowding out the space that allows me to connect with God, with the source. Some people get that connection from going to church. I don't go to church unless I happen to be in a town where there's a really great service. Years ago I went faithfully, 8 o'clock service, 12 o'clock service. I was a tither. I was making 227 dollars a week, and I tithed 22 dollars and 70 cents every week. But after Jim Jones led the mass suicide in Guyana, I started to feel differently. The church I went to had a really charismatic pastor—you had to show up early to get a seat—and I remember sitting there one Sunday while he was preaching about how "the Lord thy God is a jealous God, the Lord thy God will punish you for your sins." I looked around and thought, *Why would God be jealous? What does that even mean?* And I'm looking at the people in the church, and everybody's up, shouting. And I started wondering how many of these people—including myself—would be led to do whatever this preacher said. That's when I started exploring taking God out of the box, out of the pew. And eventually I got to where I was able to see God in other people and in all things—in graciousness and kindness and generosity and the spirit of things. Okay? Okay, let's do a few more questions.

Kristy: **You know you've had a good day when...**

Oprah: I know I've had a good day when, after all the work I put into creating a show that goes out to ten million people around the world, somebody e-mails back and says, "What you said really mattered to me." That's a good day.

Kate: **Your name's so unique. What's the origin?**

Oprah: From the Bible. Ruth, first chapter. It's misspelled. It's supposed to be *Orpah.*

Kate: **Was that on purpose?**

Oprah: No. The *p* got put before the *r* on my birth certificate.

Gayle: **Who's your favorite musician on your iPod right now?**

Oprah: Gaga.

Vanessa: **If you could sing any karaoke song, would it be Lady Gaga?**

Oprah: It would definitely be a Tina Turner song. Because if I see myself as anybody, I can't be Gaga but I can be Tina. I have the wig to prove it! I actually got to sing "Simply the Best" onstage with her. Now I would wear a short dress and do "Steamy Windows." To me, nobody stands up to Tina Turner, because she turned 70 a couple of years ago and she's still rocking it out.

Gayle: **What advice would you give a young Oprah?**

Oprah: I would say, "Hold on to yourself, 'cause it's all going to be all right." When I was 28 years old in Baltimore, I was doing an event, and the gospel singer Wintley Phipps was performing there. Wintley Phipps, who I did not then know at all, came up to me backstage and said, "God has impressed me to tell you that He holds

you in His hand. And that He has shown great favor to you. And that you will speak to millions of people in the world in and through His name."

Gayle: **And you were just a local news anchor then.**

Oprah: I said, "Who are you? What? In Baltimore?" He said, "I don't know. God has just impressed me to tell you that." And it was one of those eerie, crazy moments, because I had always believed those things myself, even before that conversation. In the time just before I left Nashville for Baltimore, I was speaking in churches a lot. I remember speaking at a women's day service—I had my red Cutlass outside, packed and ready to drive to Baltimore. And my sermon was, "I don't know what the future holds, but I know who holds the future." I have no fear about the future. I have no fear about anything, because I really do understand that I am God's child and that He has guided me through everything and will continue to until the end.

Vanessa: **In your best-case scenario, how would you balance your time?**

Oprah: Still trying to figure that one out. If I knew the answer, I'd have managed to open my Christmas presents by now. I'm not kidding. I left California and came in a day early this week because I wanted to get through my Christmas presents here in the office—it's February and I haven't opened them yet. But I ended up getting stuck with all the requests that were on the desk: Will you do this, will you do that, will you speak here, will you go there? The thing is, when you're on TV, you're in people's homes every day. You are familiar. So it's like, "Oprah, come on over here! Stay right here while I go get my camera—and hold on, my sister wants to get a picture with you, too!" You wouldn't say that to Angelina Jolie.

Keisha: **You've sacrificed a lot to live the life you have.**

Oprah: Actually, I've had a great time. But I would have to say that at this particular time in my life, I look forward to being able to take a rest. I was just saying to someone the other day, "What do women do when they wake up in the morning?" One of my favorite lines from *Beloved*—the movie nobody went to see, and thank you if you did, since as you can tell [*laughs*], I still carry a little pain about it—is spoken by the character Sethe. She says, "Twenty-eight days, 28 good days of a free life... I'd wake up in the morning and decide for myself what to do with the day.... Twenty-eight days of freedom. And on the 29th day, it was over." I can't imagine what it's going to be like to wake up in the morning and decide for myself what to do with the day. I don't know what it is to have free time. I really don't know. If I get to leave here and be home early, I won't know what to do. What do people do?

Lisa: **Watch Oprah. 〇**

Oprah Talks to Thich Nhat Hanh

He's been a Buddhist monk for more than 60 years, as well as a teacher, writer, and vocal opponent of war—a stance that left him exiled from his native Vietnam for four decades. The man Martin Luther King Jr. called "an apostle of peace and nonviolence" reflects on the beauty of the present moment, being grateful for every breath, and the freedom and happiness to be found in a simple cup of tea.

Sharing a warm
greeting before
our talk,
October 2009.

The moment I meet Thich Nhat Hanh at the Four Seasons Hotel in Manhattan, I feel his sense of calm. A deeply tranquil presence seems to surround the Zen Buddhist master.

But beneath Nhat Hanh's serene demeanor is a courageous warrior. The 85-year-old native of Vietnam, who joined the monastery when he was 16, valiantly opposed his own government during the Vietnam War. Even as he embraced the contemplative life of a monk, the war confronted him with a choice: Should he remain hidden away in the monastery tending to matters of the spirit, or go out and help the villagers who were suffering? Nhat Hanh's decision to do both is what gave birth to "Engaged Buddhism"—a movement that involves peaceful activism for the purpose of social reform. It's also what led Martin Luther King Jr. to nominate him for a Nobel Peace Prize in 1967.

As part of his denunciation of the violence inflicted on his countrymen, Nhat Hanh founded a relief organization that rebuilt bombed Vietnamese villages, set up schools and medical centers, and resettled homeless families. Nhat Hanh also created a Buddhist university, a publishing house, and a peace activist magazine—all of which led the Vietnamese government to forbid him, in 1966, to return home after he'd left the country on a peace mission. He remained in exile for 39 years.

Before his exile, Nhat Hanh had spent time in the West (studying at Princeton and teaching at Columbia University in the early 1960s), and it was to the West that he now returned. Seeing an opportunity to spread Buddhist thought and encourage peaceful activism, he led the Buddhist Peace Delegation to the Paris Peace Talks in 1969, established the Unified Buddhist Church in France, and went on to write more than 100 books, including the 1995 best-seller *Living Buddha, Living Christ*—a volume that never leaves my nightstand.

Nhat Hanh eventually settled in Southern France and founded Plum Village, the Buddhist meditation practice center and monastery where he still lives. Thousands of people travel there each year to join him in exploring the tenets of Buddhism—including mindfulness (intentionally tuning in to the present moment), the development of a practice (a regular activity, such as mindful walking, that redirects you toward right thinking), and enlightenment (the liberation from suffering that comes when you wake up to the true nature of reality). These principles were introduced to the world more than 2,000 years ago by Siddhartha Gautama, or the Buddha, the Indian-born prince who left a life of ease and indulgence in order to seek enlightenment—and founded a religion along the way.

Thich Nhat Hanh—or, as his students call him, Thây, the Vietnamese word for "teacher"—brings along a group of Plum Village monks and nuns to listen in on our conversation. In some spiritual traditions, there is a concept called "holding the space"—or showing up as a compassionate listener. Thây's friends are the space holders who have traveled with him from France, and as we take a photograph together just before our chat, they usher in a peaceful mood by collectively singing a Buddhist song: "We are all the leaves of one tree; we are all the waves of one sea; the time has come for all to live as one."

Oprah: Thank you for the honor of talking to you. Just being in your presence, I feel less stressed than when the day started. You have such a peaceful aura. Are you always this content?

Nhat Hanh: This is my training, this is my practice. And I try to live every moment like that, to keep the peace in myself.

Oprah: Because you can't give it to others if you don't have it in yourself.

Nhat Hanh: Right.

Oprah: I see. I know that you were born in Vietnam in 1926. Is there any wonderful memory of your childhood that you can share?

Nhat Hanh: The day I saw a picture of the Buddha in a magazine.

Oprah: How old were you?

Nhat Hanh: I was 7, 8. He was sitting on the grass, very peaceful, smiling. I was impressed. Around me, people were not like that, so I had the desire to be like him. And I nourished that desire until the age of 16, when I had the permission of my parents to go and ordain as a monk.

Oprah: Did your parents encourage you?

Nhat Hanh: In the beginning, they were reluctant because they thought that the life of a monk is difficult.

Oprah: At 16, did you understand what the life would be?

Nhat Hanh: Not a lot. There was only the very strong desire. The feeling that I would not be happy if I could not become a monk. They call it the

> "People sacrifice the present for the future. But life is available only in the present."

beginner's mind—the deep intention, the deepest desire that a person may have. And I can say that until this day, this beginner's mind is still alive in me.

Oprah: That's what a lot of people refer to as passion. It's the way I feel about my work most days. When you're passionate about your work, it feels like you would do it even if no one were paying you.

Nhat Hanh: And you enjoy it.

Oprah: You enjoy it. Let's talk about when you first arrived in America. You were a student at Princeton. Was it challenging as a Buddhist monk to form friendships with other students? Were you lonely?

Nhat Hanh: Well, Princeton University was like a monastery. There were only male students at that time. And there were not many Vietnamese living in the United States. During the first six months, I did not speak Vietnamese. But the campus was very beautiful. And everything was new—the trees and the birds and the food. My first snow was in Princeton, and the first time I used a radiator. The first fall was in Princeton.

Oprah: When the leaves are changing.

Nhat Hanh: In Vietnam we did not see things like that.

Oprah: At the time, were you wearing your monk robes?

Nhat Hanh: Yes.

Oprah: Never have to worry about buying clothes, do you? Always just the robe.

Nhat Hanh: Yes.

Oprah: Do you have different robes for different occasions?

Nhat Hanh: You have a ceremonial robe, saffron color. That's all. I feel comfortable wearing this kind of robe. And it happily reminds us that we are monks.

Oprah: What does it mean to be a monk?

Nhat Hanh: To be a monk is to have time to practice for your transformation and healing. And after that to help with the transformation and healing of other people.

Oprah: Are most monks enlightened, or seeking enlightenment?

Nhat Hanh: Enlightenment is always there. Small enlightenment will bring great enlightenment. If you breathe in and are aware that you are alive—that you can touch the miracle of being alive—then that is a kind of

Leading a capacity crowd in meditation at New York City's Beacon Theatre, October 2009.

enlightenment. Many people are alive but don't touch the miracle of being alive.

Oprah: I'm sure you see all around you—I'm guilty of it myself—that we're just trying to get through the next thing. In our country, people are so busy. Even the children are busy. I get the impression very few of us are doing what you just said—touching the miracle that you are alive.

Nhat Hanh: That is the environment people live in. But with a practice, we can always remain alive in the present moment. With mindfulness, you can establish yourself in the present in order to touch the wonders of life that are available in that moment. It is possible to live happily in the here and the now. So many conditions of happiness are available—more than enough for you to be happy right now. You don't have to run into the future in order to get more.

Oprah: What is happiness?

Nhat Hanh: Happiness is the cessation of suffering. Well-being. For instance, when I practice this exercise of breathing in, I'm aware of my eyes; breathing out, I smile to my eyes and realize that they are still in good condition. There is a paradise of form and colors in the world. And because you have eyes still in good condition, you can get in touch with the paradise. So when I become aware of my eyes, I touch one of the conditions of happiness. And when I touch it, happiness comes.

Oprah: And you could practice that with every part of your body.

Nhat Hanh: Yes. Breathing in, I am aware of my heart. Breathing out, I smile to my heart and know that my heart still functions normally. I feel grateful for my heart.

Oprah: So it's about being aware of and grateful for what we have.

Nhat Hanh: Yes.

Oprah: And not just the material things, but the fact that we have our breath.

Nhat Hanh: Yes. You need the practice of mindfulness to bring your mind back to the body and establish yourself in the moment. If you are fully present, you need only make a step or take a breath in order to enter the kingdom of God. And once you have the kingdom, you don't need to run after objects of your craving, like power, fame, sensual pleasure, and so on. Peace is possible. Happiness is possible. And this practice is simple enough for everyone to do.

Oprah: Tell me how we do it.

Nhat Hanh: Suppose you are drinking a cup of tea. When you hold your cup, you may like to breathe in, to bring your mind back to your body, and you become fully present. And when you are truly there, something else is also there—life, represented by the cup of tea. In that moment you are real, and the cup of tea is real. You are not lost in the past, in the future, in your projects, in your worries. You are free from all of these afflictions. And in that state of being free, you enjoy your tea. That is the moment of happiness, and of peace. When you brush your teeth, you may have just two minutes, but according to this practice, it is possible to produce freedom and joy during that time, because you are established in the here and now. If you are capable of brushing your teeth in mindfulness, then you will be able to enjoy the time when you take a shower, cook your breakfast, sip your tea.

Oprah: So from this point of view, there are endless conditions of happiness.

Nhat Hanh: Yes. Mindfulness helps you go home to the present. And every time you go there and recognize a condition of happiness that you have, happiness comes.

Oprah: With you, the tea is real.

Nhat Hanh: I am real, and the tea is real. I am in the present. I don't think of the past. I don't think of the future. There is a real encounter between me and the tea, and peace, happiness, and joy are possible during the time that I drink.

Oprah: I never had that much thought about a cup of tea.

Nhat Hanh: We have the practice of tea meditation. We sit down, enjoy a cup of tea and our brotherhood, sisterhood. It takes one hour to just enjoy a cup of tea.

Oprah: A cup of tea, like this? [Holds up her cup.]

Nhat Hanh: Yes.

Oprah: One hour.

Nhat Hanh: Every moment is a moment of happiness. And during the hour of tea meditation, you cultivate joy, brotherhood, sisterhood, and dwelling in the here and the now.

Oprah: Do you do the same thing with all food?

Nhat Hanh: Yes. We have silent meals eaten in such a way that we get in touch with the cosmos, with every morsel of food.

Oprah: How long does it take you to get through a meal? All day?

Nhat Hanh: One hour is enough. We sit as a community, and enjoy our meal together. So whether you are eating, drinking your tea, or doing your dishes, you do it in such a way that freedom, joy, happiness are possible. Many people come to our center and learn this art of mindful living. And go back to their hometowns and set up a sangha, a community, to do the same. We have helped set up sanghas all over the world.

Oprah: A sangha is a beloved community.

Nhat Hanh: Yes.

Oprah: How important is that in our lives? People have it with their own families, and then you expand your beloved community to include others. So the larger your

beloved community is, the more you can accomplish in the world.

Nhat Hanh: Right.

Oprah: On the subject of community, let's go back to 1966. You were invited to come and speak at Cornell University, and shortly after that, you weren't allowed back into your country. You were exiled for 39 years. How did you deal with those feelings?

Nhat Hanh: Well, I was like a bee taken out of the beehive. But because I was carrying the beloved community in my heart, I sought elements of the sangha around me in America and in Europe. And I began to build a community working for peace.

Oprah: Did you feel angry at first? Hurt?

Nhat Hanh: Angry, worried, sad, hurt. The practice of mindfulness helped me recognize that. In the first year, I dreamed almost every night of going home. I was climbing a beautiful hill, very green, very happily, and suddenly I woke up and found that I was in exile. So my practice was to get in touch with the trees, the birds, the flowers, the children, the people in the West—and make them my community. And because of that practice, I found home outside of home. One year later, the dreams stopped.

Oprah: What was the reason you weren't allowed back in the country?

Nhat Hanh: During the war, the warring parties all declared that they wanted to fight until the end. And those of us who tried to speak about reconciliation between brothers and brothers—they didn't allow us.

Oprah: So when you were a man without a country, you made a home in other countries.

Nhat Hanh: Yes.

Oprah: And the United States was one.

Nhat Hanh: Yes.

Oprah: How did you meet Martin Luther King Jr.?

Nhat Hanh: In June 1965, I wrote him a letter explaining why the monks in Vietnam immolated themselves. I said that this is not a suicide. I said that in situations like the one in Vietnam, to make your voice heard is difficult. Sometimes we have to burn ourselves in order to be heard. It is out of compassion that you do that. It is the act of love and not of despair. And exactly one year after I wrote that letter, I met him in Chicago. We had a discussion about peace, freedom, and community. And we agreed that without a community, we cannot go very far.

Oprah: How long was the discussion?

Nhat Hanh: Probably five minutes or so. And after that, there was a press conference, and he came out very strongly against the war in Vietnam.

Oprah: Do you think that was a direct result of your conversation?

Nhat Hanh: I believe so. We continued our work, and the last time I met him was in Geneva during the peace conference.

Oprah: Did the two of you speak then?

Nhat Hanh: Yes. He invited me up for breakfast, to talk about these issues again. I got caught in a press conference downstairs and came late, but he kept the breakfast warm for me. And I told him that the people in Vietnam call him a bodhisattva—enlightened being—because of what he was doing for his people, his country, and the world.

Oprah: And the fact that he was doing it nonviolently.

Nhat Hanh: Yes. That is the work of a bodhisattva, a buddha, always with compassion and nonviolence. When I heard of his assassination, I couldn't believe it. I thought, *The American people have produced King but are not capable of preserving him.* I was a little bit angry. I did not eat, I did not sleep. But my determination to continue building the beloved community continues always. And I think that I felt his support always.

Oprah: Always.

Nhat Hanh: Yes.

Oprah: Okay. We've been talking about mindfulness, and you've mentioned mindful walking. How does that work?

Nhat Hanh: As you walk, you touch the ground mindfully, and every step can bring you solidity and joy and freedom. Freedom from your regret concerning the past, and freedom from your fear about the future.

Oprah: Most people when they're walking are thinking about where they have to go and what they have to do. But you would say that removes us from happiness.

Nhat Hanh: People sacrifice the present for the future. But life is available only in the present. That is why we should walk in such a way that every step can bring us to the here and the now.

Oprah: What if my bills need to be paid? I'm walking, but I'm thinking about the bills.

Nhat Hanh: There is a time for everything. There is a time when I sit down, I concentrate myself on the problem of my bills, but I would not worry before that. One thing at a time. We practice mindful walking in order to heal ourselves, because walking like that really relieves our worries, the pressure, the tension in our body and in our mind.

Oprah: The case is the same for deep listening, which I've heard you refer to.

Nhat Hanh: Deep listening is the kind of listening that can help relieve the suffering of another person. You can call it compassionate listening. You listen with only one purpose: to help him or her to empty his heart. Even if he says things that are full of wrong perceptions, full of bitterness, you are still capable of continuing to listen with compassion. Because you know that listening like that, you give that person a chance to suffer less. If you want to help him to correct his perception, wait for another time. For now, you don't interrupt. You don't argue. If you do, he loses his chance. You just listen with compassion and help him to suffer less. One hour like that can bring transformation and healing.

Oprah: **I love this idea of deep listening, because often when someone comes to you and wants to vent, it's so tempting to start giving advice. But if you allow the person just to let the feelings out, and then at another time come back with advice or comments, that person would experience a deeper healing. That's what you're saying.**

Nhat Hanh: Yes. Deep listening helps us to recognize the existence of wrong perceptions in the other person and wrong perceptions in us. The other person has wrong perceptions about himself and about us. And we have wrong perceptions about ourselves and the other person. And that is the foundation for violence and conflict and war. The terrorists, they have the wrong perception. They believe that the other group is trying to destroy them as a religion, as a civilization. So they want to abolish us, to kill us before we can kill them. And the antiterrorist may think very much the same way—that these are terrorists and they are trying to eliminate us, so we have to eliminate them first. Both sides are motivated by fear, by anger, and by wrong perception. But wrong perceptions cannot be removed by guns and bombs. They should be removed by deep listening, compassionate listening, and loving space.

Oprah: **The only way to end war is communication between people.**

Nhat Hanh: Yes. We should be able to say this: "Dear friends, dear people, I know that you suffer. I have not understood enough of your difficulties and suffering. It's not our intention to make you suffer more. It is the opposite. We don't want you to suffer. But we don't know what to do, and we might do the wrong thing if you don't help us to understand. So please tell us about your difficulties. I'm eager to learn, to understand." We have to have loving speech. And if we are honest, if we are true, they will open their hearts. Then we practice compassionate listening, and we can learn so much about our own perception and their perception. Only after that can we help remove wrong perception. That is the best way, the only way, to remove terrorism.

Oprah: **But what you're saying also applies to difficulties between yourself and family members or friends. The**

> "Holding our suffering, looking deeply into it, we find a way to happiness."

principle is the same, no matter the conflict.

Nhat Hanh: Right. And peace negotiations should be conducted in that manner. When we come to the table, we shouldn't negotiate right away. We should spend time walking together, eating together, making acquaintance, telling each other about our own suffering, without blame or condemnation. It takes maybe one, two, three weeks to do that. And if communication and understanding are possible, negotiation will be easier. So if I am to organize a peace negotiation, I will organize it in that way.

Oprah: **You'd start with tea?**

Nhat Hanh: With tea and walking meditation.

Oprah: **Mindful tea.**

Nhat Hanh: And sharing our happiness and our suffering. And deep listening and loving speech.

Oprah: **Is there ever a place for anger?**

Nhat Hanh: Anger is the energy that people use in order to act. But when you are angry, you are not lucid, and you might do wrong things. That is why compassion is a better energy. And the energy of compassion is very strong. We suffer. That is real. But we have learned not to get angry and not to allow ourselves to be carried by anger. We realize right away that that is fear. That is corruption.

Oprah: **What if in a moment of mindfulness you are being challenged? For instance, the other day someone presented me with a lawsuit, and it's hard to feel happy when somebody is going to be taking you to court.**

Nhat Hanh: The practice is to go to the anxiety, the worry—

Oprah: **The fear. First thing that happens is that fear sets in, like,** *What am I going to do?*

Nhat Hanh: So you recognize that fear. You embrace it tenderly and look deeply into it. And as you embrace your pain, you get relief and you find out how to handle that emotion. And if you know how to handle the fear, then you have enough insight in order to solve the problem. The problem is to not allow that anxiety to take over. When these feelings arise, you have to practice in order to use the energy of mindfulness to recognize them, embrace them, look deeply into them. It's like a mother when the baby is crying. Your anxiety is your baby. You have to take care of it. You have to go back to yourself, recognize the suffering in you, embrace the suffering, and you get relief. And if you continue with your practice of mindfulness, you understand the roots, the nature of the suffering, and you know the way to transform it.

Oprah: **You use the word** *suffering* **a lot. I think many** people think suffering is dire starvation or poverty. But when you speak of suffering, you mean what?

Nhat Hanh: I mean the fear, the anger, the despair, the anxiety in us. If you know how to deal with that, then you'll be able to handle problems of war and poverty and conflicts. If we have fear and despair in us, we cannot remove the suffering in society.

Oprah: The nature of Buddhism, as I understand it, is to believe that we are all pure and radiant at our core. And yet we see around us so much evidence that people are not acting from a place of purity and radiance. How do we reconcile that?

Nhat Hanh: Well, happiness and suffering support each other. To be is to inter-be. It's like the left and the right. If the left is not there, the right cannot be there. The same is true with suffering and happiness, good and evil. In every one of us there are good seeds and bad. We have the seed of brotherhood, love, compassion, insight. But we have also the seed of anger, hate, dissent.

Oprah: That's the nature of being human.

Nhat Hanh: Yes. There is the mud, and there is the lotus that grows out of the mud. We need the mud in order to make the lotus.

Oprah: Can't have one without the other.

Nhat Hanh: Yes. You can only recognize your happiness against the background of suffering. If you have not suffered hunger, you do not appreciate having something to eat. If you have not gone through a war, you don't know the value of peace. That is why we should not try to run away from one thing after another thing. Holding our suffering, looking deeply into it, we find a way to happiness.

Oprah: Do you meditate every single day?

Nhat Hanh: We try to do it not only every day but every moment. While drinking, while talking, while writing, while watering our garden, it's always possible to practice living in the here and the now.

Oprah: But do you ever sit silently with yourself or recite a mantra—or not recite a mantra?

Nhat Hanh: Yes. We sit alone, we sit together.

Oprah: The more people you sit with, the better.

Nhat Hanh: Yes, the collective energy is very helpful. I'd like to talk about the mantras you just mentioned. The first one is "Darling, I'm here for you." When you love someone, the best you can offer is your presence. How can you love if you are not there?

Oprah: That's a lovely mantra.

Nhat Hanh: You look into their eyes and you say, "Darling, you know something? I'm here for you." You offer him or her your presence. You are not preoccupied with the past or the future; you are there for your beloved. The second mantra is, "Darling, I know you are there, and I am so

happy." Because you are fully there, you recognize the presence of your beloved as something very precious. You embrace your beloved with mindfulness. And he or she will bloom like a flower. To be loved means to be recognized as existing. And these two mantras can bring happiness right away, even if your beloved one is not there. You can use your telephone and practice the mantra.

Oprah: Or e-mail.

Nhat Hanh: E-mail. You don't have to practice it in Sanskrit or Tibetan—you can practice in English.

Oprah: Darling, I'm here for you.

Nhat Hanh: And I'm very happy. The third mantra is what you practice when your beloved one is suffering. "Darling, I know you're suffering. That is why I am here for you." Before you do something to help, your presence already can bring some relief.

Oprah: The acknowledgment of the suffering or of the hurting.

Nhat Hanh: Yes. And the fourth mantra is a little bit more difficult. It is when you suffer and you believe that your suffering has been caused by your beloved. If someone else had done the same wrong to you, you would have suffered less. But this is the person you love the most, so you suffer deeply. You prefer to go to your room and close the door and suffer alone.

Oprah: Yes.

Nhat Hanh: You are hurt. And you want to punish him or her for having made you suffer. The mantra is to overcome that: "Darling, I suffer. I am trying my best to practice. Please help me." You go to him, you go to her, and practice that. And if you can bring yourself to say that mantra, you suffer less right away, because you do not have that obstacle standing between you and the other person.

Oprah: "Darling, I suffer. Please help me."

Nhat Hanh: "Please help me."

Oprah: What if he or she is not willing to help you?

Nhat Hanh: First of all, when you love someone, you want to share everything with him or her. So it is your duty to say, "I suffer, and I want you to know"—and he will, she will, appreciate it.

Oprah: If he or she loves you.

Nhat Hanh: Yes. This is the case of two people who love each other. Your beloved one.

Oprah: All right.

Nhat Hanh: "And when I have been trying my best to look deeply, to see whether this suffering comes from my wrong perception and I might be able to transform it, but in this case I cannot transform it, you should help me, darling. You should tell me why you have done such a thing to me, said such a thing to me." In that way, you have expressed your trust, your confidence. You don't want to punish anymore. And that is why you suffer less right away.

Oprah: Beautiful. Now I'm going to ask just a few questions about monkdom. Do you exercise to stay in shape?

Nhat Hanh: Yes. We have the ten mindful movements. We do walking meditation every day. We practice mindful eating.

Oprah: Are you vegetarian?

Nhat Hanh: Yes. Vegetarian. Complete. We do not use animal products anymore.

Oprah: So you wouldn't eat an egg.

Nhat Hanh: No egg, no milk, no cheese. Because we know that mindful eating can help save our planet.

Oprah: Do you watch television?

Nhat Hanh: No. But I'm in touch with the world. If anything really important happens, someone will tell me.

Oprah: That's the way I feel!

Nhat Hanh: You don't have to listen to the news three times a day or read one newspaper after another.

Oprah: That's right. Now, the life of a monk is a celibate life, correct?

Nhat Hanh: Yes.

Oprah: You never had trouble with the idea of giving up marriage or children?

Nhat Hanh: One day when I was in my 30s, I was practicing meditation in a park in France. I saw a young mother with a beautiful baby. And in a flash I thought that if I was not a monk, I would have a wife and a child like that. The idea lasted only for one second. I overcame it very quickly.

Oprah: That was not the life for you. And speaking of life, what about death? What happens when we die, do you believe?

Nhat Hanh: The question can be answered when you can answer this: What happens in the present moment? In the present moment, you are producing thought, speech, and action. And they continue in the world. Every thought you produce, anything you say, any action you do, it bears your signature. Action is called karma. And that's your continuation. When this body disintegrates, you continue on with your actions. It's like the cloud in the sky. When the cloud is no longer in the sky, it hasn't died. The cloud is continued in other forms like rain or snow or ice. Our nature is the nature of no birth and no death. It is impossible for a cloud to pass from being into nonbeing. And that is true with a beloved person. They have not died. They have continued in many new forms and you can look deeply and recognize them in you and around you.

Oprah: Is that what you meant when you wrote one of my favorite poems, "Call Me By My True Name"?

Nhat Hanh: Yes. When you call me European, I say yes. When you call me Arab, I say yes. When you call me black, I say yes. When you call me white, I say yes. Because I am in you and you are in me. We have to inter-be with everything in the cosmos.

Oprah: [Reading from the poem] "I am a mayfly metamorphosing on the surface of the river. And I am the bird that swoops down to swallow the mayfly…. I am the child in Uganda, all skin and bones, my legs as thin as bamboo sticks. And I am the arms merchant, selling deadly weapons to Uganda. I am the 12-year-old girl, refugee on a small boat, who throws herself into the ocean after being raped by a sea pirate. And I am the pirate, my heart not yet capable of seeing and loving…. Please call me by my true names, so I can hear all my cries and laughter at once, so I can see that my joy and pain are one. Please call me by my true names, so I can wake up and the door of my heart could be left open, the door of compassion." What does that poem mean?

Nhat Hanh: It means compassion is our most important practice. Understanding brings compassion. Understanding the suffering that living beings undergo helps liberate the energy of compassion. And with that energy you know what to do.

Oprah: Okay. At the end of my magazine, I have a column called "What I Know for Sure." What do you know for sure?

Nhat Hanh: I know that we do not know enough. We have to continue to learn. We have to be open. And we have to be ready to release our knowledge in order to come to a higher understanding of reality. When you climb a ladder and arrive on the sixth step and you think that is the highest, then you cannot come to the seventh. So the technique is to abandon the sixth in order for the seventh step to be possible. And this is our practice, to release our views. The practice of nonattachment to views is at the heart of the Buddhist practice of meditation. People suffer because they are caught in their views. As soon as we release those views, we are free and we don't suffer anymore.

Oprah: Isn't the true quest to be free?

Nhat Hanh: Yes. To be free, first of all, is to be free from wrong views that are the foundation of all kinds of suffering and fear and violence.

Oprah: It has been my honor to talk to you today.

Nhat Hanh: Thank you. A moment of happiness that might help people.

Oprah: I think it will. ⓞ

UPDATE Thich Nhat Hanh's latest book is Our Appointment with Life: Sutra on Knowing the Better Way to Live Alone *(Parallax Press).*

Oprah Talks to Tyler Perry

The director, playwright, and actor is the first black studio mogul in American history—but at one time he was living in his car. Perry sits down with Oprah to talk about his journey from struggling artist to superstar.

It doesn't surprise me that Tyler Perry and I have become close friends in recent years.

There's a similarity in our paths: Each of us has been on a journey that can only be called a miracle.

Tyler, 42, grew up in New Orleans, in a physically abusive home. Outside the home he was also sexually abused, as he revealed on my show. The trauma left him confused and angry—one especially "nasty" outburst got him kicked out of high school—but he found an outlet in writing about his life.

In 1992 Tyler moved to Atlanta with the dream of staging his first play. When that effort failed (and failed, and failed, six times over), he was left homeless, disheartened, and broke—but not broken. He kept on pursuing his dream, and in 1998 it finally took flight, when hundreds of mostly African-American fans lined up to buy tickets for the seventh staging of the show he'd devoted his life to, *I Know I've Been Changed.*

Since then millions of people have turned out to see Tyler's work. His first movie was 2005's *Diary of a Mad Black Woman,* adapted from his 2001 play and featuring his most famous character, the outspoken, gun-toting, 6'6" grandmother, Madea. After his second film, *Madea's Family Reunion,* he opened Tyler Perry Studios, in Atlanta, and went on to direct and produce seven other movies and create two successful TBS shows, *Tyler Perry's House of Payne* and *Meet the Browns.* Now he's pushing his self-honed directorial talents to a new high with a drama that debuted in November 2010: *For Colored Girls,* based on Ntozake Shange's 1975 play, *For Colored Girls Who Have Considered Suicide When the Rainbow Is Enuf.* When I visited him on the set last year, he was in his element, and I loved watching him. It made me so proud to see the respect everyone had for him—there was a lot of "Mr. Perry, sir" going on.

I sat down with Tyler on a rainy Sunday morning. He was in Washington, D.C., to perform in *Madea's Big Happy Family,* and we met up in a parking lot, in his favorite place to unwind on the road: a double-wide mahogany-paneled bus, complete with kitchen, sitting room, two bathrooms, and bedroom. "This is my home away from home," he told me. "I love having this bed. And now I don't have to worry about getting bedbugs when I travel, 'cause I have my own mattress!"

The fact that Tyler's work began with a play he scribbled in a notebook—and that he has grown it into such a powerful bond with so many millions—still blows me away. When I'm near him, I have the same experience I had back when I first went to one of his stage productions: I leave feeling more connected to others, like I just came from church.

Oprah: I love the idea of miracles because I think my whole life is a miracle, and I wonder if you think yours is also.

Tyler: I know it is. There are a lot of people who have dreams, goals, and hopes, but there aren't a lot who get to see them realized.

Oprah: What's your definition of a miracle?

Tyler: A prayer answered. I remember being a kid and praying in the hell of my house to have somebody love me and somebody that I could love.

Oprah: Did you ever feel loved growing up?

Tyler: I knew that love was around. I truly believe my mother loved me. But feeling it all the time? I didn't.

Oprah: You caused quite a stir when you wrote on your Web site about your extensive abuse as a child. What made you do that?

Tyler: My intention was to free myself. My mother was very ill at the time. I was told she had only a month or so to live, which turned out to be true. And I'd just turned 40. I was frustrated with so much in my life. I had been carrying so much heaviness for so long and trying to smile my way through it. It was cathartic to write things down. That's what I do when I need freedom from something. Because it's hard to keep smiling. Even when my mother was well, it was hard to go home and sit with my father and try to smile. It didn't matter that I was 40; I still felt so much fear around him.

Oprah: What was life like for you with your father?

Tyler: My father was a man who didn't know his parents. When he was 2 years old, he was found in a drainage canal by a white man and brought to a 14-year-old black girl called May to be raised. This girl's parents only knew to beat her, so what she knew was to beat my father. Beat, humiliate, ridicule, all his life. So this is what I was born into. I didn't understand it for a very long time—why so much disdain and hatred. It wasn't until I got older and my mother and I had some conversations that I started to get where his anger came from. And that it was his issue, that I didn't own any of it.

Oprah: When you're a little boy, you don't know that.

Tyler: You don't know it. I think about the child I was, the tremendous debt I owe him now. There wasn't anybody there to protect him or make sure he was okay, but he made it through. He died to give birth to me.

Oprah: Oh, that makes me want to cry!

Tyler: And me, too, when I say it, but it's so true. I feel like he had to endure so much so that I could be here.

Oprah: What would your father do to you?

Tyler: Well, I hated the food that was in the house with a passion. Maybe it was just disgusting to me because I didn't like seeing dead animals lying on the table—raccoons and squirrels.

Oprah: And possums. That was in my grandmother's house, too. We were country folk.

Tyler: Those eyeballs looking at you. I wouldn't eat that food. Which meant that I was always hungry. But my father knew I loved cookies, so he would buy them and put them on top of the refrigerator and wait for me to go get them. And then he would beat me.

Oprah: What's the worst thing he did to you?

Tyler: I don't think I allowed myself to single out one moment. He would scream at me, "You're a dumb mother-f---er, you got book sense but you don't have no street sense!" 'Cause he hated the fact that I would read and draw and get straight A's in school. But even though he would humiliate me to my face, I would sometimes hear him talking to the neighbor, telling him what a great kid I was. How smart I was. It confused me to no end. That was one of the most agonizing things, because I didn't understand it.

Oprah: I read that he once hit you with an electrical cord.

Tyler: Yeah. He cornered me in a room one night and I still to this day don't know why. I've racked my brain to

From left: Perry dons a fat suit, wig, and dress to play the title character in his second film, *Madea's Family Reunion*, 2006; Celebrating Christmas in New Orleans at age 6, 1975; Directing Janet Jackson on the set of his new movie, *For Colored Girls*, in June 2010; laughing—and lounging—it up in the tour bus's luxurious bedroom.

figure out, what did I do? He came in drunk. That was his thing. Friday about 5 or 6 o'clock in the evening, we'd be waiting for him to get home. He'd come in, give us our allowance, and then leave to go get drunk. And as it got closer to 10, 11 o'clock, we all became very quiet.

Oprah: **Because you knew he was going to come home and raise hell?**

Tyler: He would walk in the door raising complete hell. Sometimes he would come home in such a rage that he was a totally different person. Then he'd get on his knees, pray, and go to sleep. The vacuum cleaner cord—that was one of those nights. He beat me till the skin was coming off. He was much bigger than me, so I couldn't get away. When he finally went in and did his prayer and lay down, I ran out of the house to my aunt who lived around the corner.

Oprah: **That's a slave whipping. I had a couple of those, too, growing up....**

Tyler: Mm-hmm. So I went to my aunt, who is one of those strong black women. She got her gun and came around to the house and put it up to his head. Her husband had to come take the pistol from her. And she told my mother then, "Wherever you go, you take this boy with you. Don't you leave him with that crazy mother-f---er." That's when I started going to Lane Bryant and beauty salons and everywhere else with my mother.

Oprah: **I know you had great, deep love and affection for your mother. But what was your feeling about her when you were a child? Because you want your mother to stand up for you.**

Tyler: Children love their mothers. Especially with a boy child and his mother, there's a bond that's unbreakable. I love my mother to this day. One of the most painful things I ever had to do was bury her, realizing that even though I was her hero, I couldn't help her with this last thing. I couldn't help her get better. All I wanted was to give her everything she wanted. Everything my father didn't give her, everything she never had.

Oprah: **You were never angry with her?**

Tyler: Not as a child. I would never say this if she were alive, but there was a time when I was older when I was angry with her, yeah, sure. But my love would override that.

Oprah: **All right. But now, in the midst of all the physical abuse, you were also sexually abused. Was this by a neighbor, a friend of the family, somebody you knew?**

Tyler: Neighbor, friend of the family, all of that. The first time, I was 6 or 7; it was a guy across the street. We built a birdhouse together and then suddenly he's got his hand in my pants.

Oprah: **Did you tell anybody?**

Tyler: Didn't tell a soul. But felt completely guilty about it. Felt betrayed.

Oprah: **Mm-hmm. Did it happen more than once?**

Tyler: Yes.

Oprah: **Did it happen regularly?**

Tyler: No.

Oprah: **But you were molested by other people, too?**

Tyler: Yes. One was a woman who lived in the apartment complex two doors down, when I was about 10 or 11. And there was a guy in church.

Oprah: **That must have been a lot for you to carry. A lot of hurt and anger and betrayal and confusion and shame. So how did all of this—*all* your experiences growing up—prepare you for the life you're now living? First of all, the aunt who came with the gun—the moment you said that, I thought, *Here comes Madea!***

Tyler: Yeah. The Bible says that all things work together for the good of those who love the Lord and are called according to his purpose. I believe that. Because I've seen it all work. I know for a fact if I had not been born to this mother, this father, this family, if I had not been born into this situation, then I wouldn't be here using my voice and my gifts to speak to millions of people.

Oprah: **When you left home, did you have this dream to become who you are right now?**

Tyler: I had watched your show. This is another thing that could just make me cry, you sitting here now. I watched your show, and you were speaking to me. There was nobody around me that told me I could fly. Nobody at school, no teacher, nobody who said, "You're special." But I saw you on television and your skin was like mine. And you said, "If you write things down, it's cathartic." So I started writing. And it changed my life.

Oprah: **You weren't writing before then?**

Tyler: Never wrote.

Oprah: **Wasn't I talking about journaling?**

Tyler: Yes. But I started writing my own things—using different characters' names because I didn't want anybody to know that I had been through this. A friend of mine found it and said, "Tyler, this is a really good play." And I thought, *Well, maybe it is.* So that's where it started.

Oprah: **How old were you then?**

Tyler: Nineteen or 20.

Oprah: **You were still living at home?**

Tyler: Still living at home.

Oprah: **You didn't go to college.**

Tyler: No. Got kicked out of high school before graduation. But I went back for my GED.

Oprah: **And what had you gotten kicked out for?**

Tyler: I was arguing with a counselor. I said some pretty nasty things. You know, after all the abuse, I was a pretty angry person.

Oprah: I was going to say, wouldn't that make you either angry or so introverted that you couldn't function?

Tyler: It made me both. An angry introvert, which is dangerous.

Oprah: But then you started to write about your life. And somebody says, "This is pretty good." Now, lots of people think, *There's something special about me,* and they wait for something good to happen—and it doesn't. Why you?

Tyler: Because I never stopped chasing it down. I don't think the dreams die—I think that people give up. I think it gets too hard. There were so many dark days when I wanted to lie there and die.

Oprah: You actually considered suicide?

Tyler: Yes. When the rainbow wasn't enough.

Oprah: When was this?

Tyler: Well, it was twice. Once when I was very young—I slit my wrists. And the other time—

Oprah: Whoa. You can't just say "I slit my wrists" and then move on. How old were you?

Tyler: About 11 or 12.

Oprah: And you had to be taken to the hospital?

Tyler: No, it wasn't that deep, wasn't that bad. I don't know if it was more a cry for help—

Oprah: Well, it was obviously a cry for help. And when was the second time?

Tyler: Probably when I was around 22. It was winter, and I was living in Atlanta, trying to get a play going. I was carrying a lot of frustration, I was homeless, and I had just scraped together enough money for this pay-by-the-week hotel that was full of crackheads. Every morning all the people who lived in the hotel—it was very cold that winter—would start their cars to warm them up. And the exhaust would fill my room. The cars would be out there warming up—at least ten, 15 cars—and I would get up and ask them to move. But I got to a point where that morning, I just lay there waiting.

Oprah: For the fumes to kill you?

Tyler: Absolutely.

Oprah: What does that feel like, to want to die?

Tyler: You feel there's nothing better for you.

Oprah: It's the end of hope.

Tyler: It's the end of a lot of things.

Oprah: So this was after you had written the play *I Know I've Been Changed,* and it failed.

Tyler: Yes. Moved from New Orleans to Atlanta, wrote the show, had every bit of my money tied up in it. I had worked selling used cars, I had worked at hotels, I had saved my tax return, I had saved $12,000 to put this play up, and I thought 1,200 people would see it over a weekend. Thirty people showed up. It was pretty devastating, because to do this, I had to leave the job I had.

Oprah: What was your job?

Tyler: At the time I was a bill collector. But there are at least 40 companies in Atlanta with a record of me working there over a period of five or six years. I was a used car salesman, shoe-shine boy, bartender, waiter…. And listen, I use all those skills today—I can pour a mean drink!

Oprah: So you believed that after saving that $12,000, now you're going to be on your way. But the play failed. The end of the dream as you knew it.

Tyler: Not necessarily the end of the dream. I went back to work, started trying to do the show again. And then I got an opportunity to do it and went to my boss and said, "I need time off." They wouldn't give it to me, so I had to quit. I tried to do the show again the following year. It failed again. But there was something in me that said, *This is what you're supposed to do.*

Oprah: Even though it had failed twice.

Tyler: Yes. I stayed the course. I tried it again the following year. Had a job. Lost the job.

Oprah: You failed a third time.

Tyler: Yes. Then there's the rent, car payment, everything. So I'm out on the street.

Oprah: And that's why you ended up in the pay-by-the-week hotel.

Tyler: Yes—when I could afford it. Other than that, I was sleeping in my car. I'd get another job and fail again. This happened once a year, from 1992 until 1998.

Oprah: And when did the play finally hit?

Tyler: March 1998. A few months before that, I had gotten into an argument on the phone with my father. He's yelling at me, cussing and screaming, and something happened in me. I started saying things I never thought I'd be able to—things I did not even know were in me. "How dare you? Who do you think you are? You are wrong." It was as if the little boy in me was screaming out everything he'd never been able to say. And my father is silent on the phone because he has never heard this side of me. And at the end of it, I hear him say, "I love you," which at the age of 27, *I* had never heard before. I hung up the phone, and I knew something had changed. My entire source of energy had been ripped from me. From the time I'd left my father's house until that moment, I had been plugged into negativity. I was plugged into anger to keep moving, to do the play, to work, to get up every day. It was based on "F--k you; I'm gonna prove you wrong." But that day, when I finally said those things, I had to find a new source of energy.

Oprah: Before that, you'd been coming from anger.

Tyler: And wanting to be around negativity. I enjoyed being a bill collector because I could make other people miserable. That's why I made so much money—I got to pass on the hurt.

Oprah: But after you hung up the phone with your father...

Tyler: It was like a car that runs on diesel fuel and now suddenly diesel doesn't work.

Oprah: Because you had released all the energy you'd been carrying. Big, big, big.

Tyler: That took me back to the times when my mother would bring me to church, which took me back to God, which took me back to my faith. And prayer.

Oprah: So you felt peace?

Tyler: Instantly. And I think the reason a lot of people don't want to have that kind of confrontation is that once that anger is gone, you're faced with, *Do I continue to thrive on the negativity? Or do I make the shift into what is going to work for me now?* I had to make that conscious choice.

Oprah: Well, that was a miracle. That was a holy moment for you. What is your relationship with your father now?

Tyler: It's very respectful. I helped him retire a few years ago. But we still can't have a conversation, because all I get are tears. Tears and shrugging his shoulders. That's about as much emotion as he can give.

Oprah: So you've tried to talk?

Tyler: I've tried to get as much information as I can, because I don't know him.

Oprah: I also believe in being respectful because that's what the Bible says you're supposed to do: Honor thy father and thy mother. But do you hold any resentment toward him?

Tyler: I can't walk up to him and throw my arms around him and say, "I love you, let's go fishing." Honoring him is doing what he did for me. He took care of me. He made sure we ate, and that we had shelter. So I give him the things he gave me.

Oprah: Yes. And then after that phone conversation, after you released all that negativity—the next time you did the play, it succeeded.

Tyler: The very next time. March 12, 1998. I had made the choice to do this last show. And this time there was a line of people around the corner trying to get in the place. From that moment on, the houses have been sold out everywhere.

Oprah: What's the most people you've played to in a weekend?

Tyler: About 55,000.

Oprah: When you first realized that people were showing up, did you think that was it—you'd made it?

Tyler: No, because then I was afraid every day that it was going to end tomorrow. You know the feeling.

Oprah: Yeah, I used to think that same thing every time

someone else came out with a new talk show. But let's get to Madea. I heard that you originally weren't even going to play her, that it happened by accident. Is that true?

Tyler: No. I was going to do Madea. The accident was that it was supposed to be a very quick five-minute scene, but when the lead actress didn't show up, Madea ended up onstage the entire time.

Oprah: Do you love her?

Tyler: What she does for people gives me great joy. What she's done for me, yes. But as far as, you know, actually doing it every night, it's pretty much a pain, wearing the fat suit and talking in that high voice for hours.

Oprah: Let's talk about how she came to be. She's a combination of your aunt who came to the house with the gun, and your mother.

Tyler: Yes. The softer, more sympathetic side is my mother. 'Cause I would often say, "She will beat the hell out of you, then turn around and offer you some pie and a Band-Aid or a ride to the hospital."

Oprah: How was Madea created?

Tyler: I have to thank Eddie Murphy, 'cause after I saw him do the Klumps [in *Nutty Professor II*], I said, "I'm going to try my hand at a female character." It was the brilliance of Eddie Murphy. I need to write him a check. Say thank you.

Oprah: Do you remember the exact moment that she came to be?

Tyler: Absolutely. There was a sold-out house at the Regal Theater in Chicago, and five minutes before the show, I put on the costume and stood at the mirror for the first time. I'm saying, *Damn, are you really going to do this?* Then the show started and I had no choice—they pushed me out onstage. Madea had a cane and she didn't talk very loud and her voice was much deeper and she sat in one spot the whole time. But after a while, I finally had to move. And when I moved there was laughter. And then I said a joke, and it was funny. I wish I had that first night on tape. It was pretty damn scary. But at the end, man, there was a standing ovation.

Oprah: For her?

Tyler: For the show, for her, for me.

Oprah: But she got the loudest applause?

Tyler: Yeah. And I was blown away. I'm 6'6" and a man. I'm thinking, *Who knew?*

Oprah: Who decided that Madea should become a movie?

Tyler: I did.

Oprah: You weren't scared to make a movie?

Tyler: No, because I didn't know what the hell I was doing. I just saw all those people coming out to the plays.

Oprah: By the time you did that first movie, *Diary of a Mad Black Woman,* you'd been doing the plays how long?

Tyler: Eight years on the road.

Oprah: And for your new movie you took on an iconic book and play and story, *For Colored Girls*. Were you scared to do that?

Tyler: Sure. But I enjoy a challenge.

Oprah: During the process of filming this movie, I think that something happened to you. The difference between doing a serious drama and having done Madea—

Tyler: It elevated my thinking of what film is. It made me understand that there is an art and a style to it. But here's the thing: Steven Spielberg got to start messing around with a camera as a kid, and Jason Reitman got his father to help. Me, it took nine films to be ready.

Oprah: You just sort of taught yourself how to be a director. How did you do that?

Tyler: I learned in progress. My first time directing was *Madea's Family Reunion,* which I cannot watch.

Oprah: Why not?

Tyler: Because I didn't know that the cameras should actually move! The camera is the eye of the audience. But it's all a part of learning, and I'm grateful for the journey, and I'm proud of the work—every bit of it. In every film I have learned something to propel me to the next level. I don't know what else will come in the future, but *For Colored Girls* is the absolute best that I can do at this time.

Oprah: I was talking to somebody the other day who was saying that you are a performer's director.

Tyler: Well, first of all, the caliber of acting in this movie is just top-notch. I don't think it gets any better. You cannot have Phylicia Rashad, Kimberly Elise, Thandie Newton—

Oprah: Anika Noni Rose...

Tyler: You cannot have them in a scene together and not expect there to be sparks.

Oprah: The film is a big risk. The audience that has supported you is used to being able to laugh every time they go to your movies.

Tyler: It will be interesting to see what happens.

Oprah: Okay. Shifting gears now: Are you comfortable with your wealth?

Tyler: I'm comfortable with the wealth. It took me a minute. 'Cause the first year I gave every dime away. There was something in me that felt like I didn't deserve it.

Oprah: And are you over that now?

Tyler: You're sitting on my tricked-out bus! I'm over that.

Oprah: What about the attention your wealth brings?

Tyler: That I don't like. I don't like the *Forbes* list. I also don't need to be in the biggest hotel and walking through the lobby and shopping and everybody looking at me. I'd rather just do the show and go live my life privately.

Oprah: Do you think you're shy?

Tyler: Until you put me onstage and put me in a situation where I'm supposed to perform, yes. I'm not good at all in small crowds.

Oprah: You may be reserved, but I wouldn't call you shy. You'd just rather be at home by yourself—

Tyler: With the dogs—

Oprah: —than out at a big glamorous party.

Tyler: Not going to do that. I hate it with a passion.

Oprah: All right. So why aren't you with someone? I cannot figure that out.

Tyler: I love being by myself too much.

Oprah: Maybe you haven't met the right person. Do you think it's that?

Tyler: I keep hearing that.

Oprah: Have you been in love?

Tyler: I was, a few years ago, with the wrong woman. And it was really bad for me and hurtful. Maybe I'm still dealing with that. 'Cause I never cried in a relationship before.

Oprah: You cried in that relationship?

Tyler: Yeah.

Oprah: You didn't tell me that. I didn't know you were in love. I thought it was just that thing in the beginning where it's intense, and you can't even call it love yet 'cause you haven't been through enough for it to be love. Are you open now?

Tyler: I'm open to whatever God has for me. I really am. However it comes.

Oprah: So as we sit here now with you looking at how far you've come and where you still have to go, what is it you know for sure?

Tyler: What I know beyond a shadow of a doubt is that God is with me. I know that. I know that He's always been with me. It is evident in everything I have endured—and the fact that I made it through with some sanity.

Oprah: Can you see the future for yourself?

Tyler: After my mother died, I realized that one of the reasons I was always running so hard was that I'd made some promises to her as a child that I was trying to keep. All those years of working and working—a lot of it was for her. Now that she's gone, I've had to reevaluate. So when you ask what's next, it makes me take a step back and go, *What do I want to do? What's going to make me happy? And do I want to continue working this hard?* At this point, I'm still looking for the answers. ◖

UPDATE Tyler Perry's latest film, Madea's Big Happy Family, *was released in April 2011.*

Oprah Talks to Elizabeth Edwards

She lived to 61 with cancer, buried a child, and withstood an excruciatingly public blow to her marriage. But in a warm, intimate, and startlingly honest discussion with Oprah, Elizabeth Edwards left no doubt that, even toward the end, she was standing tall.

Nestled amid majestic pine trees near Chapel Hill, North Carolina, sits Elizabeth Edwards's dream home: the 28,200-square-foot property she and her family moved into in 2006, four months before her husband, John Edwards, announced his run for president. Though the house is enormous, there's nothing ostentatious about it. "We're not fancy people," Elizabeth tells me as we settle in on a sofa in the living room. "All we need is a comfortable place to sit and have a conversation." Of course, little did she know as she was making plans for the house how painful some of the conversations taking place here would prove to be.

The Edwards family has survived a series of crises that began long before their dream home was built. In 1996, 16-year-old Wade—the eldest of Elizabeth and John's four children—was killed when his Jeep overturned after being forced off the road by high winds as he drove to the family's North Carolina beach house. In October 2004, Elizabeth discovered a lump in her right breast; she subsequently underwent a lumpectomy and chemotherapy to treat what turned out to be stage II cancer. Then, on December 30, 2006, two days after John announced his presidential run, he confessed to Elizabeth that he'd been unfaithful—once—with a videographer who'd worked on his campaign. Three months later, doctors discovered that Elizabeth's cancer had metastasized and was now stage IV: treatable, but not curable. And as if all this weren't devastation enough, in 2008 John told Elizabeth that his infidelity had in fact been more than a one-night stand. The *National Enquirer* reported that John had visited the woman and her infant daughter at a Los Angeles hotel, and rumors began spreading that the child was his.

Elizabeth says that even if John were to take a paternity test, the results wouldn't matter. She tells me she's not concerned with the other woman's life; her priority is her own life, the one she's worked so hard to build for her family. She is fiercely protective of her children: Cate,

A WELCOMING
PRESENCE:
Arriving at the
Edwards's home,
March 2009.

49

1. Touring the house with Elizabeth and daughter Emma Claire. 2. Meeting up with John, as Elizabeth, Jack, and Emma Claire look on. 3. Withdrawing from the 2008 race in New Orleans, joined by elder daughter, Cate. 4. Elizabeth and John holding Wade, not yet a year old, in 1980. 5. On the campaign trail in Iowa, 2008. 6. The Edwardses on their wedding day, 1977.

Emma Claire, and Jack. And she has made her home a place of comfort and peace. It was here, in this haven, that she wrote her book, *Resilience*—a memoir of the trials and triumphs of her journey. It is here, too, that she has managed to find perspective. Painted above a doorway leading into the home's master suite is a verse from the 1992 song "Anthem," by Leonard Cohen. Befitting this moment in Elizabeth's life, the lyrics are an ode to human frailty and transcendence: *Ring the bells that still can ring. Forget your perfect offering. There is a crack in everything. That's how the light gets in.*

Oprah: **When you walk into this house, it really feels like a family home. And you designed it?**

Elizabeth: I did the first layout, and then I have to give a nod to [Raleigh-based designer] B.A. Farrell, who turned my little drawings into something that they could actually build.

Oprah: **But you created it.**

Elizabeth: I did.

Oprah: **For your family. For Emma Claire and for Jack. We were just in their rooms, and I was saying that when you tell your kids, "Go to your room!" they're probably like, "Great!"**

Elizabeth: The entire house is really built with the kids in mind.

Oprah: **It's a beautiful home.**

Elizabeth: Thank you, Oprah.

Oprah: **And you're doing well?**

Elizabeth: I'm doing pretty well. I mean, you watch the news; there are so many stories of incredible hardship that it's hard to sit in this house—even with the things I face—and think, *Boy, my life really stinks.* It doesn't.

Oprah: **Your prognosis is...what?**

Elizabeth: You know, they don't really tell you.

Oprah: **The doctors don't say how long you have to live?**

Elizabeth: They never have. I think they're trained not to—in the same way that when I talk to my children, I'm honest but I know when to be vague. A year, ten years—based on what my doctor tells me, it could be either one. But I get scans periodically. And I switch up medications.

Oprah: **Are you on chemo or radiation?**

Elizabeth: I get a kind of chemotherapy. Some I take by pill, at home. And intravenous, I get every two weeks.

Oprah: **Are you in pain?**

Elizabeth: I'm not. But you know, I'm 60 this summer. I

get achy sometimes, with two little kids. So it's hard to tell whether that's something to do with cancer or not.

Oprah: But you don't feel sick.

Elizabeth: I don't. I just get worn out.

Oprah: It was during this last presidential campaign that you were given the new diagnosis, that it was terminal. And the first thing you did was...

Elizabeth: Cry. I admit it. We were sitting in a little room in the hospital, and it was hard not to break down. But then we said we're going to keep pushing. You can fight for yourself or you can just throw your hands up and say, "Okay, I'm through. I'll just wait to die."

Oprah: At the time, I thought, how brave of you to take that on—to keep going with the longest campaign anybody's ever seen. And now that I've read *Resilience,* **I see you already knew your husband had had an affair.**

Elizabeth: I knew there'd been *a night.* That's all I knew. And I'd been around politicians long enough to figure there were a lot of people for whom there'd been *a night.*

Oprah: Let's go back to that story. December 30, 2006. John had announced that he was running for the presidency two days prior. And on December 30, he comes home and tells you....

Elizabeth: He told me as little as he thought he could and still hold on to his life—and me.

Oprah: So—I'm clarifying this for the people who haven't read your book yet—December 30 he comes and he tells you he's had this indiscretion. Did he use the word *indiscretion?*

Elizabeth: You'd think I'd remember, but it's sort of a fuzz.

Oprah: You screamed and cried....

Elizabeth: I did everything you would expect.

> "You can fight for youself or you can just throw your hands up and say, 'Okay, I'm through. I'll just wait to die.'"

Oprah: And you asked him at that time to just get out of the race.

Elizabeth: I did. I was afraid for my family, afraid for him. And he said—and it made sense—"You know, I've just gotten in. We're going to get the most questions if I get out two days after I got in. Let it run its course and see if this woman's a problem or not." And he didn't expect her to be.

Oprah: You asked your husband for just one gift when you got married. What was that?

Elizabeth: I wanted him to be faithful. It was enormously important to me.

Oprah: You said, "No rings, no flowers...."

Elizabeth: I don't care about those kinds of things. But I'd seen what happened to my mother when she thought my father had cheated on her. And I didn't want to go through that.

Oprah: How did you learn about that?

Elizabeth: Well, of course, I don't know whether—Father's now dead, and my mother is not particularly cogent. But when I was in eighth grade, I found my mother's journals. I spent a lot of time reading journal after journal. And I got to see how it engendered a lot of self-doubt in an incredibly accomplished, intelligent woman, and how it undermined her in so many ways—just the thought of it. It made her less than she could be. I did not want to see that happen to me.

Oprah: You say that your husband's affair started with just four words.

Elizabeth: What he's said is that this woman had spotted him in the hotel in which he was staying. He was meeting with someone in the restaurant bar area. This is in New York. And then he went to dinner at a nearby restaurant, and when he walked back, she was standing in front of the hotel and said to him, "You are so hot." I can't deliver it—I don't know how to deliver such a line as that.

Oprah: I think she probably said it a little differently….

Elizabeth: You think so? You want to try? Because I'm not going there in any way. I know he's had people come on to him before. You know, you do rope lines, people hand you their phone numbers all the time. But you just smile nicely and hand their phone number to your aide.

Oprah: So on December 30 he came home and told you that he'd had….

Elizabeth: This relation, or indiscretion. And that she was out of his life and he regretted what he'd done.

Oprah: And it was only one time.

Elizabeth: Yes—which still leveled me. But it was something I came to be able to manage, partly because no one's perfect. This is certainly a place where I had hoped for perfection, but people make mistakes. So I was able to try to work with him and understand what happened and what that meant for us.

Oprah: You're smart people. Were you not afraid that at any moment, this woman could show up, go to the press, make life difficult?

Elizabeth: I was enormously afraid. I don't understand the psychology of someone who stands in front of hotels and tries to meet rich or successful or well-known people. Is that person after some sort of fame? Could I expect her to try to get something out of this? Probably.

Oprah: Did you believe that it was only one time with her?

Elizabeth: I did.

Oprah: Did you believe it was the only time ever?

Elizabeth: I want to believe that. But he has a lot of trust to rebuild, because after he first told me, I spent a year and a half thinking that he was being completely open with me and that we were on the same team.

Oprah: So when you were out campaigning, saying what a great husband and father and man he was, were you being honest?

Elizabeth: Well, I changed the way I talked. And I canceled a lot of things right at the beginning. But you know, his *positions* were things I could really embrace. When he talks about poverty, it's not a campaign statement. This is something he deeply believes in. But, yes, the "great husband" part

was missing from many of the things I said then. I made a decision not to put myself in a position where I was somehow complicit in some sort of cover-up. And sometimes it would be too much for me and I would leave the campaign trail for a few days.

Oprah: You were still angry.

Elizabeth: Still angry and hurt, and I had a lot of self-doubt.

Oprah: And that's when you believed it was just one night.

Elizabeth: Right. I do believe that John deeply loves me. I've been married to him now for over 30 years. He is a part of my being, just like my children are. And I want it to work out. I do. So I'm giving him a chance to rebuild the trust. I've made a decision to forgive him. If I had led an absolutely brainless life, I suppose I would find that harder to do. But I know that I've made a lot of mistakes—maybe not of this magnitude and certainly nothing that would hurt him in the same way, but we're all imperfect.

Oprah: But when you found out that what your husband had told you about the indiscretion wasn't true, how did you handle that?

Elizabeth: That was like starting over, from a worse position.

Oprah: How did you find out?

Elizabeth: John told me.

Oprah: After he had been discovered by the tabloids?

Elizabeth: Most of it he told me before. He was gradually more forthright with me as he was more confident that he wasn't going to lose the life he cherished. Then after the tabloid stuff, a few more things came out. I think we went through a process over the summer of 2008.

Oprah: Did you want to know every detail?

Elizabeth: Yes. I'm a puzzle doer. I had some pieces of the puzzle, and I felt it was going to make sense if I had all the pieces. You know, I once read a short story about how much you could tell about people from their shoes. You could tell where they had been, what they did, whether they were real walkers. So sometimes I wanted to know a detail because I was just curious, and sometimes I wanted to know a detail because I thought it was going to open some window for me to try to understand.

> "I'd seen what happened to my mother when she thought my father had cheated on her. It engendered a lot of self-doubt in an incredibly accomplished woman. It made her less than she could be. I did not want that to happen to me."

Oprah: Did you want to know whether he loved her?

Elizabeth: I'm sure I asked, but it seemed impossible to me. And I think impossible to him. This person is very different from me, and really very different from him. We're basically old-fashioned people. I remember the first time we went shopping for a jacket for him, and when I pulled one out, he said, "That seems a little loud to me." I said, "It's herringbone!"

Oprah: As toned down as it gets!

Elizabeth: That's right. So this was a pretty big leap for him. Maybe its being so different is what was attractive.

Oprah: What do you know about her?

Elizabeth: Just what I've read. I've only seen this person one time.

Oprah: So after the tabloid story, did you immediately make a decision that you would stay with John, no matter how thick the story got?

Elizabeth: No. I didn't know. I wanted to sit down with him. I wanted to scream at him. I wanted him to have to look me in the face. And I also wanted to protect him. I wanted all of us to come out of it like we had been, so we could keep our story.

Oprah: I've had friends who've been through this situation, and I've never heard anyone say she wanted to protect her husband.

Elizabeth: I saw him go through an enormous amount of pain. And after living with him and loving him for so long, I'd be lying if I said I didn't wish his pain could end, too.

Oprah: When the story came out, there was a deep feeling of empathy for you. We all felt the blow.

Elizabeth: That's the reason I didn't tell my sister at first. She had been through infidelity and a terrible divorce. And she would always talk about how our marriage was so great. If you take out this single piece and the lying about it, I do have a perfect marriage. I have a husband who adores me, who is unbelievable with my children, who has provided for us in ways we never could've imagined—and who has, in times when I've been in enormous pain, been by my side.

Oprah: He has literally fed you when you were sick.

Elizabeth: He has. So he's done this terrible thing, a thing that he thinks is terrible, too—do I say, I'm sorry, all of those other things don't count?

Oprah: You write that John can try to treat your wound— and he has tried. He can try to make you less afraid—and he has tried. But the way you were is no longer the way you can be. What does this new reality mean for you?

Elizabeth: I was a pretty self-confident person. I had a pretty good idea of who I was—my limitations and virtues. I was comfortable with that. I didn't worry about speaking my mind. And I looked like I looked: I was always struggling with weight or something else—

Oprah: Hello!

Elizabeth: Hello, sister! And at home, I'd put a hair band in and put on my silly striped socks and not worry about too much. But now I thought, *Do I look awful at home? Is that it? Or am I too strident?* There was a lot of questioning about what it was about me that had caused this to happen. But I've come to the conclusion that it never was about me.

Oprah: Did you both sit down with your children and talk with them about what happened?

Elizabeth: We did. John told them that he behaved inappropriately, but that our family was the most important thing to him and that he was going to do everything he could to make it up to us.

Oprah: What did he say to your older daughter, Cate?

Elizabeth: That's a conversation John and Cate had by themselves.

Oprah: Okay. Before this interview, you said you had only one condition: that we not mention the other woman by name.

Elizabeth: Right. If somebody wants to work at destroying my family and my home in order to get into the light, I'm really not interested. My book is not about this woman. It's about this family.

Oprah: The other woman has a baby.

Elizabeth: That's what I understand.

Oprah: There is great speculation that your husband, John Edwards, is the father of that baby.

Elizabeth: I've seen a picture of the baby, and it doesn't look like my children—but I don't have any idea. This is the part where you have to concentrate on your own life. Whatever the facts are, that doesn't change my life.

Oprah: But the truth is that most of us don't know men who meet women in hotels and hold babies that are not their own.

Elizabeth: Oh, golly, then you don't know many politicians! Holding babies is our business.

> "If the walls could talk, yes, sometimes I think about my prognosis. Mostly when I feel a pain: *Is this the beginning of the end?* You're just overwhelmed by what you've left undone and who you're going to leave behind."

Oprah: But not at a hotel after midnight.

Elizabeth: Well, first of all, I don't know anything about that picture except that he's wearing clothes he supposedly wasn't wearing the night they talked about. Some sort of sweaty running clothes. So I have no idea where it was taken. I have no idea when it was taken.

Oprah: Have you asked him if it is his child?

Elizabeth: He's talked to me about questions people ask. He doesn't know any more than I know.

Oprah: So if he had a paternity test and it turned out that it was or it wasn't his child, it wouldn't change your life.

Elizabeth: I could try to *make* it change my life. I could beat myself up about it if I thought that he was trying to start a family with this woman. But do I think that's true? Not by any stretch of the imagination.

Oprah: Do you blame her?

Elizabeth: I blame John. But I think that women have to have more respect for other women. I've created this life. It takes a lot of work to put together a marriage, to put together a family and a home. You can't just knock on the door and say, "You're out, I'm in." You have to have enough respect for other human beings to leave their lives alone. If you admire that life, build it for yourself.

Oprah: The big question for everybody who's going to read *Resilience:* How do you rebuild trust? Especially when you were lied to and then lied to again.

Elizabeth: It's a slow process. It means that sometimes John has to have conversations he doesn't want to have, to let me try to make sense of it for myself.

Oprah: Is it a day-by-day thing?

Elizabeth: Neither one of us is out the door, so I guess it's day by day. It's not that we don't argue….

Oprah: But you're still living together.

Elizabeth: Still living together.

Oprah: There are rumors that you're not—but I saw him in the kitchen.

Elizabeth: His clothes are in the closet.

Oprah: It looks like he lives here. Are you still in love with him?

Elizabeth: It's a complicated question. It's really hard. But I wouldn't be here if I didn't love him. I wouldn't be here if I didn't want to be. He's provided us with enough that we could work on this while living separately. But I want him near me. I've stayed with him because this is a really good man who has done a very, very bad thing—but who really cares about things a lot of people just ignore. Though this may seem like an odd word, he's a very moral person, with an idea of right and wrong. And so my disappointment in him is matched by *his* disappointment in him.

Oprah: **What's a typical day like for you now?**

Elizabeth: When Emma's on safety patrol, she has to be at school at 7:25. So I get up at 6:20 and get everybody fed and dressed and to school by 7:25. Then I come home and do whatever needs to be done here—laundry, feeding the dogs, then writing. I do speeches, and I try to write a new speech for different places.

Oprah: **Why did you want to write *Resilience*?**

Elizabeth: When I was first asked about writing it—

Oprah: **When were you first asked, by the way?**

Elizabeth: Right after my first book was published.

Oprah: **Because usually after you have one successful book, the publisher wants another, right?**

Elizabeth: Right.

Oprah: **Everybody thought you were going to write about why your husband got out of the campaign.**

Elizabeth: There was a lot I didn't know at the time that I said yes. And when I learned a lot more, I called my editor and said, "No, I can't write it." But then you start to think, *Am I going to say I can't do these things, or am I going to take my life back?* So although it was hard and in some ways painful to write, it was a statement that I own my own experiences. Nobody else has control of them.

Oprah: **You write, "This is the life we have now, and the only way to find peace, the only way to be resilient when these land mines explode beneath your foundation, is first to accept that there is a new reality." After your son Wade's death in 1996, there had to be a new reality.**

Elizabeth: Right. It took me a long time to get there. I continued to look for him in odd places. I would open drawers, thinking, *He's going to be in that drawer, I'm going to find him, and we can go back to the way it was.* Of course, that was ludicrous, but you want it so badly that logic flies out the window.

Oprah: **It's so interesting that you can write a book about resilience and yet be in the midst of starting a new story that could last anywhere from one year to ten.**

Elizabeth: Who knows?

Oprah: **Do you want to know?**

Elizabeth: I want to know a range. Should I be organizing the costume closet right now? Do I need to do it right this second or can that wait for a couple of months? I'm so afraid to die with things a mess. Without the Legos organized. Without our photos scanned.

Oprah: **You were telling me you just did Jack's Legos, and it took you how long?**

Elizabeth: Three weeks.

Oprah: **And do you think about your prognosis?**

Elizabeth: If the walls could talk, yes, sometimes I think about my prognosis. Mostly when I feel a pain: *Is this the beginning of the end?* And sometimes I get really, really down. You're just overwhelmed by what you've left undone and who you're going to leave behind.

Oprah: **Two small children.**

Elizabeth: And this magnificent daughter who went through a brother's death.

Oprah: **Have you talked about it with Cate?**

Elizabeth: I have.

Oprah: **What have you told Jack and Emma Claire?**

Elizabeth: I tell them that I have this disease, that this disease is what will probably kill me. And we ask them, "Is anybody at this table not going to die?" You know, I happen to know what I'm going to die from. But everybody's end is the same.

Oprah: **In your book, you say, "Death looks different to someone who has placed a child in the ground."**

Elizabeth: It's not as frightening. If there's an ever after—please, please, please—I would be leaving part of my family, but I can go and join another part, and wait for that day when we're all together again. In some ways, it's something you yearn for.

Oprah: **And a relief.**

Elizabeth: A relief. That's my expectation. Though I don't think it takes all the fear away.

Oprah: **How do you want to be remembered?**

Elizabeth: It's going to sound funny for somebody who is trained as a lawyer, but I wouldn't mind being remembered as a homemaker—someone who made a home for this family.

Oprah: **As the mom who organized her son's Legos. It's very clear that your family is everything to you.**

Elizabeth: I'm deeply in love with my family.

Oprah: **What do you know for sure?**

Elizabeth: Nothing ever stays the same.

Oprah: **The new reality is always evolving.**

Elizabeth: It's always evolving. And it is what you make of it. And that's a very important lesson. **O**

UPDATE In January 2010, John Edwards publicly stated that he is the father of Frances Quinn Hunter. Elizabeth Edwards filed for legal separation shortly thereafter. She passed away peacefully on December 7, 2010.

Oprah Talks to Jerry Seinfeld

He redefined TV comedy. Here an American cultural icon opens up about his stingingly funny film, *Bee Movie*, his kids, his cars, his wife—guys: memorize what he learns from Oprah!—and his top three rules for living well.

Over a late-night cup of coffee at Manhattan's Westway Diner in 1988, co-medians Jerry Seinfeld and Larry David had an idea: a sitcom based on the life of a New York stand-up comic. In July 1989, their brain-storm became *The Seinfeld Chronicles,* a quirky pilot that...yada yada yada. Everyone knows what happened next. *Seinfeld* redefined television comedy, won ten Emmys, and became a cultural phenomenon. Lines from the show are still lodged in our lexicon—not that there's anything wrong with that.

After Jerry decided to end the show in 1998 (an incred-ible 76 million viewers tuned in to the finale), he returned to his first love, stand-up comedy, and also happened to find a new love: In the year and a half following *Seinfeld's* last episode, he met and married Jessica Sklar, then a publicist. They've since had three children, Sascha, Julian, and Shepherd.

But Jerry, 57, still makes time for brainstorming ses-sions over coffee. Several years ago, he had dinner with legendary director and DreamWorks Studios cofounder Steven Spielberg; it was a serendipitous meeting that gave birth to an entirely new type of Seinfeld project. *Bee Movie*—the title is a twist on Hollywood slang for a second-rate film—is an animated story about Barry B. Benson, a bumblebee who leaves the predictable life of his hive in search of adventure. Jerry cowrote and copro-duced it, and provides the voice of Barry; the cast also includes Renée Zellweger, Matthew Broderick, and Chris Rock. (And if you hear a familiar voice during the court-room scene, yes, that's me.)

In August 2007, Jerry and I sat down in his living room on what he called one of the happiest mornings of his life: He'd just completed four years of work on *Bee Movie.*

Oprah: How do you feel?

Jerry: This is the day I step into the next place in my life. I didn't walk in the house last night, I stumbled in. I had no idea how much is involved in making a movie.

Oprah: You've never made a movie before.

Jerry: No. I've *been* to movies, and I'll tell you, it's better to see them than make one.

Oprah: Tell me how *Bee Movie* came about.

Jerry: I asked Steven Spielberg to direct a commercial I was going to make for American Express. I'd never met him, but I thought, *What the hell—why don't I call? I'm Jerry Seinfeld, I'm not just* nobody. [*Laughs*] Steven says, "I can't do it, but why don't we have dinner tomorrow in East Hampton?" I say, "That sounds great." Then I hang up the phone and go, "Oh my God! I'm a Jewish boy from Long Island, and I'm having dinner with Steven Spielberg!" It was like my second Bar Mitzvah. So I get up the next morning, I shower, and I sit down on a chair at 9 A.M. I was too excited to do anything but wait.

Oprah: I know what you mean!

Jerry: There I was, waiting until 6 P.M. when my wife, Jess, and I would meet Steven and his wife, Kate Capshaw. Now, my wife is one of the best-dressed women I know, but at 20 minutes before 6, she comes out and says, "What do you think?" and her blouse was just slightly see-through. Slightly. I then said something

Jerry and Oprah
in his 1959 Porsche
GT Speedster,
August 17, 2007.

I'd never said before: "I'm not crazy about the top."

Oprah: **Twenty minutes before you were supposed to meet Steven Spielberg!**

Jerry: Exactly. Every husband knows when he has moved into DEFCON 2. My mind was spinning with all the right and wrong ways to talk to a woman about her clothes.

Oprah: **Why couldn't you just say, "Honey, I can see through your top"?**

Jerry: Because when you're a good husband, you don't "just say" anything! You *think* first, especially in a moment like this. We'd only been married for three years then, so I wasn't very experienced. Being a good husband is like being a good stand-up comic—you need ten years before you can even call yourself a beginner. My skills were stretched to the max. I had to get this wife into another blouse without a fight.

Oprah: **And the clock is ticking!**

Jerry: And ticking. I started with compliments. Then I accepted all the blame for taking too long in the shower, or for showering in the first place, or for whatever I did wrong—it was all my fault. So I engineered the blouse change, we got into my Porsche—the one that's 43 years old and has a piddly ignition—and we have exactly the amount of time we need to get to the restaurant. I had wanted to get there early; instead of gushing about his movies, I wanted to show respect by being there when he arrived. But on Long Island, the police write tickets to the fancy-pants New York City people who flood their little towns in the summer.

Oprah: **And they'd know you're one of those people because they'd spot your Porsche.**

Jerry: Right. I'm on a straight road that I could have gone pretty fast on, because I really want to be sitting in that booth before Steven gets there, but I did 33 in a 30 miles per hour zone. So a day that started off with me waiting in a chair for hours turned into that scene in *Star Wars* where the walls are closing in on Luke Skywalker. Just as I'm pulling in to the place, I spot Steven and Kate driving in behind me. I think, *I could run into the restaurant and hope that Steven doesn't recognize me from behind.* But when I get out of the car, he sees me and says hello.

Oprah: **And you walked in together. Now, is that so bad?**

Jerry: It wasn't. And at least I got this funny story out of it. That's the end.

Oprah: **What about *Bee Movie*?**

Jerry: Oh, right! I forgot. [*Laughs*] In the middle of dinner, we're chatting away, and it's all going nicely. When we started talking about kids we were off to the races, but then the conversation ground to a halt.

Oprah: **I know—there's that awful moment...**

Jerry: It happens to the best of us. As an entertainer,

EARNING HIS STRIPES: *Left:* Jerry in costume to promote *Bee Movie*. *Below:* Drawing on his comedy roots, Jerry opened most *Seinfeld* episodes— like this one, from 1993—with a bit of stand-up material.

that's when I kick into gear and say something witty to jump-start the conversation. The night before, I was sitting with a couple of friends, eating a Twizzler, and I said, "What if somebody did a film called *Bee Movie,* and it was about bees?" So during the dinner with Steven, I said this to relieve the lull we'd just crashed into. I figured, he's a director, he'll relate to the term "B movie." But he didn't laugh; he fixed his eyes on me and said, "We're going to make that movie." I was like, "What do you mean *we,* Kemosabe?" He said it was a great idea, and when he gets excited, it's almost scary. He can get everyone else in the room excited! You don't meet older people like that too often. It's wonderful.

Oprah: **Is Steven considered "older" now?**

Jerry: I don't want to shock you with a calendar, but it's 2007.

Oprah: **When I did *The Color Purple* with him, I never thought of him as older.**

Jerry: That's because he wasn't then—that was over 20 years ago!

Oprah: **Thanks for reminding me. After four years of working on this film, do you feel as though you can breathe again?**

Jerry: Yes.

Oprah: **Does it feel like a burden off your shoulders—**

Jerry: Yes.

Oprah: **—like you have a new self?**

Jerry: Keep going, honey! All that. Now, I'm a guy who

did a show that was pretty well received, and—

Oprah: **That's how you think of *Seinfeld*, as "well received"? Not as a cultural phenomenon?**

Jerry: I'm just happy people liked it. I think of it as a gift: When you give someone a gift, you don't call him up every day and say, "How do you like it today?" You enjoy the moment of giving, and that's the end of it.

Oprah: **Earlier today, you told me something that resonated so deeply with me.**

Jerry: Really? This is making my day!

Oprah: **I was saying that I have just one last week before I have to start working on the next season of the show. You said, "It's yours to design." Your decision about the right time to end your show was one of the best designs I've ever seen.**

Jerry: Thank you. That means a lot to me. My managers and I still wonder: Did we stop at the right time? Before we ended the show, Jack Welch [former CEO of General Electric, which owns NBC] told me, "Your ratings are still rising." "Yes," I said, "but the only way to see the end of a hill is to go past it and realize you're going down."

Oprah: **I heard he offered you $50 million to continue.**

Jerry: I don't like to talk figures, and besides, I never even went into negotiation. We just ended the show. I did the show for the people watching it, and I didn't want them to say, "That show was great in the beginning, but..." The Beatles created something that never trailed off. What a gift that was to their fans. If you're into the Beatles, you loved them from beginning to end.

Oprah: **I was just saying to Gayle the other day, I'm really surprised I never married Paul McCartney, since all my other dreams came true.**

Jerry: It's not too late! In fact, your timing could be inspired.

Oprah: **When I first interviewed Paul in 1997, I was so nervous. We were live on a stage in New York, in front of a big audience, and I said, "I used to have your picture on my wall, and you were on the back of my cereal box. As I was eating breakfast, I'd wonder, *Is Paul eating his cereal, too? Is he thinking about me?*" Oh, well. New topic: If I were to run into you on a Saturday or Sunday, what would you be doing?**

Jerry: I'd be with the kids. Then I'd look for a moment to go for a drive in one of my old cars. Taking in a baseball game on TV is also a big treat.

Oprah: **That sounds so normal. Someone once said you were the most normal, balanced, and collected guy, unless you were crossed. Then, whoever crossed you became dead to you. True?**

Jerry: And somebody else said, "He's as normal as someone with 30 Porsches could be." I've had many of the same friends for 30 years; I haven't been crossed enough to even speak to that.

Oprah: **What makes you feel crossed?**

Jerry: I'm big on civility.

Oprah: **So what are your top three incivilities?**

Jerry: Number one, cutting people off on the road. Why are we fighting over eight feet? I love to just let others cut

Below: Jerry and his wife, Jessica, on the lawn of their East Hampton home, 2004. *Right:* Channeling *The Wizard of Oz*, the *Seinfeld* cast (*from left,* Jason Alexander, Michael Richards, Julia Louis-Dreyfus, Jerry Seinfeld) made the cover of *Rolling Stone* in May 1998, just after the show's finale.

in front of me. I'm like, "Please—be my guest." It's a little thing that can change someone's day. That's what civility does.

Oprah: I used to give big tips to mean cabdrivers. I figured if I gave him $20, it might change his mood for the next passenger.

Jerry: I tried to build that principle into *Bee Movie.* When someone does a small task beautifully, their whole environment is affected by it. Incivility number two: the BlackBerry. You can throw the cell phone in there, too. We've fallen into a trap of ever-widening orbits of contact, and there is a total disregard for the present moment. I recently sat down for breakfast and asked a friend about a trip she'd taken. Eventually, she looked up from texting someone and said, "You mean *me?*" I said, "No, I'm talking to the stack of logs behind you." Then my wife got upset because she thought *I* was being rude. Then I got steamed.

Oprah: Not long ago, I took my senior producers on a retreat where there was no wireless service. For the first time in five years, people were present and engaged with one another. By the end of the retreat, everyone said, "This has been the most amazing time." All because they couldn't get a signal! What's the third thing on your list?

Jerry: Interrupting. It's a communication felony. If someone is talking—and I don't care what they're saying or how excited you are to say what you have to say—wait until he or she is finished.

Oprah: Interrupting is like saying, "What I have to say is more significant than what you have to say."

Jerry: Right. When you interrupt, you've stopped listening. People need to be heard.

Oprah: Yes. See, that's another way you're so normal! Everyone says that happy-go-lucky people don't make great comics, that comedians need a dark side. You don't seem to have one.

Jerry: It probably helps that I had a long early career; things didn't just happen for me overnight. I'd been working as a comedian since I was 21, and I didn't get the sitcom until I was 35; by then I'd been knocked around quite a bit. Then I did the show for nine years, and I wasn't going out every night afterward. So at 44, I was unleashed on the world for the first time as a famous person of means. By then I'd gotten a good education in life. But what I had, and more, landed in Eddie Murphy's lap when he was around 22. That's a different puzzle.

Oprah: How so?

Jerry: In every conceivable way. I read about a study that

> "Being a good husband is like being a good stand-up comic—you need ten years before you can even call yourself a beginner."

says your brain goes from impulsive to thoughtful over the course of living. So when some old guy comes back to talk to young kids in prison, for instance, and he says, "Don't make the mistakes I made," he can't reach those kids. Their brains are actually built differently. How come we all have a story about some insane thing we did at 22 that we would never do today? Because we're built the same way.

Oprah: I get it. By the time you became successful, you already knew who you were.

Jerry: Right. Being an actor is the art of becoming other people; being a comedian is the art of learning who you are. A good comedian is someone who allows his or her personality to come out. Five minutes after Bill Cosby has been on a stage, you're thinking, *I know this guy.*

Oprah: Was Cosby your idol?

Jerry: Still is. I have all his albums.

Oprah: What was it like to meet him for the first time?

Jerry: It was great! I was in Vegas with a friend and we called him up because we'd heard that he talked to young comedians. Next thing I know, I'm in Bill Cosby's dressing room at the Hilton, and he talked to me for two hours! I couldn't believe it. If some guy I'd never heard of called me, he wouldn't be coming to my dressing room. I wish I could be like that, but I'm not. [*Laughs*]

Oprah: Would you call yourself an introvert?

Jerry: Yes.

Oprah: Then when you're onstage, you suddenly become an extrovert.

Jerry: Yes. Well, the stage is dark. You don't see any faces. You're essentially alone up there, yet you're reaching people, communicating with them without the intimacy of face-to-face. That's a very free place to be. Every human being wants to connect with humanity in whatever way we can. For me, stand-up comedy is a way to do that, but with gloves on. That's the appeal to a certain personality type. I love people, but I can't talk to them. Onstage, I can.

Oprah: How fascinating.

Jerry: A comedian who has some ability to function socially is tremendously handicapped on the stage. If you have another outlet for connecting with people, you'll use it. But when stand-up comedy is your only outlet, you put all your energy into it. That's what makes a good act.

Oprah: Lightbulb moment—that's why Chris Rock is as good as he is! When you put him in a small group of people, he closes himself off.

Jerry: If Chris could function in that room, he wouldn't be the genius he is onstage. All his energy is forced through that little hole.

Oprah: Does stand-up comedy still feed you?

Jerry: I love it. I love this intimate moment with the audience—

Oprah: Who gets the most from it, you or them? I'm sorry—I interrupted you!

Jerry: That's okay. Who gets the most from it? Well, I do. What could be better than making others happy?

Oprah: Speaking of happiness, you once said that men want the same thing from women that they want from underwear: a little bit of support and a little bit of freedom. Do you get that from Jessica?

Jerry: I get a lot of support. My wife is an amazing person.

Oprah: Some people thought your marriage was sudden, but it seems you give everything you do a lot of thought.

Jerry: Marriage is a subject that does not give way to analysis, sadly. Who *should* I marry? You can make all the charts and have all the discussions, but it doesn't guarantee anything. I knew I felt right, and that's all you have. Marriage is a big bet. It's the only bet of its kind, one in which you say, "This feels right…I think I'll change everything."

Oprah: After you decided, were you thinking, *Maybe this will work, maybe it won't*?

Jerry: No. I'm fiercely determined when I make a commitment. Fiercely. And nurturing. I nurture my commitments.

Oprah: Are you as supportive of Jessica as she is of you? For years I've done shows with women who say they want romance, and they get all worked up about whether the guy remembers Valentine's Day. But that's not really the issue—it's whether the woman feels appreciated.

Jerry: What makes a woman feel that way?

Oprah: Knowing that her presence is valued.

Jerry: Thank you for that—and I'm not joking. You can know things in so many different ways, and then when someone puts it a certain way, it suddenly becomes new.

Oprah: That's exactly what you've done for me today. So, do you appreciate Jessica?

Jerry: Do I? Yes!

Oprah: Does she know it?

Jerry: I hope so. I'm going to work on it more now—especially since this comes from the leader of the pack! How often does a woman need to know that she's appreciated?

Oprah: She just needs to know it, period. It's not a one-time statement. It's ongoing foreplay.

Jerry: So the foundation of appreciation has to be there, and then the little things highlight that appreciation.

Oprah: Yes. Are you romantic?

Jerry: We've started e-mailing each other. At the end of mine, I tell Jess how much I love her. She likes that, especially since she's not used to getting e-mails from me.

Oprah: And especially considering how you feel about BlackBerrys! Do you like being married?

Jerry: I love being married. But I would never want to be married to anyone else, so I can't say I like marriage. I love my wife.

Oprah: What do you love most about her?

Jerry: I just always want to be with her. Even if she's talking to someone on the phone, I want to be there. I enjoy her around-ness. I'll go into her office and just sit. I wonder if she thinks, *What is he doing here?* I'm interested, stimulated; I just like watching her live her life. Quincy Jones had that fantastic line about being with his friend Ray Charles: "It was just good air."

Oprah: Yes—I love that. On the subject of memorable quotes, I've heard that you're one of the most sought-after public speakers at college commencements.

Jerry: Really? I didn't know that. I seldom do it. Tony Bennett, one of my heroes, asked me to speak at the first commencement for a high school for performing arts in New York. So I wrote a speech, and it actually turned out to be pretty good.

Oprah: What's the essence of what you said?

Jerry: I gave them my three rules for living. First, bust your ass. That's a universal law, no matter what you do. Second, pay attention. Learn from everything and everyone all the time. One of my favorite expressions is "Wherever you look, there's something to see." Finally, I gave them my third rule: Fall in love. Fall in love with your street, your tennis game, a pillow.

Oprah: Have some passion about life.

Jerry: Exactly. You can be passionate about anything. Someone could say, "I love this fork," and I'd think that was great. Pay attention; don't let life go by you. Fall in love with the back of your cereal box.

Oprah: Last question: What do you know for sure?

Jerry: That you are one cool cat.

Oprah: I think you're the coolest. I've learned so much from you today. You're the kind of person I could be friends with.

Jerry: The door is open.

Oprah: Come on over!

Jerry: I will! ⬛

UPDATE In 2010, Jerry Seinfeld premiered a new reality television show, The Marriage Ref.

Oprah Talks to Barbra Streisand

The legendary singer/actress/director (Oscars! Grammys! Emmys! a Tony!) opens up about her wild-child Brooklyn girlhood, the mother who told her she'd never make it, the limits of perfectionism, her worries for today's world, and why touring is "about believing I am enough."

Y ou'd think Barbra Streisand—the eight-time Grammy and two-time Oscar winner—would have a long list of records she loves. Then again, maybe it shouldn't be any surprise that she's selective. "If I hear a record once, I usually never listen to it again," she tells me the day I visit her Malibu house. "I rarely listen to music—unless it's Billie Holiday. Or Shirley Horn...Maria Callas...and Mahler, Symphony NO. 10. Those are things I never get tired of." Which is why, Barbra told me, she thought about singing a Billie Holiday song, "out of respect," in October 2006 (her first extended tour in 12 years).

Leaving her dream house won't be easy. This is the refuge Barbra says she has longed for since the days when she shared a cramped Brooklyn apartment with her mother,

At Barbra's Malibu house, with her 3-year-old Coton, Sammie, July 23, 2006.

63

brother, and grandparents. "Even after I became famous," she says, "I lived in a house I didn't like. I looked out my window and saw traffic going by. I never really saw the sky." Now, the skies have it: On the cloudless day of our conversation, we look out over an eternity of blue heaven and sea.

Beyond the main house, Barbra and her husband, actor James Brolin, are building a farmhouse—or, more precisely, Barbra is building it. ("I tried to find people to help me," she says, "but no one cares as much about the details as I do.") As architect in chief, she swirls from one unfinished room to the next, explaining to me her vision for a retreat that's like an 18th-century barn, complete with a water wheel in the front yard. At her heels is her frisky puppy, Sammie, an anniversary present from James. ("Give Oprah a kiss!" she cajoles.) She is crazy about this dog! She even had a birthday party for her.

"What do I know for sure?" Barbra says when I pose the question at the end of our time together. "I'm sure that I don't know everything I want to know. I have so much more to learn." Maybe, but having snagged an award in every medium she has worked in (music, theater, movies, TV), she is hands down one of the greatest, most enduring performers around.

Oprah: I was just listening to my old Barbra CDs. You are truly one of the musical legends of our time.

Barbra: I think of myself as a girl from Brooklyn.

Oprah: How can you, when you're sitting in this house, looking at that ocean?

Barbra: I have two sides. For instance, I have no problem giving away lots of money, but the Brooklyn part of me still has to ask, "Is that tile $10.95 a square foot?"

Oprah: I understand. But can you acknowledge what your voice and art have meant to the world?

Barbra: At times. But that's like contemplating your navel. Every time I look out over that ocean and see the lights of the city at night, I am in awe. To have this house now feels like being 21—like I've just made it on Broadway and I get to have all this. On one hand, you're talking about me as a legend. On the other hand, I remember trying to get an apartment on Park Avenue in the early sixties when I was a big star, and either because I was Jewish or an actress, I couldn't get in. I had letters from the mayor, the governor, the attorney general....

Oprah: And you still couldn't get in.

Barbra: Right. And no matter how many sold-out shows I do, I also understand when my records don't sell as many copies anymore. I think, *Well, I've been around for what, 40-some years?* I mean, it's the next person's turn. I could believe it if nobody came to see me.

Oprah: No!

Barbra: I wouldn't *like* it. But I'm also grateful that I've been around this long. I'm told I've had a number one album in every decade since the sixties.

Oprah: When did you know you had the voice?

Barbra: When I was maybe 5 or 6 years old, the neighborhood girls would sit on the stoop and sing. I was known as the kid who had a good voice and no father.

Oprah: I read that you resented your father for many years because he wasn't there.

Barbra: I wouldn't say resent, but maybe subconsciously. He died when I was 15 months old.

Oprah: Didn't your mother talk about him?

Barbra: No. Later in life, I asked her, "Why didn't you ever tell me about my father?" She said, "I didn't want you to miss him."

Oprah: Were you angry?

Barbra: Maybe. I just didn't know I was angry.

Oprah: Did your mother remarry?

Barbra: Yes, and my stepfather didn't like me. Maybe because he had three kids from another marriage who didn't live with us. I tried to make him like me for a while. I tried calling him Dad and got him his slippers at night when he came in. I'd get down on my belly and crawl so I didn't walk in front of the TV while he watched wrestling. But did he like me? No way.

Oprah: Why not?

Barbra: Good question. When I was 7 or 8, my mother sent me away to a camp where I couldn't stand the food. I was throwing potatoes down to the other end of the table. She came to visit, and I said, "You're not leaving without me." I was a very powerful kid. I had no reins on me. I said, "I'm packing my bags and going home with you." Little did I know, the guy with her in the car was my new stepfather. My mother never actually told me she had remarried. And later, she didn't tell me she was pregnant, either. I'm convinced this is why I cannot stand to be lied to. I can take any truth; just don't lie to me.

Oprah: Who did you think he was?

Barbra: I didn't know. At the time, my mother, brother, and I were living with my grandparents. My grandmother and grandfather slept in one room, and my mother and I slept in another with my brother sleeping

> "I have two sides. I have no problem giving away lots of money, but the Brooklyn part of me still has to ask, 'Is that tile $10.95 a square foot?'"

Cuddling her first Oscar, for Best Actress for her role as Fanny Brice in *Funny Girl,* 1969.

all the presents? Where are my presents?" That's when I realized that she wanted to be famous, too. She had a beautiful coloratura, a soprano voice.

Oprah: Is she still living?

Barbra: No, she died a couple of years ago.

Oprah: Did you make peace with her?

Barbra: Yes. Because I realized she never had her dreams come true.

Oprah: Do you believe your mother loved you?

Barbra: I'm sure she loved me in the way she knew how. For her, love was food. When I graduated early from high school and moved out of the house at 16 to study acting, she would schlep to my place to bring me half a cantaloupe and some chicken soup. She didn't encourage me to become an actress—maybe she didn't want me to experience rejection. She never thought I would make it.

Oprah: Did she actually say those words?

Barbra: She would say it in other ways. When she first saw me act, her comment was, "Your arms are too skinny." She wanted me to forget acting and become a school secretary like she was.

Oprah: Barbra Streisand working as a secretary? What a great tragedy that would have been!

Barbra: "You'll get paid vacations and summers off," my mother would tell me. "It's a steady job." But I knew I had some other destiny. I have a picture of myself singing at P.S. 25—skinny legs, pigeon-toed. I remember people saying I had a good voice.

Oprah: There's not another one like it. When did you know that?

Barbra: I don't know.

Oprah: You *still* don't know it! Do you ever listen to your own music?

Barbra: Never. Lately, I've had to play my old records because I'm preparing a show. For a few of the songs, I thought, *This girl's good.*

Oprah: Which songs?

Barbra: Seventies songs like *Since I Fell for You* and *Kind of Man a Woman Needs,* which I may try to sing again.

Oprah: Let me ask you this: When did you first know who you were?

Barbra: Very early. I was kind of a wild child, like an animal. I could never sit still at a table—not that my family ever sat down and ate a meal together. I used to stand over the stove and eat out of a pot. There was no mealtime. I have no idea when my brother and sister ate, because I came in whenever I wanted. I also taught my mother how to smoke when I was 10.

Oprah: She let you smoke?

Barbra: Actually, I went up on the roof and smoked Pall Malls.

next to us on a cot. We didn't have a living room, so we didn't have a couch, which is probably why I love couches now. When we drove back from that camp, we pulled up to a new apartment in a project.

I remember once riding in my stepfather's Pontiac with him and my friend Roslyn Arenstein. My mother had told me he was color-blind, so I was saying things like "Oh, what a pretty red light that is," thinking he doesn't see the red and the green, thinking I'm helping. My stepfather said to me, "Why don't you be more like your friend—quiet?"

Oprah: Your stepfather really did a number on you, but what about your mom?

Barbra: I remember one Christmas when I was doing *Funny Girl,* she went nuts. With tears running down her face, she closed her eyes and said, "Why is Barbra getting

Clockwise from above: Knocking 'em dead in third grade. Barbra's teacher, Beatrice Weisselberg, was one of her first fans. With her husband, James Brolin, in Sun Valley, Idaho. Sammie's third birthday party, May 2006.

Oprah: When did you stop?

Barbra: When I was 12.

Oprah: What a childhood! Did you have any refuge?

Barbra: Well, I didn't have my own room. I slept in the living room till I was 13. My brother had this tiny room, and one day when my stepfather was being mean, I went in there to get away. I was lying on my brother's bed and I had an out-of-body experience. I actually saw myself down on the bed from the ceiling. It scared the hell out of me.

Oprah: I heard that you once tried to contact your father's spirit with a medium.

Barbra: I did. My brother is a very meat-and-potatoes guy, no woo-woo. But he told me about a woman, a regular housewife, who had a spiritual guide who could call up "Daddy's spirit." My brother said he'd seen the table move across the room when he'd met her. I was very skeptical, and I said, "I've gotta see this for myself." For 39 years, I hadn't even visited my father's grave. So first, I went there and took a picture with my arm around his tombstone.

It's the only picture I have with him. Then we met with the woman, and let me tell you, the table moved.

Oprah: Were there cards on the table?

Barbra: No. You start listing letters—A-B-C-D-E-F-G— and the table leg lifts when you get to the right one. It spelled M-A-N. So we asked, "Is it Manny?" That was my father's nickname. If the leg stomps yes, which it did, then you don't have to spell the rest of the letters. Then it spelled B-A-R—you know, a message for Barbra. I was totally freaked out. And that message was the simplest word: Sorry.

I'm sure he was sorry. He didn't see my life. I couldn't talk to him about intellectual things. My father was a teacher and a scholar. He taught high school and juvenile delinquents at a reformatory.

On the plane home from that experience, I read one of my father's two doctoral theses. It was about how to teach English to prisoners. It was all about Ibsen and Shakespeare and Chekhov. When I was 16, I had devoured

Chekhov and Ibsen—all the plays I wanted to act in. By the way, a week after I got home, my brother sent me the picture from the cemetery. On the tombstone next to my father was the name Anchel, which I hadn't seen when I was there. That happens to be the name of the character I played in the movie *Yentl*. I hadn't yet decided whether to direct the film or not. This made my decision.

Oprah: **So you felt connected to your father.**

Barbra: Totally connected. Just like my father, I've always loved education. In school I was a member of the honor society. My teachers called in my mother and said, "Why isn't this kid going to college?" But my book reports were on Stanislavsky—I'd always wanted to be an actress. I don't know why—I went to very few movies when I was a girl. For my family, going to a 25-cent movie was a big deal.

Oprah: **Some people become actresses because they don't like being themselves.**

Barbra: That was probably true for me.

Oprah: **Is part of the reason you became so famous that you never altered the way you look? You never changed your name or got a nose job?**

Barbra: People told me to change my last name. But I thought, *That's not real.* So instead, I decided to take an "a" out of my first name and shorten it to Barbra. I did that when I was 18. As for my nose, I was afraid of the pain. And how could I trust a doctor's aesthetic sense? How would I know he wouldn't take too much off?

Oprah: **If you hadn't been afraid, would you have changed your nose?**

Barbra: From certain angles, I liked my nose—still do. Some people would tell me, "You could take the bump off." And I would say, "But I like the bump."

Oprah: **I'm glad you didn't. Aren't you glad?**

Barbra: Yes.

Oprah: **Would you consider any other kinds of plastic surgery?**

Barbra: Yes, but it's scary. I don't even have pierced ears.

Oprah: **I just pierced mine recently. It was major. And now one has closed up. Yesterday I had to stick a needle through to open it.**

Barbra: Each ear is a different length, so how could you possibly put a hole in exactly the same place on two different ears?

Oprah: **You do know you're a perfectionist, right?**

Barbra: Yes, but much less now. I really don't like being called a "perfectionist" as if it's a crime. I strive for excellence.

Oprah: **And you like that.**

> "I really don't like being called a 'perfectionist' as if it's a crime. I strive for excellence."

Barbra: I have no choice over it. I'm less of a perfectionist than people think. When I'm directing a movie, I'm pretty forgiving. There's a moment in the novel *The Prince of Tides* that I tried to capture on film. In the scene, the sun and moon are out at the same time. That only happens once a month, so we waited for the right time of the right day with the right camera. But it was impossible to get the shot because that day turned out to be cloudy in South Carolina. For some reason, I could accept that easily because that is what the universe was presenting. Compromising while being conscious is very satisfying.

Oprah: **Do you live a conscious life?**

Barbra: I try to, but I make terrible mistakes. Every day I try to be a better human being. Many days I don't succeed.

Oprah: **People use the word "diva" to describe you. That word is thrown around so much that I don't even know what it means anymore.**

Barbra: It means they think you're demanding.

Oprah: **Are you?**

Barbra: Mostly of myself. I find that the myth of the "diva" is much bigger than me. If you look at the ad for my concert, the shadow is much bigger than the person.

Oprah: **Tell me about your husband, Jim. I read that after you met him, you went home feeling hopeful.**

Barbra: Yes. I remember being in a supermarket around that time. I was at the checkout counter and read the headline of one of those tabloids that said an astrologer predicted I would marry again that year, but I hadn't met anyone special. I thought it was crazy. Time goes so fast. It's hard to understand where all the years go.

Oprah: **How did you meet?**

Barbra: At a dinner party, a blind date. I walked in and saw him with a buzz cut. No hair! It wasn't pretty. I went and played with the children, but eventually I had to come back to the table and sit next to him. We started talking about architecture, because I was building things and his father was a contractor. Then I touched his head, which I'd normally never do, but because I was in director mode—I was working on *The Mirror Has Two Faces*—and dealing with male actors all day, I was much freer. So I said, "Who f---ed up your hair?" He now says that's when he fell in love with me—because I told him the truth.

Oprah: **Does his presence make you calmer?**

Barbra: Yes. My husband is much more easygoing than me. He'll live to be 100! [*Laughs*] The night we met, he wouldn't let me go back to editing my movie. Before the dinner, I'd told the crew, "I'll be back." But he took me home. I was a nervous wreck in the car. Dating is the worst.

Oprah: What is it about him that made you say yes?

Barbra: He's the yin to my yang. I wanted a companion in my life. My husband and I still have to work at our marriage every day. Relationships are about kindness. You have to constantly watch what you say and how you say it.

Oprah: Tone of voice is so incredibly powerful. You and James seem very easy together, but I'm sure it's not because *you're* easy.

Barbra: Neither is he. He has a lot of quirks. I like things in their places. He doesn't.

Oprah: Do you have a lot of quirks?

Barbra: Probably. I'm just not aware of them as quirks.

Oprah: Tell me about your relationship with your son [Jason Gould, whose father, actor Elliott Gould, was Barbra's first husband].

Barbra: It's really good. He's a kind, thoughtful, intelligent person. I am so proud of him. It's hard for a child of famous parents. But as Jason has grown older, he has understood how many people go through challenging childhoods. Who has it perfect? Very few. And sometimes difficulty builds character. As we become more conscious and less angry, we become more grateful.

Oprah: That's right. What matters the most to you in your life?

Barbra: The happiness of my son, my relationship with my husband and friends, and the state of the world. The unconditional love a mother has for her child is amazing and rare. My puppy, Sammie, has that kind of unconditional love for me, and it's so satisfying. She's happy every time I walk into a room. Jim made the perfect choice for me.

Oprah: And you're perfect for her. Are you looking forward to your tour?

Barbra: I'm looking forward to the challenge.

Oprah: So when I come to see you onstage, you're not going to be having fun up there?

Barbra: Well, I did have fun during the final shows of the last tour. I surprised myself. What I like about music is that it marks time for people—like "I got married to that song." One reason I can perform now is that they have pills for stage fright. I wish somebody had told me about these pills years ago.

Oprah: Will you use a teleprompter?

Barbra: Yes, or I might go blank. I'll think, *What am I doing on this stage? Holy mackerel!* But then I realize that fear has an energy behind it. The whole point is to go beyond the fear and do it anyway, because I know I'm singing for a good cause.

I can sing before a full stadium because it's like looking into a black hole. I can't perform in front of a few people in a living room. I was once with Donna Karan and Liza Minnelli, and Liza just got up and sang. I was fascinated. I'm thinking, *Where do you look in a room lit up like this?* In a black hole—a theater—I can escape into my own little world.

I never remember my good reviews, so when I hear something good about myself, I go, "Really?" But I can tell you about the bad ones, because there's part of me that thinks, *They're right.* And that's an age-old point with many performers. That goes so deep. On the surface, I can tell you that I'm famous and I'm good at what I do. But there's also that part of me that never quite hears the nice things. But I'm much better than I used to be. First of all, I care less about what critics say about me, I don't read reviews, I just want to live each day to the fullest.

Oprah: And you'll be living a lot of those days on tour.

Barbra: I haven't really performed much. In my entire career, I've played in a handful of cities in the United States and only three outside of America. Performers like Neil Diamond, U2, and Madonna tour every two years and

Streisand: Five decades of number one albums

People
1964

The Way We Were
1974

A Star Is Born
1976

Guilty
1980

The Broadway Album
1985

Back to Broadway
1993

Higher Ground
1997

Love is the Answer
2009

sing in hundreds of cities all over the world. My friend Diana Krall told me she used to tour 300 out of 365 days a year. I've worked so little, which is why the idea of retirement is ridiculous. Actually, I didn't sing in public for 27 years, except for charity. That's the main reason I'm going back on the road now—to give to organizations that my foundation supports.

Oprah: So, you want to do big things?

Barbra: Yes. That's why my foundation just gave the first million-dollar grant from my upcoming tour to the Clinton Climate Change Initiative, which will fight against global warming. I'm interested in setting up more professorships in universities, perhaps one about truth in journalism. Why are the facts so often distorted?

Oprah: It's propaganda. People are fed whatever makes money.

Barbra: There are stories about me that are so ridiculous. My husband looked it up. He said there are 36 unauthorized biographies about me. One day I'm going to write my own book.

Oprah: What is the worst thing that you've ever heard about yourself?

Barbra: Well, there have been so many silly things. One story was that I walk into a room full of musicians, and if a guy plays the wrong note, I fire him. It's all just diva crap. I'm a normal person. Why would I fire a musician because he played the wrong note? If I sing the wrong note, do I get fired? It's absurd.

You know what it's about? It's about the Aristotelian rule of drama. It's about the fall of kings and queens. The Greek tragedies are not written about the common man. They're written about the fall of people in high places. Part of me understands it: People want to see kings and queens fall because it's the great equalizer; it makes them less envious. The gap between the rich and the poor has become so huge, so terrible. The world is in a chaotic state. People are living in fear and denial.

Oprah: There's a lack of critical thinking on the part of the public.

Barbra: Well, you can't listen to negative news 24/7. But the public should be informed to make intelligent decisions, especially about who they vote for. I value intelligence. If you were to go into surgery, would you want to put your life in the hands of a C student or an A+ student? I'm sure President Bush is a very nice guy, but some people voted for him because they thought he was a person they could have a beer with. What is that about? Do you

> "From certain angles, I liked my nose—still do. Some people would tell me, 'You could take the bump off.' And I would say, 'But I like the bump.'"

want to have a beer with the doctor who's going to operate on you, or do you want him to be the top of his class...be a bit in awe of him?

Oprah: You are not optimistic at all about these times.

Barbra: Yes, I am, because people are finally realizing the truth about what happened in Iraq, even though, sadly, some of the public is still confused by the way the administration bent the facts. In 2002 I had a meeting with Scott Ritter, a weapons inspector who'd been in Iraq for seven years. He told me there were never any weapons of mass destruction. Even if they'd had biological or chemical weapons, he said, they would be dust, because they have no shelf life. Experts agree that Iraq had *nothing* to do with 9/11.

Oprah: Do you fear for our world?

Barbra: Oh, yes. I fear global warming. I fear nuclear proliferation. I think we have to do everything we can to prevent self-annihilation. I have a knot in my stomach all the time. How can I not? Before the election, the public gave President Bush high marks on fighting terrorism, but he ignored all the warnings. Before 9/11 he didn't even beef up airport security. He was negligent. During the 2004 election, I begged John Kerry to attack Bush on terrorism, to make his "strong" point his weak one...because it was true! Imagine how different it would have been if Al Gore had been president. We would not be in a war.

Oprah: I once did a show titled "Is War the Only Answer?" In the history of my career, I've never received more hate mail—like "Go back to Africa" hate mail. I was accused of being un-American for even raising the question.... In the coming months, what are you looking forward to?

Barbra: On tour I want to be in the moment and really appreciate the love that's given to me. During my last tour, when I kicked off my shoes and said whatever I wanted, I actually enjoyed myself. Performing is not about perfection. I could never perform live if it were. For me, it's about raising the money to do good in the world. It's about self-acceptance. It's about believing that I am enough. **O**

UPDATE In 2008, Barbra Streisand endowed $5 million to Cedars-Sinai for the creation of The Barbra Streisand Women's Cardiovascular Research and Education Program.

Oprah Talks to Tina Turner

The triumphant queen of rock 'n' soul—that 1,000-watt voice! Those killer legs! That hard-earned don't-mess-with-me-ness!—lets her glorious mane down to talk about growing up in Nutbush, Tennessee, surviving Ike Turner's brutal physical abuse (and the night she got away), younger men, growing older, plastic surgery, and why "all the best" is yet to come.

When Tina Turner's Wildest Dreams tour stopped in Houston back in 1997, I stood (let me tell ya, you seldom *sit* at a Tina performance) next to a woman whose story I'll never forget. "I came because I was looking for the courage to leave the man who beats me," she said. "Tonight I found that courage."

Watching Tina perform is what I call a spiritual experience. Each electrifying swing of her miniskirt, every slide of her three-inch Manolos across the stage, sends a message: *I am here. I have triumphed. I will not be broken.* When I leave a Tina concert, I feel the same way I do after I've seen any great art: I want to be a better human being.

Before Tina Turner—a stage name Ike Turner gave her—there was Anna Mae Bullock, a girl born to share-cropping parents in 1939. Her father and her mother, who was part Native American, left her during World War II to be raised by her grandmother in Nutbush, Tennessee, while they worked in Knoxville. In Nutbush, Anna fanta-sized about stardom while singing in talent shows and at church. After moving to St. Louis at age 16, Anna was discovered by Ike, the leader of the R&B band the Kings of Rhythm. Within a few years, her stirring vocals and energetic dance moves catapulted her from backup singer to the act's dominating force, which was renamed the Ike & Tina Turner Revue.

In 1960 the couple had a son, Ronnie. (Ike already had two sons, and Tina had one.) The same year, they landed their first hit, "A Fool in Love," and in 1962, they were married in Tijuana. The band's crossover to pop came with "River Deep—Mountain High" (1966)—a song that, while not a chart topper in the United States, propelled them to European acclaim. Onstage Ike and Tina soared, but offstage she suffered through his violent attacks. One night in 1976, after arriving in Dallas to begin a tour, he beat her bloody en route to the hotel. As soon as he fell asleep, Tina put on sunglasses to disguise her bruised face and escaped with 36 cents in her pocket. She found refuge in a nearby Ramada Inn, then fled to Los Angeles.

After the split, Tina paid her rent by cleaning houses. She eventually broke into cabaret, performing old hits, and later played Las Vegas. Finally, in 1984, with her own manager and a new record label, Tina released her break-out solo album, *Private Dancer.* The record sold more than ten million copies; she won three Grammys and scored her first number one hit: "What's Love Got to Do with It." In 1986 her autobiography, *I, Tina,* was published, ex-posing the shocking abuse she'd endured. (The book was

made into the 1993 movie *What's Love Got to Do with It.)* Since leaving Ike, Tina has become an international rock and soul legend whose packed concerts are among the top selling in history. For more than 20 years, she's been living in Zurich with her longtime partner, Erwin Bach.

Although she officially hung up her high heels from the big tours in 2000, she returned to the United States in 2004 with the release of her double CD anthology, *All the Best.* I spent my birthday, January 29, 2005, with her at the Hotel Bel-Air in Los Angeles. At 65 she was more gorgeous than I'd ever seen her. "I've never been happier," she said. Her face and demeanor showed it. I've talked to Tina many times on TV, and in this interview, I found her at her most candid—about the years with Ike, rocking on through her 60s, loving a man 16 years her junior, and the one dream she still has.

Oprah: You look good! Those legs—is that just genes?

Tina: Yeah, I always had long legs. When I was young, I used to think, *Why do I look like a little pony?*

Oprah: Your legs aren't just long, they're shapely and beautiful.

Tina: I never put a lot of praise on myself because of my relationship with Ike. I was just happy when I started to like myself—when I divorced and took control of my life.

Oprah: You didn't just divorce. You broke out.

Tina: That's right.

Oprah: Growing up, how poor were you? Every time I hear your song "Nutbush City Limits," I think of my little hometown in Mississippi.

Tina: We weren't in poverty. We had food on the table. We just didn't have fancy things, like bicycles. We were church people, so on Easter, we got all done up. I was very innocent and didn't know much else. I knew the radio—B.B. King, country and western. That's about it. I didn't know anything about being a star until the white people allowed us to come down and watch their television once a week.

Oprah: Which white people?

Tina: The Poindexters. My [maternal] grandmother lived on their farm. That's when I saw Loretta Young on TV. I thought someday I'd have a star on *my* dressing room. But guess what? When we did "A Fool in Love," and we went to the clubs, we were in a storage room full of beer bottles, Coke bottles. We had to dust and clean up. We were on the road, sleeping in the car.

Oprah: But you started to dream when you first saw Loretta Young?

Tina: Before that. Remember Betty Grable?

Oprah: No.

Tina: You're 15 years younger than me. Betty Grable [a World War II pinup girl and actress] had beautiful short legs. She was in proportion.

Above: Tina with son Ronnie and dog Onyx at home in Baldwin Hills, California, 1973. *Left:* In London with Ike, 1975—a year before she left him.

Oprah: Your legs are endless.

Tina: That's what I didn't like. I didn't know how to buy clothes for that. As I grew up, I learned what worked for me. That's where the short dresses came from. And you can't dance in a long dress.

Oprah: No, no. But let's start with Nutbush. What carried you to the next point?

Tina: Fate. When my parents went off to Knoxville to work, I lived with my father's mother. She was strict—the kind who starched and ironed dresses. I had to sit more than I played. Oh, I was miserable. I liked being out with the animals. I'd come in the house with my hair pulled out, sash off the dress, dirty as heck. I was always getting spanked. When my parents returned, they separated. Oooh, Oprah! You know what happens to children sometimes when their parents separate—school can be really cruel. I got teased, and it interfered with my learning. But

I grew out of that, and I fell in love in high school. Why did I fall so deeply in love? I think when you haven't had that much love at home, and then you find someone you love, everything comes out.

Oprah: The first love can be the most difficult to get through because you've had no experience.

Tina: That's right. When I think of Harry now, my heart beats faster. He was the most good-looking guy. Everything was in the right place—his eyes, his nose, his mouth. He was a basketball star. Sometimes I'd wear his jacket. It was fainting hot, but because it was his jacket, I wore it. It was magical.

Oprah: I can see that.

Tina: Harry also took my virginity. I don't regret it. I came home that night and folded the dress I'd been wearing and put it away. The next day, my grandmother was doing spring cleaning and everything got washed. When I came home, she said, "I knew you were running around. You're gonna get pregnant." Oh, Oprah! I felt embarrassed. I didn't know what to say. She didn't wash the dress. She just left it out. There was this big spot on it. She didn't let me go dating Harry anymore.

Oprah: Your eyes still light up when you talk about him.

Tina: At the time, I wanted to get married and have children. Harry would have been the one. Years later, after "What's Love Got to Do with It," I ran into his son. He came up to me and said, "Harry Taylor is my father." He looked just like Harry. I thought, *My God, that must have been from another lifetime.*

Oprah: It's so interesting what maturity does. What did the Ike years teach you about yourself?

Tina: That's when I learned that I was truly talented. Before I met Ike, I was singing at church and at picnics— but lots of people sing at church and picnics. After I moved with my mother to St. Louis, my older sister and I went to see Ike Turner, who was the hottest then. His music charged me. I was never attracted to him, but I wanted to sing with his band. Ike thought I couldn't sing because I was a skinny-looking girl. Oprah, you were Ike's type. He liked the ladies with the hips.

Oprah: Oh, I really missed out on that one! What is Ike's phone number?

Tina: There was a girl named Pat, and she looked a lot like you, Oprah. He let her sing because she was his type. Pat couldn't sing nearly as well as I could. One evening when the drummer gave my sister the mike, I took it. I could do B.B. King songs with all the emotion. Ike said, "Girl, I didn't know you could sing!" I was so happy, because he was bigger than life. That's when I knew I wanted to be an entertainer. Forget marriage, children, and living happily ever after as a housewife. That was gone. Ike went out and bought me a fur, a dress, some high-heeled shoes. He got my hair all done up. I rode to work in a pink Cadillac. I even got my teeth fixed.

Oprah: How old were you?

Tina: Seventeen. Ike had to come to the house and ask Ma if it was okay for me to sing with him. He knew I had the potential to be a star. We were close, like brother and sister. We had so much fun, Oprah. On his off nights, we'd drive around town, and he would tell me about his life, his dreams. He told me that when he was young, people found him unattractive. That really hurt him. I felt bad for him. I thought, *I'll never hurt you, Ike.* I meant it. He was so nice to me then, but I did see the other side of him. He was always fighting people—but I just thought that was because they'd wronged him. That had nothing to do with me.

Oprah: That's what you thought?

Tina: Yes. I also saw that he had a temper when he would fight with the girl he was dating. Then I learned that his father had been beaten up by some whites for going out with the same woman one of them was going out with. His father later died. I learned a whole story about Ike.

During the time when I didn't have a boyfriend and Ike had broken up with his woman, he started touching me. I didn't like it, but I didn't know what to do or say. We were sitting in the backseat of a car. In those days, everybody did what Ike said. He had the power. He had never been mean to me, so I felt loyal to him. But I didn't want a relationship with him.

Then came the recording. I went to a studio, recorded "A Fool in Love," and Ike sent it to New York. Soon after, Ike and I had a little run-in and I said to myself, *I think I'd better get out of this.* So I told the girl who was managing everything that I didn't want to be involved with the recording. That was the first time I really got a beating from Ike.

Oprah: A beating?

Tina: With a shoe stretcher.

Oprah: Wait a minute. He hit you with a wooden shoe stretcher?

Tina: Yes.

Oprah: Where were you?

Tina: At his house in East St. Louis. I was afraid of Ike— I'd talked to the manager because I felt the vibration of what was about to happen. I wanted out.

Oprah: Even if it meant giving up your music?

Tina: I had a reputation around town as Little Ann. I could have gotten jobs with other bands—but I was loyal to Ike. That's how I am. Ike would ask me over and over: "Oh, you want to hurt me like everybody else, don't you?" I'd be saying, "No, no, no," but the more I said no, the more he'd say, "Yes, that's what it is." Later on, that pattern of dialogue became so familiar that when he'd start with it, I'd know a beating was coming. He'd walk around biting his lip and working himself up. I'm sure he needed a bit of therapy.

Oprah: A bit?

Tina: Anyway, *wham!* I was shocked. How could you hit someone with a shoe stretcher? Then he hit me with the heel of a shoe.

Oprah: In your face?

Tina: Always. Later he'd hit me in the ribs, and then always try to give me a black eye. He wanted his abuse to be seen. That was the shameful part.

Oprah: Over the years, I've told women that when it happens the first time, you need to walk.

Tina: I did not walk.

Oprah: What happened after he hit you?

Tina: He told me to get in the bed, and he had sex with me. When I met Ike, I couldn't have orgasms. He used to get angry with me. He'd say, "You're not trying." Later it became, "You're not trying to get a hit record." All the blame was on me. When I look back on that time now, it was just hell. So why didn't I walk out? I had nowhere to go. I didn't have money—and neither did my mother. I found out later that my mom had this worship thing for Ike. When Ike and I eventually separated, she tried to find me for him.

Oprah: Is it true that he would beat you before you went onstage?

Tina: Yes. I never knew what would trigger him. He was tired, he didn't eat properly, and he'd drink peach brandy with his drugs. So his emotions were never in control.

Oprah: He was obviously unhappy with himself.

Tina: And so fearful of failure. We hadn't had a hit for a while. He was spending most of the money on drugs. Expenses were mounting. I was upset because I wasn't receiving a dime. I knew that he was buying for all the ladies around him.

Oprah: What was the greatest humiliation for you?

Tina: There were so many. He liked to show the public that he was in control and that he was a woman hater. He also liked for his women to get up and walk across the floor for display so that other men could see what he had. I didn't know how to get out of the whole situation. There were many times when I picked up the gun when he was sleeping. I once moved all his clothes from the house down to the studio. He had a fit.

Another night we had a fight in the dressing room, and when I went onstage, my face was swollen. I think my

> "I believe that if you'll just stand up and go, life will open up for you."

nose was broken because blood was gushing into my mouth when I sang. Before, I'd been able to hide under makeup. But you can't hide swelling.

Oprah: Did people around you know what was happening?

Tina: The band knew. But it was probably difficult for them to get work and I think they wanted drugs from Ike. I didn't know where to go. And I still had a sisterly love for the man. I did my best to make him happy. I shopped for him. I did his hair. I was his Cinderella.

Oprah: Some part of you must have believed that you deserved the abuse.

Tina: Oprah, if I thought I deserved it, I never found that out. It was just karma. I came into this lifetime with a job to finish. I finished it well. I've been told many reasons for why I lived through what I did. But I have never felt that I deserved it.

Oprah: Was it a self-esteem issue? There's no way this could happen to you today. I just ran across a letter I wrote in my 20s, when I was in an emotionally abusive relationship. I'd written 12 pages to one of the great jerks of all time. I wanted to burn the letter. I want no record of the fact that I was ever so pitiful.

Tina: I had pity for myself. That started way back when I felt my mother didn't love me. A psychic in England told me that when my mother was pregnant with me, she didn't want me. When I confronted Ma about that, she told me the whole story. When I was born, she felt trapped into staying with my father. I didn't blame her, but I felt sorry for myself.

Oprah: Not being wanted is a terrible feeling. My mother didn't want me, either.

Tina: Did you feel pity for yourself?

Oprah: No. But it affected my self-esteem for years. It's unnatural to not be wanted by your mother. That takes some overcoming.

Tina: Right. I don't think about my years with Ike a lot because I don't need to. It was the worst time in my life.

Oprah: Did your children witness the abuse?

Tina: They saw the black eyes. Ike's children never reacted, but my oldest son, Craig, was a very emotional kid. He'd always look down in sadness. One day when Ike was fighting me, Craig knocked on the door and said, "Mother, are you all right?" I thought, *Oh, please, don't beat me at home.* I didn't want my children to hear. I tried to have meals with the children, talk to them about life. But Ike had no sense of that. He'd always come home late from the studio. It was awful.

Clockwise from top: Tina, Ike Turner, and the Ikettes heating up the stage in Las Vegas, 1970. Bringing the house down on her final big tour, London, 2000. Tina with Erwin Bach, her longtime companion, 1990.

Oprah: What did you learn from that time?

Tina: That I have to depend on myself. When you stay in a situation like that, you're trapped in negative energy. I believe that if you'll just stand up and go, life will open up for you. Something just motivates you to keep moving. When I left, I simply said to that white manager at a hotel in Texas, "Can you give me a room?" I was shaken, nervous, scared. But I knew I wasn't going back.

After my plane landed in California, my heart was in my ears. I was afraid Ike would be there because when I'd left once before, he tracked me down on a bus. I'd been sleeping, and when I sat up and looked out the window, there he was. That was the first time I got beat with a hanger.

So when I got off that plane, I ran like mad. I said to myself, *If he's here, I'm going to scream for the police.* And I had one chant in my head: *I will die before I go back.*

Oprah: After surviving that, did you feel you could do anything?

Tina: Oh, yes.

Oprah: Were you still scared of him for a long time?

Tina: When he finally found me, he asked if I would see him. I went out and sat in the car to talk with him. I knew exactly where the door handle was. So when he said, "You motherf---er," I was out of the car and back in the house. I think he told my mother that he was happy I'd gotten out of the car because he had a gun and was planning to kill me.

Oprah: Weren't you afraid?

Tina: I wasn't afraid of death. And I knew there was nothing he could say or do that would make me go back to him. In court, during the divorce, he tried to give me a mean look. I wanted to say, "You're such an idiot. Do you think your vibes can even reach me now?" He had no power over me. For anyone who's in an abusive relationship, I say this: Go. Nothing can be worse than where you are now. You have to take care of yourself first—and then you take care of your children. They will understand later.

Oprah: I got that.

Tina: Your children are blessed. They possibly have good karma, or someone will take them in. People take care of children. But they don't always take care of you.

Oprah: I understand that in a way that I've never understood it. How old were the kids when you finally left?

Tina: Old enough. Craig had graduated from high school. My youngest son, Ronnie, was still in school. The housekeeper was there. I made sure they would be all right. But before you can really help them, you have to strengthen yourself. You're the priority.

Oprah: How did you get on that plane with only 36 cents?

Tina: I called one of our lawyers who had often looked at me with a face that said, *Why do you stay?* I said, "I've left Ike. If you can send money, I promise to pay you back one day." The lawyer called some friends in Fort Worth, and the next day, a couple came to the hotel. They didn't say a word to me. I just got in their backseat. The country was still very segregated, yet these white people were doing something for a black woman. When I arrived in California, I took a taxi to a hotel in Hollywood to meet the lawyer. He paid for the cab, and from there, we went to his home. The next day was the Fourth of July—Independence Day. That holiday had never meant so much.

Oprah: You've been a Buddhist for a long time. What brought you to that?

Tina: The women who sold drugs to Ike said, "What are you doing here, Tina? How can you live with this madness?" Then one day, someone told me, "Buddhism will save your life." I was willing to try anything. I started to chant. Once, I chanted, went to the studio, and put down a vocal, just like that. Ike was so excited that he gave me a big wad of money and said, "Go shopping!" I thought, *This chanting stuff works.* I was hooked. I still believe in the Lord's Prayer. I find a form of the Lord's Prayer in Buddhism. Every religion has rules for living a good life. If you practice any kind of spirituality, it moves you to stages where you gather other ways of communicating.

Oprah: That's exactly what I believe. You evolve new parts of yourself.

Tina: I never close a door on any other religion. Most of the time, some part of it makes sense to me. I don't believe everyone has to chant just because I chant. I believe all religion is about touching something inside of yourself. It's all one thing. If we would realize this, we could make a change in this millennium.

Oprah: I believe that. I also believe it's not going to happen in our lifetime.

Tina: The seed is planted. People are feeling it. We're becoming more aware. There's a whole new way of thinking about age, too. People are not that worried about being old anymore.

Oprah: Is it that people don't care, or is it that we just don't care?

Tina: There are some who think that when you're 60, you have to cut your hair and wear certain shoes. But a lot of people aren't doing that now. They don't think, *Oh, I'm old, I really have to start behaving differently.* In this millennium, a new world is coming. After destruction, there's always something good.

Oprah: A rebirth.

Tina: Yes. It's that feeling you have when you're sick. You suddenly know how good you feel when you're well. People are open to new things now.

Oprah: I hope you're right. What do you want to accomplish with your life?

Tina: I believe I'm going to learn something about how to help people think. We are not thinking correctly. I want to tell people how to live spiritually. After you've bought all your houses and your clothes, you want something bigger. I want my gift to become a gift for others. We're caught in a stagnant belief system passed on to us from our parents and what's been given from the churches. I believe there's another truth. Dancing and singing is all good, but the ultimate gift is to change people's minds. What else is there?

Oprah: There isn't anything else. When people hear your story, they are changed.

Tina: And yet I've never seen myself as a star. That's why traveling to America this time has been incredible. These people are acting like I'm...

Oprah: Tina Turner.

Tina: But I always felt that my show was second-class, because I'm not a star like Barbra Streisand or Maria Callas. I'm just dancing and singing.

Oprah: You don't see yourself as a star?

Tina: Stars can be bitchy and full of themselves. I've never had that attitude. I feel like my dress is great, I can sing, and I'm here to put on a good show for the people.

Oprah: But don't you see yourself as a legend? Not even during your last three sold-out world tours?

Tina: I finally accepted that, and it is incredible. I never had as many records as Whitney Houston or Aretha Franklin. But after years and years of work, people finally came to see me in my 60s. I said, "Why are these people still coming? What is it? I dance and I sing and I make the people feel good. So what?"

Oprah: You don't just dance and sing. You represent possibility. When people see you performing, they know you've come up from the ashes, from the depths of despair. It means that however down a woman is, she can be like you.

Tina: Thank you for saying that.

Oprah: Do you think that it is because of the constant

performing that you've stayed in such great shape?

Tina: Well, my legs are starting to go a little bit. I've been able to get by with short dresses, but I've had to make sure that each dress is absolutely perfect. I'm not complaining, but I've got some cellulite, and I've lost some tone.

Oprah: I don't see it.

Tina: I'm not going to let you see it, Oprah.

Oprah: Did you make a decision to defy age? It was because of you that I decided to rock on through the 50s. It was because of you that I said: "I'm not going to stay where I am. I'm going to get better."

Tina: That's wonderful.

Oprah: Are you happy in your life?

Tina: Very happy.

Oprah: I know I get annoyed by the marriage question. Do you?

Tina: Yes. People often ask me why I don't marry. I have love. I have a good life. I don't need to interfere with that. For some people, marriage means "You're mine now." That can be the beginning of the failure of a relationship. Psychologically, something happens when someone says, "You're my husband or wife. You can't do this or that." It's about ownership. That freedom of two people loving each other and wanting to be together—and being able to leave if anything is wrong—is gone. Neither Erwin nor I feel that we need to get married. We've been together for years. What would marriage give me that I don't already have? Marriage would be about pleasing the public. Why do I need to please the public if I'm already pleased?

Oprah: Did the age difference ever bother you?

Tina: I don't worry about age or color. In the past, I knew the difference when whites made us remember that we were black. But that has passed. And age? When I went for Erwin, he was 30 — just three years older than my oldest son.

Oprah: How old were you then?

Tina: Forty-six. I didn't know he was 30, and I didn't care. Erwin was more mature than most 30-year-olds. I've observed older men, especially the more conservative ones who wear suits all the time. There's a grumpiness that doesn't allow for laughter and fun.

Oprah: Boring!

Tina: Yes. They don't mean to be. It's a male thing. They hope that a young woman can wake them up and make them feel good. But it doesn't happen a lot, so she ends up a decoration. If I were with an older man, I'd have to work very hard. I would refuse for him to be old. He would have to wake up, laugh, and have fun. If I were single, would I give an older man a chance? Only if I saw life in him. Only if he didn't say, "Now that I'm 60 or 80, I have to get to

bed at a certain time." Many older men have set rules. And they still have that "I am the man" attitude. I refuse to live in that culture.

Oprah: It's oppressive. When you're with Erwin, do you remember that he's younger?

Tina: No. It just feels like me and Erwin. Even at night, there's nothing that makes me feel like I have to work at looking pretty in bed. We're past that. What's love got to do with it? A lot!

Oprah: A lot! But you've really never worried about getting old?

Tina: There's an expression, "You'll never get out of this world alive." It's true. We won't. Go forward. Do your best with your makeup, hair, and clothes.

Oprah: Would you ever have plastic surgery?

Tina: No. I'm afraid I might end up not looking like myself. I had my nose done [because Ike broke it]. That drove me nuts for such a long time. What might happen if I had plastic surgery on some other part of my body? No. I'll use makeup, and I don't mind wrinkles—though I don't have any yet.

Oprah: Do you mind people saying your age?

Tina: No problem.

Oprah: That's fantastic. I don't, either. I own every damn year. What principles do you live by?

Tina: I think health has a lot to do with happiness. When you're healthy, you think more clearly, and you can work on yourself. But it's not about extremes. I eat everything I ever ate, just not too often.

Another principle is that I shouldn't allow others to influence me. I lived a whole life with Ike and the drugs. Once when Ike tried to give me drugs, I blew it in his face. That doesn't mean I think I'm better. It just means I have principles I feel good about. I like me very much. When I look in the mirror and my skin glows back at me, I think, *Wow, that sure is pretty.* I have a simple, childlike view of life, and I want to keep it. That's why I never got into that Beverly Hills world. So many pretentious people. They just aren't real.

Oprah: Yes. Your CD is called *All the Best*. Do you believe that better is still to come?

Tina: I don't limit myself. I feel good, and I'm happy. My home is great, and I'm doing as much as I can for my family. My wish is to give the kind of truth to people that will help them change their minds. When that happens, I'll be the best that I can be. **O**

UPDATE In 2008, Tina Turner embarked on a sold-out tour, Tina!: 50TH Anniversary Concert Tour.

Having a laugh in Jon Stewart's living room in Manhattan. At his office, the TV's always on, but home is the place where, Stewart says, "I shut everything down."

Oprah Talks to Jon Stewart

For those of us who like our current events with a side order of satire, Jon Stewart's *The Daily Show* is the best thing that's happened to the nightly news. Here, the man who never met a politician he couldn't laugh at riffs on his early years, the boos he's bounced back from, the comedians he admires, the infamous *Crossfire* incident, and how a blind date changed his life.

on Stewart and *The Daily Show* is to Comedy Central what *Nightline* is to ABC: the voice of reason in a world gone off its rocker. In Stewart's ever-growing corner of the cable universe, nothing—from the Terri Schiavo controversy to the war in Iraq—is sacred, which, thanks to his barbed-wire wit and benevolent brain, leaves 1.2 million viewers going to sleep feeling amused, challenged, understood, and a little less alone every Monday through Thursday night. As for those nights he's not on the air, I suggest you survive them by reading his very funny 2004 best-seller, *America (The Book)*—you'll laugh, you'll cringe.

I laugh the minute Jon Stewart opens the front door to his lower Manhattan townhouse (he assures me it's not normally filled with many bouquets of fresh flowers) and introduces me to his little "man-wich," Nathan, who burrows into the crook of his arm, as his wife, Tracey, comes to join us from the other room. It's a lazy Sunday morning, the perfect time to curl up on an overstuffed sofa and reflect on how Jonathan Stuart Leibowitz, the product of divorce, the class clown, the nice Jewish boy from Lawrence, New Jersey, went from kid with a college degree in psychology to brilliant stand-up comic to serious contender in the battle for talk-show-host supremacy. Contemplative, grounded, and awfully cute, Jon Stewart settles his son in for a nap and sits down for a chat.

Oprah: When did you know you had the gift of comedy?
Jon: When I got fired from everything else.

Oprah: Really?
Jon: Some people can paint. I can't. Some people can sing. I can't. Some people make a joke of everything. I've done that since I was 4 or 5 years old. I don't remember a time when people didn't think I was a wiseass. I hope I've gotten more artful over time, because when I was younger, I was just obnoxious.

Oprah: I've heard a lot of comedians say their humor is born of pain. Do you believe that?
Jon: If you looked at anybody's life, you could find the pain in it and say that what they do is born of that pain. Everybody's got their shit. I come from a straight-up middle-class existence. It was the seventies—"I'm OK, you're OK"—and we got hit with all of that.

Oprah: How did that affect you?
Jon: Man, I wish I knew. I'm sure I'll find out ten years from now. Someone will spill the gravy, and I'll flip out and start yelling. Anyway, what I'm trying to say is this: I don't think what I went through is any more remarkable than what anybody else goes through. My way of handling it was with humor.

Oprah: I read that you were teased as a child.
Jon: Who wasn't?

Oprah: But weren't you teased about your last name?
Jon: Yes. There's a lot that rhymes with the "itz" in Leibowitz. But if it hadn't been that, it would've been something else.

Oprah: I was called Okra.
Jon: Did you tell them, "I'm going to have an Angel Network"? Did you say, "I'm going to have a Wildest Dreams bus one day, and you're going to need a house—and I'm not gonna flippin' give it to you"?

Oprah: No, my big thing was that I never heard my name called on *Romper Room*. So you said earlier that you were fired a lot. Wasn't it hard to keep your self-esteem?
Jon: That wasn't a problem, because I didn't have any. I was good at what I cared about—like playing sports and drinking—but unfortunately, there wasn't a big market for those things.

Oprah: In 1993 you were a finalist to replace Letterman on NBC. Weren't you disappointed when you didn't get it?
Jon: Oh, yes. The Letterman job was big. But, you know, this is a business of rejection. I remember my first night onstage was at the Bitter End at 1 in the morning on a Monday. I was heckled almost immediately. On your first day of work at McDonald's, there's at least someone behind you who knows how to work the register. At some point, you can say, "Could you come over here, please? This guy just ordered a McFlurry, and I don't know what the hell that is." In stand-up, there's just you. You have no idea whether what you say will work. I was always funny in a back-of-the-room way. I can make my friends laugh. But the people at the Bitter End weren't my friends. They were drunk—and they thought I was going to be good.

Oprah: Is it harder to perform when the audience is drunk?
Jon: Easier. Inhibitions are gone. These days when people come to see me, it's more of a theater experience. They've paid their money, they're sitting down....

Oprah: And their expectations are higher.
Jon: Yes, but their willingness to believe I'm funny is also greater. It's like, "I've paid $60 to see this man, so clearly, he must be good. Otherwise, why would I have paid such ridiculous money?"

Comedy is the only form of entertainment where the audience doesn't know what to expect. In an evening, you might get ten comics doing ten different things. That's not what happens when you go to hear music. There isn't a classical performance followed by a hoedown followed by rap.

Oprah: Comedy is a ride.

Jon: Some people respond to wordplay, others to props. Everybody thinks they're funny or knows somebody who's funny, so people don't view comedy as a talent. They view it as a cry for help.

Oprah: I beg to differ. There are many people who realize you have a talent they don't have.

Jon: Do you mind if I put you on the phone with my father right now so you could repeat that last sentence to him?

Oprah: Oh, absolutely. You say what everybody else is thinking but can't articulate, in a way that makes people laugh. That's a gift. Chris Rock also has it.

Jon: Chris is unbelievable. I'm very able to appreciate it in other people.

Oprah: So who impresses you as a comedian?

Jon: Chris. David Letterman, Garry Shandling, Adam Sandler.

Oprah: What's a typical workday like for you?

Jon: We usually work ahead—being a fake news program is a huge advantage. On a weekday morning, we might think of the most visceral aspect of the Iraqi elections—like "Now that we've had an election, we can leave." What's the best way to express that through stand-up? Someone might throw out an idea: Could we have the

At the College of William & Mary, 1983. Stewart majored in psychology.

correspondent stand in front of a green screen that's moving? And on the reveal, you'd see he's doing his commentary while running the heck out of Iraq. But then we figure out, okay, we can't do that. It's all about having an ear for the right idea.

Oprah: Did you know that when you took over the show?

Jon: No. I just knew I wanted to do something different.

Oprah: But I've heard the staff wasn't with you on that?

Jon: That's correct. Tracey can attest. Many times she'd find me in the living room at 4 in the morning, smoking and having arguments with myself.

Oprah: How did you convince them to go your way?

Jon: I didn't. Those who were with me stayed; others left.

Oprah: Was it a conscious decision to move to politics?

Jon: It was a conscious decision to move to relevance—to make the show something people care about. I had done a talk show where it was, "Ladies and gentlemen, tonight we're doing three segments instead of two with Maria Conchita Alonso. Because it turns out the guy with the falcons is not going to come tonight." I thought, *This can't be how I live my life.* So I decided not to give a crap about what anybody else thought anymore. I did what I wanted to do, with like-minded people who'd bring passion, competence, and creativity to it.

Oprah: Did you feel that even when people started walking out?

Jon: I can't tell you how relieved I was when people started walking. I didn't have to fire them.

Oprah: I hate firing.

Jon: But anytime you can weed out crazy and bring in sane, it's worth it. A friend of mine used to say, "Why shouldn't a good person get the job? Why shouldn't competence be rewarded?" So I brought in Ben Karlin, a guy from *The Onion* [an online newspaper parody], and Stephen Colbert, and we developed a team that felt right. We got better at structuring the show. I always hear quarterbacks say the difference in the NFL now is the speed of the game. The difference in *The Daily Show* is the speed with which you have to digest material and turn it into a comedy-like pulp. When you look at Johnny Carson's old shows, you want to smoke a pipe, have a cup of tea, and relax. But our show moves. That's how TV is now.

Oprah: I've heard that the faster you tell a joke, the funnier it is. True?

Jon: I don't know, but I will definitely talk faster from now on.

Oprah: You really became part of the public's consciousness during "Indecision 2000." Do you deny that you are powerful?

Jon: Yes—I deny that I am powerful. Power implies an

agenda that's being acted on.

Oprah: But more than anyone else, you have us thinking about politics differently.

Jon: Every generation has had its people who stand at the back and make fun of those in charge. When the Nazis came to power in the thirties, it created an incredible underground scene of satirical comedy. Peter Cook [a British comedian] once said with a straight face, "Yes, they really showed Hitler." That's how I see it. I'm not saying I'm powerless and in a vacuum. But if I really wanted to change things, I'd run for office. I haven't considered that, and I wouldn't—because this is what I do well. The more I move away from comedy, the less competent I become.

Oprah: I got that. People ask me all the time whether I'd run for office. What I do well is television. I wouldn't be effective sitting in an office trying to push legislation.

Jon: But if power were your aphrodisiac, you would do it anyway. You could translate your influence into political power.

Oprah: I agree. I question your denial that you have a powerful effect on the way people think about politics.

Jon: Honestly, I'm not trying to be self-deprecating or even obtuse. What we're doing on the show is not original. If it weren't me, it would be somebody else. We set out to deconstruct the process [of politics] and give people a glimpse at what we think the reality is—and while we're doing that, we tell jokes. If I didn't do jokes, nobody would give a crap.

Oprah: When did the media become the be-all and end-all for influencing people's opinions?

Jon: When Gutenberg came up with that printing press. After that it was over. It's not about the media; it's that a means of communication will always be co-opted by people who want to use it for powerful purposes. And when we say "the media," do we mean me, Ted Koppel, or Rush Limbaugh? Those are very disparate voices. The media is really a bunch of feudal kingdoms that exist in a larger structure.

The Bush administration is actually doing something really smart: They're blurring the line between what's a voice of authority and what isn't. They've paid guys like Mike McManus and Armstrong Williams to go out and tout their programs and create news pieces. [Federal agencies allegedly paid several newspaper columnists to help promote the No Child Left Behind campaign and other initiatives.] These guys are government advocates

> "I don't remember a time when people didn't think I was a wiseass…but I hope I've gotten more artful."

working under the guise of "analysts." What's more confusing than that?

Oprah: Isn't that the ultimate in propaganda?

Jon: Yeah. The media started winning in 1960. That was the first time—when Nixon went up against Kennedy in the debate and said, "I don't need any makeup. I look freakin' great." Everybody watching went, "Oh my God. Who's Sweaty McSweatington?" They all voted for Kennedy. In the same way that Franklin D. Roosevelt recognized the power of radio, politicians now recognize the power of TV—and power doesn't want scrutiny. Noise is an advantage. I'm not even making sense anymore, am I?

Oprah: I get it.

Jon: I've got to ask, or else we'll be sitting around like, "Don't you get it, man? It's the media, dude."

Oprah: I think what your show has done, especially during the election, is allow people to ask, "Are we just being sold a bill of goods?"

Jon: There are a lot of people saying what we're saying, but I hope we're doing it in a funny and artful way.

Oprah: You are.

Jon: I'll take that. It's not about power. It's about allowing more people to sample knowledge because it's baked in a delicious chocolate cake.

Oprah: And you don't have an agenda?

Jon: We do have an agenda—just not the one that many people think we have.

Oprah: Do you have an intention?

Jon: Ooh, well done! Yes, and it's a selfish one. The barometer I use is mostly internal. A bad day for me is when I feel incompetent, not when I feel powerless.

Oprah: What makes you feel incompetent?

Jon: Poor execution. The show is a recipe of the silly, the relevant, the didactic, and the bawdy. We try to mix it in just the right measure so that it tastes delicious but still has enough nutrients. I would love for this show to be as competent as *Seinfeld.* I just want to be really good at what I do and feel good about doing it.

Oprah: Do you?

Jon: On more days than I deserve. But some nights, I'll come home to Tracey and go, "Honey, I got no mojo." It takes a while to hustle your way out of that—especially after a kid.

Oprah: Has parenting surprised you?

Jon: There's always talk about the red-blue cultural divide. But I'm surprised at the difference between having kids and not having any. Tracey says she now sees everyone as somebody's kid. When I look at Nathan, I think, *I could kill someone for him.* In fact, I could do it almost every day. When I see people walking down the street, it's like, *Somebody is crazy about this person in a way that hurts his heart.*

Oprah: Or somebody needed to love that person.

Tracey: Now we sometimes see people and think, *Somebody wasn't so good to them.*

Oprah: Since you've hit your stride on *The Daily Show,* do you feel successful?

Jon: I feel comfortable in my own skin. For me, that was the battle.

Oprah: When did you win it?

Jon: What time is it? When you walked in the door and I didn't cry. No, really—it was gradual. After college, I bartended while working for the state on a puppet show about disabilities—I was literally helping and hurting people, all on the same day. While the show was a noble effort, it was completely unsatisfying for me because I didn't feel part of it. When I dreamed, I dreamed of being somebody else. I realized I needed to create something I felt part of. Then slowly, that feeling of wanting to be someone else went away.

Oprah: You'd rather be yourself.

Jon: Right. I think that's a huge victory.

Oprah: I think so, too. If I come back in a second life, I want to come back as me.

Jon: [*Laughs.*] You know what? I'd like that, too.

Oprah: In the early nineties, I realized I'd been imitating others because I thought I needed to. I now know that the show has to come out of me.

Jon: Otherwise, how could you sustain it? When I first got on *Letterman* five years into my career, I thought, *This is it—the end of my rainbow.* He was the Carson of my generation. On the show, I did as well as I could. When I woke up the next morning, I wasn't any taller, I had a head cold, my apartment still had roaches. That's when I realized, *This isn't about moments; this isn't about getting to the next place. It's just about being good.* Then I got a show on MTV.

Oprah: What was that called?

Jon: Such an original title—*The Jon Stewart Show.* That did well enough for me to get Arsenio Hall's job after he quit. I was scared shitless. About four months into it, I thought, *Wow, this unbelievable opportunity will be taken away from me, and when someone asks, "Did you even enjoy it?" I'm going to say no.* I remember the night when I just exhaled.

> "In that moment, I realized I had suddenly become competent. I had lived through the loss I feared."

Oprah: That happened to me when I was onstage dancing with Tina Turner. The song was only three minutes and 27 seconds long, and I was so nervous. Suddenly, a voice in my head said, "You've already wasted a minute. You'd better enjoy this!"

Jon: If this were Hollywood, the story would be that I relaxed and then built an empire, and 30 years later, that show is still going strong. Well, I relaxed, and five minutes later they locked my door and didn't let me back in the building. I got fired. But I had a hell of a time. I woke up the next day and it was the opposite of the *Letterman* experience. I thought, *Okay, my apartment is no worse and I can still write jokes.* In that moment, I realized I had suddenly become competent. I had lived through the loss I feared.

Oprah: That's a pivotal adult moment.

Jon: A month later I met Tracey.

Oprah: How did you meet?

Jon: On the only blind date either of us had ever been on, at a Mexican restaurant.

Tracey: The date wasn't blind for me.

Jon: Tracey had seen me on TV.

Tracey: It's a fairy tale from my end. I had just gotten out of a seven-year relationship. I was depressed, and my friends were trying to set me up all the time. After a bad date, they'd ask, "What are you looking for?" I had discovered *The Jon Stewart Show,* so I said, "Someone funny and sweet, like Jon Stewart." My roommate was working on a movie set, and Jon knew someone who worked on that set. So Jon stopped by to say hello. They were all sitting around talking about how they weren't having much success with dating. My friend said, "I have a roommate who thinks you're cute. She saw you on TV." And, of course, Jon immediately thought...

Oprah: Loser!

Tracey: Right. Because my roommate was always setting me up with actors, I'd said, "No more performers." So she told Jon, "Actually, it goes against you that you have a television show." Then she told him more about me. Jon said later that he'd never heard someone talk in such a loving way about a friend.

Oprah: So was there chemistry at the Mexican restaurant?

Jon: I thought she hated me.

Tracey: I was embarrassed by how we met, and so nervous that I couldn't eat.

Jon: The date was literally me talking and eating. I cleaned my plate and part of hers. Then after I got a couple of drinks in her...

Tracey: I wouldn't stop talking.

Brainstorming with writers at *The Daily Show*, December 2003.

Jon: So now I just keep her drunk.

Oprah: How long have you been married?

Jon: Since May 2000. But we have been together much longer.

Oprah: Did marriage change you?

Jon: Tracey would probably say it didn't change me fast enough.

Tracey: I think it changed your living environment.

Jon: Let me put it this way: If I were single, this interview would have been a much different experience. You'd be surrounded by boxes.

Oprah: Where do you see your show going? I know that's tough to answer when you work on a daily program.

Jon: Right. After every show, we have a two-minute postmortem where we go, "Jesus, I can't believe we did that" or "We should have moved that piece up higher." And then it's "What are we doing tomorrow?" When I come home, Tracey says, "Who was on the show tonight?" and I have no idea because it's not about that. It's about hitting the next night.

Oprah: People come up to me and say, "I was on your show two years ago," and I have no idea who they are.

Jon: At least we only have one guest a night. *The Daily Show* is really about the writing. We've realized that people will become accustomed to our voice, and we have to evolve it in a way that's inspired. You can exist on television for a long time as mediocre. You can become comfort food. We don't want that. I can't imagine doing this 20 years from now.

Oprah: Are there topics you consider off-limits?

Jon: I hope our humanity saves us from producing nasty or mean-spirited shows.

Oprah: You caused a media storm by calling *Crossfire* host Tucker Carlson a dick when you went on his show in 2004. Do you regret that?

Jon: I regret losing my patience. That's about it. But calling him a dick? Not really. I was calling that guy who was on that show right there a dick—I don't pretend to know Tucker as a person. But I regret going on air as tired as I was and not being more articulate with what I wanted to say.

Oprah: That's what happens when you're on the edge.

Jon: I thought, *Let's just end this on a sneeze!*

Oprah: A-choo!

Jon: The TV networks have an opportunity to bring noise or clarity. So much of what the government and corporations do is bring noise because they don't welcome scrutiny. They don't necessarily want you to know what they're up to. So if you're working in a medium that has an opportunity to bring clarity and you instead choose to create more distraction, that's theater—which is what these news channels have become.

Oprah: Theater that isn't really challenging.

Jon: The reason everyone on *Crossfire* freaked out is that I didn't play the role I was supposed to play. I was expected to do some funny jokes, then go have a beer with everyone. By stepping outside of my role, I stunned them. Imagine going on *Crossfire* and expressing an opinion that causes a problem. Apparently, the only people you cannot put in the crossfire are the hosts of *Crossfire.* What they do isn't real. It's talking point, talking point, talking point. It's like, "We all understand this is a game. Now let's go have dinner." But for those of us watching at home, it's not a game. It's frustrating. And it wasn't their dismissiveness that riled me; it was their condescension. It was like, "How dare you come on here and not do what you're supposed to do?"

Oprah: Because you're supposed to be a comedian.

Jon: Right. What I ultimately said was, "Tomorrow I'll go back to being funny, and you guys will still blow." I have no respect for them. It was as if they thought I was suddenly taking myself too seriously. What do you think *The Daily Show* is about? Just because we're comedic doesn't mean we don't care about this stuff. We do.

Oprah: I love that you told John Edwards he'd have to announce his candidacy someplace else because it didn't count on a fake news show.

Jon: Right. And my interview with John Kerry wasn't very good.

Oprah: You don't think so?

Jon: No. Our interviews either have to be really funny or find some humanity in the subject. I didn't do either. He remained guarded throughout, so it struck me as a boring fencing match.

Oprah: When I'm talking with politicians, I can't break that wall.

Jon: Politicians are salespeople. If you're trying to sell a product, what's more powerful than an appearance on

> "I surprised the crap out of everyone. I wanted something different. I yearned, and I went for it."

Oprah's show? In the last four months, one book overtook America on Amazon. It's called *He's Just Not That Into You.* When I saw that title, I said, "What the hell is that?" Somebody told me, "The author was on *Oprah.*" So politicians see your show as their chance to display their theatrical humanity, not their real humanity. They come on my show to display their theatrical sense of humor—and to show that they're down with the kids.

Oprah: Kerry didn't accomplish that.

Jon: No, he didn't. Because he was—like I was on *Crossfire*—tired and in a certain mood.

Oprah: Right. So you don't think you'll be doing *The Daily Show* in 20 years?

Jon: I don't want to be. I love my wife, and we want more kids. I'm not going to disappear, but I don't want to work this hard.

Oprah: What kind of daddy do you want to be?

Jon: The kind who stays. The kind who doesn't say to a 9-year-old kid, "This doesn't mean your mother and I don't love you" as he's heading out the door.

Oprah: What's important to you?

Jon: That. I've achieved far more than I ever thought I would. I'm not complacent, but I don't think long-term. I tell myself, *If I get good at this, it'll be fun to do.*

Oprah: Can you taste your success?

Tracey: I can taste it.

Jon: For her, it actually tastes like an online catalog. I just don't think it's in my nature to savor things. But I no longer live with a gnarly void, like an angry troll under a bridge.

Oprah: Isn't that what defines a real man?

Jon: That seems genderless to me.

Oprah: It's also what makes a real woman.

Jon: Yes. What I'm proudest of is moving to New York.

Oprah: You left the puppets.

Jon: Yes—and I surprised the crap out of everyone. I might have become a bitter guy at the end of the bar, complaining about how I could've been somebody. But I sold my car and moved up to New York with no job because I wanted something different. I yearned, and I went for it. **O**

UPDATE In 2010, Time *named Jon Stewart's* The Daily Show *one of the 100 best TV shows of all time.*

Barbara Walters and her Havanese, Cha Cha Cha, greet Oprah in the library of Walters's Manhattan apartment.

Oprah Talks to Barbara Walters

She's sat down with world leaders, probed the inner lives of presidents, interrogated film stars, gotten the unguarded truth out of royalty, and inspired generations of female TV journalists, including a young Oprah Winfrey. Here, a broadcasting legend who can coax a fascinating answer out of a rock opens up about her life, her passions, her peaks, her regrets—and, yes, she makes Oprah cry.

hen I was 17, I entered the local Miss Fire Prevention Contest. I knew the judges would ask what I hoped to do with my life, and I'd planned to say, "I want to become a fourth-grade teacher." But I'd seen the *Today* show that morning, and it popped into my head to say my goal was to be a TV journalist. "What kind of journalist?" one of the judges pressed. I've never forgotten my answer: "I want to be like Barbara Walters."

Thirty-three years later, I was delighted to get a tour of Barbara's Manhattan apartment, which is filled with antiques and artwork from her travels around the world. If these walls could talk, one of them would speak volumes—she calls it her wall of fame and infamy, lined with framed photos of every president and first lady since Lyndon Johnson, as well as Fidel Castro, Yassir Arafat, Muammar al-Qaddafi, and dozens more leaders, dictators, and cultural icons she's interviewed. The photos, many signed with personal notes, are a testament to one of the most extraordinary women of our time.

Barbara was born 81 years ago to nightclub owner and theatrical producer Lou Walters and his wife, Dena. The couple had already lost a son and had an older daughter who was mildly retarded. The family bounced back and forth from Boston to Miami to New York, where they lived in penthouses until her father lost his fortune in the mid-1950s. Barbara, who'd just graduated from Sarah Lawrence College, helped support her parents with her income from a secretarial job.

Following a brief first marriage, Barbara landed a position as a writer for the *Today* show. By 1964 she'd become a "*Today* girl"—her job was essentially to make the male anchor look good, and to look good herself. Eventually, she became the cohost. With her second husband, theatrical producer Lee Guber, she adopted a daughter, Jacqueline.

The couple divorced in 1976, the same year Barbara moved from NBC to ABC for an unprecedented $1 million salary. Male colleagues complained that she was overpaid; some decried her "infotainment" style. After less than two years, the president of ABC removed her as coanchor of the nightly news and reassigned her as a correspondent. Early in her ABC stint, the first prime-time *Barbara Walters Special* aired. A couple of dozen pre-Oscar interviews later, Walters signed on as cohost of *20/20*. In 1997 she also became co-executive producer of *The View*—a responsibility she kept when, after 25 years, she gave up her weekly *20/20* gig. Sitting in her living room overlooking Central Park on a beautiful sunny afternoon, she talked about ambition, regret, heads of state, children, and what's next for her.

Oprah: By the time this interview appears, you'll be doing your last regular episodes of 20/20. Why are you leaving?

Barbara: I've worked all my life, and I've never had time to go to a city or country where I haven't been in the studio. I watched your special [Diane Sawyer devoted an hour of *Primetime* to Oprah's work in South Africa] not just with tears but with yearning. I've been to China four times—but I've never really seen China.

Oprah: Because you were always working.

Barbara: Yes. While I'm still healthy and young enough, I want time to do these things. And I want more time with my daughter before I turn around and say, "Where did that go?"

Oprah: Your daughter, Jackie, is a grown woman. Hasn't there already been a moment when you turned around and said, "Where did the time go?"

Barbara: Oh, yes. I tried to be with her a lot—but why wasn't I there more? My new arrangement gives me the opportunity to stay in television, because I'll still do five specials, and I'll do *20/20* from time to time.

Oprah: Up until the moment you leave, won't you feel the sense of competition—of needing the next big "get"?

Barbara: Well, I can't pretend that I didn't go after the big interviews. Years ago I traveled to Cairo and threw pebbles against Anwar el-Sadat's window before the signing of the Camp David peace treaty, hoping he'd come out and do one more interview. I mean, that's insane. Then I'd get on a plane and do an interview in New Orleans. During the years when I covered the Middle East, I was constantly traveling. Now I don't have that burning ambition.

Oprah: When Martha Stewart was first indicted, did you think, *I have to get that interview?*

Barbara: No. I thought, *I'd like this interview, I hope I get it.* A few years ago, I would have said, "I *must* have it." Now I want something I haven't had since I was in my 20s—time. I'll miss certain things. I love my producer. But I also feel very content with my choice. I want to write a book, and I want to do it myself.

Oprah: I still have your first book, *How to Talk with Practically Anybody About Practically Anything.*

Barbara: I did that in my 30s. Now I've got to write about growing up and my father, who was such an extraordinary person, and my poor sister, who was borderline mentally challenged.

Oprah: You've got to write about what this life has meant to you.

Barbara: And I want to learn Spanish.

Oprah: Me, too.

Walters started in television as a newswriter (*top*, in 1953), then went on to become the *Today* show's first female cohost (*above*, with anchor Frank McGee in 1971), though her role was limited: She was allowed to ask a hard-news question only after McGee had asked three.

Barbara: I find it fascinating that you told Bill Clinton you'd never want to be in politics. I feel the same way.

Oprah: Why would we want politics?

Barbara: Never.

Oprah: You've sat at the center of the world, doing what you do, and for so many years. I've said what a mentor you've been for me. Had there not been you, there never would have been me. Do you feel like the leader on the frontier?

Barbara: No, because I didn't deliberately pave the way. I wasn't Gloria Steinem. When I look back at the kinds of things I wasn't allowed to do when I began as a writer, even on the *Today* show...

Oprah: What year?

Barbara: Around 1960. I could write only the so-called female pieces. The big breakthrough was when I could write for men. I remember when I was there with an anchorman named Frank McGee. He had to ask three hard-news questions before I could ask one.

Oprah: Wow.

Barbara: I also remember writing to the president of NBC News and saying, "We should do something on the women's movement." And he wrote back, "Not enough interest." Now I'm very encouraging and admiring of women. The other night I was on with [CNN anchor] Paula Zahn and I said, "I feel I'm your fairy godmother." I feel that way about quite a few of the younger people on the air. And I want to say something else. There's been a rumor rattling around for years, and it drives Diane Sawyer and me crazy. It's been said that we're competitive because Roone Arledge [the late president of ABC News] brought Diane over to do a newsmagazine show, and I did a newsmagazine. I just want to say that I have such admiration for Diane. We feel very good about each other. Always have. We can laugh together. This whole business that we've always been out to kill each other is such an old story. We're sick of it.

Oprah: So you are competitors with respect for each other.

Barbara: Great respect. If I don't get the interview, I want Diane to get it. I think she feels the same way.

Oprah: That rumor never would've happened about men.

Barbara: If Ted Koppel and Peter Jennings competed, we'd never hear about it. But we still have these clichés.

Oprah: I was in broadcasting when you made the move to do the *ABC Evening News*. I remember your first night on the air like it was happening to me.

Barbara: Then you must have felt awful. It must have been the worst time of your professional life. You must have been thinking, *I'm drowning and there's no life preserver.*

Oprah: No, no. Barbara, do you remember that this was the biggest deal? A million dollars.

Barbara: I keep saying this, and no one is listening. I did not get a million dollars for doing the news, which is what everyone thought. And I'm not saying that a million dollars isn't a great deal. It is. But I made $500,000 to do the news—with Harry Reasoner, my unwilling coanchor. Then I made another $500,000 to do four one-hour prime-time specials. The first special had Jimmy Carter and Rosalynn Carter and Barbra Streisand. But everybody seized on the million dollars. One magazine headline said she's a flop. When I saw the editor, I said, "That's so painful. Why would you say that?" He said, "Because, Barbara, you are a flop."

Oprah: Oh, no.

Barbara: At that point, Harry Reasoner was the bigger star. I was the upstart. I hadn't learned everything from the Associated or United Press. I was a child of television, and I was a woman. How dare I even think I could do the news?

Oprah: Wasn't that in 1976?

Barbara: Yes. The first night I did an interview—I talked with [Egyptian president] Anwar el-Sadat. Then the second night I interviewed [Israeli prime minister] Golda Meir. My publicity was so hideous. I got killed for it. That's when I did the now famous interview with Anwar el-Sadat and [Israeli prime minister] Menachem Begin, which was the first joint interview the two had ever done. Then I went to Cuba and spent ten days with Fidel Castro.

Oprah: That was your way of saying, "I'm not gonna let 'em have me."

Barbara: What was I going to do? I had a child to support. I was supporting my family then.

Oprah: Were you devastated, Barbara?

Barbara: I really did feel that my career was over. What saved me were my friends and my child. I'd decided to go to ABC because it was time to see my child in the mornings without always being so exhausted. Then I had four years of all these big interviews. It was a different time— we wanted to see heads of state. Now heads of state call up and ask, "What's your rating?" I'm not kidding. It's like, "Hello, this is Saddam Hussein. How many viewers do you have? Do you reach a young audience?"

When I went over to *20/20,* I felt I needed a home. The show's anchor, Hugh Downs, was very honest and said, "Look, I like her very much, but I don't really want her." ABC said, "It will make the ratings better to have a partner." He was wonderful. So it's good to fail sometimes. When you fail, you have to prove yourself. That's often the best thing that can happen, because then you're sure your success isn't just luck.

Oprah: Have you ever been nervous before a big interview?

Barbara: No. Thirty years ago, I used to smoke one cigarette beforehand. You know when I did get nervous? When I'd go on Johnny Carson or David Letterman. Now with David, I just let it fly.

Oprah: So you weren't nervous before the Sadat and Begin interview?

Barbara: No. It helps that I do so much homework.

Oprah: How about with Castro?

Barbara: I was concerned that it might be a boring interview, but I wasn't nervous. However, put me on a dance floor, and if I have to dance by myself, I can't do it. I also don't drive.

Oprah: You don't?

Barbara: No. Years ago I heard my daughter on the phone saying, "My mommy doesn't drive. My mommy burns the meat loaf. My mommy doesn't do anything except television." There are whole areas in which I feel very inadequate. Who doesn't drive except me?

Oprah: Quincy Jones. You're the only two people I know.

Barbara: Thank goodness. We can share a car.

Oprah: But how can you not be nervous with some of the people you talk to?

Barbara: During an interview, I'm in control. It's in other aspects of my life where I'm not. And listen, when I say I'm not nervous, I want you to know that I'm hardly the most self-confident person. I second-guess almost everything I do, except editing. I love to edit. But I can't tell you whether I should wear the red dress or the green, or whether I should take the trip or stay home. It's torture. Years ago when I was covering fashion for the *Today* show, I remember trying to decide whether I should stay in Paris another week. I decided I should take the money and go to a psychiatrist because I couldn't make up my mind. But then I couldn't make up my mind which psychiatrist to go to!

Oprah: Is that a true story?

Barbara: Yes. Anybody who knows me knows this. At work I know what questions to ask. In real life, I'm asking myself, *Should I marry him?* until the day I get married. The only thing I've been certain of is my love for Jackie.

Oprah: When you sit down to talk with a major head of state, do you use a certain technique?

Barbara: No. I know I have to ask certain tough questions, though I sometimes don't want to. You're damned if you do and damned if you don't.

Oprah: You're really damned if you don't.

Barbara: Exactly. I might ask, "What's the biggest misconception about you?" That gives the person the opportunity to discuss the difficult issues. I did the first live interview with Richard Nixon after his resignation. I asked all kinds of foreign policy questions, and he was wonderful about them. When I wanted to ask about him personally, I said, "What got you through it? Was it your spirituality? Was it your family?" He said, "Oh, Barbara, you don't want to ask these personal questions. Nobody's interested." I said, "They really are, Mr. President." When he griped about it, I tried to go back to my list of foreign policy questions—but I couldn't find them. Before an interview, I write hundreds of questions on little cards, then boil them down. For this interview, I'd written so many that, fortunately, I remembered some. I usually know more about the person I'm interviewing than he knows about himself. When the interview was over, Nixon was perspiring. I was ice-cold. I stood up to shake his hand, and I realized that I'd put the questions under my fanny.

Oprah: What a great story! Back in '77, during your interview with Sadat, didn't you know you were making history?

Barbara: Yes. But with other interviews, I often have to decide whether I want to make *The New York Times* or

In 1977 Walters broadcast her groundbreaking joint interview with Israeli prime minister Menachem Begin and Egyptian president Anwar el-Sadat.

to ask a question that the audience wants to hear. There must be a balance.

Oprah: **Are celebrities difficult?**

Barbara: Young celebrities are difficult because they haven't done much [to talk about]. Comedians are also difficult.

Oprah: **Yes. I saw an interview you did with Richard Pryor.**

Barbara: He's fascinating because he's more than a comedian. I interviewed him four times. The second time was after he'd set himself on fire. The third was when he admitted to me that he'd set himself on fire. I'm touched by Richard Pryor because I saw this brilliant man self-destruct. I'm going to make a comparison, and you're going to think I'm nuts, but I'm also touched by Margaret Thatcher. I'd talked with her before she was prime minister and while she was in office. I also did an interview with her after her fall. So I saw all those years in a progression. You become emotionally involved. Those are memories I treasure.

But yes, young celebrities are hard, and I won't have to do many of them anymore. When I do a special, it really has to be special—and I worry a little about that. I'm contractually committed to specials for far longer than I ever thought I'd be working. But I'm also proud, because I'll probably have been in news longer than any other woman. That's not the kind of thing you put in *Ripley's Believe It or Not!*, but maybe we'll have less age discrimination.

Oprah: **You're still on the frontier.**

Barbara: Yes, and that will affect other women. That makes me feel good. All I need is good lighting and a little Botox [*laughs*].

Oprah: **It took me years to get good lighting.**

Barbara: It's more important than makeup. Shall we tell people about that in their own homes? Watch your lighting.

Oprah: **It's everything. So you were talking about areas in your life where you don't feel in control. Do you think you were a great mother?**

Barbara: I was a loving mother. But a career is a difficult thing to balance with a very young child. These days you can bring your child into some workplaces. If I had brought Jackie in with me...

Oprah: **Can you imagine?**

Barbara: I wanted my child so much. She was indeed the chosen child. She was adopted after I'd had three miscarriages. I used to say that you could have a great marriage and a great career, a great marriage and great children, or great children and a great career, but you couldn't have all three. Now you can, with the support of a mate, if indeed you have one. It's a different time, and there are many women who do it. I was traveling so much, and I rationalized it by saying, "If I hadn't worked all those years, I wouldn't have been able to help my daughter accomplish some of the things she has accomplished." Do you know what my daughter does? She runs a therapeutic wilderness program for adolescent girls in crisis. Isn't that wonderful?

Oprah: **Yes, it is. Is there anything you would have done differently?**

Barbara: I would have been home more—and you and I wouldn't be talking today.

Oprah: **Really?**

Barbara: Yes. It's not just about spending quality time. It's about time in general. There are kids who don't need quite as much. But you really have to think about it.

Oprah: Is that a regret?

Barbara: Jackie's so wonderful now that it's not. But had she not been, it would have been a very deep regret. When she was going through the turmoil of her teen years, which I don't want to talk about, it was a terrible heartache. But maybe I did something right, because look how she turned out. She sometimes says to me—though not always with great pleasure—"I'm just like you, Mom. I'm a workaholic."

Oprah: Do you spend a lot of time with her?

Barbara: We spend much more time together these days. She used to live on the West Coast. She moved to Maine to be nearer to me. She doesn't really like New York, but Maine is two hours away by plane.

Oprah: Maya Angelou said that her mother was a better mom to an older child than she was to a younger child.

Barbara: I'm not sure which is true for me. I love babies. Jackie used to say that she had to watch me in the park 'cause I'd kidnap one. My daughter doesn't particularly want to have children. I would love to have a grandchild. I've told her, "Have a grandchild and give it to me." But I understand women who don't want children. That's one of the good things about our society today. Nobody says, "You don't want children? What's wrong with you?" My mother had friends who were childless, and people looked down on them.

Oprah: That's right.

Barbara: See, Jackie adores what she does. She feels these [girls she works with] are her kids. And she doesn't want to have children. I did—desperately. If you don't want them desperately, and you've got a big career, don't have them.

Oprah: Thank you, Miss Barbara!

Barbara: You're very welcome. Anytime. Just lie down on my couch.

Oprah: My friend Gayle [King] goes, "You never wanted kids?" She was one of those people in high school who was already naming her sets of twins. I've never done that.

Barbara: Then I'm so glad you didn't have them just to show them off or to be able to say, "Now I've experienced everything."

Oprah: Yes. Is there anything that frightens you?

Barbara: Other than driving and cooking?

Oprah: Well, as a woman on the front lines, you've always seemed to know how to handle yourself.

Barbara: Oh, I don't know. Listen, I certainly haven't been very good at marriage. [A third marriage, to producer Merv Adelson, ended in 1992.]

Oprah: Don't you think it would have been difficult for you to be great at marriage with your dedication to your career? It takes a very special man to understand that.

Barbara: Maybe if he were also very busy.... Those types of marriages seem to work.

Oprah: You couldn't have had a man with a lot of time. He'd be saying, "Where are you?"

Barbara: I've always been attracted to men who were busy and successful in their own lives. And by the way, I do want to mention the one thing that has changed others' perception of me: It's *The View.* People realized I could be silly and funny. I had to think about whether being on that show would interfere with my interviews with heads of state. Would I still be able to do hard news? I'd been around long enough that I had the reputation, so I could do both.

Oprah: Was that a serious consideration?

Barbara: In the beginning, yes. The news department didn't want me to do *The View.*

Oprah: Especially because of the places you all go sometimes.

Barbara: That's right. There are still times when I put my face in my hands on *The View.* The news department is a very holy club, H-O-L-Y. Though more and more, people can be human and show both sides.

Oprah: As we were walking past your wall of fame, my eyes started to water because there's such history and depth and meaning there. Do you still get impressed with yourself?

Barbara: I forget what I've done until I start working on a retrospective. Then I'm amazed. I was never supposed to be in front of the cameras. I wasn't beautiful. I didn't speak perfectly. At the time, the very few women on TV were weathergirls. Isn't it funny that we now have all these weathermen?

Oprah: Yes.

Barbara: I consider myself blessed. But I also know I'm normal. I don't walk around saying, "Look what I've done."

Oprah: But what do you feel when you walk down that hallway?

Barbara: I wish I'd kept a diary. In the beginning, I was so sure I was a failure that I didn't. Then I got too busy, too tired at night.

Oprah: You thought you were a failure?

Barbara: At ABC I *was* a failure.

Oprah: But did you still feel that way once you'd landed the Sadat and Begin interview?

Barbara: I'm still auditioning.

Oprah: But you don't have to anymore, Barbara.

Barbara: Well, up until a couple of years ago, I was auditioning.

Oprah: I understand. Up until a couple of years ago, I thought, *If I don't have this job, I don't know if I'll ever work again in TV.*

Barbara: Having had a life with such great economic uncertainty—my father lost everything and I supported the family—financial security meant a great deal to me.

Oprah: Once you have that security, you can do what you do for the pure joy of the craft. You can't live from airplane to airplane if it's only about the money.

Barbara: None of us does it just for money. I used to say I would do my job for nothing, and I was afraid that ABC would say, "Okay!" Giving up *20/20* will make a financial difference.

Oprah: Aren't you set for life?

Barbara: Yes. That's why I'm able to walk away. It's actually not that I'm still auditioning. I just know people who are far more confident than me. Maybe you have to be the way I am to have the kind of drive I've had. Make sense?

Oprah: Yes. When you interviewed Martha Stewart, she said work was her whole life. How has work fit into the scheme of things for you?

Barbara: What sustained me during bad press, or when I didn't get an interview, were my close friends. When Martha Stewart said, "My work is my life," I understood that. She also has a child she is close to. But my life is my life. Part of my life is my work. Another part is Jackie. Then there's my social life. I love to be with my friends. I find great joy in that.

Oprah: You're always out.

Barbara: Too much.

Oprah: Three nights a week?

Barbara: Yep. I've often joked that after I leave *20/20,* I won't be sitting next to the prime minister. But I have to tell you, sometimes sitting next to the prime minister is extremely boring. It's more fun at the other table.

Oprah: You always get the best seat.

Barbara: That may change, and that's okay.

Oprah: Wait a minute, that won't change! You're Barbara Walters!

Barbara: Do you think to yourself, *I'm Oprah?*

Oprah: No.

Barbara: So I don't think, *I'm Barbara Walters.*

Oprah: When I see my image on a magazine cover or hear people talk about me, I try to imagine what they see.

Barbara: We've known each other for a long time, so we can talk about this. You're extraordinary. Look at the lives of people you've changed, the schools, your work in Africa. Plus you're funny and you're cute and you're sexy.

Oprah: But I don't think about it like that.

Barbara: You want to know what people think of you? I think you're the most remarkable woman I know.

Oprah: Thank you, Barbara.

Barbara: I don't do what you do. I have not changed the world.

Oprah: But you're Barbara Walters!

Barbara: But I don't see myself as "Barbara Walters."

Oprah: What does being "Barbara Walters" mean?

Barbara: Sometimes it's okay—and sometimes I can't drive. Most of the time when I look back on what I've done, I think, *Did I do that?* And you know what I say to myself? *Why didn't I enjoy it more? Was I working too hard to see it?*

Oprah: Because you were just going from one airplane to the next.

Barbara: And worrying about the shows and getting them on the air—and then thinking, *Was it right?* What I'm trying to do now, before it's too late, is to finally smell the roses. I know it's a cliché, but I want to enjoy it. I want to get rid of the alarm clock every day. I've done enough.

Oprah: What you just said in that moment changed me. That resonates with me to the core, big-time. I got it. I'm trying not to cry. Everybody always ends up crying in your interviews.

Barbara: Time is what it's all about. Look at all those pictures in the hallway. Look at what I accomplished. Yet I was always onto the next thing.

Oprah: Wow, Barbara. That was the most powerful insight you could have given me.

Barbara: Good. Then maybe I've changed someone's life.

Oprah: Bravo. Barbara, what do you know for sure?

Barbara: That you've got to have someone you love—and not necessarily that you have to have someone who loves you. You've got to have a reason to get up in the morning. That doesn't mean you have to have a career. But you must have something you really care about. And you have to have friends. I don't want to do all the clichés for you, but the older I get, the more I think you must be kind. That's why I probably will be less and less of a good interviewer.

Oprah: Really?

Barbara: Sometimes you have to ask the tough questions. I can't be quite as brash as I used to be. I know it hurts. I've become a kinder person.

Oprah: When you walk out of that 20/20 studio, what will you do?

Barbara: I plan to go to a spa the next day. I haven't been to a spa in ten years, maybe 15. I'll go somewhere with no television because I don't want to watch—it will make me cry. Then I'll come home and I'll be fine. I would love to be your age, Oprah. I would love to be a kid of 50. But I have never been at a better place in my life. **O**

UPExpected UPDATE In 2008, Barbara Walters published her memoir, Audition *(Knopf). She is co-host, co-owner, and co-executive producer of* The View.

THE

CHAPTER 3

Living a Healthy Life

DR. OZ	94
BOB GREENE	116

O

EXPERTS

CHAPTER 4

Living Intelligently

SUZE ORMAN | 136

DR. PHIL | 156

CHAPTER 5

Living Thoughtfully

MARTHA BECK | 182

LISA KOGAN | 220

CHAPTER 6

Living Beautifully

NATE BERKUS | 242

ADAM GLASSMAN | 256

10 Things I Know For Sure

During the past ten years, I went from being a doctor to being a doctor/*Oprah* guest/ book author/TV host, and in the process, I've learned a lot about my viewers, my patients, and myself:

1 **The latest thing isn't always the greatest thing.** I work at a cutting-edge hospital, but I also put stock in ancient remedies like treating burns with silver (long known as an antibiotic) or healing surgical wounds using leeches (yes, hospitals continue to do this). If it's still used today, the practice likely has some merit or it would have died off long ago.

2 **Change is possible—but only if you believe it.** The more we learn about genetics and disease, the more we realize that DNA isn't nearly as important as lifestyle.

People think that if their parents had heart disease or were overweight, they're doomed to the same fate. But you can change your health—if you commit yourself to making good choices.

3 **We regret the actions we don't take more than the ones we do.** A few years ago, I appeared on *Oprah* with Randy Pausch, the Carnegie Mellon professor who was dying of pancreatic cancer. He told me that he had recently taken his family on a trip to Discovery Cove to swim with dolphins. It was something that he'd always wanted to do, but it wasn't until he was dying that he made it happen. The next day, I booked the same trip with my family. If there's something on your wish list for life, make plans today to do it.

Hosting a TV show is not that different from doing open-heart surgery. In both the TV studio and the operating room, you depend on highly skilled professionals doing their jobs correctly so you can excel at yours. As a team leader, I recognize that each player—from the anesthesiologist to the camera operator—is better at what they do than I would ever be, and I appreciate their ability to make me look better.

To achieve your goals, make the right thing to do the easy thing to do. I recently replaced the couch in front of my TV with a stationary bike. Now I can pedal while viewing my favorite shows (like *House*). Since the average American watches more than 30 hours of TV per week, it could mean a lot of activity for your body, with little inconvenience.

Knowledge doesn't lead to change—understanding does. If I tell you, "There were a million heart attacks last year"—unless you're one of those million, you don't care. But if I can show you a picture of an artery, and you can see the plaque rupturing—now the heart attack isn't abstract, it's a real story. And you're much more likely to take care of your own heart, because you don't want that same story to affect you.

Going to bed 30 minutes earlier will change your life. I spent years surviving long hospital rotations on little sleep, and I learned that if I don't get seven hours of shut-eye a night, I won't perform well the next day. Less than half of Americans over age 50 get enough sleep, but if you make it a priority, I guarantee that you'll have more energy, less stress, and (most important for a doctor) a clear head.

If you want a healthier community, fight for it. I used to ride my bike across the bridge from New Jersey to Manhattan every morning. I noticed that many bikers stopped riding during the winter, in part because you had to haul your bicycle up and down a flight of 50 stairs on each side of the bridge. So we petitioned for a new bike path that didn't involve stairs—and got it. We all have the power to improve the health of our community, whether it's getting better bike lanes, more sidewalks, or

> If there's something on your wish list for life, make plans today to do it.

a farmers' market that sells fresh produce.

Better patients make better doctors. People are often hesitant to challenge their doctor, but a good patient is someone who raises her hand and says, "I don't understand this" or "This isn't working for me." Your physician will be able to take the knowledge she gains from your open, honest dialogue and pass it on to the next person she treats.

It's not about living longer—it's about living better. I once had a patient who was in danger of having a heart attack if he didn't change his habits. So he changed them. At his next checkup I congratulated him on adding years to his life, but he said, "That's not why I did it. I just wanted to feel better." The idea of living into your 80s or 90s is nice, but what really motivates people to make a change is having a healthy body today. ◖

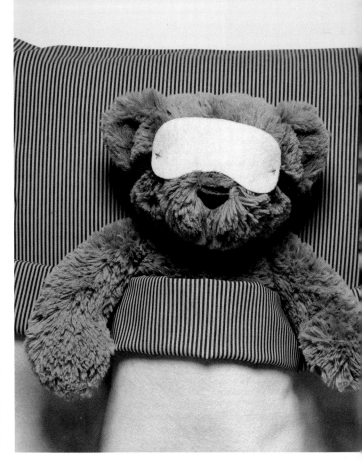

7 Ways to Reduce Stress

1. **Take more restroom breaks.** There's a reason it's called the restroom: It's the one place—at work or at home—where no one will bother you. If you're overwhelmed, steal away for a five-minute meditation break. Inhale deeply into your belly and try to focus on your breathing. You'll emerge calmer, and maybe even more productive. Research shows that meditation can improve your ability to concentrate.

2. **Show up five minutes early.** Everyone knows the feeling: You're running late, stuck in traffic, glancing at your watch every 30 seconds in frustration. Give yourself extra time to get wherever you need to go. Being an early bird will kill stress by giving you more control over your day and your commitments.

3. **Change your stress eating.** The best stress-quashing foods are made by Mother Nature, not Baskin-Robbins. Berries are naturally rich in vitamin C, which helps fight increased levels of cortisol, a stress hormone. A handful of pistachios can lower your blood pressure, which means less of a spike when you get that next rush of adrenaline.

4. **And quit stress drinking.** Yes, a few cocktails can relax you, but alcohol also prevents your brain from entering stages of deep sleep. And sleep and stress are bound together: Chronic stress can keep you up at night, and a lack of sleep can also lead to further stress. Limit yourself to no more than one drink a night.

5. **Get your heart pumping.** Stress makes your body spew out two hormones: cortisol and adrenaline. These chemicals put your body into fight-or-flight mode, ratcheting up your energy level and causing your heart to pound and your muscles to tense. Exercise gives you an outlet to release some of that tension. A good workout also increases your levels of "feel-good" chemicals called endorphins.

6. **Make it a comedy night.** Researchers say that merely anticipating a laugh can jump-start healthy changes in the body by reducing levels of stress hormones, which have been linked to conditions like obesity, heart disease, and memory impairment, to name just a few.

7. **Enjoy the company of friends.** Socializing releases oxytocin, a chemical that can help combat stress hormones and lower your blood pressure. Whether it's spending time with dog lovers, book club buddies, or siblings—whatever group you like—just knowing you're not alone can go a long way toward coping with stress.

4 Ways to Keep Your Brain Sharp

1. **Eat more fresh vegetables.** They're rich in vitamins and nutrients (like E, B6, and folic acid) that protect against brain cell damage. But don't forget that as soon as you pick a tomato off the vine or pull a carrot out of the ground, its nutrient content starts to decline. So the longer it sits on store shelves (or inside your refrigerator), the less good it's doing you. Buy the freshest produce you can, or freeze it at the height of freshness for later use.

2. **Play mind games.** This is the best way to slow the mental decline that can come with aging. Take up a musical instrument. Try to recall the addresses of the last four places you lived. Renew your local library card—and use it.

3. **Sign up for dance lessons.** Exercise boosts the brain's rate of neurogenesis—the generation of new brain cells—throughout your life. To really sharpen your gray matter, pick a workout that stimulates you both mentally and physically. One great example is dance. Moving the body in a coordinated fashion and following along with complex movements in sync with music requires lots of brainpower. Dancing also works your heart, so you're pumping more blood upstairs.

4. **Choose red wine over white.** Red wine contains a compound called resveratrol, which research shows may help prevent the buildup of plaque. Brain plaques are often seen in Alzheimer's patients, and they cause a breakdown in the communication between neurons. ⬤

9 Ways to Improve Your Family's Health

1 Quench cravings with water. Thirst and hunger both originate in the hypothalamus and are sometimes hard to differentiate from each other. So offer your kids a glass of water before you give them a snack. If they don't like plain water, toss slices of fruit or vegetables into a carafe of filtered water for a healthier alternative to sugary beverages.

2 Scrub up like a surgeon. Cold germs, the flu virus, and even bacteria that cause diarrhea are all commonly spread through hand-to-hand contact. Every time you enter your house, wash your hands—including your wrists, the backs of your hands, and underneath your fingernails—with soap for at least 15 to 20 seconds.

3 Eat more meals together. Kids who eat dinner with their families tend to eat less fried food, drink less soda, and consume more fruits and vegetables. Those kids also have a higher intake of vitamins and nutrients and a lower intake of saturated and trans fats. And a regular family meal provides a way to keep the lines of communication open and strong.

4 Stop wearing shoes indoors. Your shoes don't just track dirt into the house, they also track in countless germs, as well as pesticides, smoke and toxins, dust mites, and allergens. One study from the University of Arizona found that the outsides of our shoes contain an average of 421,000 bacteria. So kick them off at the door.

7 **Teach your family to give back.** Volunteering has been linked to increased life expectancy, greater life satisfaction, and reduced rates of depression. Check out servicenation.org or serve.gov for opportunities across the country.

8 **Check your air quality.** Radon is the second leading cause of lung cancer in America, after cigarettes. This gas naturally wafts up from the ground and can get trapped inside your home, where it builds to dangerous levels. You can get a radon-testing kit for less than $20 at www.radonzone.com; the best time to test is winter, when our homes tend to be most tightly insulated. If your levels are elevated, contact your state's radon program (find it at epa.gov/radon/whereyoulive.html) and ask about ways to reduce your exposure.

9 **Feed your dog organic.** Pets have high cancer rates (50 percent of dogs over the age of 10 will develop cancer), and one possible cause is the chemical compounds found in most processed pet foods. Filling Fido's bowl with organic food means you're not exposing him to dangerous additives. **◖**

5 **Stretch.** Flexibility will make daily activities—such as bending over to tie your shoes or running to catch the bus—easier and less tiring. Stretching also improves your circulation as well as your range of motion, which helps keep you balanced, preventing falls and other injuries as you age. Try this stretch as soon as you wake up: Stand with your feet three feet apart, hips directly over your ankles. Interlace your hands behind your back and straighten your arms. Inhale and draw your shoulder blades in toward each other, then exhale and bend forward at the pelvis. Allow your arms to move down toward your head. Hold for ten seconds, taking three to five deep breaths. To release, unclasp your hands and place them on your thighs, bend your knees slightly, and roll back up.

6 **Upgrade your sunscreen.** Look for a product that protects against both UVB rays (which cause sunburn) and UVA rays (which affect the skin on a deeper level and can cause cancer). The SPF number applies only to UVB protection, so check the list of ingredients for a UVA-blocking agent like avobenzone. If you're using a product (or applying one to your kids' faces) that doesn't have UVA blockers, your skin may be getting damaged even if you're not burning.

5 Secrets of "Waist Loss"

Rules to help you fight your body's cravings and stay slim for life.

The unfortunate truth is that most diets do not succeed, and it's easy to blame that fact on a lack of willpower. But restricting food intake runs counter to the body's natural urges. Our ancestors needed extra calories to survive times of extreme stress (say, a famine), and today, when our stress hormones spike—whether due to job frustration or a fight with our spouse—it's as if we're stranded on the tundra of the last ice age.

The good news is that you can outwit your evolutionary biology by implementing these five rules of successful "waist loss" that I developed with Michael Roizen, MD, for our book *YOU: On a Diet.*

Rule 1 Spoil your dinner.

Remember the plant from *Little Shop of Horrors,* with its demands to "Feed me"? The hormone ghrelin is your body's version of Audrey II, only it gets your attention with stomach growls instead of musical numbers. Once you've started eating, it takes about 30 minutes for ghrelin levels to fall and that "full" feeling to kick in. But if you eat a 100-calorie snack (like a handful of nuts) about a half hour before mealtime, your ghrelin levels will already be subsiding by the time you pick up your fork.

Rule 2 Nix soft drinks with meals.

Leptin is a hormone that signals the brain that you can stop eating once your body has stored enough energy from food. Yet fructose (a sugar found in soft drinks) interrupts the feedback loop, preventing your brain from getting the message. Quench your thirst with water instead.

Rule 3 Fill up on fiber.

The ileum is a part of the small bowel that can squeeze, or "brake," to slow the transit of food through the intestines. When that happens, you get a slow but steady supply of fuel, which keeps you feeling satiated. A high-fiber breakfast triggers this mechanism, because the bowel needs more time to absorb nutrients from fiber. The result: No more 11 A.M. stops at the vending machine.

Rule 4 Eat with awareness.

That means eating at the table, not sprawled across the couch. It also means no zoning out in front of *American Idol,* checking your BlackBerry, or surfing the Web during meals. Not only will mindful eating increase the satisfaction you get from food but the extra time will allow your ghrelin levels to drop even further as you eat.

Rule 5 Build more muscle.

You may have heard that muscle burns more calories than fat, but did you know that it burns *a dozen times* more? Aim to walk 10,000 steps a day, and begin a muscle-strengthening program, which will help steel your skeleton as well. Trainer Joel Harper has an excellent program at oprah.com/omagextras. O

DR. OZ WILL SEE YOU NOW

Antidepressants

Feeling down? Dr. Oz explains why drugs aren't always the best answer.

For years now, we've been led to believe that if we are falling behind in the joy department, we need only take a pill to feel calm and content. Yet, as many people are aware, antidepressants have been linked to significant side effects, including decreased sexual desire, weight gain, even an increased risk of suicide. Adding insult to injury, the drugs may not work as well as advertised; a 2008 study found that some can be no more effective than sugar pills. And according to a report in *The New England Journal of Medicine,* many negative antidepressant study results have never been published. All in all, the prescription route to happiness may be less safe or effective than even doctors realize. To help cut through the confusion, I've identified four common misconceptions about happiness and depression. The truth just might surprise you.

Myth 1 You should feel happy all the time.
Sadness is not necessarily a sign of illness—it's a normal part of being human and can even be beneficial. For example, grief is a natural and healthy response that helps us adapt to major losses (of a loved one, a marriage, a job). In the face of stressful challenges, unhappiness can also serve as a beacon to spur positive change. In fact, depression likely evolved to help us cope with environments that are unsatisfying or even harmful. Low moods can signal that it's time to reevaluate what's happening in our lives.

Myth 2 It's all about serotonin.
The most popular antidepressants are drugs called selective serotonin reuptake inhibitors (SSRIs). These work by increasing levels of a brain chemical called serotonin, which regulates mood. But newer research suggests that two areas of the brain called the hippocampus and Brodmann's area 25 can also influence how we experience despair. In addition, we know that depression is often closely linked to anxiety, against which stress-reducing practices like yoga or meditation can be powerful weapons.

Myth 3 Pills offer the easiest fix.
About 15 percent of adults will experience major depression at some point in their lives, but many others suffer from mild to moderate forms of the disease. In those cases, research has shown that lifestyle interventions, such as therapy and exercise, can be as effective as medication. And they're free of one of the most common side effects of antidepressants: weight gain.

Myth 4 Depression looks the same on everyone.
Everyone experiences depression differently. Some patients eat too much and sleep too long, others find that they wake too early and have no appetite. The bottom line is that depression tends to magnify each sufferer's unique vulnerabilities, and as such, physicians often have trouble making a clear-cut diagnosis. If your doctor says that you're depressed and recommends antidepressants, consider seeing a mental health specialist for a second opinion. While untreated depression can be dangerous, taking medication when you don't need it can expose you to potentially harmful side effects. ⬤

Frequent Headaches

An analysis of the different treatments.

The feeling is familiar: a band cinching your skull, a dull ache in the back of your neck. It's a tension headache, and it's by far the most common type—about 90 percent of women and 70 percent of men will experience one during their lifetime. Neurologists don't completely understand the reason your head hurts, but they do know that many headaches are linked to stress, contraction of the neck muscles, poor sleep, and, in women, monthly hormonal fluctuations. Which is why most headache experts recommend relaxation techniques, exercise, limiting caffeine and alcohol (which interfere with sleep), and, for women, discussing birth control pills with a gynecologist. Here, you'll find four approaches to treating headaches.

Neurology

The first thing a neurologist would do is order a CT scan or MRI to rule out potentially serious causes such as a tumor, aneurysm, or stroke, says Marc Sharfman, MD, director of the Headache and Neurological Treatment Institute in Longwood, Florida. If those are ruled out, then, besides the nondrug treatments that follow, Sharfman might suggest biofeedback: He connects patients to devices that monitor muscle tension, blood pressure, and heart rate, then has them practice breathing patterns to identify what helps them relax. Drugs—over-the-counter and prescription—are part of a neurologist's arsenal, but Sharfman notes that patients do best by combining nondrug approaches with minimal medication use.

Acupuncture

A primary goal for an acupuncturist is to wean the patient off prescription and over-the-counter painkillers that can trigger rebound headaches (people who regularly take these medications can suffer a headache as soon as the pills wear off), says Daniel Hsu, a practitioner of traditional Chinese medicine and founder of New York AcuHealth, an acupuncture clinic. Acupuncture can help patients relax as well as transition off medications; what's more, a recent review of research found that the technique could halve the number of days a month a person experiences head pain.

Homeopathy

Along with prescribing a remedy for the headache, a homeopath will typically offer advice on improving diet or, say, reducing exposure to chemicals in the environment, says Dana Ullman, who runs Homeopathic Educational Services in Berkeley. Because homeopaths believe the body's response to an illness is the correct one, they give heavily diluted substances—often the herbs nux vomica and belladonna for headaches—that are supposed to mimic the patient's symptoms, thereby helping the body defend and heal itself. (Though these two herbs are poisonous, the doses contain no toxins.) Often, the patient can begin to feel much better after one treatment, Ullman says.

Nutrition

Alexander Mauskop, MD, director of the New York Headache Center, has performed numerous studies on the interplay of nutrients and headaches, and has found that many sufferers are low in key nutrients—primarily magnesium, coenzyme Q10, riboflavin, and vitamin D. "Up to 50 percent of headache sufferers can be magnesium deficient," he says. Magnesium can ease muscle spasms and alter brain chemicals thought to play a role in headaches; what the other nutrients do is less clear. Mauskop uses sophisticated blood tests to measure nutrient levels. But if a patient doesn't eat plenty of fruits and vegetables, is under a lot of stress, or is a frequent drinker, Mauskop might prescribe supplements without testing. "All these things can reduce nutrient levels," he says.

My Recommendation: Acupuncture and homeopathy are worth considering as adjunct therapies once you are sure that the headache is not a sign of a serious disorder. Like Alexander Mauskop, I believe that magnesium can help—it relaxes arteries and muscles in the body, both of which can help with headaches.

Exercise helps, too—and yoga is a great choice since it can also help you unwind. Biofeedback is useful; in headache research, it has proven its worth. As far as medications go, I prefer ibuprofen and aspirin. And although no one mentioned this, lavender or sandalwood aromatherapy can help you relax. Just take a dab of the oil and rub it into your temples.

DR. OZ WILL SEE YOU NOW

Fibromyalgia

Demystifying the chronic disorder.

Though classified as a disorder of the musculoskeletal system, fibromyalgia is now seen as a central nervous system problem. Symptoms include increased sensitivity to pain, achy and stiff joints, fatigue, and specific tender points on the back, chest, arms, and legs. Migraines, sleep disorders, and irritable bowel syndrome are also common complaints. Up to 3 percent of the population may suffer from fibromyalgia, but with no clear cause, the condition is difficult to diagnose.

Western medicine approach
A formal diagnosis for fibromyalgia didn't exist until 1990, but now there are three FDA-approved meds to combat the pain. Still, says Nancy Klimas, MD, director of the Allergy and Immunology Clinic at the University of Miami, "there is much more to treatment than a pill." Strategies are needed to improve sleep, stretch and restore symmetry to muscles that have been shortened by spasm, and raise overall conditioning through exercise.

Energy-based approach
Practitioners believe the root of fibromyalgia is a disturbance in nerves that blocks energy. The disturbance, says Devi S. Nambudripad, MD, PhD, and a licensed acupuncturist, is caused by sensitivities to substances ranging from pollen to vaccines to chemical agents in fabrics. Anxiety and depression may also play a part. Practitioners use acupuncture to release energy and allergy testing to identify problem substances.

Psychological approach
"The pain of fibromyalgia is not caused by depression," says Leonard Jason, PhD, professor of psychology at DePaul University, "but depression can deepen a patient's experience of pain." Mental health professionals may play a complementary role in treatment, but it's a vital one.

Cognitive behavioral therapy can relieve depression and help patients identify sources of stress that magnify their symptoms.

Nutrition-based approach
Fibromyalgia is a systemwide breakdown, says Jacob Teitelbaum, MD, medical director of the nationwide Fibromyalgia & Fatigue Centers. After suffering from the disease in the 1970s, he developed his own protocol; in studies, patients improved by as much as 91 percent. He recommends supplements to help sufferers sleep, balance hormones, boost immunity, and improve nutrition. He also prescribes regular exercise.

My recommendation: Because Western medicine was slow to accept fibromyalgia, it is behind in its work; this is an area where patients will want to take a serious look at alternative approaches. Energy-based medicine could offer some important advances in treatment over the next decade, but since it has yet to be tested by independent research, I think it's premature to base your therapy solely on this approach. I'm more impressed by Teitelbaum's supplement regimen (find it at oprah.com/omagextras), and not only because he has tested his theories: I've put patients on this program with very good results. I would add counseling, as it should always be a part of fibromyalgia treatment. If after a couple of months you don't see improvement, talk to your doctor about drug therapy. O

Lower Back Pain

A look at your options.

About 80 percent of Americans will experience back pain at some point in their life. The connection to a physical source isn't always clear, since some people show no spinal abnormalities on an X-ray yet suffer excruciating pain. Here are the treatment options:

Chiropractic treatment

Even when the pain is in the lower back, the problem tends to be with the entire spine, says Victor Meir Nazarian, a Los Angeles–based chiropractor. Chiropractors employ manipulation—adjustment of the vertebrae—to help align a patient's spine, and often prescribe regular visits. "People come in only when they're in pain," Nazarian says. "But we need to think of our spine the way we do our teeth, using preventive care to stay healthy."

Physical therapy

The lower back must flex, extend, and rotate, says physical therapist Peggy Brill, author of two books on managing pain through exercise. Yet most of us sit immobile for hours at a time. That's why physical therapists prescribe walking and other gentle exercise, such as stretching and core strengthening, following a flare-up of back pain. Usually, after 72 hours patients will begin to feel better, says Brill.

Stress relief

Stress is the source of most low back pain, according to John Sarno, MD, professor of clinical rehabilitation medicine at New York University. Though Sarno doesn't dispute that the pain is real, he believes it stems from buried emotional issues that trigger tension in the body and ultimately deprive nerves and muscles of oxygen; relief comes through understanding this link and by learning to deal with negative emotions constructively.

Surgery

"Think of this as the last resort," says Paul McCormick, MD, a professor of neurological surgery at Columbia University. Surgery may be necessary in some cases of curvature of the spine, narrowing of the cavity that surrounds spinal nerves, and nerve inflammation or disk degeneration—but these conditions are rare, McCormick says: "Ninety-nine out of one hundred patients will recover without surgery."

My recommendation: The research is positive on chiropractic treatment, physical therapy, and stress relief—they all help ease back pain. (As Paul McCormick says, with rare exceptions, surgery is unnecessary.) The key is to get moving again as soon as possible after the pain hits, and then make sure you take steps to prevent a return. I see low back pain as a warning about overall fitness: If you're active, your hips and back are flexible, your core strength is good, and you're coping well with the emotional challenges in your life, your back probably won't bother you. Overlook one of those areas, however, and your back will let you know. And while the emotional link to back pain is controversial, there's no question that stress can play a part in muscle tension, especially in the lower back and hips, leading to trouble. **◑**

Pap Smear
Skin Exam
Mammogram
Colonoscopy

Ace Your Next Health Test

You don't have to pull an all-nighter to pass your next medical exam, but that doesn't mean it's okay to arrive completely unprepared. In fact, if you don't prep properly, the test's reliability can be compromised—meaning you may need to have a not-so-pleasant procedure redone, or problems may be missed. In addition to following your doctor's advice, these simple steps can make your next screening go a lot more smoothly.

MAMMOGRAM

For the best results:
- Use a testing facility that specializes in mammograms, and stick with it. Not only will you get to know a few familiar faces, but your results can be more easily tracked and compared from year to year.
- Skip deodorants and lotions the day of the test. Many contain aluminum, which can show up on your X-ray film and mimic an abnormal result.
- Ask about your breast density score. Dense breasts can make it difficult to see tumors on traditional X-ray film. If you have a high score (a three or higher), request a digital mammogram—it's better at detecting tumors in dense breasts.

Make it easier on yourself:
- Don't schedule your appointment during the week just before your period, when your breasts are most sensitive. And take an aspirin one to two hours before the test—it will kick in by the time the mammogram starts.

PAP SMEAR

For the best results:
- Continue getting regular Pap smears even if you've been vaccinated against HPV. While the vaccine guards against four virus strains, two of which are responsible for about 70 percent of cervical cancer cases, it doesn't protect you from all types of the disease.
- Try to schedule your appointment 10 to 20 days after the first day of your period. Blood and cells from the uterus can sometimes interfere with the accuracy of your results.
- Abstain from sex, baths, and tampon use beginning two days beforehand. Semen can change the pH inside your vagina and irritate the cervix, while baths and tampons can wash or rub away abnormal cervical cells.

Make it easier on yourself:
- If you have vaginal dryness, it's okay to apply a prescription estrogen-based cream or over-the-counter lubricant to your labia before the exam.

COLONOSCOPY

For the best results:
- One or two weeks before the exam, stop taking supplements that contain iron. The mineral can cause black stains that make the colon wall more difficult to see.
- Cut out red meat and raw vegetables several days before the test. These foods are tough for your body to digest and need time to be cleared from your gastrointestinal system.
- Avoid grape juice, or foods and drinks that contain red or purple dye, which can mimic the appearance of blood in the colon.

Make it easier on yourself:
- You may be starving after the exam, but gorging on food can cause uncomfortable bloating—the most common complaint after a colonoscopy. Start off with semisolid foods like oatmeal or yogurt, and avoid gas-producing fare like cabbage and beans.

SKIN EXAM

For the best results:
- See a dermatologist. An Emory University study found that dermatologists were able to find thinner tumors than nonspecialists.
- Ask your partner or a close friend to help you check your skin beforehand, and circle any troublesome spots with a marker. Often patients arrive concerned about a particular mark but can't find it because it's in a hard-to-see area.
- Remove your nail polish. Acral lentiginous melanoma accounts for about 5 to 10 percent of melanomas, and it commonly develops beneath the nail.

Make it easier on yourself:
- Avoid taking aspirin the day of the test, and tell your doctor if you're on prescription blood thinners. If he needs to perform a quick biopsy at your appointment, these drugs can cause excess bleeding. O

This Is What's Up, Doc!

An insider's guide on talking to your doctor.

Let's face it, there's a reason your MD majored in biology instead of English—doctors aren't always the best communicators. And though most physicians get some training on how to interact with patients during medical school, if you have a doctor who's as old as I am, that could have been two or three decades ago.

That's why it's often up to you, the patient, to make sure you and your doctor understand each other. Poor communication has persistently been shown to be a leading cause of patient complaints against doctors, and, scarily, it occurs often: In a recent study of arthritis patients and their doctors, researchers found that nearly one in five visits ended in a complete miscommunication about whether knee replacement surgery was recommended for the patient. Here's my five-part prescription for getting the most out of every checkup.

1 Take along a list of your concerns. If you get interrupted—which is a likely prospect, since research has shown that it takes doctors only 23 seconds, on average, to interrupt their patients—having a list of the topics you want to discuss will remind you to return to your most important points.

2 Don't spare the details. More than 80 percent of health problems can be diagnosed by the information that you provide to your doctor—so be specific. If you have belly pain, for example, be prepared to pinpoint whether it's piercing or throbbing, how severe it is on a scale of 1 to 10, when it occurs and how often, and what makes it better or worse.

3 Ask the tough questions. If your doctor suggests a new medication, why is it better than the drug you're currently taking? If she advises that you get a diagnostic procedure, are there any less invasive alternatives?

4 Don't tweak the truth. Some of the most common white lies we hear: (falsely) swearing that you don't smoke or drink, that you're eating a healthy diet, and that you're following our instructions. Some researchers estimate that as many as half of all patients tell their doctor they're taking their medication as prescribed, when in fact they're not.

5 Insist on understanding. Can you guess how often doctors ask their patients whether they understand what's being discussed? Less than 2 percent of the time. Don't be afraid to interrupt and say, "I'm confused—can you explain that in layman's terms?" If it helps to take notes or record the conversation, do so. One study showed that after the visit was over, on average, older patients forgot more than 75 percent of what their doctor had said. ◘

What's in Dr. Oz's Medicine Cabinet?

And what should be in yours?

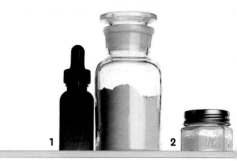

It may not look as cluttered as your garage or basement, but of all the storage spaces in your home, your medicine cabinet probably needs a makeover the most. Once you've cleared out the expired bottles, restock with my medicine cabinet must-haves:

1 Tea Tree Oil Applying this naturally antimicrobial oil straight to the skin can treat a range of fungal infections, including athlete's foot.

2 Tiger Balm This nearly 100-year-old remedy contains active ingredients, including camphor, that create a heating effect and help ease pain.

3 Band-Aids Protecting small wounds helps prevent infection—and discourages scabs from forming, which helps reduce the chance of scarring.

4 Ibuprofen Take this drug a few days before menstrual cramps hit. It blocks the formation of compounds called prostaglandins, which cause your uterus to contract.

5 Aspirin If you're over 40, ask your doctor about taking two low-dose aspirin daily to help prevent heart disease and reduce the risk of breast and colon cancer.

6 Neti pot Using a neti pot to cleanse your sinus cavity can help fight congestion—without the side effects of allergy pills and nasal sprays.

7 Pepto-Bismol This pink medicine can treat all manner of GI ailments, from nausea to diarrhea, by fighting inflammation and acid buildup.

8 Dental floss Flossing is essential to help prevent gingivitis, a chronic infection of the gums that increases your risk for heart attack and stroke.

9 Toothbrush Keep it inside your medicine cabinet, not on the counter. Flushing the toilet can send tiny bacteria everywhere—including onto your bristles.

10 Toothpaste Check the label. Sodium lauryl sulfate creates foam when you brush, but you don't need it for a clean mouth—and it can cause canker sores.

11 Valerian root This ancient insomnia remedy may affect the neurotransmitter GABA, the chemical targeted by many prescription sleep medications. **O**

How I Stay Well All Season Long

Secrets for beating winter bugs.

Every year I dread cold and flu season—not just because I hate feeling sick but because, like most of you, I'm already spread thin between work and family responsibilities; being stuck in bed for days just isn't an option. Luckily, over the years, I've picked up a few scientifically proven tricks that have helped me stay healthy when the mercury drops.

Have H2O in flight. Canadian researchers have found that air passengers are over 100 times more likely to get a cold than those who travel by bus, train, or subway. My rule for air travel: Hydrate. The plane's dry air can sap moisture from the lining of your nasal passages, creating tiny cracks that make you susceptible to infection. Water can help moisten those membranes.

Forget echinacea. There's actually no conclusive research proving echinacea to be effective against the common cold. What do I take instead? Vitamin D. Studies have found that D can stimulate the production of a virus-killing protein, and taking D supplements (aim for 2,000 IU a day) can lead to fewer viral infections.

Brave the cold. No matter how low the temperature, I take a brisk walk every day. Exercise boosts the circulation of immune cells throughout the body, and research shows that walking 30 to 45 minutes a day, five days a week in winter can cut your sick days in half.

Warm up with tea. Research from the University of Michigan supports the growing body of evidence that the antioxidant quercetin may protect against infection by preventing viruses from replicating. Black and green teas are packed with quercetin, so sip a hot cup once a day.

Avoid antibiotics. These drugs are not only ineffective against the flu—which is caused by a virus, and not by bacteria—but can lead to adverse effects like upset stomach, diarrhea, and even yeast infections. If you get the flu, ask your doctor for an antiviral drug such as Tamiflu. But act fast—studies have found that these drugs work best within 48 hours of the first symptoms.

Dodge germs. Flu viruses can survive on surfaces for over two hours, but you can't wash your hands 24-7—so when is it most important to scrub up? Scientists from the University of Virginia pinpointed the areas of your home most likely to harbor germs: refrigerator handles, remote controls, and doorknobs.

Enjoy a comfort food. Chicken soup really can treat a cold. The hot vapor expands your airways, which helps to clear mucus from the nasal cavity. Plus, University of Nebraska researchers found that chicken soup has an anti-inflammatory effect that may soothe a sore throat. ⬤

Hurt Alerts

These five pains could be a sign of big trouble.

I once had a patient who checked into the hospital as she was having a major heart attack. As it turned out, she'd been experiencing intermittent chest pain and nausea for weeks, without realizing that these symptoms can signal impending cardiac crisis.

Everyday aches are a part of life—especially as we age. But before you brush off your symptoms, as so many people do (one survey found that 70 percent of people delayed seeking medical attention for a sharp pain), take note of the five warning signs you should never ignore:

Spreading chest pain
If the pain is creeping up to your shoulder and jaw, or you feel intense pressure (like you're being tightly squeezed), a blocked blood vessel may be impeding the flow of oxygen to your heart. **WHAT TO DO:** Call 911 and take one full-strength aspirin. When you get to the hospital, an EKG can determine if you're having a heart attack.

Numbing lower back pain
An aching back that also feels numb or pain that starts in the buttocks and extends down the back of your legs may be signs of a herniated (slipped) disk. This occurs when a portion of a spinal disk ruptures and presses on the nerve. **WHAT TO DO:** A physical exam by your doctor can usually diagnose the problem. Nonsurgical treatments, such as rest, painkillers, and simple strengthening exercises, will relieve symptoms in more than 90 percent of patients, but if the pain continues, you may need surgery to remove the disk.

Tingling foot pain
You're probably familiar with the fiery sensation that develops after a long day in four-inch heels. But if the pain is accompanied by a pins-and-needles feeling, you could have nerve damage in your feet. One surprising culprit: diabetes. **WHAT TO DO:** A blood sugar test can diagnose diabetes. Diet and exercise, blood sugar monitoring, and medication can prevent further damage.

Severe headache
Migraine sufferers are more than familiar with severe headaches. But *extremely* acute pain—imagine the worst headache of your life—can signal a ruptured blood vessel in your brain, known as an aneurysm. **WHAT TO DO:** Because the escalating pressure in your skull could reduce the oxygen supply to your brain, this symptom requires an immediate trip to the ER. The doctor will likely perform a CT scan to check for hemorrhaging, then surgeons will work quickly to drain the excess fluid and repair the vessel.

Leg pain with redness and warmth
You may be tempted to chalk it up to muscle cramps, but if you also experience swelling, redness, and warmth, it could be deep vein thrombosis (DVT), a blood clot that forms in the veins of your legs. If the clot breaks free, it could travel through your bloodstream and cause a pulmonary embolism (a blockage of the arteries that supply your lungs with blood). **WHAT TO DO:** Don't try to massage away the pain—doing so could cause the clot to break loose. Instead see your doctor, who can diagnose DVT using an ultrasound. You may need blood thinners to help dissolve the clot.

In the Hot Seat

The consequences of America's "sitting epidemic."

ere's a health tip that sounds too easy to be true: Stand up. If you're like the average American, you spend nearly eight hours a day—more than 50 hours per week—planted on your behind, according to Vanderbilt University researchers. There's a cost to all that downtime (and it's not just a spreading lower half).

When you're sitting, your body undergoes a metabolic slowdown. You use less blood sugar for energy, and you burn fewer calories. Sitting also decreases the activity of an enzyme called lipoprotein lipase, which works to eliminate fats in the blood. The worst part: Even regular exercise won't protect you. Research has shown that if you spend long periods sitting, you'll have a larger waist, greater body mass index, and higher levels of blood sugar and blood fats than someone who takes frequent breaks to stand or stretch—regardless of how often you lace up your running shoes.

Ultimately, spending more time on your feet means a longer life. However, even desk-bound workers aren't doomed. These simple changes can create a more active routine.

Try TV training.
For every hour you add to your average daily tube time, you increase your risk of metabolic syndrome (a group of conditions that can predispose you to heart disease, stroke, and diabetes) by more than 25 percent. I've made the area around my television a workout space. Try walking on the treadmill while you watch your favorite programs, or swapping your La-Z-Boy for an energy ball, which forces you to engage your muscles while you sit.

Use technology to your advantage.
Thanks to instant messaging, cell phones, and wireless Internet access, we can shop, catch up with friends, and chat with colleagues—all without taking a single step. However, technology also allows us to communicate and get work done while simultaneously staying active. Why not take your next conference call while strolling through the park? You'll stay fit and maintain productivity.

Think NEAT.
Nonexercise activity thermogenesis (NEAT) is the energy you expend for activities other than direct exercise, and it can have an even greater impact on your health than the amount of time you spend on the treadmill. There are countless simple ways to increase your NEAT. Wash the dishes instead of using the dishwasher, walk to a neighbor's house instead of driving, cook dinner instead of ordering in, or take the stairs instead of the elevator at work. ◗

The Quiet Killer

This life-threatening disease afflicts millions of Americans—many of whom have no idea they're even at risk.

There's a dangerous health problem on the rise in the United States, affecting more than 20 million adults—25 percent more than a decade ago. It's more common than diabetes and twice as prevalent as cancer. More alarming: New evidence shows that the majority of those stricken by the condition don't even know they have it. What is this insidious epidemic? Chronic kidney disease.

Located just below the rib cage on either side of the spine, the kidneys act like a laundry service for your blood. Each bean-shaped organ, about the size of a computer mouse, contains approximately one million tiny filters, or nephrons, that separate the nutrients and other substances your body needs from waste products and excess fluid, which you eliminate as urine.

Chronic kidney disease (CKD) occurs when the organs' tiny filters are progressively damaged over the course of several months to years. Eventually the damage leads to a dangerous buildup of waste in your blood, which can cause inflammation in the blood vessels, setting you up for heart attack, stroke, even brain damage. Without treatment to help slow the progress of the disease, many patients will require either dialysis or a kidney transplant.

One reason CKD is on the rise is that it's linked to two other increasingly common conditions—diabetes and hypertension, which together account for two-thirds of CKD cases. (High blood sugar and high blood pressure damage the kidney's nephrons and impair blood vessel function, making it more difficult for waste to be removed.) But although more and more Americans are being screened for these two conditions, CKD often goes undiscovered until obvious symptoms—numbness in the hands or feet, a halt to menstruation, or severe joint pain—appear. The bad news: These symptoms usually don't arise until kidney function has fallen to less than 25 percent of normal and irreversible damage has occurred. The good news: With your doctor's help, you can detect the disease earlier and even prevent it altogether.

WHAT YOU CAN DO

Watch for warning signs. Many symptoms of kidney disease are ignored because they don't seem serious. Keep an eye out for loss of appetite, nausea, fatigue, swollen ankles or feet, and difficulty sleeping and concentrating.

Get screened. Even if you have no symptoms of CKD, you should still get screened if you have diabetes (about 40 percent of those with diabetes develop CKD), high blood pressure, or a family history of kidney disease, or you are over age 60. Screening typically includes a urine test to check for protein, which can show up months to years before symptoms occur. Your doctor may also order a blood test to measure the buildup of waste products (specifically urea and creatinine) as well as an ultrasound of your kidneys.

Block the damage. To combat diabetes and hypertension, the primary instigators of CKD: Maintain a healthy weight and diet, exercise, and quit smoking. Your doctor may prescribe a special low-salt, low-protein diet, or medication to regulate your blood pressure and blood sugar. (Aim for a blood pressure below 115/75 and a fasting blood sugar below 100.) Also ask your doc to check your levels of hemoglobin A1c, which can indicate the average amount of glucose in your blood over several weeks. One recent study showed that for every 1 percent drop in A1c level, the risk of kidney disease drops by up to 40 percent. ◐

Ask Dr. Oz

Advice from America's MD.

Q Is one drink a day okay if I have a family history of breast cancer?

Dr. Oz: How's your heart health? While alcohol has been shown to increase the risk of breast cancer, it can also lower the risk of heart disease. Each year far more American women die of heart disease than die of breast cancer; thus, for the average person, the benefits of alcohol outweigh the risks. But if you've inherited a harmful BRCA gene mutation, your risk of breast cancer is dramatically higher than that of the average woman. For a known carrier, drinking any alcohol is probably a bad idea. For others, the odds still favor having the occasional glass of wine.

Q Should I be doing colon cleanses?

Dr. Oz: Some colon cleanses involve taking laxatives at home; in other cases, a therapist performs an irrigation using a device inserted into the rectum. In either case, cleanses are not only unnecessary but potentially dangerous. Your colon is designed to clear out waste every 24 to 48 hours or so, and eating lots of fiber helps speed things along. Doing regular colon cleanses can lead to dehydration and an electrolyte imbalance, resulting in dizziness, fatigue, vomiting, and cramps.

Q Is there an easy way to naturally elevate my mood?

Dr. Oz: Just inhale. And don't stop reading—because I'm not talking about deep breathing, although that can work, too. I'm talking about tapping into the power of scent. The nose is a gateway to the mind, and researchers have discovered that scents can influence your mood in powerful ways. For example, one recent study from the Medical University of Vienna found that the smell of both oranges and lavender lifted the moods of patients about to undergo dental procedures. If that's enough to make people facing a root canal happy, imagine what it could do for you. Try placing some lavender oil on your desk at work and taking a whiff when you're feeling down.

Q Do antibiotics interfere with the effectiveness of birth control pills?

Dr. Oz: This association emerged in the early 1970s, when women taking oral contraceptives reported high rates of irregular bleeding and unwanted pregnancies while being treated with a specific antibiotic called rifampin. For the

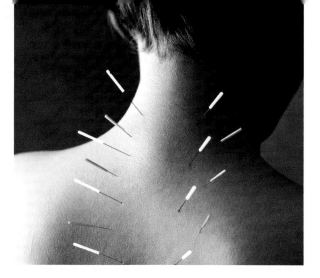

sake of caution, women are still warned against relying on the Pill while taking antibiotics. Yet there's very little evidence that any drug other than rifampin interferes with the efficacy of the Pill. If you're really worried, you can use a condom as a backup, but it's generally unnecessary.

Q What can I do to reduce my risk of Alzheimer's?

Dr. Oz: The same healthy habits that boost your overall brain function can also help ward off Alzheimer's disease. That means engaging in regular physical and mental exercise, and making sure your diet includes lots of leafy greens and foods rich in omega-3s (like nuts and fish). I'd also suggest eating more curry, because it contains the spice turmeric. Research shows that turmeric may help prevent the accumulation of plaques that build up in the brains of Alzheimer's patients and that can interfere with communication between neurons.

Q Does acupuncture really work?

Dr. Oz: Those little pinpricks can be an effective way to manage pain. Specifically, studies show that acupuncture can alleviate the debilitating symptoms of osteoarthritis and fibromyalgia. There are several theories as to why acupuncture works. One is that it triggers the release of endorphins, part of the body's pain-control system. Another is that it increases blood flow to the areas of needle insertion. Regardless, find a practitioner who is certified by the National Certification Commission for Acupuncture and Oriental Medicine.

Q Does using a microwave increase my risk of cancer?

Dr. Oz: While it's true that microwave ovens emit tiny amounts of radiation, studies have shown that they're not nearly enough to cause cancer. A microwave could cause other injuries (like burns or cataracts), but only if it's been damaged and starts leaking large amounts of radiation—an unlikely occurrence. If you're worried your appliance may be faulty, replace it, or ask your state health department to test your level of exposure.

Q Is there a natural way to ease allergies?

Dr. Oz: One remedy I've long espoused is nasal irrigation, which can wash away allergens (like pollen) and excess mucus. When you experience a flare-up, fill a neti pot (a small, spouted dish) with saline water, then tilt your head to one side and pour it into the upper nostril. The water will then flush out of the lower nostril. Certain supplements can also help (consult your doctor before taking them): Bromelain may reduce inflammation inside the nasal passages, while some studies have shown butterbur to be an effective natural antihistamine.

Q I'm trying to quit smoking. Are electronic cigarettes a healthy way to go?

Dr. Oz: Electronic cigarettes are smokeless, battery-operated devices shaped like cigarettes. These devices are marketed as a less damaging alternative to regular cigarettes because they contain no tobacco (users get a fix by inhaling a vaporized liquid nicotine solution). But they have been found to contain other carcinogens and toxic chemicals, such as diethylene glycol, an ingredient used in antifreeze. And unlike other nicotine-replacement products—like the patch, the gum, or the lozenge—e-cigarettes are not FDA approved, and there's no way to know how much nicotine you're receiving. If you're trying to quit smoking, a better solution is to start by working with your primary care physician. Research has shown that you're more likely to succeed with doctor support.

Q My husband occasionally experiences erectile dysfunction (ED). Could this be a sign of a bigger health problem?

Dr. Oz: Yes. In fact, up to 90 percent of ED cases can be attributed to a physical problem (the other 10 to 20 percent of cases are linked to psychological issues). Often the condition is an indicator of early stage cardiovascular disease. Clogged arteries, for instance, can slow the flow of blood to the penis. And diabetes, over time, can damage the blood vessels and nerves that control erection. (The average man with diabetes will develop ED ten to 15 years earlier than a man who doesn't have diabetes.) Impotence may also be the result of obesity. Fat cells in the belly help convert testosterone into estrogen, and low testosterone levels can decrease a man's libido or interfere with his ability to achieve or maintain an erection. Your husband should talk to his doctor, who can help him determine the cause behind his ED and come up with solutions.

Q Is it safe to take antidepressants during pregnancy?

Dr. Oz: Though some drugs (like Wellbutrin) have no established risks, no one can say for sure that any antidepressant is completely safe during pregnancy—and several drugs (like Paxil, which has been associated with fetal heart defects) definitely pose a known danger. Still, you shouldn't stop taking your medication cold turkey. That's because untreated depression can weaken your motivation to maintain a healthy lifestyle, as well as raise your risk of early delivery and postpartum depression. If you're pregnant or thinking about becoming pregnant, talk to your doctor about the best course of action.

Q I've been under a lot of stress lately, and my stomach is always churning. Could I have given myself an ulcer?

Dr. Oz: Doctors used to think that ulcers (sores on the inside lining of your stomach, small intestine, or esophagus) were caused by stomach acid, which does increase during times of stress, and may be causing your churning feeling. But we now know that the majority of ulcers are caused by a type of bacteria called *H. pylori,* which can trigger inflammation in the gut. It's estimated that 20 percent of the population carries *H. pylori* in their digestive tract, putting them at greater risk of an ulcer, though it's not clear how the bacteria are transmitted.

Q Short of surgery, is there anything I can do about my bunions?

Dr. Oz: Unfortunately, surgery is the only way to remove a bunion (a bony bump around the joint at the base of the big toe), and there are drawbacks: Recovery can take up to six months, and the bunion may return. So you might consider a more conservative approach first. For pain and swelling, try anti-inflammatory drugs (such as ibuprofen) or an ice pack two to three times a day. Orthotic shoe inserts can help prevent bunions from getting worse; you can buy them at a drugstore, or your podiatrist can prescribe custom-fitted ones.

Q Is kosher food safer or healthier?

Dr. Oz: While research is scant, kosher food is carefully supervised by certifying agencies as it's processed and prepared. (The most reliable agencies are OU, OK, KOF-K, CRC, and Star-K.) Every butchered animal is examined for disease, and produce is inspected for insects. Moreover, kosher companies must keep records of where their ingredients come from and demonstrate that their products contain only what's on the label. So it can be argued that you know more accurately what's in your food.

Q I recently went through menopause, and now I'm putting on weight in my middle. Why is this, and what can I do?

Dr. Oz: You're not alone. Before menopause, women are predisposed to gain weight in their hips and legs (i.e., become pear shaped), but afterward the drop in estrogen can redirect body fat distribution toward the abdomen. Unfortunately, from a health perspective, your midsection is the worst place you can gain fat. Research shows that having a waist size measuring more than 33 inches—no matter how much you weigh—increases your risk of developing cardiovascular disease, diabetes, and even certain types of cancer. Try to stop or reverse your weight gain by eating right and getting 30 minutes of cardiovascular exercise a day. Moves that target the transverse abdominal muscle can strengthen your midsection. Try this exercise, called abdominal hollowing: Get on your hands and knees, letting your belly hang toward the floor. While breathing normally, slowly draw your belly button up and in toward your spine, as if you were being held in by a girdle. Hold the contraction for ten seconds, then rest for ten seconds. Work up to ten repetitions.

Q I get so anxious before parties that I often end up staying home instead. What can I do?

Dr. Oz: While it's normal to feel a little shy or nervous before entering a roomful of people, it sounds like you may be struggling with social anxiety disorder, which affects about 15 million American adults. People with social phobia feel intensely afraid of being negatively judged, and so tend to avoid mingling altogether. You may also have panic-attack-like symptoms, such as sweating, heart palpitations, or chest pain. This disorder can be treated with cognitive behavioral therapy, which involves mental strategies and relaxation techniques that help you conquer your fears. ◻

10 Biggest Health Mistakes

Over the past decade, I've noticed that people tend to make the same mistakes over and over again when it comes to losing weight and staying healthy. Luckily, you don't have to follow in their footsteps.

1 They work out simply to burn calories. What matters more is the intensity of your exercise. Vigorous exercise dulls your appetite, while moderate exercise stimulates it.

2 They strength train with two-pound dumbbells. Heavier weights will help you build bone mass. You should be able to complete only eight to ten repetitions of each exercise.

3 They substitute pie for the pie chart. Draw a circle and divide it into wedges, like a pie. Label each wedge with some aspect of your life—your finances, your kids, your spouse—then, using a plus or a minus sign, note whether each area is going well. Work on nurturing areas that you're unhappy with, and your weight will be easier to control.

4 They aren't aware of third-hand smoke. These foul-smelling toxins can linger on your hair, clothes, carpet, and furniture. Even if your partner isn't lighting up in the house, third-hand smoke can harm all of you.

5 They keep eating until they go to bed. Make a hard-and-fast rule: No eating within two hours of bedtime.

6 They don't pay attention to the hunger scale. Imagine a scale from one to five—one being full, and five being ravenous. If you're hitting a three—your stomach's grumbling, you're physically dragging—it's time to eat. Any lower than that, and you're eating to fill an emotional need, not a physical one.

7 **They don't think about how relationships affect their motivation.** If you've got a strong support network, you're less likely to de-stress by crashing in front of the TV or eating poorly.

8 **They think a finite goal is the only thing that matters.** I've seen clients reach their goal weight, then gain it back once they realize that life isn't suddenly perfect—

even at a size 6. Make your goal to live a healthy life, no matter what's on the scale.

9 **They fall for the latest fad.** A "cookie diet" is not a sound nutritional plan.

10 **They underestimate the power of 80 percent.** People tend to have an all-or-nothing attitude when it comes to living healthy. But if you can put these tips into practice even 80 percent of the time, you're still going to be successful. ◖

When Oprah Met Bob

Her life was mostly win-win—so why was it so painfully difficult for Oprah to lose-lose? Then a personal trainer galloped into her world with a life-changing question.

I feel like I've always known Bob Greene, though the truth is it's been 18 years since we first met. My life has not been the same since.

At the time, I was 237 pounds, miserable, and so ashamed to have joined the ranks of the perpetually obese that I had trouble maintaining eye contact. I couldn't understand why I was able to triumph over so many other challenges and adversities in life, and yet when it came to losing weight I was a big fat failure.

I had spent years bouncing from one diet to another, from the time I was 22. That was when I landed a big job as a news coanchor in Baltimore and discovered that food—especially corn dogs and six-inch chocolate chip cookies with macadamia nuts—could provide a great deal of solace. I had no friends and no furniture, not even curtains on the windows of my new apartment. My coanchor seemed to resent me, and I worried that I was in way over my head. I'd had almost no experience as a writer, but every day I was given news copy to rewrite. It's an awful feeling when you know you can't make the mark. No matter how hard I tried, I could not bang out the copy fast enough for my superiors. Every day as we neared the 6 o'clock news hour, I'd hear John, the copy editor, yell across the room: "WINFREY, WHERE'S THE GODDAMNED COPY??!!!!"

I was humiliated but put on a smile and got through the days, reading the news and chitchatting with my fellow anchors on air. I felt blessed to have my job, but I truly hated some of the things I was required to do. I always felt as if I were chasing bodies, waiting for the worst to happen. The bigger the fire or collision, the more excited my bosses became.

Working in that environment was an affront to my spirit. The reporter's objectivity I needed to maintain went against everything in my nature. Many times I was an eyewitness to the most devastating moments in people's lives, but I was not allowed to express any emotion. So I ate those emotions, and along with them, just about everything I could buy at the mall food court. I thought I was fine; I just had a little weight problem. Now I realize I didn't have a weight problem. I had problems that I was burying by eating, but it wasn't until years later, after many conversations with Bob, that I finally made the connection.

When I first met Bob and he asked me why I was overweight, I thought he was being a smart-ass. I was overweight for the same reason everybody else is, I answered smugly. I loved food.

It took me a while to get to the truth. I didn't love food. I used food to numb my negative feelings. It didn't matter what the feeling was: a phone call from someone I didn't want to talk to, a confrontation of any kind, being late, feeling tired, anxious, or bored. No matter how insignificant the discomfort, my first reaction was to reach for something to eat, unaware of how much I was consuming. Living unconsciously was like being the walking dead. All my fat years—my unconscious years—are a blur to me now.

I grew up believing that people with money didn't have problems. Or certainly none that money couldn't solve. When I started my working life in Nashville and Baltimore, paying the rent and the electric bill and making payments on my car left me with just enough to buy groceries and get my hair done. Then, in 1986, my show went national. It changed the trajectory of my life. Now I had more money than I'd ever imagined, and everybody wanted some. The first thing I did was to retire my mother, father, and a cousin who helped take care of me when I was growing up. My father let me buy him a new house and a Mercedes, but he refused to quit working in the barbershop. He's still there.

   Then everybody came out of the woodwork. Distant family members I barely knew wanted me to completely take care of them or wanted to work for me. Relatives I hadn't seen since I was 10 years old showed up demanding thousands of dollars "because we're family." Helping my family was something I wanted to do, but I didn't know how to handle the total strangers who came to Chicago claiming to have spent their last dime leaving a battering spouse, or the teenagers who'd run away from home.

   The first year, I helped almost everyone who asked me, family and strangers alike. It was stressful trying to figure out how much to give to whom, and before I knew it, they'd return for more. I was overwhelmed, but I never

felt it. Once again, I just ate until I couldn't feel. By the end of the year, I weighed 200 pounds.

   In 1988, totally frustrated and up to 212 pounds, I turned to Optifast, a liquid diet supplement program. For four months, I ate not a single morsel of food. I lost fat—and muscle—and I dropped to 145 pounds. Now I know that it's impossible to starve your body for four months, then feed it, and not expect to regain the weight.

   It would take seven more years of gaining and countless attempts to follow diets that I wasn't really prepared to stick to before I discovered the truth. In the meantime, I was racing through 200 shows a year, leaving my apartment at 6 A.M., and getting home at 10 at night. My entire life was work.

   In 1992 I won another Emmy for best talk show host. I had prayed that Phil Donahue would win so that I wouldn't have to embarrass myself by rolling my fat butt out of my seat and walking down the aisle to the stage. By now I'd reached the end of believing I could be thin, though I was scheduled to leave for Colorado the next day to visit yet another spa. At 237 pounds, I was the heaviest I'd ever been. I had filled journals with prayers to God to help me conquer my weight demon.

   Bob Greene was the answer to my prayers. When I first met Bob at that last-ditch-effort spa in Colorado, I thought for sure he was judging and labeling me as I had already judged and labeled myself: fat and out of control. Bob, it turned out, wasn't judging me at all. He really understood.

But he did have some tough questions for me. One of them was the hardest question that anyone had ever asked me: What is the best life possible for you?

"You of all people in the world can have your life be what you want. Why don't you do it?" he asked. "What do you really want?"

"I want to be happy," I replied.

"Happy isn't a good enough answer. What does that mean? Break it down for me. When was the last time you were really happy?"

"When I was filming *The Color Purple,* seven years ago."

"What about filming *The Color Purple* made you happy?"

I didn't have to think to answer. "Doing that work filled me up. I was playing a character who was meaningful to me, surrounded by the brilliance of Alice Walker, Quincy Jones, and Steven Spielberg. I was so charged and stimulated every day, I just wanted to do better and be better."

"So what would it take for you to have that feeling again?"

In answering that question, I realized that the show had gotten away from me. In order to stay competitive, we had become more and more salacious, covering topics like "My sister slept with my husband" and "Is my husband or my boss my baby's father?" I didn't want to put junk on the air that perpetuated dysfunction instead of resolving it. It wasn't who I wanted to be.

And so, while I worked out and changed what and how much I ate, managing the rest of my life became my real focus. I started asking myself the same questions Bob had asked me. For every circumstance, I asked myself:

"What do I want?"

"What kind of show do I want?"

"What kind of body do I want?"

"What do I want to give to all the people who are asking me for my attention, my time, my money?"

I finally made a decision about that last one. I set up trust funds with a finite amount of cash for the people to whom I wanted to give money. And to those with whom I had no connection, I said no and meant it. And just to be sure, I changed my home phone number. I've never visited a psychiatrist, but working with Bob has been priceless therapy.

One thing I know for sure now is that you've got to ask yourself: What kind of life do you want and how close are you to living it? You cannot ever live the life of your dreams

> ## It all comes down to another question Bob asked me: "How much do you love yourself?"

without coming face-to-face with the truth. Every unwanted pound creates another layer of lies. It's only when you peel back those layers that you will be set free—free to work out, free to eat responsibly, free to live the life you want and deserve to live. Tell the truth, and you'll learn to stop eating to satisfy emotional hunger and to stop burying your hopes and dreams beneath layers of fat.

The Best Life Diet plan on the following pages mirrors the way I eat and live now. I lost weight in stages. First, I became active. I still work out, even though I really hate it. But I know if I don't, I will end up 200 pounds again. Then I started working on my eating. I stopped eating past 7:30 at night. When Bob told me it would make a big difference in my weight, I resisted. I thought it was going to be too hard. It was at first, but it gradually got easier and turned out to be one of the most effective changes I made.

I've now taken most of the unhealthy foods out of my diet and replaced them with better choices. I eat smaller portions and healthful foods as a way of life, not as a diet to go on and off.

I still work constantly at not repressing my feelings with food. If you turn on the TV and see that I've picked up a few pounds, you'll know that I'm not managing and balancing my life as well as I should.

I pray or meditate—or do both—every day. I pray to be used by a power greater than myself. It takes consistent effort to live my best life. The mistake I've made in the past is not realizing how constant a struggle it really is not to turn to food for comfort. It all comes down to another question Bob asked me years ago: "How much do you love yourself?"

"Of course I love myself," I'd snapped. "It's the first law of self-preservation. I firmly believe in it."

"You may believe in it, but you don't practice it," he said. "Otherwise you couldn't let yourself be 237 pounds."

I wanted to cry, and later I did. He was so right. I cared more about everyone else's feelings than my own. I'd overextend myself to do anything anyone asked, to honor his or her feelings. I didn't want anyone to think I wasn't "nice," or worse, that "the money has gone to her head."

This, too, I know for sure: Loving yourself means honoring yourself and your own feelings *first.*

My hope is that you can learn from my mistakes and liberate yourself from this struggle. I finally know it doesn't have to be so hard. Make a decision. Know that you deserve the best life possible. It's there for the asking, the answering, the taking. Go out and get it! ◑

The Plan: Three Sane Phases

Start slow, go easy, think hard, and find success: Bob Greene's guide to making healthy changes that last.

How you lose weight is no great mystery; it's just a matter of eating fewer calories than you burn. The puzzling question is why, after managing to shed the pounds—often a lot of them—so many people return to their old ways. Even more puzzling: When I ask those who have been on the weight loss roller coaster how they felt when they were thinner, most of them say, "Great. I never felt better in my life." So what makes them regress?

After working one-on-one with many clients and talking to thousands of people through the years, I think I can say with some authority that the fast and furious approach to weight loss is also the fastest route to failure.

Human beings don't respond well to sudden change. When changes come in measured amounts, however, the body and mind have a powerful ability to adapt. If you've always relied on food for emotional sustenance, you're going to have to get used to the idea of turning to other things to help you through tough times. Most important, you've got to figure out why you need food to make yourself feel better in the first place. If you're eating because you're stressed or angry or bored or lonely, you've got to find what's at the root of that and change it. For Oprah, becoming aware and dealing with her habit of burying her emotions under plates of food was the most critical component of her weight loss. For many people, it will be, too.

The Best Life Diet plan is not something you go on and off of. It is a diet in the traditional sense of the word: a way of eating for life. Because there's a logical order to how we adapt to new habits, this program is divided into three phases. When you follow the sequence, you will build your body into a better weight loss machine.

Phase 1: The Rev-Up

In the first four weeks, you're going to focus on moving more and changing your eating patterns. You don't have to worry about subtracting foods from your diet just yet. There's a good reason for this: Increasing your activity and restructuring your meals and snacks is going to rev up your metabolism, which will eliminate some of the problems you might otherwise bump up against when you begin cutting calories later. The changes you make in this phase will help you regulate your appetite more effectively, and that, too, is going to enhance your ability to handle the challenges to come. Before you go any further, step on the scale to get your starting weight. Then put it away—you won't need it this month.

I could bore you with the details of how physical activity lowers the risk of almost every disease imaginable and significantly improves your quality of life, but you've heard all that before. So let me get right to what might convince you to increase the amount you're presently doing: The more you move your body, the easier losing weight is going to be. Activity burns calories, allowing you to eat more food while shedding pounds, and it revs up your metabolism beyond its normal capacity. Also, because being active counteracts your body's tendency to put up a fight when you drop weight by slowing metabolism to a crawl.

First determine where you are on my activity scale (*see next page*).

For those of you who are already exercising regularly (with the exception of level five), your best bet is to move up one level. But if you're at level zero, I encourage you to go up two levels and start engaging in formal workouts right away, as long as you check with your physician first. With exercise, the hardest part is getting started; after that your body adapts, and it becomes easier and easier to increase how much you move.

The other change I want you to make is to eat three meals and one snack daily. Plan to get 25 to 30 percent of your total calories from each meal with the remainder going toward your snack. Dividing your calories wisely throughout the day will keep hunger at a reasonable level and maximize your calorie burning.

I'm sure you've heard many times that breakfast is the most important meal of the day. This isn't just rhetoric invented to sell cereal; breakfast can have a significant impact on controlling your weight. It not only gives your metabolism a little jolt; if you forgo a meal at the beginning of the day, chances are your appetite is going to roar to life right around the time you're perusing the lunch menu or gazing at the mac and cheese peering out at you from behind the counter. If you wake up without an appetite, give it an hour to develop; then, no matter how you feel, have some food anyway. This is the only time I'm going to tell you to eat when you're not hungry. Breakfast is that important.

Aside from adding exercise and reorganizing your eating, I have just a few other rules for you at this stage: Eliminate alcohol (you can add it back in later). Have a glass of water at every meal. Take a multivitamin, an omega-3 supplement, and a calcium supplement if you're not getting enough from your diet. And (as anyone who is familiar with my other books knows, I'm a stickler for this one) stop eating at least two hours before you go to bed.

After four weeks of making these changes, take out the scale. If you dropped a pound or more per week, you should actually consider staying in this phase two or three more weeks, because simply making these lifestyle shifts is working for you. If you didn't lose much weight, that's fine—you're right where you should be. Your body is now prepared for the aggressive weight loss that's coming in the next stage of the program. You're ready to move on.

The Activity Scale

Level 0
Any activity beyond what it takes to get through your day is accidental.
Aerobic exercise: none.
Strength training: none.

Level 1
You see value in activity, so you look for creative ways to move throughout the day, but you don't formally work out.
Aerobic exercise: none.
Strength training: none.

Level 2
You have a moderate but consistent exercise schedule.
Aerobic exercise: three times a week, at least 90 minutes total.
Strength training: none.

Level 3
You make sure to exercise at least five days a week, usually the same workout.

Aerobic exercise: four times a week, 150 minutes total.
Strength training: at least two times a week, a minimum of six exercises.

Level 4
You work out almost every day, cross-training with multiple activities.
Aerobic exercise: five times a week, at least 250 minutes total.
Strength training: at least three times a week, a minimum of eight exercises.

Level 5
Exercise isn't just how you stay healthy; it's a way of life.
Aerobic exercise: six times a week, a minimum of 360 minutes total.
Strength training: at least three times a week, a minimum of ten exercises.

Phase 2: The Switch

In this phase, which should last a minimum of four weeks, the pounds will really drop off. I'm going to ask you to eliminate just a few foods from your diet and replace them with foods that in addition to being less fattening also dampen your appetite. Banned for now:

Soft drinks: Soda is probably the number one source of empty calories in America. Instead, have water (plain or flavored), herbal iced tea, or skim milk. If you crave a sweet drink, have one glass of fruit juice a day—better yet, cut it with seltzer water. If you feel diet sodas help you lose weight, drink them, but try to get down to one a day, or you'll never lose your taste for supersweet foods.

Foods containing trans fat: Big offenders are margarine and vegetable shortenings (although there are trans fat–free versions of both) and processed food such as frozen meals, crackers, ramen soups, cake mixes, chips, and candy. To see if a product has trans fat, check the ingredients list for partially hydrogenated vegetable oil. My top pick for replacements are heart-healthy olive and canola oils.

Fried foods: Even when they don't have trans fat, fried foods in restaurants are often cooked in oil that's reused, which can create by-products that have been linked to a variety of diseases, including cancer. And fried foods are highly caloric. As an alternative, try oven-frying: Cut potatoes into strips, toss with a little olive oil (or use a spray), salt, and pepper, and cook in a 400° oven until brown. And if you can't live without potato chips, choose baked varieties made without trans fat.

White bread and regular pasta: Don't panic—you can still have your carbs; they just have to be whole grain. Compared with refined "white" flour, whole grains not only are more nutritious, they also have lots of fiber, which keeps you fuller longer. Be aware that packaging can be misleading. (Some brown "wheat" breads, for example, don't even contain whole wheat.) To make sure you're getting a meaningful amount of whole grains, check that they show up at the beginning of the ingredients list. Bread should have at least 2 grams of fiber per slice and pasta at least 4 grams of fiber per 2 dry ounces. You may continue eating some refined grains, such as white rice, but the ultimate goal is an almost all-whole-grain diet.

High-fat dairy products: Although dairy food (cheese, milk, yogurt, ice cream, whipped cream) is an excellent source of calcium and protein, there is absolutely no reason

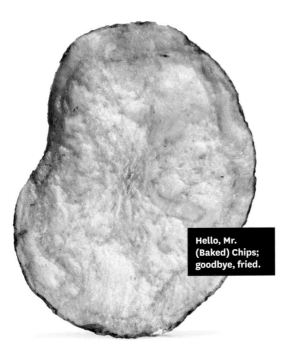

Hello, Mr. (Baked) Chips; goodbye, fried.

to have the full-fat version. A cup of whole milk has 146 calories, 7.9 grams fat (4.5 grams of it saturated), and 24 milligrams cholesterol. Compare that to a cup of nonfat milk: 83 calories, 0.2 grams fat (0.125 grams of it saturated), and 5 milligrams cholesterol. The one exception here is cheese—low-fat is fine, but nonfat tastes pretty awful.

In this phase, you'll weigh yourself once a week. If the number goes up, don't be hard on yourself—weight loss hardly ever occurs in a completely straight line. Look over the changes you've made and see where you may need to fine-tune your efforts.

I also strongly suggest that you refer to the activity scale and go up another level. This is optional, but by producing pleasure-inducing brain chemicals called endorphins, exercise can provide some of the comfort you might otherwise find from eating. As you make these changes, bear in mind that to achieve permanent weight loss, you must give yourself the time and attention you deserve. I'm not saying you should shirk your responsibilities to others, but you really have to take a stand and do what's right for you.

At the end of four weeks, it's time to reevaluate. If you've met your goal weight, you're ready to move on. If you are 20 pounds or less from your goal and still dropping pounds, you have two options: You can stay in Phase Two until you reach your goal, or go to Phase Three, where you'll continue to lose but at a slower rate. Those who have more than 20 pounds to lose but are consistently dropping pounds should stay in Phase Two—it's working.

Some of you may have stopped losing and still have 20 or more pounds to go. Please don't be discouraged. Make

Breakfast—or Else!
Here are a few great choices:

Toast: Spread a slice of 100 percent whole-grain toast (or whole grain bagel or English muffin) with peanut butter. Or try almond, cashew, or soy butter. Add apple or pear slices and a drizzle of honey, and drink a glass of 1 percent milk.

Cereal: Choose a 100 percent whole-grain cereal (it should have at least 4 grams of fiber and no more than 5 grams of sugar per 100 calories) plus 1 percent milk. Top with fruit and, if you like, 1 to 2 tablespoons of nuts. For a hot breakfast, do the same thing with oatmeal (the fruit can be dried).

Smoothie: Mix in a blender a small banana, 1 cup of frozen berries or other fruit, ½ cup of nonfat or 1 percent milk or soy milk, ½ cup of low-fat yogurt, a spoonful of honey, and no more than 2 tablespoons of wheat germ or ground flaxseed.

Yogurt: Top plain low-fat yogurt with fruit, nuts, a little honey, and, if you like, a spoonful of wheat germ or ground flaxseed or a couple of spoonfuls of low-fat granola.

Healthy snacks: Like breakfast, these will stabilize your blood sugar and keep your appetite in check (all are between 100 and 200 calories):

- 1 or 2 whole-grain pretzels (1 ounce)
- 1 cup red pepper strips or celery sticks with ⅓ cup hummus
- ¾ cup carrots with 3 tablespoons low-fat ranch dressing
- 2 to 3 tablespoons peanuts, almonds, walnuts, or cashews
- 1 slice (1 ounce) low-fat cheese on 2 whole grain crackers (½ ounce)

Earn foods containing more than two teaspoons of sugar by being active.

Level 0	100
Level 1	100
Level 2	150
Level 3	210
Level 4	280
Level 5	300

Your goal should be to make vegetables the foods you eat most of. You might want to go easy on potatoes, corn, and peas because they're as starchy (and about as caloric) as grains. Try to get beans into your diet a couple of times a week—they are superfoods in terms of nutrition. And I recommend at least two servings of fruit a day.

I'd like you to continue to replace refined grains with whole ones. Ideally, 75 percent of the grains in your diet will be whole. You've already made the switch with bread and pasta. Now try doing the same with whole grain pretzels, crackers, waffles, tortillas, and pizza crust. There are a variety of delicious whole grains out there—oats, barley, quinoa, buckwheat groats (a nutty-tasting grain), bulgur, millet, wild and brown rice (brown rice sushi is great), and popcorn (stick with the air-popped and low-fat versions).

As for sweets, you can have fruit anytime. Frozen berries, mango, even rhubarb taste terrific in smoothies or stewed and served with a dollop of fat-free yogurt. Otherwise, look at the packaging: All desserts and snacks containing more than 8 grams of sugar (2 teaspoons) per serving count as Anything Goes calories.

Getting to indulge in a few more of these extra calories may be one incentive to increase your activity level, which I suggest you do again when you enter this last phase. And I hope you will keep that option open for the rest of your life. Exercise not only is going to help you maintain the weight loss you've achieved and allow you to eat more food without regaining, it's also going to help slow down the aging process. Weigh yourself no more than once a week and no less than once a month.

Above all, keep working toward your goal and find pleasure in each small victory—that's what separates those who keep pushing from those who throw in the towel. Don't take for granted turning down a piece of cake or eating a healthful breakfast or going for a walk at lunch, or any of the small but significant efforts you make as part of your commitment to this program, because every step is truly a thrilling accomplishment. If you can become less concerned with achieving big, exciting results, you're going to get more satisfaction and enjoyment from the process of change. And that, ironically, is going to help you get big, exciting—and, yes, lasting—results. **◘**

sure you're fulfilling all the objectives of the first two phases and haven't unconsciously let extra calories start slipping back into your diet. (Keeping a food diary can help you get a good picture of what's really going on.) If you've been true to the program, try cutting your calories or increasing your exercise another notch. You may have hit a plateau, and this will help jump-start your progress.

Phase 3: Happily Ever After

Welcome to the rest of your life. I don't expect you to incorporate all the recommendations of this phase at once. Do the best you can, and consider the way you eat and exercise as works in progress. I hope you'll use the workouts and recipes on thebestlife.com Web site to keep the process going.

I'm going to ask you to maintain all the changes you achieved in Phases One and Two, but I'm making it a little easier by adding Anything Goes calories—the chance to have foods you still hanker for. Everything you eliminated in the last phase is now allowable under this category. My preference is that, rather than doughnuts and French fries, you put these Anything Goes calories toward "luxury foods" that are indulgent but still have something beneficial to offer: dark chocolate, full-fat cheese and yogurt, pretzels, pizza with whole-grain crust, berry sorbet, fruit crumble, or a glass of wine. How many of these Anything Goes calories you get per day depends on your activity level:

Oprah's Boot Camp

Trainer Bob Greene shows no mercy.

When Oprah asked me to design a six-week boot camp program of exercise and healthy eating, her goals weren't only to look stunning for the Emmy Awards and for the covers of *O*. She also wanted to jump-start a rededication to health, strength, and self-nurturing. Oprah signed a contract with herself—a powerful motivator, most people find—committing to consistent exercise, healthful food choices, and a daily cutoff time for eating. Since your metabolism slows as you approach bedtime, the later you eat, the harder it is to burn calories. I also suggested that during boot camp she give up alcohol, since it slows the metabolism. Oprah launched this program just three weeks before Emmy night. [Editor's note: Before you try an intense exercise program, consult a trainer and your doctor.]

Cardiovascular Workouts

Six mornings a week: Forty-five minutes of aerobic exercise, including at least two of the following: Power walking on a graded treadmill (up to 10 percent), jogging, elliptical exercise, stair stepping, or rowing.

Four or five evenings a week (before dinner): A 20-minute workout using one of the above exercises. These sessions gave Oprah a chance to reflect on her progress toward her goals.

Once a week: On a day with no strength training, Oprah replaced her usual aerobic exercise with a 75-minute run.

Strength Training

Four or five times a week: Thirty to 40 minutes of strength training, usually two days in a row, followed by a day off. Oprah preferred to train before her aerobic workout. Her warm-up: a 15-minute power walk.

Day One

Squats: Three sets of ten using 50 pounds of weight. Remember: This is a customized program; these weights may not be appropriate for everyone. (Works the buttocks, quadriceps, and hamstrings.)

Leg extensions: Three sets of ten using 60 pounds. (Quadriceps.)

Leg curls: Three sets of ten using 60 pounds. (Hamstrings.)

Chest presses: Three sets of ten using 50 pounds. (Chest.)

Incline presses: Three sets of ten using 40 pounds at a 45-degree angle. (Upper chest.)

Lat pulls: Three sets of ten using 50 pounds. (Upper back.)

Seated pull-downs: Three sets of ten using 50 pounds. (Biceps, chest, and shoulders.)

Standing flies: Three sets of ten using 20 pounds. (Chest.)

Seated rows: Three sets of ten using 50 pounds. (Back and shoulders.)

Back extensions: Three sets of ten on a back-extension device or a Roman chair. (Lower back.)

Day Two

Shoulder presses: Three sets of ten using ten-pound dumbbells. (Shoulders and upper back.)

Lateral raises: Three sets of ten using ten-pound dumbbells. (Shoulders.)

Frontal raises: Three sets of ten using ten-pound dumbbells. (Shoulders and arms.)

"Thumbs down" raises: Three sets of ten using five-pound dumbbells. (Shoulders—rotator cuff—and arms.)

Standing cable-cross curls: Three sets of ten using 20 pounds. (Biceps.)

Rotary torso: Three sets of ten on each side using 20 pounds. (Abs—obliques.)

Back extensions: Three sets of ten. (Lower back.)

Abdominal work

Incline crunches: Three sets of 30 at three increasingly difficult inclines (every day).

Stretching

After every workout, Oprah preformed stretches for her whole body, although 80 percent of them focused on her legs.

The Emmy Awards fell halfway through boot camp, and there were many toasts in Oprah's honor after she won the Bob Hope Humanitarian Award. She declined even a sip of Champagne, because that was part of her commitment. But I think she was feeling bubbly enough already. ◐

Bob Greene's
Best Life Diet: The Basics

These lists will help rev up your motivation, curb your appetite, and pinpoint exactly how hungry you are (or aren't).

3 Big Questions

Before you start any program, I want you to give some serious thought to one thing: yourself. If you've dropped and regained pounds many times over, it's an indication that you may not be facing up to the reasons you misuse food. Answering these questions will help you change the pattern:

1 **Why am I overweight?** Rather than "I don't have time to make healthy food" or "I have to eat out a lot," I want you to recognize the authentic feelings that lead you to overeat—for example, you're really anxious about work (and ice cream calms you down) or your husband is emotionally distant (and eating fills the void).

2 **Why do I want to lose weight?** If you say, "To look better," push further to *why*? Maybe you're afraid your significant other will leave you for someone prettier. But what does that mean about your relationship? Maybe you're trying to meet someone. Fine, but are there other changes you should be thinking about? (It's not only thin women who have partners.) When people think that getting thinner will make them happy, only to find it doesn't, it almost always leads to the misuse of food and a return to being overweight.

3 **Why have I been unable to maintain weight loss in the past?** Think back to the trigger that turned you from staying on a healthy program to eating out of control. Was the diet too rigorous? Did your spouse think you would fail? Many people have a core belief that they're not meant to be happy, so they continually find ways to sabotage themselves. Figuring out what drives you to relapse is the beginning of success. **O**

8 Ways to Curb Your Appetite

These proven techniques will help keep hunger from overriding your best intentions:

1. **Eat every three to four hours.** Your blood sugar won't have a chance to drop so low that you get famished and then binge.

2. **Load up on foods high in fiber and water**—they'll keep you full at a low-calorie cost.

3. **Make every meal and snack a combination of protein, fiber-rich carbs, and fat.** It can buy you an extra hour of satiety. (A salad with no dressing will just make you hungry again.)

4. **Wait 20 minutes before having seconds or another course.** That's how long it takes for your brain to receive the "full" signals. If you're in a restaurant, go somewhere else for dessert—by the time you get there, chances are you won't want it.

5. **Avoid being around food when it's not time to eat.** We are programmed to react to the sight and smell of anything edible by wanting to consume it.

6. **Exercise.** Research suggests that physical activity increases the brain's receptors for pleasure chemicals. This may help some overeaters who have fewer pleasure receptors (which is why it takes more food for them to get the same satisfaction others get from eating less).

7. **Try to resolve emotional issues that trigger you to eat.** Also find alternatives to eating that make you feel good, such as talking to friends, listening to music, or planning a vacation.

8. **Go to bed.** Research has suggested a link between not getting enough sleep and being overweight. Good shut-eye helps prevent the disruption of some of the hormones that control appetite. ◖

The Hunger Scale

This tool is going to help you avoid eating mindlessly. The more in touch you are with your hunger, the less you need to count calories. **Eat only when you're feeling 1, 2, 3, or 4.** Put your fork down at 5 or 6, and wait until the next scheduled meal or snack. If you're trying to lose weight, stop at 5, the point at which you're eating a little less than your body is burning.

10
Stuffed. You are so full you feel nauseous.

9
Very uncomfortably full. You need to loosen your clothes.

8
Uncomfortably full. You feel bloated.

7
Full. A little bit uncomfortable.

6
Perfectly comfortable. You feel satisfied.

5
Comfortable. You're more or less satisfied, but could eat a little more.

4
Slightly uncomfortable.
You're just beginning to feel signs of hunger.

3
Uncomfortably hungry. Your stomach is rumbling.

2
Very uncomfortable. You feel irritable and unable to concentrate.

1
Weak and light-headed. Your stomach acid is churning. ◖

"I can't stand the idea of wearing a swimsuit. I don't want to gross everyone out."
—CINDY COX, 48

"All the models are my height—I should look like Elle Macpherson."
—JILL SCHROEN, 36

"I'm so mad at my thighs—they never grew up with the rest of me."
—CARLA FRANK, 45

"At ten pounds less, I'd have more confidence, more energy, and my clothes would fit better."
—MIYA GRAY, 29

"I saw a photo of myself onstage with my stomach sticking out and was horrified."
—LANA SPENCE, 43

These women are convinced

What do you think? Ten women of assorted shapes, sizes, and ages. One thing they have in common: Each believes—truly, deeply, and possibly madly—that if she were only ten pounds lighter, her clothes would fit, she'd feel fine in a bathing suit, and she'd go out into the world happy and confident....

By Emily Yoffe

"I weigh myself every day. I'll see how much my food weighs, then I weigh myself after I eat it."
—KAREN RENDULIC, 31

"I walk into a room and think, *Look how great she looks.* All my friends talk about weight."
—SALLY HEREDIA, 34

"Food and television became my best friends after my son died."
—GAIL JOHNSON, 50

"I don't know if my 'last ten pounds' is really correct. It might be the 'last 15!' *Yuck!*"
—GRETCHEN SCHELDORF, 29

"I don't feel comfortable in my body at this weight."
—ELIZABETH POLYCARPE, 59

they need to lose ten pounds.

O magazine posted this question on oprah.com: "Do just ten pounds stand between you and happiness?" We were inundated with e-mails answering a resounding and agonized "Yes." Not that we were surprised. Women famously think they're heavier than they are. But the misery bound up in those "extra" ten pounds was staggering; the remarks acridly self-disparaging—"See how chubby I am"; "That's my gut"; "Fat belly" (photo with arrow pointing to offending spot). It was all too clear that the consuming desire to lose the weight is smothering the pleasure so many of us could be getting out of life.

Wondering how we—you, every woman—can be freed from this self-inflicted torture, *O* brought together ten of the respondents in New York City to meet with a panel of experts for a reality check. Did they really have ten pounds to lose? Or did they just need to firm up by working out more effectively? Then again, could dressing smarter make all the difference? Or did the real answer have nothing to do with diet or waistlines but rather with getting the "fat" label out of their heads?

Bob Greene, Oprah's trainer and the author of *Bob Greene's Total Body Makeover,* was onboard to assess and advise the women about exercise and eating habits. Stacy London, cohost of TLC's *What Not to Wear* and coauthor of *Dress Your Best,* came to coach the women on how a different style of pants or jacket could visually take off ten pounds.

Cracking the mind-set would be tougher. Psychologist Margo Maine, PhD, body image and eating disorder specialist and the coauthor of *The Body Myth: Adult Women and the Pressure to Be Perfect,* agreed to work with the women in teasing out the emotions tangled up in their weight anxiety. But even with insight, how do you shake off the self-image of "fat," which, we realized, has a hold on women equal to the fanaticism of a cult? We turned to a mind control expert who helps people leave cults, Steven Hassan, author of *Releasing the Bonds: Empowering People to Think for Themselves.*

Weight: The Obsession

Millions of Americans struggle with the medical consequences of being enormously overweight, from diabetes to collapsing knees. Not our ten women. They range in age from 29 to 59, in height from 5'2" to 5'11", and in weight from 125 to 165 pounds. Meeting them for the first time in New York, the experts are struck by how attractive they are—and how unable to accept that fact they seem to be.

Addressing the group, Steve Hassan asks everyone to consider how much of her fixation on ten pounds is a form of self-sabotage—a way of buying into a society that says there should be less of you. People wildly underestimate the extent to which we channel outside influence—billboards, fashion ads, movie images—and assume it's our own opinion, he says.

To illustrate, he shows a video of a conformity study in which people are instructed to inspect a series of straight lines and select the two of equal length. One at a time, the unknowing subjects are placed in a group of people who had all been prepped to give the wrong answer. Hassan's tape shows subject after subject buckling to the pressure of the group, eventually declaring that two clearly unmatched lines are the exact same length.

The women laugh, and a few say they would never bow to such coercion.

But is that true?

Karen Rendulic, 31, a single mother from Omaha, wrote in her e-mail, "If only I could lose ten pounds and feel healthy, I know I would be 100 percent happier."

It's hard to see Karen—a graceful 5'11" and 155 pounds—as anything but stunning. A surgical nurse who works night shifts so she can spend time during the day with her son, Karen will cancel a dinner engagement if her pants feel too tight. A major cause of her angst is how she looks in a bathing suit. She tells Margo Maine, "I don't go to the pool with my son. If I'm not perfect, people will be staring."

It seems almost beside the point to tell Karen that she's positively slender. Instead Margo encourages her to take the focus off her body and go after the enjoyment she is missing. "If you went out to dinner, something pleasant might happen," Margo tells her. "But you stay home and ruminate about your pants." As for the bathing suit, Margo says, "in ten years your son probably won't want to go to the pool with you, and you'll wish you had done it now."

Karen takes a deep breath, as if about to plunge into the water. "I'm going to get into a swimsuit. I'll hate it, but I'll do it."

Like Karen, Cindy Cox, 48 and from Covington, Georgia, is seeking perfection, only she is after the ghost of her younger self. A bubbly mother of five—the youngest is 9 and the oldest about to

Good Advice DIET

"Two of the best ways to lose weight: (1) Make a food cutoff time two or three hours before going to bed, and (2) eat a good breakfast."
—*Bob Greene*

make her a grandmother—Cindy is 5'3" and 130 pounds; her white top tucked into slacks shows off her small waist. When she visualizes herself, she tells Margo, she's still in her 20s. "I love the water, we have a boat, I love to swim, but when I look at my body in a bathing suit I think, *Where did this come from?* How do you accept it? Why am I flabby?"

Bob Greene says Cindy can absolutely firm up her so-called flab with regular resistance training. But he explains (as he does endlessly) that muscle weighs more than fat. "Cindy thinks she needs to lose ten pounds," he says. "No—she needs to tone up. She may or may not lose weight; she might even gain some."

Margo is struck by Cindy's unrealistic expectations and gently reminds her that no matter how much she exercises or starves herself, a woman who's almost 50 and has had five children simply is not going to have the body of a 25-year-old. "Would you give up your five children to have that body back?" she asks.

"Of course not," Cindy says, adding, "but society tells you that you can have that body."

"It tells you that you should want to," replies Margo. "Whole industries are devoted to it: diet, undergarments, working out. These are huge industries."

Listening to many of the married women in the group describe their spouses' reactions to their bodies, one starts to feel sorry for the adoring men whose wives can't take a compliment. As Cindy wrote in her e-mail, "My darling husband tells me on a regular basis how beautiful I am, but I can't believe him because I don't see what he sees."

Sally Heredia also can't accept her husband's appreciation. Standing 5'5½", the 34-year-old mother from San Antonio appears athletic at 145 pounds. "I want people to say, 'She's had three kids and she looks great,'" Sally says, explaining her longing to lose ten pounds.

"How about if they say, 'She's a great mother?'" Margo asks her.

Sally considers that. "My husband doesn't think I need to lose an ounce," she admits. "He thinks I'm perfect as I am. I say, 'Thank you, but....'"

"Why don't you hug and kiss him? Really thank him," suggests Margo.

"But it's not up here," Sally acknowledges, pointing to her head.

Margo recommends that Sally stop making an inventory of all her flaws and just practice enjoying her husband's praise. "This is a way of avoiding intimacy," she says of women's incessant self-criticism. "It's a way to be disengaged. It takes away from your relationship; it distances you to say, 'Thank you, but....'"

The Problem with "This"

In their frustration at not having the bodies they yearn for, several women grab a part of their anatomy, hold it out to the experts, and say they want to get rid of "this." Miya Gray, 29, who is 5'10" and 165 pounds, makes a chopping motion at her knee, then one at her waist. "This is my problem area," she says.

Bob has news for Miya, and for all the others who have a "this" they hate. "Every woman on planet Earth has a problem area—classically it's the hips, thighs, or backs of the arms," he says. This is where those seven to ten pounds insist on settling themselves, and "it's genetically predetermined." But the idea that you can target a body part and spot-reduce, says Bob, is a myth. Even if you work off those ten pounds, the hard truth is, you may not lose the weight where you want to.

"People get obsessed with their problem area," Bob says. "They lose weight and end up looking gaunt and unhealthy because they've gone after the last seven pounds instead of just living with them." Not that he suggests relaxing in the recliner with a box of doughnuts. He says an intense but relatively short workout—20 to 30 minutes of cardio five days a week and 15 minutes of resistance training three days a week—will rev up anyone's metabolism and sculpt the body by replacing fat with muscle.

131

He asks Miya to stand up. She's a software consultant from Washington, D.C., who lost 60 pounds about four years ago and now works out almost every day. Bob tells Miya she has a "beautiful hourglass figure" and that instead of trying to shrink the bottom, why not strengthen the top? He describes specific exercises to add to her routine to develop her shoulders. "They will respond enormously quickly," he promises. Without her losing a single pound, her silhouette will be better balanced.

Like Miya, Carla Frank, a creative director, believes the problem is all in her lower half—she wants to delete a good portion of it. She wants it so much that throughout her intensely busy days, she's aware of a constant refrain: "Lose ten pounds, lose ten pounds." It's a voice, she knows, that comes from a lifetime of both external and internal pressures. At 45, Carla is recently divorced, and despite her good looks and professional success, dating is a daunting prospect. "In New York, there are so many great-looking women. You have to be perfect." Of course, she adds, "there is no such thing. But I know I'd be more confident if I were five to ten pounds lighter."

Perhaps the man who would be attracted to her only if she were that much lighter, Steve suggests, isn't worth having. Carla understands his point. The two talk further about where her dissatisfaction is coming from. Appearance was very important in her

> **Good Advice**
> ## ATTITUDE
> "'Normal eating' is flexible—not perfect—and it includes sometimes having too much just because we feel like it."
> —*Margo Maine, PhD*

family, she says eventually. As a teenager, Carla rebelled by gaining weight—up to 142 pounds on her 5'2" frame. Though she's down to 125 pounds now, she thinks she should lose more.

Hassan talks about how difficult it is to change your behavior when you're motivated by negativity. "Going toward what you want is very different from going away from what you don't," he says. "Can you tell yourself, *I'm fine however I look?*" It's such a simple thought, but one that Carla never learned when she was young. "That's what I wish I would have learned," she says, her eyes welling with tears.

Stacy has a suggestion: "You have a great little body, but who can tell when you look like you're going to ride the Tour de France with Lance?" Carla is wearing tapered black pants with a side zipper, and a black top with a racing stripe down the sleeves. "Tapering makes your ankles look skinny and the rest of you look bigger," Stacy continues. "It's the ice-cream cone effect." The side zipper, she adds, creates what looks like a tundra of fabric across the midriff. Carla good-naturedly accepts the critique. "These pants are outta here!" she says.

Is It Really Worth the Work?

Everyone here, Bob says, could lose ten pounds if she wanted to—it means seriously cranking up her daily activity and watching what she eats (in particular, limiting refined carbohydrates)—but he has a question for them all: "Is it worth the work? Is it worth it to throw your life off for the last five to ten pounds? The body will defend those fat stores—that's survival. The last five to ten pounds are the hardest ones to lose."

Gretchen Scheldorf, 29, knows exactly what Bob is talking about. "Right now I can eat what I want," says the 5'7", 156-pound schoolteacher from Louisville, Kentucky. She worries that while she could maybe get to her 146-pound goal, the effort to do it, and then stay there, will turn her into what she doesn't want to be—"a person who's obsessed with weight all the time."

The truth is, says Bob, if she's not willing to put in the time and continual sacrifice necessary to meet her goal, she doesn't want the goal. And

> "Focusing on your physical flaws is a way of avoiding intimacy."
> —MARGO MAINE, PhD, BODY IMAGE CONSULTANT

that's fine, but then she should stop wasting energy on pining after the ten-pound loss and take the pressure off herself.

Jill Schroen, who's 5'10" and 160 pounds, also admits ambivalence about doing what it would take to get from a size 10 to an 8. "I don't want to give things up," she says with a smile and a great deal of self-knowledge. One of those people who used to be able to eat whatever she wanted, at 36 the mother of two from Memphis has to think about her weight. "I love food. I love it! I know I should stop, but it's so yummy."

With a little questioning, Steve finds that food is Jill's indulgence at the end of a day spent caring for others. She left a teaching career to stay home with her two young children. He proposes that since she's not bringing in an income, she believes she doesn't deserve to do something for herself like go to the gym.

Jill starts nodding and says she sees that if she can reward herself with both food and exercise, she wouldn't feel as if she's depriving herself. "My whole life, I'm doing for others," she says. "I'm going to allow myself to join a gym—to take two hours for 'me' time."

Stacy London makes a pitch for a shopping spree. "Do you follow the Grateful Dead?" she quips, pointing to Jill's pink

tie-dyed pants, "because they died." Though Stacy verbally shreds their clothes, the women love her wit and directness. Jill has fabulous long legs and should showcase them, Stacy says: For a pants update, she suggests a wide waistband that fits across the stomach (where Jill carries her weight), a front or back zipper—never the side—and a roomy leg cut.

If Jill is tie-dye, Lana Spence is denim. A bluesy rock singer from Falling Waters, West Virginia, she was plunged into menopause seven years ago, at age 36, when she had a hysterectomy due to ovarian cancer. She is 5'2" and was 112 pounds then; now she weighs 125. Bob doesn't see an extra ten pounds here—maybe two or three—but regular exercise, he says, would do wonders.

Steve asks her what is tripping her up. "I guess that little voice in the head," says Lana. Whose voice is it, he prods? What is he or she saying? Lana's not sure. He asks her to visualize the voice, hear it and see it. Finally she manages, "I see something that's trying to defeat what I want to be."

He suggests that the voice—it could be a mother's, father's, former husband's—might not be totally malevolent, that it might contain resources she needs.

"Just tap into it, like, let it grow?" Lana asks.

"Well, engage it," Steve answers. "Say something like 'What's up when you tell me I'm a fat slob?' Maybe the voice is actually trying to motivate you to lose weight. 'Well,' you tell it, 'that's not working—it just makes me feel lousy. If your intention is really to encourage me to lose weight, try saying, "Hey Lana, why don't you, when you finish the plate of food, wait 20 minutes to decide if you're still hungry before you have seconds?" ' My strongest advice is, instead of fighting that part of you, use it to help you."

When Ten Pounds Is Unhealthy

For two women in the room, Bob Greene says, losing ten pounds is a good idea, even critical. They look fine—it's not about that; they both have health issues.

Three years ago, Elizabeth Polycarpe, 59, had a heart attack. Diagnosed with high cholesterol, high blood pressure, and high blood sugar, she was ordered by her doctor to lose weight. She managed to drop 30 pounds, but at 163 now (she's 5'5"), ten of them have crept back on. The irony is that of all the women, Elizabeth is the least troubled by her weight. In Haiti, where she grew up, she says, "women wanted to be shapely, have a nice behind. They didn't worry about being skinny."

A moderate exercise program, perhaps walking on the treadmill, six days a week (if cleared by her doctor) could be a lifesaver for her, says Bob. Elizabeth knows this, and she knows she should watch her diet. But she's having trouble doing both.

Steve asks about her day-to-day life and discovers that she is under almost unrelenting pressure. She works in Skokie, Illinois, as a customer data analyst all day, then comes home to care for her elderly, ailing mother, who lives with her. Monday through Friday, Elizabeth never gets an uninterrupted night of sleep. Steve explains that all of this is impeding her ability to lose weight. "It sounds like you spend 80 percent of your energy taking care of your mother and 20 percent taking care of you," he tells her, "and that's not going to work in the long run. A heart attack is your body saying no, no, no, no."

Elizabeth gets it. "I have to say no to some people," she says—so her body isn't always saying no to her. Learning relaxation techniques such as self-hypnosis, Steve says, could really help. (For information, check out the American Society of Clinical Hypnosis at asch.net.)

So could a different color, says Stacy, on a lighter note. She's inspecting Elizabeth's jacket, a pale pink, which, she deadpans, "would be good for drapes." Stacy recommends structured jackets with high armholes—much more flattering than blousy tops, although she approves of the soft peach wrap sweater Gail Johnson is wearing. Like Elizabeth, Gail is under tremendous stress and has high blood pressure.

Gail, 50, never had a weight problem until March 2004, when her 30-year-old son, Jason Armstrong, was murdered. After his funeral, she went home, sat on the couch, turned on the television, and ate—for a year. "I was numb," says the operations planning manager for an electronics company in Tucker, Georgia. "Nobody who hasn't lost a child can really understand." Food was the safest way she could find to ease her grief. Over time the agony finally started to recede. But the weight—30 extra pounds of it—seemed there to stay. "How do you deal with emotional eating?" she says, now carrying 149 pounds on her 5'5" frame.

Margo rests a hand on Gail's knee. "Everyone uses food emotionally—everyone," she says. "Don't get too stringent with yourself. You do need comfort. Allow yourself food that tastes good." She says that losing weight slowly is the best way to do it and adding an activity she likes will help. Gail nods. She explains that during the year she spent inside, she avoided her friends. "I didn't want people saying, 'Oh, I'm so sorry.'" But she says she is ready, literally and figuratively, to "take small steps to find myself again." She loves to walk, and feels able to face the world and start living again.

As much as Bob Greene advocates the benefits of strenuous exercise, he believes just as much in building more chances for movement—such as walking—into people's lives. E-mail is convenient, but Bob suggests instead of sending it to colleagues in the same building, deliver the message in person. "Most calories are not combusted during structured exercise," he says. "Routinely walking down the hall could mean a four-pound weight loss at the end of the year."

Stacy challenges Gail to play with patterns. No, she's not suggesting it as a method of camouflage but as an approach that's at the heart of her whole philosophy: Dressing well is really about how you feel inside, she believes. If you're having fun with your clothes, using them to express your uniqueness—rather than disguise your flaws—you'll feel better about yourself and worry less about your thighs or stomach. "Don't let the covers of fashion magazines be your standard," Stacy encourages the whole group. "You can use style as your personal weapon to create your own standard of beauty—and that's empowering."

Then Stacy, whose own reedy figure is cover-worthy, tells them a story to explain that she understands, really understands, how they feel. When she was a senior in college, she decided to lose some weight because she wanted to go into the fashion business. "In three months, I lost 60 pounds. People thought I was sick. I just figured, *They're jealous.*" She developed an eating disorder and wound up in the hospital with pneumonia. After she got out, she couldn't stop eating: "I ate boxes of cereal, loaves of bread. I doubled my weight in a year." She went to work at *Vogue* and at one point was carrying 180 pounds on her 5'7" frame. But, amazingly, even at that weight she learned to feel good about herself by dressing to enhance her body, not hide it. It took her seven years to get back to the weight she started at.

Incidentally, how much weight had she originally decided she had to lose to be perfect? Ten pounds.

Good Advice
FASHION

"Don't get hung up on the size. If you feel bad about yourself because a 12 is what fits, take a Sharpie, and write '6' on the label."
—*Stacy London*

Two Weeks Later

From the e-mails our women sent when they got home, it sounds as if many of them spent most of their return plane ride reading Bob's book. Several of them have already adopted parts of his program into their daily routine and have also incorporated pieces of the other experts' advice, from shaking up their closets to looking at their bodies through new eyes.

Cindy resolved to stop obsessing about what she calls her "flabby, waving back at ya" arms. "One thing that really hit me was when Bob talked about not just concentrating on one area," she writes. "Now I'll push for overall firming up, and hopefully [my arms] will slim down." She is also trying to integrate the lesson Margo taught about how women's dislike of their bodies can damage intimacy with their husbands. "I still don't see what Jerry sees," she says, "but I'm working on that."

Jill and Gretchen both came away deciding not to devote their lives to battling ten pounds. Of the hard body she formerly fixated on, Jill writes, "I was floored when Bob said that only 10 to 20 percent of the population has the drive to look like that. I've come to the realization that I don't have, or want to have, that type of motivation. Being healthy and happy with what I've got is most important." Ironically, after letting go of the fantasy, Jill lost three pounds.

Gretchen, too, is accepting where she is with her weight. "I do have to say that seeing all those other gorgeous women worried about their last ten pounds (and thinking to myself that they really didn't need to) made me a lot more secure in my own body and all its lumps and curves."

For Miya, the day in New York helped her address larger issues in her life. "I am very focused on finding my purpose (beyond losing my last ten pounds)," she writes. And Karen has made it a priority to look for a new job—one without the crazy night shifts that leave her so tired and overwhelmed.

Gail started wearing a pedometer to help her increase how much she walks. Elizabeth, too, is exercising six days a week for at least 45 minutes. "I feel good, and I hope the extra effort will help me enjoy a healthier life," she says. But, she adds slyly, "I am keeping the pink jacket." ●

> "Don't let the covers of fashion magazines be your standard. You can use style as your personal weapon to create your own standard of beauty—and that's empowering."
>
> —STACY LONDON, FASHION CONSULTANT

The Clothes Diet

The next time you find yourself heading for a weight-anxiety bender, Stacy London, cohost of TLC's *What Not to Wear*, has two words: *Go shopping*. You can look ten pounds thinner just by zipping on a different pair of jeans or adding a well-placed pinstripe. Here's a snippet of her book, *Dress Your Best: The Complete Guide to Finding the Style That's Right for Your Body*, written with cohost Clinton Kelly.

If you're...bigger on the bottom: Don't try to hide your "problem areas" with long shirts or jackets; you'll only make your legs look shorter. Shorter tops (ending above the hip) that enhance your waistline are the way to go for you. The one must-have item is a nonpleated pair of trousers that sits at the top of the hip and has a midwidth leg. Always go with a pointy shoe (fun prints are a good thing)—you'll add instant legginess.

...bigger on the top: Stay away from skinny pants because they'll throw you way out of proportion. The same is true for straight and narrow skirts. A softly draped A-line, however, will balance out the bust and slim you down. Look for dresses that have an Empire seam, which supports the bustline and raises the eye above the natural waist, creating length in the whole body.

...carrying a little extra in the middle: To create more of an hourglass, structured jackets are key. Look for one that nips in at the waist and falls over the top of the hip; it should also fit closely in the shoulders. Choose pants and skirts with a little volume. And for a suit, consider a dress-and-jacket combo.

...shaped like an hourglass: Forget those super-low-rise pants and skirts (they'll emphasize your hips and give you love handles). Try a straight-cut, wider-leg pair of jeans that fits at the broadest part of your hip. Your must-have is a faux-wrap dress in cotton or nylon jersey (faux meaning it's sewn to look like a wrap so you don't have to get all tied up in it)—great for emphasizing your narrow midsection and accenting your assets.

10 Priceless Strategies for the Next Decade

Lasting wealth is not found in the numbers flickering from the ATM screen. It's built on the foundation of who you are, how you act, and what you believe in. Follow these steps over the next ten years to ensure financial security:

1 Take an oath of financial honesty. A crushing credit card balance caused by your need to impress others is a costly lie. Living within your means is living honestly. Find ways to save $25 a week and you'll free up $100 a month. Invest it, and in 25 years you could have $80,000.

2 Stop settling for what the world offers. You need to be your own best advocate. If there's no raise this year because of the economy, meet with your boss to determine grounds for a raise next year. If you're self-employed and haven't increased your rates in years, I have

to ask, why are you putting yourself on sale? I say it's fear. Recognize that this fear is keeping you from having more in your life.

3 Avoid debt bondage. Yes, debt is necessary; it's how you own a home or get a college degree, but the trick is to respect it. Take on only what you can afford. Have a credit card balance? Use the $100 from step one to increase your minimum payment on a $10,000 balance that charges 18 percent interest and you could save almost $24,000 in interest fees.

4 Make your financial life work within the new normal. The best move you can make today is to let go of what was and focus on what has been dubbed the new normal: a period of more moderate growth. That means, for instance, you need to expect that your house will appreciate at roughly the rate of inflation.

5 Get in great credit shape. I've always said a high FICO score is a key component to security—but it's even more important now that lenders are so circumspect about making loans. A FICO score of at least 700 is your best defense. And if you find yourself in the job-hunting pool, be sure to check that your credit report (annual creditreport.com) doesn't have any glaring mistakes. (Yes, many employers check credit reports. It's considered an insight into your sense of responsibility.)

6 Remember that every no leads you that much closer to a yes. The pain and anxiety of shocks like layoffs or divorce are unquestionably destabilizing. But you make things worse when you see these events as major setbacks, instead of starting points for you to re-imagine and reclaim your life. I also believe you can reduce the pain by adopting a "hope for the best, plan for the worst" mind-set (i.e., have an emergency fund).

7 Open up. Most people in financial trouble hold tightly to what they have. To put yourself in position to receive more in life, you must first open your hands— and your heart—by giving to others today. If you want to learn about a specific charity, check out the free service charitynavigator.org.

8 Save for indulgences. Assuming you're on track with your retirement savings, have no credit card debt, and have an emergency savings fund, I'm not going to deny you fun—so long as you've saved up for it. If you want to have $5,000 for a milestone birthday trip in two years, you'll need to put away about $200 a month now, given today's low bank rates.

9 Eliminate the "I shoulds." Now is the time to take care of every major must-have document—a will, a healthcare power of attorney, etc.—you've sworn for years that you'd get to.

10 Choose your legacy. This is all about the deathbed test. Will loved ones describe you in terms of what you bought for yourself, or will they talk about who you were and how fiercely you loved? Make that question your guidepost, and I will 100 percent guarantee that life will be richer than you can imagine. **O**

Why Tidy Files = Tidy Finances

A surefire way to build wealth—without spending a penny.

have a surefire way to build wealth that won't cost you a penny. Even better, it's so easy, you can do it while watching a DVD. Here's the deal: You are going to clean up your finances by trashing old paperwork that serves no purpose other than as a dust magnet, and developing a system for keeping your important documents, bills, and statements organized. Like your home's closets, your financial clutter needs an overhaul every now and again, and the payoff will go far beyond the psychic satisfaction of neatening up.

I am a big believer that orderliness begets wealth. A pile of bills and statements—whether paid or not—is a sign that someone is clueless about what's coming in and going out. When you consciously open, read, and file away your bills and statements, you are connecting with your money and taking control of your life.

Being organized also makes it infinitely easier to give yourself the financial health screenings I advocate month in and month out. For example, if I told you to go check your home insurance policy right now to make sure your coverage is for "guaranteed replacement" or "extended replacement," would you have any idea where your policy is? If not, you could have insufficient coverage, which could mean tens of thousands of dollars in uncovered claims.

If you're not staying on top of your money, you are putting your financial well-being at risk. Here's how to launch an invigorating spring cleaning:

FIRST, ORGANIZE.

Let's begin by gathering up your docs. Pull out stray files, snatch the latest round of bills, and empty that overflowing kitchen or office drawer stuffed with papers you've been meaning to get to for ages. Sort everything into six piles:

- **Monthly bills, bank statements, and pay stubs**
- **Investment statements** (pension updates, 401(k) statements, brokerage and fund statements, and so forth)
- **Tax returns and supporting docs**
- **Policy documents and deeds** (insurance policies, home deed, car title...)
- **Warranties and user manuals**
- **Forever docs** (things like marriage license, will, birth certificate)

Next, create a folder for each type of document (except forever docs; see next paragraph) and add new papers as they come in. Then create folders within the folders: Take ongoing bills, for example. Store all gas bills in one folder, electricity bills in another, cable bills

> **If you're not staying on top of your money, you are putting your financial well-being at risk.**

in a third, and so on. If possible, keep all folders in a fireproof, water-resistant file cabinet or box; if not, a drawer or shelf will do.

It's an entirely different ball game for the forever docs. Because of their importance, they must be put in a portable fire-and-water-resistant home safe or file container—something that you can grab at a moment's notice. Why not a bank deposit box? Because you don't have access 24/7. If, God forbid, you die or become incapacitated, your relatives may not be able to access it; besides, the maintenance fee is a waste of money compared with the onetime cost of simply buying a safe.

For everything you're sending to the trash, I have one word of advice: shred. The FTC estimates that up to nine million Americans each year are victims of identity theft, in which personal documents are stolen and the data is used to run up charges on existing accounts or to obtain new credit or debt. That can wreak havoc with your financial life, and low-tech Dumpster diving—where a crook rifles through your garbage to find financial data—remains a big risk. At about $150 a pop, a crosscut paper shredder is a great investment; it will make mincemeat of any important papers.

Tips for Going Paperless

Step back and size up the clutter. A lot of those piles sitting in front of you are wholly unnecessary in our cyberfriendly world. You can receive bills electronically via your bank or credit union's Web site—it should be free (if not, consider switching banks)—and with just a few clicks you can authorize direct e-payments from your checking account. **Bye-bye, (manual) checkbook balancing.** Moving monthly bill paying online will help you stay on top of your income and outgo because all debits and credits are tracked for you; no input necessary. You can also set up e-mail alerts to remind you when you need to log on and take care of business, or create ongoing automatic monthly transfers (so you'll never forget to pay a bill again!).

Take proper caution. Worried about cybersafety? Just make sure to use a password-protected secure network when logging on to your account; that means no bill paying from public Wi-Fi hotspots.

Clutter be gone. Since most statements are readily available via the Web, you don't have to obsess about keeping records at home. For example, because you can see your annual benefits estimate from the Social Security Administration online, you can toss paper statements from years past and even the current one once you verify it's up-to-date. (Go to ssa.gov and click on Estimate Your Retirement Benefits.) —*S.O.*

NEXT, KNOW WHAT TO KEEP AND FOR HOW LONG.

Okay, now we're ready to tackle each of the piles. (If you ever need a reminder, I also have a cheat sheet on my Web site, suzeorman.com/finclutter.) Here we go....

Ongoing Bills

▨ **Utility bills:** Hold on to these for one year—just in case there are any billing issues. If you claim a home-office deduction, keep statements for three years because that's how long the IRS generally has to challenge tax returns.

▨ **Pay stubs:** Save one year's worth. Once you receive a year-end W-2 statement, check it against the last pay stub. If it all matches, chuck the backup.

▨ **Bank and credit card statements:** Keep for one year, but with this caveat—if you expect to apply for a mortgage, HELOC, or car loan in the near future, hoard two years' worth of bank statements. After being burned by their own no-doc policies prior to the credit crisis, many lenders are now asking for a ton of income verification before granting loans, especially for the self-employed. If you bank and pay your bills online, you can typically access at least six months of statements at no charge. Save pdfs of them on your hard drive (or print out copies) in case you need the information; you may be slapped with a fee if you have to ask your bank or credit card company to cough them up later.

Investment Statements

▨ You probably receive monthly or quarterly updates, as well as an annual summary. Once you get that annual statement, toss the others.

▨ If you make any trades during the year, keep a record of each transaction for at least three years.

▨ For nondeductible contributions to a traditional IRA or conversions to a Roth IRA, save the IRS form 8606 you filed when making the deposits. When you withdraw during retirement, it will be a piece of cake to prove you've already paid the taxes.

Tax Returns and Supporting Docs

▨ Since the IRS has three years to challenge anything, you *must* keep three years' worth of returns and supporting documents.

▨ Remember: If the IRS suspects you haven't reported income, it can challenge returns from the past *six* years. So if you are self-employed or have multiple income sources, hold on to six years of files to be safe. (By the way, there is no statute of limitations if you fail to file or if the government suspects you of fraud.)

Keep it or Not?

Get rid of... ATM slips more than a month old. Toss them after checking them against your monthly statement.
Be sure to save... Receipts for big-ticket purchases that might be included in an insurance claim. And photograph the possessions; the more documentation you have, the easier the claims process will be. —*S.O.*

▨ To learn more about IRS recordkeeping guidelines, see Publication 552 on their Web site (irs.gov/pub/irs-pdf/p552.pdf).

Policy Documents and Deeds

▨ Keep the policy statement for any active account, such as auto and homeowner's insurance, as well as the deed to your home and titles to your cars.

Warranties and User Manuals

▨ Save active warranties; equally important is letting go of expired ones.

▨ Although the 100-page tomes covering operating details of shiny new gadgets are not financial documents, I've included them here because they go hand-in-hand with warranties and contribute to so much clutter. If you find yourself staring at a user manual for the cell phone you lost in a cab last month, trash it right now! And if you're comfortable Web surfing, get rid of *all* user manuals: Manufacturers have downloadable versions on their Web sites, and plenty of third-party sites amalgamate manuals from different companies (try usersmanualguide.com and manualnguide.com).

Forever Docs

▨ Some stuff should never, *ever* be tossed: birth certificates, marriage license, divorce decree, will, trust, estate planning documents, and death certificates. Make sure your family knows how to access these important records if you die.

▨ I'd also suggest keeping a permanent file of all loans you have paid off (mortgage, car, school, and so on) because if you later find a mistake with how the data was reported to credit bureaus—or if an identity thief complicates your life—having those docs handy will save you much grief. ◖

> I'm a big believer that orderliness begets wealth.

Risky Business

How to avoid the financial pitfalls you might not be aware of.

I know you've got the major risks in your financial life well taken care of: Your 401(k) is properly diversified to help you weather market volatility, and your reserve cash fund is on call to cover life's inevitable emergencies. Good work!

But I'm worried about your financial blind spots—those pesky threats to your security that lurk behind seemingly sound decisions. Here are a few common traps, and advice to ensure that you won't get taken by surprise:

The Perils of Plastic

■ **The Good News:** You've sworn off credit cards. Goodbye insane interest rates and fees! You're sticking with your debit card from now on.

■ **The Hidden Risk:** Debit card transactions aren't reported to the credit bureaus, so if you don't use a credit card, you'll have less of a payment history—which hurts your FICO credit score.

■ **How to Stay on Top:** I love, love, love that you want to use your debit card. But to keep your credit score solid, you still need to keep a few credit cards and use them at least once every few months. Even if you think you'll never need to borrow again, your FICO credit score has a big impact. It can affect your auto insurance premium and whether a landlord will rent to you, and many employers even check it when vetting a job application. Cards issued by credit unions typically charge lower rates (generally limited to a max of 18 percent) and fewer fees. Check out creditcardconnection.org to find the best options.

The Bond Issues

■ **The Good News:** You're sleeping better than ever since you moved all your retirement money out of stocks and into bonds.

■ **The Hidden Risk:** You're approaching two land mines here. First up is inflation. Make it to age 65 and there's a good chance you'll live another 20 years or longer. (More on this in the next item.) Over a 20-year period, a 4 percent average inflation rate (the historical norm since the '50s) will reduce the purchasing power of today's dollar to about 50 cents. That will make it very hard to maintain your standard of living in retirement. Bonds aren't an ideal inflation hedge, since their historical returns are typically not much better than the inflation rate. Making matters worse, because of the financial crisis and the Federal Reserve's efforts to keep the economy growing, bond yields are at unprecedented lows. This is not a permanent situation. Soon—maybe this year or next—interest rates, and thus bond yields, will start to rise. When rates rise, the market price of bonds falls. That hurts your portfolio.

■ **How to Stay on Top:** Every portfolio benefits from bonds; they provide a cushion when the stock market hits a rough patch. But avoiding stocks completely could mean your investment won't grow any faster than the rate of inflation. As a general rule, your age is a good guideline for the percentage of bonds you want—if you're 55, put 55 percent in bonds and 45 percent in stocks. If you're worried about putting money in stocks right now, stick with mutual funds or exchange-traded funds (ETFs) that focus on dividend-paying stocks. The dividend payout is a steady stream of income, much like a bond, and right now the yield on some dividend portfolios is actually higher than the yield on a five-year Treasury bond. While dividend stocks have their own risk, if you have time on your side—at least ten years—you can pocket that nice dividend income today, ride out the volatility, and, over the long term, potentially earn inflation-beating gains.

Live Long—And Prosper?
■ **The Good News:** You're likely to reach a much older age than women of previous generations. Today a woman of 65 will probably live 20 more years—60 percent longer than her life expectancy in 1900.
■ **The Hidden Risk:** That means more years that your 401(k) and IRA need to support you.
■ **How to Stay on Top:** To enjoy a long, comfortable retirement, save more today. If you're 50 or older, take advantage of the catch-up provisions: Instead of an annual 401(k) max of $16,500 in 2011, you're entitled to invest $22,000, and your IRA limit rises from the standard $5,000 to $6,000. You may also want to retire later. Working until 67 or 70 gives those funds more time to grow—which gives you more security. You don't have to keep the high-powered career you have now; a less demanding job will still bring in valuable income.

On Borrowed Dimes
■ **The Good News:** You're in a pinch, but your company allows you to borrow from your 401(k).
■ **The Hidden Risk:** Make that plural—there are three problems with taking your company up on that loan. First, if you leave your job, voluntarily or not, you'll typically have only a few months to pay back what you've borrowed. If you can't, the loan converts to a withdrawal on which you'll owe income tax, and if you're under 55 you'll also be hit with a 10 percent early withdrawal penalty. Second, when you pull money out of any investment, it's no longer working for your future. Anyone who took a loan from their 401(k) in early 2009 missed out when the S&P 500 stock index shot up more than 60 percent from March to December. That was a costly time to be out of the market. Third, your loan money will end up being taxed twice—when you repay the loan it will be with after-tax dollars, and then in retirement, when you begin using your 401(k) for living expenses, you'll be responsible for the tax due on those withdrawals.

> You may not be providing enough security for your family if something happens to you.

■ **How to Stay on Top:** Make a 401(k) loan an absolute last resort. A well-maintained emergency savings fund is a far better insurance policy against unforeseen expenses. As you know, I advise saving up eight months of living expenses—especially now, when most unemployed people need at least six months to find a new job.

Kids Need the Darndest Things
■ **The Good News:** You're expecting, or you have young kids.
■ **The Hidden Risk:** You may not be providing enough security for your family if something happens to you.
■ **How to Stay on Top:** You can't control fate, but you absolutely, positively can make sure that your children will be financially secure, no matter what. A term life insurance policy that's at least 20 times your annual income will give your kids' guardian plenty of money to raise them according to your wishes. I know that sounds like a lot, but these policies are remarkably inexpensive.

Shaky Foundations
■ **The Good News:** The steep decline in home prices means you can afford to buy your first home.
■ **The Hidden Risk:** It's easy to underestimate the real cost of home ownership.
■ **How to Stay on Top:** Property tax, insurance, and maintenance can add 30 percent to your base mortgage. To see how that expense will affect you, plug in your price range for a home at bankrate.com/calculators/mortgages/mortgage-calculator.aspx to determine your monthly mortgage payment, and then add 30 percent to that figure. If the total is more than your current rent, spend six months "playing house"—each month, deposit the difference between your rent and your probable mortgage payment into a separate savings account. If you can't afford this exercise, you can't afford to buy a home at that price just yet. And don't forget: Before buying a home, you must have an emergency fund that can cover your expenses for eight months. If anything happens to your job or a big expense pops up, you'll need to have the cash to pay the mortgage. Finally, don't buy if there's any chance you'll move within five to seven years. If you sell a newly purchased house, you risk making too little on the sale to cover the typical 6 percent agent's fee and your moving costs. I know the housing market's rock-bottom prices are tempting, but it's better to be safe than sorry. ◐

Where Does Your Money Go?

Twelve little things that can bust your budget.

No matter the size of your budget, life always costs more in reality than it does on paper. I've often been asked to evaluate women's homes and habits to see if I can figure out where the money is going. You'd be surprised at how quickly seemingly insignificant expenses—and missed opportunities—add up.

Following is a list of little things that might be costing much more than you think:

Clothing bought on sale. A bargain? Maybe not. If you weren't planning to buy new clothes before you saw that alluring half off sign, you didn't need them.

A kitchen cupboard filled with unused gizmos. Do you have a pastamaker, breadmaker, and popcorn popper gathering dust? What about the little gadgets: the apple corer, the bagel slicer, and so on? If you never use them, you should sell them, give them away, trade them, or donate them to an organization that can use them. I promise you'll feel richer with less. And you'll be richer too because you'll think through the life cycle of a gadget the next time you're tempted to buy a new one.

A messy desk. Do you have stacks of bills you haven't opened, paperwork you haven't gotten around to doing, and piles of mail-order catalogs you may or may not eventually read? Clutter gets in the way of clarity—and clarity is the gateway to financial freedom.

Every time you look at that clutter, you feel anxiety and fear—and a sense of "I can't." These feelings don't disappear when you turn away from the clutter. They're a part of your financial self-esteem, and they prey upon every aspect of your life, even in the subtlest ways. Your paperwork represents money (your own or, in the case of unopened bills, your creditors'). Show respect for yourself, for your money, and for others by facing that clutter, not hiding from it.

Your well-stocked refrigerator. Take a good look inside it. How much do you throw out in a week? Ten dollars' worth? Fifteen? Or more? That's maybe $1,000 a year in the garbage. If you go the grocery store once a week, change your schedule and shop every eight days instead of every seven. Make do with what's in the fridge for that last day. Improvise. Do something with that half cucumber, put that lonely piece of chicken in a salad, make applesauce before those apples spoil. Over the course of a year, you'll make seven fewer trips to the supermarket. If you typically spend $175 per trip, you'll save more than $1,000 per year.

Your cup of morning coffee. If you buy a $2.75 coffee concoction five days a week, you're spending more than $700 a year. Buy a travel mug for the car and make your coffee at home.

Unopened statements for your retirement plan. If you're not vigilant about preparing for your future, who will be? And if you're not planning ahead, you're sabotaging your chances for financial comfort down the road.

A bathroom cabinet filled with abandoned shampoos, hair gels, creams, lipsticks, and nail polish. When I look through a house, I often see a few hundred dollars' worth of hair care products and cosmetics going to waste. Use it or toss it!

I suggest that you start by trading the products you don't use with a friend (the way you did as a teenager), when hygiene permits. If you can't swap, then see how it feels to actually throw away an almost full bottle. You'd still be throwing away the money if you let the product grow ancient in your cabinet. But this way, you'll be much more aware of what your purchase meant in terms of dollars, and you'll begin to buy more discerningly.

That mason jar brimming with spare change. This money is not being respected. Money flows—it's that simple. It flows in and it flows out. Sometimes there's less and sometimes there's more. But stashes around the house stop the flow. If you're going to use your money wisely, every penny you have (or don't have) is important.

See how much cash you have around the house. I'll bet it's at least $30, maybe much more. If you have credit card debt, apply it to that. If you don't, invest the money and make it count.

A big bag of freshly dry-cleaned clothes. Did they all really need to be cleaned, or could you have worn some of them once or twice more after a fresh pressing? Be sparing with your dry cleaning and you'll not only save money, you'll also extend the life of your clothes.

A credit card with perks that go to waste. If those free frequent flier miles just expired, switch to a card that offers a freebie you will use.

Too many toys in the playroom. Think about the lessons you're teaching your children about money, about things, about what's essential in life. Then help your children give more value to their toys by examining each and every one. Keep only those they really play with, give the rest away— and think carefully before buying the next new goody, even if it only costs a few dollars.

A tax-refund check. Free money? I don't think so. If you get a refund check, that means you've been letting the IRS enjoy the interest on that money when you could have been putting the interest toward your future. Let's say you typically get back $2,000. What if, instead, you were to increase the number of allowances you claim on your W-4 form? (You may be able to claim yourself as an allowance if you don't already.) You might get a smaller refund or no refund at all, but you'll bring home more money in your paycheck each month.

Now what if you were to take that money and invest it each month in a no-load mutual fund? In just a few years, you'd have built a nest egg. As for the argument that it feels good to get a big IRS check every year, from what I've seen, that so-called windfall just gets spent and is gone. Why not make the money grow for you instead? **◐**

The Biggest Budget Wrecker

I've seen it a million times—people try to stick to a rigid monthly budget only to be defeated. Why? Because in order to work, a budget has to budge—to give and take and stretch.

You know what your mortgage payments will be every month, and certain other expenses are also fixed. But some months you'll have five presents to buy, and some

months none. If you pay for child care every Friday, you'll have some months when you have five checks to write instead of four.

You've also got once-a-year expenses. Do you spend $2,000 on Christmas gifts and parties? That's costing you $166.66 every month. If you buy a $500 gym membership, that's $41.66 a month. If you spend $500 for

the kids' back-to-school clothes, you pay for that all year too.

Look at what you're going to spend over the course of a year, rather than in any given month—and allow yourself some leeway. When your budget is realistic, you'll be able to live within it and you'll feel firmly in control of your money. *—S.O.*

When Is a Deal *Not* a Deal?

A few deals you never want to make.

It looks like a bargain, it sounds like a bargain, it must be a bargain—right? Not always. When it comes to the many financial options out there, what seems great at first glance is often anything but a fair shake. You'll spare yourself serious money woes if you understand the true cost of any financial decision—whether you're transferring a balance or helping your child select a college. Here are seven deals you never want to make (and three offers you'd be crazy not to accept).

DON'T: Opt for lower monthly payments with a five-year (or longer) car loan. According to Federal Reserve data, the average new-car loan term is 62 months. That's ten months longer than a decade ago, and, to put it simply, longer is a waste of money. Your car is a depreciating asset— after just one year, its value will be 30 to 50 percent lower. So don't pay interest on it for any longer than you have to.
DO: Sign up for a car loan only if it's for 36 months or less. If the shorter term makes the monthly payment too high, you need to shop for a less expensive car.

DON'T: Buy sale items on credit. Say a product you buy often is 15 percent off, so you decide to buy in bulk. Paying with a credit card could get you in trouble. If you purchase $350 worth of merchandise at a 15 percent discount, your bill will be $298. But if the $298 goes onto your credit card at 20 percent interest and you pay only the minimum due each month (usually about 3 percent), it will take you two years and $67 in interest to pay it off.
DO: Pay with cash or a debit card. If you do use credit, pay off the purchase in full when the bill arrives. If the item is nonessential, don't make the purchase at all. Use the calculator in the credit card section of bankrate.com to compute the true cost of paying only the minimum due.

DON'T: Get a low deductible on your auto or home insurance policy. Limiting your out-of-pocket costs seems smart, but with a deductible of just $250 or so, you're more likely to file small claims in the event of an accident or loss of property. That's a quick way to get on your insurer's bad side—your premium may increase at renewal time, or your insurer may decline to keep you as a customer.
DO: Raise your deductible to $1,000. Handle small issues out-of-pocket and save your insurance for major problems. Not only will you stay in your insurer's good graces, you'll reduce your annual premium by at least 10 percent.

DON'T: Let your child go to that fantastic college if it's outside your price range. Your teen understands the need to apply to a safety school—and it's your job to make sure every school she applies to is *financially* safe, too. A college education can be incredibly valuable, but it makes no sense to rack up massive debt to obtain one. And I can't stress this enough: Do not deplete your retirement fund to pay for college. That money needs to keep working for your future.
DO: Start making the numbers work in high school (if you haven't already set aside funds in a 529 plan or other savings account). If your teen is an academic achiever, scoring well on Advanced Placement tests can reduce her required coursework in college, and since fewer than 40 percent of students graduate in four years—and a fifth year can add 25 percent to the total cost—that's a huge leg up. Bear in mind that the average tuition at a four-year public college for the 2010–2011 school year was $7,605, compared with $27,293 for a private college. If your child's chosen career requires a graduate degree, spending less at the undergrad level will be a big help when it comes time to finance grad school. Once the acceptance letters arrive, make sure you fill out the FAFSA form to see if you're eligible for financial aid. And try to stick with federal loans: at a maximum 6.8 percent fixed interest rate, the Stafford loan program is the best deal going. Once your kid maxes out on Staffords, you can look into a PLUS loan; parents can borrow up to the full amount of school minus any aid, and the fixed rate is 7.9 percent.

DON'T: Fall for teaser and variable rates. Some credit card companies lure you in with a rate of 0 percent but raise it to 18 percent after the initial promotional period. Adjustable-rate mortgages that started at 2 percent or lower in 2005 have reset at much higher rates, sending thousands of people into foreclosure. And that private college loan that started at 10 percent? It could climb to 15 percent or higher if it's tied to an index that rises. The bottom line: If the interest rate isn't permanent, you could get taken for a ride.

DO: Stick with a 30-year fixed-rate home mortgage (average is currently around 5 percent), avoid credit card promotions altogether, and, as much as possible, steer clear of private college loans—again, Stafford and PLUS loans are the way to go.

DON'T: Transfer balances. A few years ago, transferring your debt to a card with lower rates would have been a no-brainer, as many card issuers charged a maximum balance transfer fee of $50 to $75. But today companies often charge a percentage of your entire balance—usually between 3 and 5 percent (and a 3 percent fee on a $5,000 transfer is $150).

DO: Try to find a no-fee transfer deal at creditcards.com. And if you are considering a deal that charges fees, use the calculator at creditcards.com to determine whether you'll come out ahead (creditcards.com/calculators/balance-transfer.php).

> **If an interest rate isn't permanent, you could get taken for a ride.**

DON'T: Use a debt settlement firm. Those TV ads that promise to negotiate a deal with your creditors so you pay only a fraction of the bill can be enticing—but you should change the channel, and quick. According to the National Foundation for Credit Counseling, debt settlement firms typically charge fees between 13 and 20 percent of your total debt, or a cut of the total debt reduction plus a hefty monthly fee of $50 or more. Not to mention that many of these companies are far from squeaky-clean—several simply collect your fees without doing much at all to improve your situation, and the Federal Trade Commission has numerous cases pending against the worst offenders. Furthermore, even if you *are* able to negotiate a lower payment, you will likely owe federal tax on the amount forgiven (the IRS considers it income), and a settlement will hurt your credit score.

DO: The negotiating for yourself. If you're unable to make your payments, call your creditors. They would rather get something than nothing from you, and they're just as willing to deal with you as they are with a debt settlement company.

Asking to settle your bill for less than the full balance will work only if you have enough funds to make a lump-sum offer—you'll need to bring cash to the table. And remember that if they accept, there could still be a tax bill coming your way. **◖**

Deal Yourself In: Three Offers Worth Their Weight in Gold

Retirement Fund Contribution Matching. Many employers offer a 50 percent match for every dollar you contribute out of your paycheck, up to a limit of around 6 percent of your salary. Despite the appeal of an automatic 50 percent gain, benefits consulting firm Hewitt Associates reports that about one in five eligible participants fails to take full advantage of the program. Don't be one of them: Call your human resources department and make sure your contribution rate qualifies you for your employer's maximum match.

The Roth IRA. It's the Swiss Army knife of investments: In an emergency you can withdraw your contributions without owing any tax or penalty; if necessary, you can use them to help pay for college; and it's great for preserving assets you intend to pass on to your heirs. Best of all, in retirement your withdrawals will be tax free—and you're not required to withdraw annually as you are with a traditional IRA or 401(k).

Term Life Insurance. Web sites such as selectquote.com and accuquote.com will shop among multiple insurers to find you the best deal, but a 40-year-old woman in good health will likely pay $30 or so a month for a $500,000 20-year guaranteed term policy. In my book, spending just $30 a month for peace of mind that your family will be taken care of is a major bargain. —*S.O.*

"We Don't Know Where To Start"

Tax debt, garnished wages, zero savings, and a faltering marriage: Repairing this family's finances was anything but simple.

Erin Mason*, 38, may be a Web-search expert, but she and her husband, Jeff, 40, have been feeling pretty lost: "We owe nearly $15,000 in back taxes," she told me last summer. "Our wages have been garnished. We have two liens on our house. We both make good money, but we can't get ahead. We don't know where to start."

Erin wasn't kidding about the good money part. Together, she and Jeff, a systems administrator, net nearly $6,800 each month. But they're so far behind on their income tax payments that the state garnishes $800 per month from Jeff's paychecks, and the couple also pays $283 toward federal back taxes each month. These payments are included in their monthly expenses of $5,900 ($2,100 goes toward the mortgage on their Portland, Oregon, home). Despite a $900 monthly surplus, Erin worries about providing for their children: Andy, 16; Meg, 10; and Joseph, 12, whose developmental disability is another financial concern. In fact, Erin has even considered filing for bankruptcy.

Bankruptcy? When you make more than $100,000? I don't think so. The Masons need to fix their own mistakes. Erin seemed ready to get down to work, but I would soon find out that she and Jeff weren't exactly on the same page.

When Erin and I first spoke, I found myself confused. Despite that extra $900 each month, the Masons had saved very little. "We're scraping by," Erin said. Yet her expense list included $60 a month for pet food and vet care, $125 for meals out, $67 for a YMCA membership, $48 for magazines, newspapers, and books, $200 for Costco runs, and $86 for charitable donations.

They clearly weren't spending responsibly. And there was another issue. Erin told me she was serious about fixing their financial mess, but that Jeff felt differently—he spent about $100 a month adding to his massive sports memorabilia collection. "He has no perception of how much he really spends," said Erin, who estimated that Jeff had dropped up to $30,000 on the collectibles over the years.

I was eager to tell Jeff that selling this collection could be their ticket out of trouble: Even if it brought only $15,000, they could pay off the entire amount due on their back taxes. I had also figured out that the Masons were heading for more tax trouble in the coming year. As an independent contractor, Erin must pay quarterly state and federal income tax, including self-employment tax. Yet she wasn't setting aside what she owed. Finally, I had my eye on Erin's $27,000 student loan (she earned her bachelor's degree in June 2010—her job lets her work at home and set her own hours). She started repaying in January 2011, meaning another $200 to $400 monthly expense. Unless the Masons made some changes, that payment would be tough to handle.

When it was time for my chat with the couple, I asked if Jeff would unload some of his collection. He said, "I'll think about it"—but his tone sounded more like "No way." To my dozens of other questions about their finances, he often just said, "I don't know." I told him that by refusing to work with Erin, he was behaving like the fourth child in this family. He went silent, but he didn't stay that way: A few days after my dose of tough love, Erin told me that Jeff had admitted their constant squabbles about money had left him uncertain he wants to stay in the marriage.

I told Erin that no matter what happens, it's time for her to make better choices. First things first: The unneces-

> It's time to make better choices—the unnecessary spending has to stop.

sary spending has to stop. Instead of buying books and magazines, they could use the library. At Costco, Erin must make a list—focusing on needs, not wants. And while charity may be noble, the Masons can't afford it right now. What Erin can't afford *not* to do, however, is follow my plan to turn things around:

Control the cash flow. Unfortunately, Erin must take a drastic step and move all the couple's money to a new checking account—in her name only. She needs to hold the purse strings from now on.

Get a will and trust. The Masons have neither, which puts their children at risk. I sent Erin and Jeff my Must Have Documents Kit (available at suzeorman.com) and asked them to fill out the forms pronto.

Purchase ample life insurance. The couple had a $90,000 policy on Jeff's life, which is equal to about 1.5 years of their living expenses. You need a death benefit equal to at least 20 times your annual living needs—and the Masons' policy should insure Erin's life, too, since she's also a breadwinner. Erin went to selectquote.com and qualified for a $1.2 million, 15-year-level term policy costing just $100 a month.

Create a special needs trust. If anything happened to Erin and Jeff, whatever inheritance Joseph received could be kept in this account to ensure that he qualified for the federal Supplemental Security Income program. SSI provides financial support to the disabled, but disqualifies any individual with more than $2,000 in assets (excluding a home and a car) from receiving benefits. Should Joseph inherit anything more, keeping the money in this trust would allow him to remain eligible for those federal funds.

Set aside money for taxes. I want Erin to arrange an automatic deposit into a savings account so the money is waiting when the quarterly payments are due. This will help prevent another massive bill next April.

Build an emergency fund. Set up an automatic monthly deposit from a checking account into a separate savings account used only for true emergencies. You can shop for the best savings accounts at depositaccounts.com.

Keep the car. Erin has 18 months left on a car loan costing the couple $415 a month. (They own Jeff's car outright.) When the loan is paid off, Erin needs to drive that car for at least five more years and put the $415 toward the emergency fund. In five years that would add about $25,000 to their savings account.

Erin was enthusiastic about following through. "After we spoke, I canceled cable, saving $35 a month, tweaked our YMCA membership to be summer only—part of Joseph's ongoing therapy is swimming—and scaled back the charitable giving," she said. She's got the life insurance, and is working on the special needs trust. Best of all, after his initial resistance, Jeff came around. Erin told me, "He's giving me a ton of stuff to sell on eBay, and he's researching ways to save energy in the house and make our own home improvements. He's taking your words as a personal challenge." Music to my ears!

Buckling down is hard, but Erin has been so willing to change. And that's the attitude that will help her become the mom she wants to be: one who's committed to doing the right thing for her family. **O**

All names have been changed.

The Courage to Begin

You may be feeling every bit as stuck as Erin was. If so, do what she did: change. Here's how:

▇ **Ask** for help. Maybe you've got a financially savvy friend—ask her how she does it. Or maybe you've been shouldering the family bills alone—ask your partner to help you brainstorm better solutions. But…

▇ **Know** that ultimately you have to fix things. Erin was considering bankruptcy—she just wanted the problem to go away. Reality check: The problem isn't going anywhere. So will you retreat in fear? Ignore it? No. You will take charge and make things right.

▇ **Accept** that you will always face obstacles. Maybe your issues aren't as extreme as the Masons', but we all have financial concerns. I'm not asking you to be perfect with your money. I'm asking you to be prepared for whatever stumbling blocks you may face.

▇ **Make** the hard choices. I know it's tough to cut the small luxuries when you're strapped—you can't swing a big vacation, so shouldn't you get to have that $100 cable package? Not if you can't afford it. That might seem harsh, but I promise, when you embrace change, your courage will be rewarded. **—S.O.**

"What's Your Money Personality?"

Are you a penny-pincher, a financial wreck, a spender, a daredevil, or on the right track?

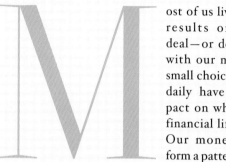

Most of us live with the results of how we deal—or don't deal— with our money. The small choices we make daily have a huge impact on what kind of financial life we have. Our money choices form a pattern, and this pattern becomes a money personality.

Do you pinch pennies? Overspend wildly on your credit cards? Find it impossible to save? Or are you someone who has her money under control? This quiz is designed to give you a better idea of how you handle your money and why you make the financial decisions you do. Choose the description under each entry that most applies to you.

Saving

A. When you receive a windfall such as a tax refund or a bonus check, you don't even consider saving it. Instead, you buy something extravagant or go on vacation.

B. Every month you sock away a larger percentage of your household income than is really comfortable for you, even when it means doing without "luxuries" such as dinner out or a movie.

C. You have no money in savings, you're behind on repaying your student loans, and while you keep promising yourself to sign up for your employer's 401(k) plan, years have gone by and you haven't done it.

D. Not only do you not save or invest, you have borrowed against the cash value in your life insurance policy and/or taken a home equity line of credit to pay off your credit cards. A few months later, you have even more debt.

E. You save a manageable amount every month, with specific goals in mind.

Spending

A. You buy what you want, when you want it—on credit if necessary—telling yourself that you'll earn the money to pay for it.

B. You put off buying the essentials, although you can easily afford to pay for what you need.

C. Shopping is a competitive sport for you. If a friend buys the latest skirt or jacket, you have to have one, too.

D. Your closet is full of clothes you've never worn. You have boxes full of products you've ordered but never use, and you probably have collections of watches, bags, or shoes.

E. You buy what you need, aren't often tempted by what you don't need, and understand the difference between a need and a want.

Bills and Records

A. You can't be bothered to balance your checkbook. Shouldn't the banks keep track of your money?

B. You check all your account statements frequently, either by phone or online, to make sure your records match exactly. You keep your ATM receipts, credit card vouchers, and canceled checks for years.

C. Because you don't pay your bills on time, you often owe a late fee, and sometimes you can't even find your bills amid the clutter on your desk.

D. You have a dozen credit cards and pay only the minimum amount due on each. Your attitude is, *It doesn't matter what I owe; it only matters what I own.*

E. Your checkbook is balanced, and your bills are paid as soon as they come in. You pay taxes when they are due, and you don't get large refunds.

Giving

A. When it comes to charity, you tend to give impulsively and you're likely to give more than you can afford.

B. You give to charity but restrict your giving to relatively small amounts—$5 or $10—compared to what you could give.

C. You repeatedly donate large amounts of your income to your favorite religious or community group, even though you don't have a retirement savings program.

D. You rarely give money to charity—unless it involves a social event you want to attend or a raffle with great prizes.

E. Every month you write a check for the same affordable amount to the charities of your choice. You've mindfully budgeted your money and your time to support the causes that are important to you.

Relationships

A. On a whim, you would volunteer to lend a relative or friend a significant sum of money—even if you suspected that he or she might not be able to pay you back.

B. Although you have money, you rarely carry enough cash to cover your share of expenses on evenings out.

C. You never discuss finances, even with people close to you—you'd be mortified if they found out how you handle your money.

D. Your spouse pleads with you not to spend so much. But you can't, or won't, stop spending, although you know you're creating a strain on your relationship.

E. You and your significant other talk openly about money. You keep separate checking accounts but also have a joint account for household expenses, to which you contribute proportionately according to income.

Planning for the Future

A. You're convinced that the likelihood of something bad happening to you is slim, so why would you need a will, a trust, life insurance, or a retirement plan?

B. You've created your own will using a self-help book and a computer program.

C. As far as you're concerned, the ins and outs of retirement planning, investment accounts, wills, and trusts might as well be subatomic physics.

D. With the high cost of living, saving money is totally out of the question.

E. You have a will, a trust, and a durable power of attorney for health care. Your retirement accounts are well funded. You and your spouse—and your children, if you have them—talk openly about how you're planning for your financial future. **O**

Scoring

Count how many of each letter you have circled, and record the number below. The biggest number will reveal your primary money traits.

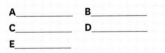

A_____   B_____
C_____   D_____
E_____

A. Financial daredevil

You relish living on the financial and emotional edge, spending more than you can afford because you crave the excitement of walking a financial high wire. You are generous, true, but you are too often reckless, and your choices are limiting tomorrow's freedom for today's thrills. You identify yourself more by what you do than by who you are, which means that somewhere along the way you've lost a sense of your own identity.

If you fall off that financial cliff you're peering over, you can get seriously hurt. Ask yourself, *Why do I take the risk of hurting myself and those who love me?* Now begin to act in your own best interest.

B. Penny pincher

Being a penny-pincher doesn't mean you're poor; on the contrary, you probably have more than enough to live on. But you won't spend your money; you hoard it because you are afraid to let it go—which means, in my opinion, that you are afraid of never having enough. Usually, people who are penny-pinchers grew up in families where either money or love was scarce; as a result the kids grew up with fear and shame—two big obstacles to wealth.

When you block the flow of money out, you also block the flow of money *in*. You need to open your clenched fist to receive—even if it's one finger at a time.

C. Financial wreck

Your friends would be shocked to know just how financially chaotic your life is, because—so far, at least—the disorganized condition of your finances remains your little secret. It's likely you have low self-esteem and don't really believe you can take care of yourself.

The first step for you is to become honest with yourself and those around you. When a car has been in a wreck—as you have been, both emotionally and financially—it needs major repairs. Ask a close friend or family member for help. Remember, when you talk about money with honesty and courage, anything can be mended.

D. Spendthrift

Your spending is way out of control. You probably know this because most spendthrifts get that way by watching a spendthrift parent. Sooner rather than later, financial reality will catch up with you—with crushing credit card interest or, in the worst case, bankruptcy. Wouldn't you rather put a stop to it before that happens?

Look around your house at all the things you've bought, and rate them on a scale of 1 to 10 by how much joy and value they have given you. Then pretend your house is on fire and you have five minutes to grab everything you want to keep. If you are like most people, not one thing you'd take is something you've bought. Remember that the next time you go out to spend.

E. On the right track

Congratulations! You are creating a life where people come first, then money, then things. Either you grew up in a family that had a very healthy relationship with money or one that was so disrespectful of money that you refused to repeat its serious mistakes. Either way, you've learned to value who you are over what you have. You're on the right road. —*S.O.*

"It's Important To Face Reality And Do What Is Right for You Over The Long Term."

Q Please help us before we have no money left. My husband and I are in our mid-60s and have lost more than half the money in our 401(k) and Roth IRA accounts. Our financial adviser suggested that we not panic and that we stay the course. We took his advice, only to watch our funds continue to shrink. Now my husband is talking about funding our Roth and SEP IRA [for those who are self-employed] accounts before tax preparation this year, but with the poor economy, the thought of putting more money into these accounts really scares me. How do we protect what we have?

Suze: It is not panicking to want to protect what you have; it's sound, rational thinking. Since you are in your mid-60s, I'm guessing you may be retiring sooner rather than later and will need to start tapping some of your savings. But I'm concerned that your accounts are down by more than half. That shouldn't be the case if you had the right mix of stocks and bonds in your investments. As a general rule, people in their 60s who are nearing retirement should have at least 60 percent of their money in individual bonds or stable-value investments. (I prefer individual bonds, such as U.S. Treasury, over bond mutual funds because they have a set maturity date, so you know when you'll get your principal back as well as any accrued interest.) If your portfolio had a big stake in these less volatile investments, your overall losses this year should have been in the vicinity of 15, not 50, percent.

I want you to sit down with your husband and your financial adviser and review your current mix of stocks and bonds. If your adviser has put all your money into stocks, he or she had better have a very good reason for doing so. And if that's indeed the case, I recommend that you rebalance your portfolio: Move money out of your stock investments and into bonds. It won't make up for what damage has already been done, but it will protect you against even more losses if the market drops.

Q My husband and I have two children. Our daughter just graduated from college, where housing and tuition ran $17,000 a year. She will repay $15,000; we assumed the rest of the debt for her. Our son is now a senior at a private college. His school gave him a few small scholarships, but his tuition alone this year was $45,000. As with our daughter, he will take on $15,000 and we will pay the balance. Of course, we don't have this kind of money saved. We applied for all the assistance we could think of, but because we each make a good living, my husband and I don't get much tax relief. We're up to a whopping $98,000 in loans. Should we max out our home equity? We're so proud of our children, but we are literally forever in their debt.

Suze: Lots of parents find your situation frighteningly familiar. The sad fact is that college costs are rising at a rate that far outpaces the growth in household income, which has necessitated both parents and their children taking on huge amounts of student loan debt. So in the spirit that tough times require making tough choices, I'm going to give you a qualified green light to use your home equity to help cover college costs. But you are never to max out your available home equity—that's too risky. Tapping 30 percent is as high as you ever want to go.

My take on this issue may surprise many of you. In the past, I've gone on the record as saying it's dangerous to use home equity to pay for college. I haven't changed my mind; the risk is still front and center. If you fall behind on your home equity payments, you could lose your house. But you face a good deal of risk with college loans, too. Failure to repay means your wages can be garnished, and even if you were to file for bankruptcy, student loans are rarely forgiven.

While there are risks associated with both, I see a few advantages to using a home equity loan (HEL). First, I'm assuming you have a strong credit score. That should allow you to qualify for an HEL with a lower interest rate than what most parents end up paying on private and federal loans for their kids. You also get a better deal with an HEL because the interest will be tax deductible; with student loans, you can deduct up to only $2,500 a year if you and your husband report less than $140,000 in adjusted gross income and your kids remain dependents for tax purposes. It's very important that you opt for a fixed-rate loan so you will never have to worry about increasing installments. HELs—as opposed to home equity lines of credit (HELOCs)—are typically the best way to go when you want a fixed rate.

Once you start borrowing against the value of your home, the hard work begins. Your family must cut all non-essential spending so you have more income to put toward paying back the HEL as quickly as possible. It's not enough to know you gave the kids a good education; you need to give yourselves the security you're now borrowing against.

Q I'm in my late 20s, and I'm determined to get smart about investing. When it comes to mutual funds, I hate not knowing exactly what I'm opting into. I try to be a socially responsible person and don't want to contribute to companies that may be harming the causes I'm passionate about. I've heard of politically and socially correct funds, but I'm not sure how to find them and which ones to trust. Please help me be an accountable, engaged member of society and still meet my financial goals.

Suze: Can I just start by saying thank you? It's not every day I get a question that makes me smile. I've said this over and over: The earlier you get serious about your money, the more successful you'll be. And your desire not only to do well with your investments but also to make sure that those investments do good for the world is a fabulous thing.

The funds you're interested in fall under the category of socially responsible investing (SRI). According to investment research firm Morningstar, there are now nearly 250 such funds, and they're all different. Some SRI funds focus on the negative, meaning they don't include any "sin stocks," such as those offered by companies that do business in areas like tobacco, alcohol, gambling, nuclear energy, or weapons manufacturing. Anything that passes the sin screen is eligible for consideration. Many funds go one step further by actively buying into companies with good records on environmental and social issues.

While I admire your not wanting to compromise your principles, you may have to make a concession on something else that's also very important: performance. I'm a huge believer in keeping costs down to maximize your net returns, which is why I always recommend index funds and exchange-traded funds (ETFs). With annual expense ratios typically around 0.2 percent, they're the most cost-effective way to invest. (The expense ratio is the annual charge all investors pay to cover fund management costs.) But many popular SRI funds have expense ratios of 1 percent or more. The difference between 0.2 and 1 percent may not sound like much, but it can add up to thousands of dollars over time, so aim to keep your costs as low as possible.

Domini (domini.com) and Pax World (paxworld.com) are two of the oldest and most respected SRI fund companies. The Vanguard FTSE Social Index Fund has very low costs (an expense ratio of just 0.29 percent), but its performance has been middling the past few years. The TIAA-CREF Social Choice Equity fund has solid performance and a 0.38 percent expense ratio. I also recommend checking out socialfunds.com.

Q In 2005, at the age of 40, I made the difficult decision to leave my marriage of 16 years. At the time, I was in school with just over a year to go before receiving my degree. Fast-forward to today: I still haven't been able to find a full-time position in my field. I've got $17,000 in credit card debt, $21,000 in student loans, a car payment, and an interest-only, variable-rate home loan that will adjust in two and a half years. I take in about $37,000 annually. How will I ever be able to save for today, for retirement, for my sons' futures? I feel completely overwhelmed. Where do I begin, and how do I prioritize?

Suze: I understand that you feel swamped, but I'm thrilled that you recognize the need for a plan. Let's dispense with what I *don't* want you to focus on: paying for your sons' college educations. There is no more loving decision you can make than to build your own financial safety net so that you'll be self-sufficient later in life rather than being so strapped that you become a burden to your children.

Your overriding goal must be to stay current on all your monthly debt. Pay at least the minimum amount due on your credit cards each month, and keep up with the car payment. That should result in a strong credit score, which means you may be able to ask to have your cards' interest rates reduced.

Next, ask your mortgage lender what your payment would be if the adjustment hit today. If the answer scares you, I want you to consider selling now and moving into a rental. Don't sit and worry for the next two and a half years or pray that your income will go up. If you can sell and make enough to cover your mortgage and moving costs, I suggest you do it now. The move will give you a better grip on tomorrow by reducing your costs today. Assuming that renting will free up some money, I want you to open two accounts that will help you establish peace of mind: an emergency cash fund and a Roth IRA. When you find full-time work in your chosen field—and you will, stay positive—you can revisit buying a home.

Q I am living with a man who's worth more than a million dollars. When we started dating, I jokingly told him that if we ever got married and it didn't work out, all I wanted was a plane ticket home. Well, we're now talking about a prenuptial agreement, and he keeps bringing up that comment. His son, who doesn't like me very much, wants everything written down so that if his father dies or we get divorced, my children and I wouldn't get a cent. My kids are older, so I'm not worried about them, but I need to be able to support myself—as far as money goes, I've got nothing to bring to the table. My boyfriend said I could live in his home, and his son (who's financially sound) would dole out cash as I need it. What should I do?

Suze: This situation is no joke. With your boyfriend hiding behind your tongue-in-cheek comment for protection, I'm not sure this relationship is going to fly. What kind of man would want his wife to answer to his son for money—especially when he knows that his son doesn't like her? If your boyfriend continues to put his son's desires ahead of yours, you need to seriously consider whether he's the right man for you. Negotiating a prenuptial agreement is the perfect way for you to talk about these important issues. Make it clear that you respect his right to leave everything he accumulated before marrying you to his son, but acknowledge in the prenup that assets and debts accrued during the marriage would be split evenly.

I also want you and your lawyer to discuss setting up a life estate on the house. This document would allow you to stay for as long as you want if your boyfriend dies first. After you move or pass away, the house would go to whomever he designated in his trust; in this case, probably his son. Everybody wins: You know you'll always have a roof over your head, your boyfriend gets to take care of his family, and his son can rest assured that he'll get his inheritance.

Now, if your boyfriend balks at any of this, I think you should run. When a person can't share his financial life, I question his ability to share his heart. The way we handle money is a manifestation of who we are inside, and how he approaches the topic signifies his love and respect for you. Without those two ingredients, you shouldn't be considering a walk down the aisle.

Q I'm 23 and recently began working as a speech therapist. I'm making decent money but don't have a plan for it. I've got a $17,000 student loan on which I pay the minimum plus a bit more each month. I also intend to get married in a year. We can't pay for the wedding out of pocket, and I don't want to stop putting extra dollars toward my loan or emergency savings. My boyfriend can't help because he's still in school and has loans of his own, which total about $85,000. Maybe I'm naive, but I want to have a dream wedding, which will cost $15,000 at the very least. Where do we get the funding—another loan? If so, can I lump it together with my existing one? Please help me come up with a strategy.

Suze: You need to stop dreaming and be honest with yourself. Neither you nor your boyfriend can afford an expensive wedding right now. I doubt any bank would loan you money for a wedding given your financial situation, and if one did, I bet the interest rate would be well above 15 percent—way too high. I don't want you planning a plastic wedding. If you charge $15,000 on credit cards and slowly chip away at the balance, you could be paying for it until your 25th anniversary. Over that quarter of a century, you will have paid nearly $15,000 in interest—that's equal to the cost of the party itself!

Instead of being so focused on your fantasy wedding, which is going to last only one day, focus on creating a marriage that can last a lifetime. That means being financially responsible to each other. Since your boyfriend already has a big loan hanging over his head (and you aren't exactly debt free yourself), I don't think you should be adding any more pressure to your relationship by borrowing money for a wedding. Digging yourselves deeper into debt is no way to start a life together.

My advice to you is to plan a wedding you can afford to pay for outright. I realize that may require you to wait a bit longer, perhaps until your boyfriend is out of school and working to reduce his loans and contribute to a wedding fund. Or you can have a small ceremony that symbolizes what's most important: your love for each other. In a few years when your finances are in great shape, you can throw yourselves an extravagant anniversary party.

Q **Two years ago, I discovered that my stepdaughter, then a college sophomore, had $1,500 in credit card debt. My husband got her an interest-free card, and they agreed she'd pay it off over the next 18 months. That never happened. Last summer she worked 40 hours a week but managed to triple what she owed. Again her father rescued her. I'm going crazy trying to accept what I consider a lack of good parenting. He even used a portion of his retirement savings to pay down her cards,** **though we still have some debt of our own. My stepdaughter works part-time, barely passes her courses, and still gets spending money. I made her a budget, which she looked at once but never used. She lives in her own comfortable world doing whatever she wants. How do I put a stop to this?**

Suze: The problem isn't with your stepdaughter so much as with your husband. Men who overspend on their children are often trying to overcome their guilt. In this instance, your husband may feel he's to blame for putting his daughter through the pain and loss of his divorce. You need to work on him, not her. He has to realize that his behavior is actually hurting his daughter. That's hard for divorced parents to come to terms with, so be supportive but firm. As straightforward as the problem is to you, it's that emotionally charged for him. You'll gain nothing by attacking.

Remember, this isn't about asking him to choose between you and his child. If there isn't enough money to pay your bills or get through retirement, you're both going to be in major trouble, to say nothing of his daughter. Show him that he must choose to take care of himself first. When he does, all three of you will be fine.

Your biggest challenge is to help your husband see his daughter's behavior for what it is: a cry for help. Her financial irresponsibility is the mark of an insecure, lost girl, not a strong woman, and his indulgence is keeping her powerless. A father should give his daughter the tools she needs to grow into a confident, self-sufficient adult. Only when she takes control of her life will she have control of her money—and the same goes for your husband. **O**

Get Smart About College Spending

Tapping your home equity to pay for your kids' education is a reasonable move only if you've exhausted all other possibilities. Here's what you should consider long before you contemplate borrowing against your home:

■ **Make sure your kids max out on student aid.** Please don't feel guilty about this; they need to take on some of the cost themselves. Besides, repayment terms for students are better than what parents can get. A repayment plan that took effect in mid-2009 ensures that your child's monthly student loan payment will not exceed 15 percent of his or her disposable income, and any outstanding balance after 25 years will be forgiven.

■ **Shop for scholarships.** Don't just take the word of your guidance counselor or college consultant—put your own elbow grease into looking for every possible bit of aid. Check out fastweb.com for a free database of scholarships.

■ **Consider a less expensive route.** By doing your homework, you can find plenty of public universities—as well as special programs within a school—that deliver a terrific education at a much lower cost than many private institutions. A solid public school education that doesn't leave you or your children owing six figures may be what's best for you and your family.

■ **Start a 529 savings plan.** There's no income limit on who can make use of these savings vehicles for college. Interest on invested money is tax deferred, and withdrawals used to pay for college costs are tax free. Parents can learn more about 529s at savingforcollege.com. —S.O.

The 10-Step Life Renewal Plan

Ask yourself these questions to figure out what's working, reject what's not, and move toward your best decade yet.

1 Does the way you spend your time reflect what's important to you? List your top five priorities—marriage, children, career, volunteer work, and so on—and track how many hours you devote to each in a week. If any numbers are too low, recalculate your time budget so you can live according to who you want to be.

2 Does your BlackBerry get more attention than your family and friends? Resolve to switch off your gadgets during private moments so you can nourish personal connections with complete focus.

3 Are you nursing a grudge or two? Let bygones be bygones, and free yourself from the emotions that weigh you down.

4 Who should be in your life? Phase out any so-called friends who offer only criticism and negative energy. Surround yourself with people you admire, who believe in you and want you to succeed.

5 Have you typecast yourself? You may cherish your responsibilities as a mother, but "Mom" is not the whole of who you are. Ask yourself if one role is draining all your energy, leaving other expressions of your authentic self unfulfilled.

6 What battle are you fighting? Is your husband really the one who's letting you down, or are you blaming him for the pain of a past relationship? Are you doing what's best for your kid, or are you parenting with a chip on your shoulder left over from your own childhood? Remember: You are not a prisoner of your legacy.

7 How can you live greener? Can you swap your gas guzzler for public transportation? Trade plastic bottles for a thermos? Go meatless once a week? Pinpoint changes you can make now.

8 What are your goals? Define your specific goals with measurable outcomes, and then assign yourself a timeline. Passion and willpower alone will not cut it—you need to have a strategy.

9 Who is standing in your way? The answer may be you. Reject self-loathing and treat yourself with the kindness and the respect that you would show your best friend.

10 What one thing can you do for yourself every day? It could be as simple as finding 20 minutes to take a bath (my wife, Robin, swears by that).

Every day gives you a brand new opportunity to pay attention to your own needs and to make choices that you can feel good about. This year, you need to claim the right to minister to yourself. ◖

Give Yourself a Mental Makeover

Adjust your view of the world, let go of negative feelings, and turn dreams into goals.

Nobody can resist a dramatic makeover, whether the before-and-after photos are evidence of a killer workout routine, a wardrobe revamping, or the genius of a makeup artist. But there's another kind of makeover that transforms your life from the inside out, and we all have the power to achieve it. Hard work is necessary, requiring you to make some major choices about how you think, feel, act, and react. But the payoff is looking in the mirror and knowing you're a better, happier, more peaceful version of yourself. No matter what or how you want to change, here's your plan for a revolution from within.

Own up.
When things aren't going your way, resist the temptation to point the finger at other people, and remember: You are the creator of your life experience. I'm not saying that your loved ones don't play a role in rocky relationships or that your boss can't be a jerk sometimes. Still, how you relate to others is completely in your hands. If you confront people with hostility, hostility is what you'll get back. If you instead rely on compassion and understanding, you'll likely see the principle of reciprocity kick in and your compassion flowing back to you. I've said it before, and I'll say it again: We teach people how to treat us.

Even if kindness isn't always repaid in kindness, remember that no one else has the power to hijack your state of mind. Your emotions belong to you alone. Start taking ownership of them now.

Be a trend-spotter.
Look for patterns in how you view yourself, your career, your bonds with friends and family—every aspect of your life. If fear and apprehension color how you raise your kids or negotiate the workplace, then you're bound to see failure and missed opportunities all around, even when things are going swimmingly. If you've become complacent in the role of put-upon spouse or saintly friend (the one who can always spare two hours on the phone to sort out a pal's latest crisis), your martyr complex will cast a negative spell on other relationships, too. Ask yourself what kind of lenses you're wearing and whether they're distorting your view of the world. When you adjust your perception, you transform your reality.

Shed toxic emotions.

If you are hampered by anger, anxiety, or the pain of betrayal, it's time to close that book and store it on your shelf; you'll know it's there, yes, but you won't have to read it every day. Or maybe guilt is your warden: You feel locked into unhappiness because you're being punished for the sins and errors of your past. Remember, guilt can be self-serving—a convenient excuse to beat yourself up on the sidelines instead of doing the harder, braver thing: jumping back in the game and giving it your best shot.

No matter what emotions burden you, closure is possible. Start by identifying what I call the minimal effective response: the simplest action you can take to satisfy your need for resolution without creating new problems. Your minimal effective response can come in all kinds of forms. Do you need to pour out your heart in a letter to a parent or an ex (even if you never send it)? Should you clear the air with someone? Apologize? Forgive yourself? Go to confession? Meditate? Cut a certain person out of your life completely? Figure out the least you can do to clear your mind of debilitating thoughts. Unless you want your past to become your future, you need to let go. You can't reach your destination if you're always looking behind you.

Adjust your approach.

At this point, you've jettisoned negative thoughts, behaviors, and maybe even people from your life. Now reflect on ways you can improve how you engage with the world and the people you love most.

For example, perhaps you can recognize that your marriage is terrific except for those same dumb arguments that flare up every few weeks. In that case, pinpoint the triggers that ignite conflict, and simply choose not to react to them. Or when you feel trouble brewing, take a long, deep breath—in midsentence if necessary—and stop yourself before you blurt out something you'll regret. Disputes will still bubble up, but they'll move toward a different outcome: one of mutual understanding, rather than a pointless battle to prove each other wrong.

Or maybe your main issue is that you're a dreamer who lacks direction. If so, recast yourself as a goal-setter. The major difference between a dream and a goal (whether it's to get in shape, save a down payment for a home, or re-tune your career) is a timeline for progress coupled with

> The major difference between a dream and a goal is a timeline for progress coupled with accountability— so mastermind your plan and get moving.

accountability—so mastermind your plan and get moving. Whatever the challenge before you, keep in mind that a feverish pace doesn't necessarily guarantee the quickest route from A to Z. Keep your tempo slow and steady, and check in with yourself to make sure that your hour-to-hour decisions and behavior jibe with your ambitious, long-term goals.

Write a new life script.

If you're stuck in the doldrums of your daily routine, it's time to draft a plan to change your behavior. Start small: If you always exercise alone, try a group class at the Y. If your circle of friends hasn't varied in years, make it a goal to talk to three new people every day. If you always sit in the back and stay quiet in staff meetings, next time grab a spot up front and speak up. Pushing yourself outside your comfort zone means that you'll find new opportunities to live differently—and better.

Accept yourself.

This may strike you as an odd directive for a makeover column. But a successful reinvention doesn't happen when you hate the person you are. It happens when you love yourself enough to believe that you can do better and deserve better. The more you understand who you are and who you want to become (someone who's not as critical, or guilt-ridden, or anxious, or bitter, or...), the less validation you'll need from others.

Picture your typical response when, say, a grocery store clerk is rude to you. Are you rude right back? Do you hold your tongue but find that the incident casts an angry cloud over the rest of your afternoon? Or do you think, *Wow, she must be having a bad day,* and move on? When you lack respect for yourself, you will cling to every morsel of respect you can get from other people—and you'll feel threatened and unmoored if they don't cooperate. But when you have an internal reservoir of dignity and self-acceptance, you won't be begging others to fill it.

Remember that life is managed, not mastered, and sometimes we need to be more hands-on in directing our behavior and outlook. Seize this moment to put yourself in the shop for an inside-out tune-up. When you've pulled off a makeover worthy of your best self, the people around you won't just marvel at your stunning results—they'll feel blessed themselves, and maybe ready for a makeover of their own. ◖

Personal Power: 6 Rules for How to Harness Yours

Whether you're negotiating relationships with family and friends, setting boundaries for your kids, or trying to make your voice heard at work, the balance of power in everyday life is constantly shifting. Sometimes subtle diplomacy is required; other moments, you just need to dig in your heels. But if you often feel cornered or guilt-tripped into making decisions that don't mesh with your goals, here are six rules for creating a purposeful, effective, self-determined life, plus strategies for tapping your inner power reserves when you need them most.

Know who you are. A strong sense of self is the foundation of personal power. If you define yourself by what someone else thinks, you've already lost the battle. Assert the right to be who you want to be.

The scenario: Your mother-in-law considers you a bad parent because you work full-time and don't share her exact views on meal prep and discipline. Her constant criticism and passive-aggressive remarks drive you nuts. But if you're doing what's right for you and your children, why should her comments matter? Have the mettle to tell her that you respect her years of parenting experience but that she ought to respect *your* hard work, too—and keep her opinions to herself.

Live passionately. If there isn't something in your life that makes you wake up curious and excited to start the day, you will never be a powerful person. Passion is what fuels the jet engine propelling you toward your goals and a meaningful existence.

The scenario: You've been hitting "snooze" on your alarm clock a lot lately, and your afternoons at work just slip through your fingers (aimless Internet surfing, perhaps?). To recharge your batteries, think of your favorite part of any given day: the endorphin rush after a long jog, the thrill of winning a new client (or the novelty of meeting prospective ones), or the fun of trying out a new recipe. Identify the things that give you a boost, then infuse more of them into your normal routine. Figuring out what nourishes you and then being disciplined about doing it—that's real power.

Keep to a plan. People with power have not only a goal but a means of reaching it. It doesn't matter how smart, energetic, and insightful you are—if you're not headed to a destination with a map to guide you, then your intelligence and ambition are going to waste.

The scenario: You haven't been promoted in six years, though you once dreamed of running your department. You're asking yourself why others move forward while you stand still, but maybe the only difference between you and them is a solid plan. Make a list of steps you can take to improve your job prospects. Can you approach your boss and discuss your future at the company? Take a class to fill gaps in your skill set? Research other firms where you'd have more room to grow? You have the power to sketch your own blueprint for a more fulfilling career.

Embrace risk. Great businesspeople don't operate on guarantees when they switch companies or launch a startup; instead they rely on a steadying belief in their abilities, their confidence to try something new, and a certain

in a dead-end job. They don't say, "Those can't be my kid's drugs; his friends must have snuck them into the house." A woman with power has the guts—and the smarts—to look the truth in the eye, even when it's painful or shocking.

The scenario: You've been friends with Jane for 15 years, and you've seethed over her gossiping, attention hogging, and undermining comments, which were amusing and forgivable in her 20s but not the stuff of friendship in middle age. But your social circles overlap, your husbands watch football together, and your kids have playdates—phasing Jane out of your life is more trouble than it's worth, right? Wrong. If you have to deny your own feelings and principles to maintain a "friendship," then you're refusing to be your authentic self. Face up to the fact that the relationship is over, and then do what you need to—whether it's a frank conversation or a quiet but firm withdrawal—to end it. Establish your right to spend your time as you wish and deserve to.

Be assertive. An aggressive person wants to advance her agenda even at the expense of others—in fact, she may secretly enjoy watching others fail where she succeeds. An *assertive* person, by contrast, will reach her goal while still considering the feelings and best interests of others.

The scenario: You have an ailing parent who requires full-time care. But your kids also need your attention, your siblings live across the country and can't pitch in much, and Dad resists moving into the assisted-living facility you've researched and recommended. Worse, he wants to make you feel terrible: "I spent decades sacrificing for you, and now look what you want to do," he says. Your response should be both compassionate and assertive. You might say, "It's because I love you—and my husband and my children—that we should establish a plan that works for all of us. Let's discuss our options and decide by the end of the week. I love you, but I will not let you make me feel guilty about a move we need to make."

focused restlessness. You can extend that kind of entrepreneurial thinking to any aspect of your life, whether it's overhauling your health and fitness habits or rejuvenating your friendships or marriage.

The scenario: You and your husband have fallen into a rut. Date nights are mundane, conversations peter out, your sex life is flagging. But what have you done lately to shake up the dynamic? You'll have to stretch yourself and reach for something more, even—or especially—if the effort feels awkward or unfamiliar. Maybe you'll book a surprise getaway, try something new in the bedroom, or consider couples' counseling. Whatever you choose, it will be a powerful feeling to take responsibility for reimagining and jump-starting your marriage.

Deal in the truth. Denial is not an aspect of powerful people's lives. They don't think it's "not so bad" to be stuck

> # A woman with power has the guts—and the smarts—to look the truth in the eye.

A final note: We may think of power as something that other people give us, but in fact we grant it to ourselves through our moment-to-moment decisions, our behavior, our thoughts. The antidote to feeling powerless is having faith in yourself—the confidence to determine the paths and outcomes of your best life. So if you're getting the short end of the stick, remember that power comes from within. You, right now, are a powerful person—you just have to plug in. **O**

Nine Holiday Headaches And How to Survive Them With Good Cheer

y dad used to joke that this is the season for people who aren't very close to crowd into a small space for far too long and make each other miserable! But that doesn't have to be you. How do you make your own season bright? First, figure out what you care about most—religious observance, quiet family time, festive meals, gift giving, or whatever. Next, set realistic expectations. To help you out, here's my advice for surviving nine typical holiday scenarios:

Scenario 1: Your uncle always comes for turkey dinner, drinks too much, then argues about politics. How do you keep things under control?

Let your uncle know in advance that this year's celebration is neither the time nor the place for him to misbehave. You can either lay down some very specific rules—no drinking and no talking politics, for starters—or you can disinvite him. If you choose the first option, you need to talk to him ahead of time; be direct because rude people don't pick up on subtle cues. Then stick to the rules, even if it means taking him aside if he acts up and asking him to leave.

Scenario 2: You have been very good about sticking to your diet and don't want to find yourself sliding backward. How can you resist the pressure from your pushy family to eat a big, decadent meal?

I grew up in a family that shared food to show love, so I know this can be a sensitive subject. To avoid hurt feelings, talk to your family ahead of time. You might say: "I have a lot invested in what I'm doing, so please don't take offense if I either bring my own food or turn down something you've worked hard to make. This is really important to me, and I appreciate your support." If you decide you're going to eat what's served, consider having a healthy snack at home first so you don't show up famished and end up overindulging.

Scenario 3: Your aunt is the worst gift giver. How do you diplomatically steer her in the right direction?

Why do you care what your aunt gives you? You don't have to like her gift—just graciously accept it, thank her, and then give it to charity. But if your goal is to encourage your aunt to be a better gift giver, come up with creative ways to do so. Suggest that she make a donation to your favorite charity in your name. Or agree to give each other books and suggest a list of titles. But no matter what, try to remember how lucky you are that your aunt is alive, that you get to spend time together, and that she cares enough to buy you a gift at all.

Scenario 4: You want to relax, but you're a perfectionist about the gifts, the decor, and the food. How do you keep from becoming so wiped out that you can't really enjoy the season?

Take a closer look at what's motivating you. You may think you're working hard to ensure that everyone else has a lovely time, but the more likely reason you're killing yourself is the need to be in control. If your goal is to create a great holiday for your loved ones, focus on them. Our home is always festive during the holidays, but we don't obsess about it. When the kids were younger, letting them decorate the Christmas tree was a family ritual. There would be a high concentration of ornaments right at the spot of their height each year, and then hardly any decorations above that. But the imperfections of the tree made it just perfect for our family. If you refocus your priorities, you're more likely to enjoy the holidays—and your family will enjoy you.

Scenario 5: Every year your kids have a long list of expensive gifts they want. How can you teach them to be happy with less this year?

Make the most of this teachable moment by asking your children to select one favorite gift on their lists and saying: "This year Christmas is going to be different. It will still be about togetherness, but because the economy is so bad, we're going to do only one gift per person. Next year may be a Christmas with more gifts, but right now we don't have the money." Depending on your kids' ages, this may be a good chance to convey the reality that the money you would have spent on gifts will pay for the food they eat and the car that gets everyone to school and work. Be honest and loving. Explain that you're cutting back not because they have been bad or aren't loved but because your top priority is to put a roof over their heads.

Scenario 6: Your husband's December mantra is "Bah! Humbug!" How can you help him get with the program?

Redefine the issue for him. This isn't about him investing in the holidays; it's about him investing in your happiness. By actively rejecting the holidays, he's rejecting you and an experience that has meaning to you. Explain why you love the holidays, and try to understand what exactly he dislikes so you can minimize his exposure to those things. For example, if he enjoys holiday music but finds the gift giving too commercialized, then blast holiday tunes all month long but don't put gifts under the Christmas tree until the very last minute. He may never find the same meaning or excitement that you do, but if he loves you, he should try to compromise.

Scenario 7: You're single and always get lonely this time of year. How can you get into the spirit of the season?

The best way to fill a hole inside yourself is to give away the thing you long for most. If you're yearning for someone to share the holidays with, then go be that person for someone else. Volunteer at a nursing home, a soup kitchen, a foster center, or a church. Help wrap presents for kids who think Santa isn't going to visit them this year. Bring the winter coat you haven't worn in years to a homeless shelter. Instead of focusing on what's missing in your life, focus on what you can give.

Scenario 8: You love your family, but after a few days cooped up together, you're ready to jump headfirst into a snowbank. How can you get some space?

You don't need to be a victim here. If your priority is to celebrate with your family while also preserving your sanity and enjoying some solo downtime, then structure your holiday in a way that gives you the space you need. It's never too late to rethink the way things have always been done so you can control your own schedule and accommodations. If everyone is going to be at Grandma's house for five straight days, maybe you show up on day two and leave at the end of day four—or stay at a nearby hotel or with a friend. But let your family know your schedule ahead of time; they'll be less likely to object to it if they have some notice.

Scenario 9: When your family gets together over the holidays they fight, often over silly old issues. How can you keep peace on Earth?

Christmas get-togethers are not the time to declare a family problem-solving session! It's not the time to say, "Since we're all here, let's talk about what happened when Grandma died and her stuff got divided up." If there's an important issue that the entire family needs to discuss, talk about it before you gather or let it wait until after the holidays. If a contentious topic comes up, say, "Let's all agree to schedule a time to get on the phone or meet in person next month. Not now. Let's just enjoy each other's company and make the most of this holiday."

> Holiday get-togethers are not the time for family problem solving!

"Forget New Year's Resolutions. Now's the Time to Audit Yourself And Make a Commitment To Real Change."

Today is your opportunity to call a time-out, reflect on what you're doing, and commit to changing the attitudes and behaviors that may be holding you back. I'm not talking about making a hollow resolution that you'll stick with for three days. Instead, let's look seriously at where you are in your life and how you can change for the better. Here are ten questions you need to ask yourself.

1 **Is what you're doing in your life working?** I hate it when I see people spending time and effort doing things that simply aren't working—and yet they do them over and over again. For example, if you're financially hanging on by your fingernails, then what you're doing is not working. You may tell yourself, *We have all these fixed expenses like house payments and car payments.* Well, let me tell you, nothing is fixed. If the life you've chosen has left you in the red, then you need to be willing to dump the house, lose the cars, and deal with the guilt when you can't afford to buy your kids what they want. If you're in a relationship that's stealing your energy, then you need to get out of your comfort zone and deal with it. Check every area of your life, and when you find one that isn't working, tell yourself, *This may have been my habit, but now's the time to change it.*

2 **Are your payoffs healthy?** People do things repeatedly because they're getting some kind of payoff. But oftentimes the rewards for your choices aren't healthy or constructive. People who smoke get a payoff

by feeling better in the moment, but over the long term, cigarettes rob them of their health and take years off their lives. You may be in a relationship in which you're neglected or emotionally or physically abused, but it's easier to stay than it is to admit there's a problem and get out. Sitting on the sidelines or putting up with less than you deserve because you don't have the courage to reach for something different is not my idea of a payoff.

3 **Are you getting in the way of your own success?** Ask yourself whether your decisions are carrying you toward what you want. For example, you may be afraid of elevators. If you work on the first floor of your building, then it's probably not a big problem for you. Let's say you hear about a better job on the 32nd floor, but you don't go for it because you don't want to get in that elevator or climb all those stairs every day. Your fear is disrupting the flow of your life. Or you might think your drinking is not a problem. But if it interferes with your relationships and sets a horrible example for your children, then it's time to make a change.

4 **Are you making everyone happy except yourself?** Maybe you don't want to work in the family business, but you feel obligated to get onboard. Maybe you don't want to stay in your marriage, but it would upset your family if you split. Maybe you dream of having a career, but now that you're a mother, you fear others will think you're selfish if you return to the workforce. It's easier to say no to yourself than to someone else, but I would hate for you to live this year—or the next 20 or 30 years—pleasing others while neglecting yourself. You need to look at why you're unwilling to stand up for who you are and what you want, and start working to change.

5 **Is the cost of what you're doing too high?** Let's assume that in order to have harmony in your marriage, you have to stop being who you are. Maybe you're an assertive woman who muzzles herself in order to get along with an overbearing husband. If you have to stop being all of who you are in order to be half of a couple, then the cost is too high. Or if the only way to make your boss happy and keep your job is to put up with abuse and insensitivity, and you head home day after day feeling drained and miserable, then the cost is too high. No matter the circumstance, you've got to weigh the price you're paying and decide whether it's worth it.

6 **Are you living with a chip on your shoulder?** Going through life motivated by anger and resistance will get you nowhere. If you resist promising ideas and opportunities because you're unwilling or afraid to care about something, then it's time to let go of negative baggage and steer your attitude in a more positive direction.

7 **Has it been too long since you relaxed?** People who are unhappy in their lives rarely take a deep breath. They don't sleep well, don't eat right, and carry tension in their bodies all the time. If you're overweight or feeling burdened by endless stress, your body is telling you something. It's time to start listening.

8 **Have you gotten too comfortable?** I think the term *comfort zone* is used inaccurately. A comfort zone is actually a stagnation zone: You're stuck because you're afraid to take a risk. People often tell me that the scariest risk is admitting that what they have isn't what they want. They're afraid to acknowledge that it's time for a change because they're scared to death about making it happen. Quit pretending that what you have is okay if that's not the case. You have the ability to create the life you want.

9 **Are you being spiritually fed?** Spirituality can be at the core of a healthy life, and yet we often neglect that aspect of ourselves because it's so difficult to quantify or even describe. But if you feel a void, then it's time to make a change from the inside out. If the path you've taken doesn't offer you peace, meaning, and purpose, then step off it and investigate new experiences. This could be as simple as trying meditation or as far-reaching as studying a new religion. Don't be afraid to explore new spiritual options.

10 **Are you low on your own priority list?** We all tend to live reactive rather than proactive lives: We wake up every day and deal with what is thrown our way. When women look at their own priorities and where they spend their time, they're usually way down on the list or not on it at all. Are you always doing for others and never taking time for yourself because you think it's selfish? The truth is that we need mothers, not martyrs. We need women, not sacrificial lambs. If you don't take care of yourself, then you can't take care of others. If you run out of time before getting around to the simple things you want—and need—to do, then you've got to make yourself a higher priority. Try that Pilates class at the gym, curl up with a best-seller, put your feet up with a cup of coffee, listen to your favorite music, or take some time away from the house with absolutely nothing to do except be with yourself. If your life has become so programmed, so scheduled, and so committed that you don't have time to nurture yourself, then it's time to make a change. **O**

Why You Deserve A Break Today—If Not Sooner

It's not selfish. It's not irresponsible. It'll send you back to your friends and family calmer, happier, and nicer. Here's how to grab a little private time for yourself.

Whenever I talk to women about making alone time a priority, it's clear to me that even the thought of it makes them feel guilty. Women have been socialized to be the nurturers, the loving mothers, wives, and domestic engineers. Between working, running a household, and raising overscheduled kids, there's no time left for "self." Unfortunately, women got the message that they were being negligent if they abandoned their posts and invested in themselves. This couldn't be more wrong.

The idea that it's selfish to take care of yourself is shortsighted and prevents you from being your best. If you're rolling your eyes because you believe private time is a luxury you can't afford, think of it this way: You can't give away what you don't have. Without a peaceful, well-rested, loving, tender spirit, you're in no position to be nurturing to your family or friends. We're like bank accounts: If we make only withdrawals (carpooling, work-

ing late, helping out a friend), we wind up emotionally and physically bankrupt. We all must make regular deposits to our minds, souls, and bodies. You must take time for you.

What does alone time accomplish?

The most important relationship you'll ever have is the one you create with yourself. How can you be a good friend to a stranger? You can't. Self-esteem and self-acceptance are dictated by how well you know yourself. If you don't talk to, listen to, and give to yourself, it's easy to forget who you are. If you don't check in, your internal dialogue—what you say to yourself every minute of every day—will run on automatic. Are you saying and believing things that add to your self-worth? Are you pausing to give yourself credit for new values you've developed? Are the labels you've created for yourself outdated? That's where alone time comes in. It can be an incredible process of rediscovery.

I'm talking to myself here unless you can cross the threshold that allows you to say sincerely, "I don't feel guilty for taking care of me." You have to really believe that you're not being selfish, egotistic, or negligent of others. You must admit that you need this and then claim it.

How do I find this elusive alone time in my schedule?

I promise you that this time is just as important as sleep in soothing the spirit and replenishing the body. Maybe get up at 6:00 instead of 6:30 so that you can take some time every day to meditate, pray, smell fresh air, or whatever it is that calms your spirit. And you also need blocks of extended time. On a Saturday morning or Sunday afternoon, make an appointment with yourself. Move yourself up on your priority list, and respect the time you set aside just as you would respect a meeting with a client or an appointment with your child's pediatrician. Plan ahead, make arrangements for anyone who would usually rely on you, and do your thing.

What counts as alone time?

When I talk about taking time for yourself, I mean one hour when you are not half of a couple, a mother of two, or one member of a group of friends—one hour when you can sit by yourself without a task in front of you. The time you spend alone at the grocery store, doing laundry, or commuting to work doesn't count. You don't do your nails during a therapy session, so don't make an appointment with yourself and do the laundry. You deserve some time alone without justifying it by multitasking.

Here's my rule of thumb about what qualifies as quality alone time: If you were doing the same activity with your kids, would it nourish your relationship with them? Watching a movie may be enjoyable, but it's not bringing you closer to the person sitting next to you. Since alone time is about building a relationship with yourself, the same holds true. You may enjoy reading the newspaper, but your brain is focused on a subject other than you. Sleep is important, but taking a nap with a friend wouldn't teach you anything about her.

It's different for everybody. You don't have to sit in a room alone and stare at the walls. A lot of people can get deeply into their thoughts and feelings when they go for a jog, but be honest with yourself about whether time at the gym gives you the chance to look inward. How about using your alone time to keep a journal or create a life plan? Like I said, it is different for everyone, so find what works for you. I get massages occasionally, and my instructions to my therapist are always the same: "I'm happy to talk until we start. Once we start, I'm not interested in conversation." Then I use the time to go over things in my mind and give myself both a physical and psychological tune-up. You have to be assertive enough to put up that boundary.

> Move yourself up on your priority list.

Script of the Month: How can I ask for alone time without hurting anyone's feelings?

What if your family or friends don't understand your need for alone time? You may say, "I need time for me," but they may hear, "I don't want to be around you, and I don't love you." You can't control that. They choose how they feel, and it's not your job to change their minds. Still, you can help them understand your needs. So that they don't perceive your investment in yourself as rejection or an affront to them, here's how I suggest you raise the discussion.

You: I want to talk to you about something that's important to me. I've realized that I don't spend much time by myself, and I'd like to get to know myself again. This is not because I don't want to be with you. This isn't about you; it's about me. I don't think I'm as good a friend to myself as I can be, so I'm going to try to devote some time to that.

If you have a partner who's prone to jealousy, insecurity, or paranoia, be very specific about what you will do with the time.

You: I was thinking I'd have some time to be still on Saturday afternoons. You can know where I am; I have no secrets about this. By the way, I recommend it for you as well, and you have my support to carve out time for solitude.

You may get resistance.

Him: We don't even have time for each other and now you want time alone?

You: You're right. We don't spend enough time together, and I think part of the reason is that I've lost myself. I need to get back in control of my world, and this is my first step.

Him: Let me guess: I'll be watching the kids while you're enjoying yourself. You're being selfish.

You: I hope you'll make an effort to think about this differently. I want to come up with a plan that works for both of us. I was hoping that you'd watch the children while I do my thing, and then I'll do the same while you're taking time to be by yourself. We could also arrange for them to have an extra playdate. It's something we have to figure out, but I do think that the benefits will outweigh the sacrifices we'll each have to make. Honey, I think this could be really good for us.

If he strongly resists this, continue to try to express your goals. If you just can't get through to him, it may mean that he's happy to be with you as long as you do what he wants when he wants. If he demands that you be constantly selfless and take care of him and his needs, that's all the more reason you need alone time—to get back on track with who you are, what you want, and what you deserve out of life. ◫

Six Rules of Talking And Listening

True or false: When you talk to other people, it's best to block your ears, dominate the conversation, and if they ask you what's wrong, chirp "Nothing." True!—if you want to live alone for the rest of your life. If not, Dr. Phil has a conversation repair kit for you.

When it comes to relating to each other, *communication* is perhaps the most overused term in our vocabulary. The problem is that most people don't really know what good communication is. But talking and listening are essential tools for learning about your partner's feelings, making your feelings known, and solving problems that arise within a relationship. As the saying goes, "It's better to light one candle than curse the darkness," so here's my attempt to shed some light on the subject and help you get better at the art of exchange.

1. **Insist on emotional integrity.** You gotta tell it like it is! You must insist that everything you say, imply, or insinuate is accurate, and if your partner challenges you on those messages, you must step up and own them. Mean what you say and say what you mean. You don't have to tell people everything you think or feel. But you do have to be accurate when you choose to disclose.

Suppose you're upset. When your partner senses that and asks, "Is something bothering you?" emotional integrity requires that you won't deny the message you're sending verbally or otherwise by saying, "Nothing is wrong; I'm fine." You may not be ready to discuss it, so the accurate answer might be, "I don't want to tell you right now; I'm just not ready to talk about it."

A lot of couples flagrantly violate this principle. Then they say, "We have trouble communicating." Of course they do—they both lie like dogs! And while we're on the subject: A material omission—leaving out something of crucial importance—is as much a lie as any actual misstatement.

2. **Be a two-way, not a one-way, communicator.** A one-way communicator talks but never listens and pays no attention to whether the listener appears to be "get-ting it." You know what I mean. For her it's all about the telling, as in, "All right. What I want you to do is go out there, get this work done, give these people this message, put those kids to bed, and come back in here."

If that's how you communicate, all you know is what you've said, and you haven't got a clue about what the other person heard. Result: conflict.

But as soon as a one-way communicator asks for feedback, look what happens:

She: "Here's what I'd like you to do: A, B, C, and D. Does that sound okay to you?"

He: "Well, L, Q, R, and P don't make a whole lot of sense to me."

No wonder they're not getting along—they're not even talking about the same thing! When she checks to make sure that he has received the message, she uncovers a communication glitch. By soliciting feedback—by giving just as much weight to what is heard as to what is said—you put a spotlight on the issues the two of you, together, need to clarify.

3. **Establish a motive.** Whether you're talking or listening, you need to be clear about why something's being said. Motive and message are important. If you've got a husband who says, "You're like the Spanish Inquisition. You're always asking me these questions and bugging me all the time," you need to look at what's behind those words. Is he trying to make you feel guilty because there's something he doesn't want you to see? Or are you trying to control too much of his life because you are insecure? In answering those questions, you'll figure out the motive and be able to move on from there.

4. **Check in with each other.** You and your partner must agree to test each other's messages and respond honestly. No more B.S. Ask your partner, "Is what you're saying really the way you feel? Is that true?" Remember that when you ask the question, you have to be ready to hear the true answer. And you've got to be willing to take the same test

yourself. If asked, "So you're really okay?" have the guts to say, "No, I'm not," when you're really not. Ask your partner the questions that will confirm his or her feelings.

⑤ Be an active listener. Most people are passive listeners. If you intend to become an active listener, you'll need to master two important tools. A famous psychologist named Carl Rogers called them Reflection of Content and Reflection of Feeling. I don't agree with a lot of what Rogers taught, but he hit the nail on the head with this one.

Reflecting a speaker's content means that you listen to the person; then you give him or her feedback that makes it clear you're receiving the factual message—but as you'll see, it ain't all about the facts. Here's an example of someone's getting the information but missing the message:

A: "Sorry I'm late. As I was leaving the house, my dog ran into the street and was hit by a car."

B (*reflecting the content*): "So your dog got hit by a car?"

A: "Right."

B: "Is he dead?"

A: "Uh-huh."

B: "So what did you do with the dog's body?"

Person B establishes that Person A has been heard, which addresses a fundamental need for A. But B has clearly missed the point. To be an active listener in an emotionally relevant situation, B has to do more than just reflect the factual information that A has conveyed. Reflection of feeling tells your partner not just that he's been heard but that you have "plugged into" his life and experienced it in some way, which is essential to his satis-

faction. Reflection of feeling sounds like this:

A: "Sorry I'm late. As I was leaving the house, my dog ran into the street and got hit by a car."

B (*reflecting the feeling*): "Oh, my gosh—you must feel terrible."

A: "Well, I do. We'd had the dog for 12 years, and my kids really loved him."

B: "I'm sure they must be so upset; I'm sorry you're going through this."

Being able to reflect the feeling, not just the content, is essential to the success of your communication.

⑥ Evaluate your filters. When you and I engage in conversation, I can't control how well you communicate; I can only control how well I receive what you're telling me. I can go on the alert to things that may distort the messages you're sending me—I call them filters. To be a good listener, you've got to know what your filters are. Maybe you're coming into a given conversation with an agenda. Maybe you're judging the speaker and don't trust him at all. Maybe you're angry. Any one of these psychological filters can dramatically distort what you hear.

Filters cause you to decide things ahead of time. You may have prejudged your partner and decided that he doesn't love you anymore. Result: No matter what he says to you, you're going to distort it to conform to what you're already thinking, feeling, and believing.

Take an inventory of your filters. If you're not aware of them, you can defeat the best communicator in the world because you'll distort the message, regardless of how well it was sent. **◻**

Talking Cures: A Crib Sheet

Choose the right communication environment. When the subject matter is weighty and emotionally charged, find a place where you won't be distracted and can devote yourself entirely to talking and listening.

Pick your battles. People's willingness to listen goes down dramatically after the first criticism in a conversation. With each successive criticism, their defensiveness goes up and their receptivity goes down. By the third criticism, you might as well be talking to yourself. Don't wander into saying, "And it also really bothers me

that…" If there's something you need to address, stick with that point and deal with other issues another time.

Beware of undoing. People will ratchet up their courage to say something extremely important, then sabotage their own communication by waffling. "You know, I think you're really mean and hurtful…and I know I probably bring that out in you." No; don't apologize for your real feelings. Deliver your message. Own it. Then stay with it.

Make use of "minimal encouragers" to let your partner know he is being heard. Minimal encouragers are the very

least you must express to make sure the speaker knows you're listening to him. They are very simple: Make eye contact, nod your head, say things like, "Uh-huh; right; gotcha." What that says to the other person is "All right. I hear you. Keep going." Let him know that he's not speaking Greek to you.

Don't disguise your feelings in a question. "Are you going out with your buddies this Friday—*again?*" Really, what you're trying to say is that you want to spend more time with your partner. When your message is true, the response will be, too. *—P.M.*

"Get Past the Awkwardness of Talking About S-E-X!"

What if you don't want it and he does? Or the other way around? Dr. Phil takes on the number one source of conflict in a relationship (and tells you how to bring back that lovin' feeling).

Having dealt with thousands of relationships over the past 25 years and literally millions through my appearances on *The Oprah Winfrey Show,* I pay close attention to the primary sources of conflict among couples. Here's my top 10 list:

1. Sex
2. Money
3. Sex
4. Kids
5. Sex
6. In-laws
7. Sex
8. Division of labor
9. Sex
10. Sex

Getting any two people to want the same thing at the same time in the same way is tough. With something as intimate as sex, it gets real tough. And God forbid we ac-tually *talk* about the Big S. We've been taught that civilized people with any degree of upbringing or fetchin' up just don't discuss such things. Gee, I wonder why sexual conflicts dominate the top 10 list?

As a society of couples, we have behaved and miscommunicated our way into a problem of epidemic proportions. I don't use that term carelessly. I'm talking about millions of relationships in which sexual appetites don't match. On egos that are all too often already fragile, this discord can have a devastating effect. Nobody likes to be rejected and no rejection strikes closer to home than when your partner, the person in whom you have invested the most, says by word or deed: "I am not attracted to you, do not desire you, and do not want you." Ouch! And the resulting frustrations spill over well beyond the bedroom—a couple's sexual relationship often mirrors the rest of their relationship.

So the question is, *Are you part of this epidemic?* You know your own desire and whether or not you're satisfied with your level of sexual activity, but do you know your partner's true feelings? The questions below can help you get a fix on where you are with regard to this vital element of your life together:

■ Is sex a source of anxiety, frustration, and/or resentment for you or your partner?

■ Are you constantly pursuing or retreating within your sexual relationship, rather than enjoying a relaxed and natural pattern?

■ Are your partner's expectations either a mystery to you or, if known, a problem?

■ Do you avoid having or initiating frank discussions about sex with your partner because they involve guilt, blame, and bitterness?

■ Is frequency (whether too much or too little) a problem for you?

■ Do you or your partner feel that any show of affection must lead to sex?

■ Does the quality of your overall relationship seem to slide up and down with the quality of your sexual relationship?

If you answered yes to even a few of these questions, your sexual relationship needs some serious work. But don't despair: Once the problem is acknowledged, it's not as unsolvable as it may seem. Before we talk about steps you can take, here are some critical *don'ts:*

Don't be embarrassed to be honest about your sexual desires and needs. Get past the awkwardness of talking about *s-e-x!* If it makes you uncomfortable, just hang with it. It gets easier, I promise.

Don't apologize or feel guilty about how you feel. There is no right or wrong here. There is no "normal." You must give yourself permission to feel what you feel.

Don't make directionless complaints: Ask for what you want.

Don't fall into the trap of blaming your partner or labeling what he wants as wrong. That's saying "You're the problem, you need to fix it, and let me know when you do." Sexual incompatibility is not an individual's problem. It's a couple's problem, and nothing short of both of you being actively involved will do the trick.

Don't lie to yourself or your partner.

The good news is that there is a formula for success in any relationship, including a sexual relationship. It's a formula that works if and only if you are totally honest. Here it is:

Step 1: Identify your personal needs. Your partner can't read your mind. You may have to broaden your definition of what sex includes. (Women: Sit on your husband and make him read this paragraph!) Sexual interaction can include much more than the act of intercourse. If you want and need something you're not getting in your sexual relationship, you have to name it and then claim it. This means you must be willing to be vulnerable enough to disclose what matters to you.

Step 2: Identify your partner's needs, and make sure they are being met to the best of your ability. You can't do that if you don't learn what they are. And men: *Do not*—repeat, do not—assume that you know what your wife's needs are. Trust me, you don't have a clue. Ask questions, gather information, do not make assumptions.

Step 3: Armed with the important information about each other's needs, reopen negotiations on this topic. Your goal is to create a win-win situation, where both partners get as much of what they want as possible—eliminating judgment and blame, and creating an atmosphere of mutual support.

Step 4: Be honest in all of your self-disclosures. If the disparity in your sexual appetites is not the actual problem but a symptom of some underlying difficulty, you must be willing to talk about the real deal. If your objection is not to the sex but to the manner and context in which it occurs, be honest about that.

Your overall goal here is to come up with a plan that both of you can be excited about. This may take a realignment of your lifestyle. You may have to reprioritize your life to create and actually schedule intimate exchanges with your partner. Don't worry that it feels contrived at first. The stranger it seems, the more you need to do it.

Many fluctuations in sex drive are due to very treatable medical syndromes. Women, if you need to see a doctor because of hormonal or biochemical imbalances, then do it. Men, if you need medical help because of a condition such as impotence or hypertension, get it.

Also, be aware that a common mistake in diagnosing sexual frustration lies in confusing quantity with quality. A whole lot of poor-quality lovemaking pales in comparison to the less frequent but high-quality kind.

In sum, freshen up your attitude, reopen negotiations, and be very specific about what you want. Look, you don't have to sell out or spend your whole life gritting your teeth and faking it. What you do have to do is get real with yourself and your partner about doing that thing you do, or used to do. A cooperative spirit between the two of you can absolutely move mountains. ◐

> Don't apologize or feel guilty about how you feel.

Couples Combat: The Great American Pastime

Fighting with someone you love can rip you apart—or it can pull you more closely together than ever. Here are the rules of the ring.

I t has been said that there are only two things you can count on for sure: death and taxes. Wrong! There's a third certainty. You may do it a little or you may do it a lot, but you do it. I'm talking about that great American pastime: fighting (verbal fisticuffs only) with the one you love. No question, no doubt—I'm talking about you.

I bet you aren't very good at this couples-combat business even if you get plenty of practice. There are three fundamental truths that you need to be aware of when it comes to fighting with your partner.

First, fighting is unquestionably painful. Even if at some level it seems to feel good to vent that rage, it still hurts. You will understand and control that pain when you look at what is really happening when you argue.

Second, fighting is an unavoidable aspect of every relationship. It is part and parcel of the lives of all couples, without exception.

Third, I am absolutely convinced there's a right way and a whole bunch of wrong ways to fight. Knowing how to disagree constructively is one of those crucial life skills that—surprise, surprise—most people were never taught.

It Hurts!

Our number one need is acceptance. But this need takes the form of wanting answers to questions that we'll go out of our way to avoid asking. Why don't we ask? Because our ego can't handle a wrong answer. The kinds of questions I'm talking about are: Do you love me? Do you value me? Do you respect me? Are you attracted to me? Will you sacrifice for me? Are you committed to me?

Our number one fear is rejection. Look back at the list of questions. For most people, a "no" to any one of these questions would be unendurable. You may feel undesired, unattractive, and sexually unappealing, but you will not even test the waters because you dread getting the answer you don't want. And you wouldn't trust the right answer even if you got it.

Eighty percent of all questions are statements in disguise. When you are motivated by fear, your question is almost always heard as a plea rather than a request for honest feedback. Quite frankly, it's much easier for your partner to tell you what you want to hear than to tell you the truth.

The result is to escape into safe topics at the expense of critically important issues. The pressure builds because you never address your real concerns and fears—so when you hit a bump in the relationship road, it's enough to send you through the roof. What was the most recent topic for you and your partner? Maybe it was money, whose turn it was to take out the trash, a catty comment by your mother-in-law, or the dirty socks that were left on the floor. After the fact, you may question your sanity for going off over some triviality, but you weren't overreacting; you were reacting to the built-up need for reassurance that you're accepted. We blow off steam by fighting about less-ego-threatening topics. We don't have the guts to say, "Hey, I want to be wanted. I want to be loved!"

When you know that you are loved, respected, and cherished—by your partner or, more importantly, by yourself—then minor irritants fall by the wayside. So he didn't give you roses on Valentine's Day—if your need for acceptance is satisfied, you say, *So what?* You go through life with a sense of peace. Missing out on some flowers means nothing.

It Ain't All Bad

A certain amount of conflict is unavoidable in any relationship, including the healthiest and most fulfilling ones. The fact that you and your partner fight is not what's important. It's how you do it that matters.

The single most common mistake people make is really quite simple: If your objective in an argument is to win, that means the other person has to lose. How can that be a win for you? Your goal must be to negotiate some compromise that creates as much of what each of you wants as possible. If your goal is not win-win, guess what: *You lose!*

The Rules of Engagement

So much for how not to argue. Let's talk about what you and your partner can do to make sure your next argument is as constructive as possible.

1 **Decide what you want before you even start the fight.** Willingness to give a voice to your needs is an essential building block for constructive arguing. Why? Because at some point during a fight you're going to have to stop complaining and state what you want with clarity. Spell it out: "I want you to help me clean up the kitchen after dinner without my having to ask." "I want you to tell me that you love me, instead of assuming that I know it." Know what you want in the first place—then ask for it.

2 **Keep it relevant.** It's easier to attack your partner for watching television than it is to reveal the real issue, which is "I feel rejected because you spend your free time without me." Have the guts to ask yourself and your partner, "What are we fighting about?" When you get an answer, focus on it. If you allow yourself to stray, then you're going to have this same fight again because the real issue wasn't addressed.

3 **Know when to say when.** Being half of a couple doesn't mean having to give up all of who you are. Claim your right to be an individual in a relationship. You may need to renegotiate. I hear lots of women saying, "I have to be a mom, be a housekeeper, hold down a job, chauffeur my kids to their games, and be available for sex. I come in third, behind my husband and my kids." Or you may have cut yourself a bad deal. Maybe your husband wants sex four times a week and you don't. Maybe he wants you to be a stay-at-home mom and you want to work. If so, reopen the trading and ask for what you want and need.

Ask yourself, *What is the cost of my being in this relationship?* If you have to give up your dreams, your spirit, and your identity, then it's too much. Ask yourself, *Am I meeting my own expectations or someone else's?* Remember, the most important relationship you can ever have is with yourself.

4 **Make it possible for your partner to retreat with dignity.** The most predictive factor for divorce isn't whether you fight or not, it's how you end your arguments. Fighting that deteriorates into name-calling and character assassination—"You make me sick with your *[fill in the blank],*" "You're nothing but a *[fill in the blank]*"—is corrosive acid to a relationship. People aren't made to withstand that kind of abuse. Hold a door open to constructive change in your relationship by making it possible for your partner to retreat with dignity. I'm talking about showing your partner courtesy and respect, even if he is clearly wrong. Be merciful, accepting, and gracious.

So what is the goal when a couple fights? It's win-win for both of you: an encounter that preserves the self-esteem and security of both partners while allowing each of you to talk about what's bothering you. Follow the rules and enjoy the "makeup" sex. It doesn't get any better than that! **◖**

> If your objective in an argument is to win, the other person has to lose. How can that be a win for you?

"You Have Taught This Woman How to Take Advantage of You."

Q I have an extremely needy friend and neighbor who asks a lot of my family, including my four kids. She is married and has three grown children, one of whom lives at home, but she comes to us constantly for favors: to feed and walk her dog, clean her house, even cook her meals. (She never wants money, just time.) Lately, she's been requesting my kids' schedules and cell phone numbers to see when they are available to help her out. I've put her off, but she's persistent. Her husband is a busy man, and she is taking medication for depression, so we've tried to be there for her as much as possible. But at this point, I just don't want to have anything to do with her. How can I get out of this lopsided friendship?

Dr. Phil: As I've often said, we teach people how to treat us. You have taught this woman how to take advantage of you. Now you need to teach her that your generosity will no longer be exploited—but first you must give yourself permission to say no. There have to be two confrontations: one with yourself and one with your neighbor.

Let's start with you. When someone makes a request, you always have the right to say no. Claim that right for yourself and for your family. It's commendable that you want to help a neighbor, but there are limits—and it's up to you to set these limits. When you get comfortable with the idea of simply saying no (and it may take quite a bit of practice), you'll discover that you don't need to lie, make excuses, or feel shame or guilt.

Once *no* takes root in your vocabulary, any confrontation with your neighbor will likely be anticlimactic. If she asks you to do her household chores, be prepared to say, for example, "Perhaps you can call a housekeeper, because we're not able to do that for you." Or when she asks for the kids' cell phone numbers, you might answer, "Their cell phones are just for me to be able to reach them." If she inquires about their schedules, respond, "The kids are so busy with activities and homework that they can't add anything else to their plates now." Speak with your kids about what to do if she approaches them directly. They need not be rude or make excuses; they can simply say, "I have to check with my mom first."

All of these scenarios will be easy to manage, provided that you have permitted yourself to say no without feeling guilty. The situation will only get worse until you do something about it. You mention that she's taking medication for depression and has a busy husband as though these facts justify her exploitative nature or your willingness to help at your family's expense. Teach her that she must respect your limits, and you will see a change in her behavior.

Q I am a 37-year-old widow. My mother lives a mile away and until recently had a key to my house. She would often come in without knocking. While dog-sitting for me, she went through some of my bills. This was not the first time she searched my things. After thinking over the situation, I asked her to return my key—and she hasn't talked to me since. How can I have a good relationship with my mother but also make her understand that my house is my house and she can't snoop around?

Dr. Phil: Your mother crosses the line when she walks in uninvited or goes through your mail, so it's understandable that you feel violated and asked for your key back. All healthy relationships have boundaries, especially one with your own mother. The challenge now is not what to do but how to do it.

Let's step back for a moment, though, and look at this from your mother's point of view. As a father of grown children, I can tell you that sometimes it's hard to break out of the parent-child dynamic and remember that the people who used to be cute, needy kids are now independent adults. Not that this justifies your mother's actions, but it may help you understand why she would encroach on your space. You should also recognize that you made yourself vulnerable by giving her a key to your house. That doesn't mean you are to blame for her behavior—only that you did hand her a kind of all-access pass to your life.

You need to redefine the relationship, welcoming your mother back into your life with certain clear boundaries. I suggest you have a conversation with your mother; if she's still too hurt to talk, write her a letter instead.

Script: Honoring privacy

Mom, I know I hurt your feelings when I asked for my key back, but that wasn't my intention. I love you, and I appreciate all you do for me. But I am a 37-year-old woman whose privacy deserves to be honored. There are parts of my adult life that are mine alone. That doesn't mean I don't want us to be close—I'm happy to discuss anything that you're curious or concerned about, and I'll try to answer any questions you may have. I value you dearly, and you are a vital part of my support system. But I would never come into your house without knocking or go through your things without asking, and I expect the same respect from you. If my reaction seems harsh, I hope you'll forgive me, because I want to put this behind us and move forward.

I hope this works out for you. But remember, too, that peace at any price is no peace at all—meaning that if having a

> Remember that peace at any price is no peace at all.

smooth relationship with your mother requires you to compromise your values and beliefs, the cost is too high. For now, let her know that your heart and arms are open, so that you can take the first steps toward a meaningful, comfortable, respectful connection.

Q I have been dating my boyfriend for three years; we've been living together for two. But I still haven't met his sons, ages 12 and 9. My boyfriend says that neither he nor the kids are ready for that. I have met his brothers but no other family members. He doesn't understand why I want to meet his family, often saying that they don't have anything to do with our relationship. Should I be concerned?

Dr. Phil: Yes, you should. In no way is it normal or natural for you to be in a long-term, cohabiting relationship with someone who chooses to keep you separate from his family.

We can only speculate about his motives. Is he ashamed of his family? Ashamed of you? Is he worried that his family members will disclose something he is hiding from you, or that you'll reveal something about him? As for his sons, it's always wise for single parents to be cautious about introducing new romantic partners to their kids—you don't want children making a strong connection with someone who may not be a long-term player in their lives. But if he remains wary three years into the relationship, it hardly bodes well.

You should be very forthcoming with him. Let him know that you find it offensive and confusing that he refuses to introduce you to people who are near and dear to him. Tell him how troubled you are that he seems to be living two versions of his life: one with you, and another that erases you.

But also give him the opportunity to explain his thinking. Let him answer your questions about what he's afraid of and what he might be hiding. If he is worried about his children bonding with a woman who might someday disappear from their lives, use this concern as an opportunity to discuss what each of you thinks the future holds for your relationship.

People who have nothing to hide, hide nothing. If your boyfriend gives evasive answers to your questions or refuses to compromise, then you need to ask yourself if you're willing to settle for a partial relationship or if you want—and deserve—much more. None of us is getting any younger. You could be burning daylight barreling down a dead-end street.

Q I have been with my husband for 13 years, and we have two daughters. We've had our ups and downs (mostly downs). Five years ago, I ran into a high school crush and we talked for an hour. Two years later, I saw him again and we started talking on the phone. Now I can't stop thinking about him. I've always been faithful, but sometimes when I'm intimate with my husband, I wonder what it would be like to be with my old flame. I'm considering telling this man how I feel so that I can let go of my illusions and get back to my family. Do you think that would help?

Dr. Phil: Thirteen years is a long time to live in a situation that doesn't make you feel good about your life. That makes you vulnerable. So let's not con each other. You don't want to meet with this guy for an emotional release. You want to see him so that you can live out the fantasy that runs through your head while you're in bed with your husband. You're playing with fire here. Sure, it's fun and exciting to dream about someone else. Of course he makes you feel good—it's easy to be charming for an hour every few years, but you don't really know anything about this man. Old sayings get to be old sayings because they're profound, like the one about how the grass is always greener on the other side of the fence. This old boyfriend could look pretty good from your side of the fence, but once you cross over, the comfort and familiarity of a family bond could look pretty good, too.

Never fix problems in a relationship by turning away from your partner. You must fix them inside your marriage. You can't improve the situation by inviting in an interloper. I recommend that you sit down with your husband and tell him that you're tired of having more downs than ups. Say that you want to try to improve the quality of your relationship. There were reasons you got married. Refocus on those reasons and see if you can create some spark between the two of you. Playing footsie with some old crush is not the solution.

Q What can I do about an abusive coworker who loves to make my life miserable? Since my first day on the job, she's yelled at me, threatened me, sabotaged my work, and pointed out my mistakes to superiors. I've tolerated this for nearly six years. I like my job, but I don't think she'll be satisfied until I quit. The stress has made me sick with headaches and stomachaches.

Dr. Phil: I am troubled by the fact that you've been working in this unpleasant situation for years. The truth is that bullies are found not just at school or on the playground; they also lurk in the workplace. Having spent many years consulting with human resource departments in corporate America, I am going to tell you what I would do.

Let's start out by being very clear about your rights. You are unequivocally entitled to be treated with dignity and respect by everyone in the workplace. You are entitled to focus on your job peacefully without being subjected to social pressure, ridicule, or attack. There are two choices to consider. Number one is to confront your bully. Let her know that you will not put up with this behavior for another minute of another hour, and if she so much as looks at you cross-eyed, you will pursue the situation aggressively and formally without delay. Number two is to take action without talking to her at all. In my opinion, after six years, she has forfeited the right to handle this casually. This has been a premeditated and ongoing pattern of behavior, and you should address it with your company. Do it before the end of today.

It's hard to imagine that your superiors haven't been aware of what's going on, at least to some extent. But assuming that she, like many bullies, acts discreetly, give your bosses the benefit of the doubt. Request a meeting with your immediate supervisor and HR director. Prepare by writing down as many instances of harassment as you can recall. (Ideally, you've been documenting them all along.) You don't want to rely on opinion or emotions to prove the conduct. Explain that you want to file a formal complaint concerning on-the-job abuse by a coworker and that you're prepared to give your statement of facts. Inform them that you're suffering mental, physical, and emotional symptoms and want therapeutic or medical support. You should also indicate that you want protection from this bully and do not wish to have a confrontation or be subjected to gossip. Ask what their intentions are, and request a follow-up meeting. Understand that they must commit to a thorough investigation; they can't just take your word and fire this creep.

Do not accept a transfer from your department if that's not what you want. Corporations often make the mistake of transferring the victim, not the perpetrator. You shouldn't have to disrupt your life by moving to another office. You didn't create the problem; you shouldn't have to make the changes. If you don't get the desired response from HR, contact an employment lawyer. But under no circumstances should you quit your job, feel guilty, or refrain from taking action.

Q One of my close friends says I'm like a Stepford wife because my children are active in gymnastics and sports and I attend all their PTA meetings, games, and recitals. She feels that I'm choosing my family over spending time with her and that I'm too active in my children's lives because I don't have a "real job." She doesn't have kids and can't understand the demands of being a full-time mother, but I don't want her to feel neglected. How can I show her that she's important to me?

Dr. Phil: Anytime you receive advice, criticism, or an opinion, you should do two things. First, evaluate the person's motivation. Ask yourself: *Is she being objective, or does she have a dog in the fight?* If somebody is telling you what a great car you're looking at and why you should buy it, and he's the one selling it to you, that's an important factor to consider. While the situation is not always so clear-cut, remember that even loved ones have their own motives. Second, regardless of the person's incentive, weigh the advice carefully to see whether there's something to learn.

I definitely question your friend's motivation. She doesn't disapprove of your parenting so much as she resents not spending time with you. I'm not saying that she's ill-intentioned, only that she's not being objective. In terms of weighing her criticism, it sounds as though you're being an attentive mother who is participating in your kids' lives in a productive way. It's important, however, to examine the decision you've made so you can be confident you're doing what's right for you. If you want to be a stay-at-home mother, then find strength in that conviction and don't allow others to guilt-trip you.

The question becomes how to help your friend feel comfortable. I would suggest having a conversation along the following lines. (Let me confess that there's some manipulation involved in the script below. People tend to live up to others' expectations and to respect boundaries. If you act as if you expect the best from her, you might get it.)

Script: Negotiating a balance between friends and family

I'm really glad you feel comfortable telling me what you're thinking. That's a great reflection on our friendship. Perhaps even more important, I appreciate that you give me your opinion without expecting to control me or to make my decisions for me. It's difficult for us to see things from each other's point of view; neither of us can walk a mile in the other's shoes. As a stay-at-home mother, I'm incredibly busy. But I love it. My challenge is to keep balance in my life, and you're a big part of that. So I would love to work out ways for us to spend some time together. I think that can help us both.

Q I'm the mother of two teenage girls, ages 17 and 13, and I've been divorced from their father for 11 years. Ours was a typical split—not very nice. The problem is that my oldest daughter and her father have grown apart. She has a lot of anger toward him, and he doesn't seem to want to work it out. He does everything for our youngest child but nothing for the oldest. This has affected her school performance as well as her personal life. I've begged my ex to be more involved, to no avail. Neither one of them will try counseling. How do I help get my teen on the road to a happy adulthood?

Dr. Phil: You're dealing with two strong-willed people, and your daughter is old enough to know her mind and heart with regard to her father. So as much as I hate to say it, your attempt to broker a peace between them is probably going to be unsuccessful. If they're not inclined to go to counseling, all you can do is make sure your daughter knows that it's her father, not her, who's got to contend with his own problems. Just be careful how you say it: I think it's a mistake to bash an estranged spouse, because it hurts the children and can make them suspicious of your motives. Explain that her father's attitude is most likely due to some personal issues that have little or nothing to do with her actions. He may feel guilt or resentment toward her because she reminds him too much of you, for example.

You can also let your daughter know that in you she has a parent who loves her, accepts her, and doesn't judge her. She has to realize that although you hope she and her father will heal their wounds, you will always support her unconditionally. While you're clearly not trying to win her over to your side at the expense of your ex, she needs to understand that you're 100 percent in her corner.

When it's appropriate, you might also caution her against letting her anger spill over into other aspects of her life. Don't let your daughter go out and indiscriminately find some man to pal around with because she's got a thirst for male attention and acceptance. At the same time, she needs to make sure that she's not projecting her bitterness toward her father onto men in general. That could one day cost her a great friend or partner. See to it that this incident doesn't push her to an extreme.

Q My boyfriend and I have been dating for nearly three years. We moved in together six months ago, and our relationship has deteriorated ever since. He's 27 years old and has lived with his parents all his life. At first he didn't know how to cook or look after himself. I taught him the basics, but he has no motivation. Somehow he thinks everything gets done magically on its own. When I come home from work, he's still sitting in front of the computer surfing the Internet, and the place is a total mess. In the beginning, I got angry and cleaned up, but I don't want to be his mother, so now I leave it alone. Nothing gets done unless I nag. Am I being unreasonable? I need to know if he and I are going to make it.

Dr. Phil: I'm not necessarily a big fan of living together before marriage. I've seen many downsides that make it not such a great idea. Statistically speaking, cohabitation does not enhance the likelihood of success in marriage. Sharing a place is only half a commitment; marriage requires full-on dedication. But one of the upsides is that you get a sneak peek at what you'd be faced with if you say, "I do."

If you're under the impression that your problems will get better just as soon as you get married, let me be the one to tell you they won't. He's not going to be any more pliable, committed, or willing once you sign the papers, and walking down the aisle doesn't guarantee that you'll find a way to live together comfortably.

This man is showing you who he is, what his priorities are, and how he intends to partner with you—or anyone else, for that matter—in the long term. And you're telling me that his behavior is unacceptable to

you. The bottom line is that you and your boyfriend are fundamentally incompatible.

He seems very entrenched in his ways, and I think you need to take this as an opportunity to start looking elsewhere. If you stay in this relationship, you're going to be very disappointed. Of course there must be some positive qualities about this guy, but if you marry him, you'll be compromising your values and wind up feeling miserable. Just be glad you found out sooner rather than later.

Q When I had my daughter, I was very young. For the past few years, I've been begging my husband to let me have another baby, but he refuses. I'm almost to the point where if he won't have another child with me, I'm going to have to find someone else. Though I don't want to leave my husband, he won't communicate further on the subject. I can't understand why he's so against having a second baby.

Dr. Phil: I think you have to regard your husband's reaction as a huge warning sign. He not only doesn't want to have another child with you but, more important, won't talk about it. Relationships are negotiations, and he's decided to stop negotiating.

Does he have the right to the opinion that he wants one child instead of two or more? Yes, and there's nothing inherently flawed in that thinking. Are you wrong to want two or more? Certainly not, and there's nothing wrong with your desire, either. What's problematic is that the two of you are on opposite ends of the debate, and communication has been cut off entirely. That's the most dangerous thing that can happen.

In all relationships, there are topics and there are issues. Topics are what we often argue about because the issues—the real underlying matters—are too dangerous, scary, or intimidating to get into. It sounds like having another baby is a topic rather than an issue. The goal is to find out why he is so closed off so you can get down to the issue and deal with it. Then there will be a natural reopening of the discussion. He's threatened for some reason you're not aware of, and I will guarantee you it's not the prospect of the second child.

Whatever you do, don't force the situation and get pregnant without your husband's full support. A new baby could come into this world as a point of contention for him and cause even more friction between you, something neither child would deserve. A failure to talk openly can be catastrophic to a marriage, and you have to

> A failure to talk openly can be catastrophic to a marriage.

broach that with your husband. I suggest you say something to him along the lines of the following dialogue.

Script: How to drive home the importance of communication

Look, I understand we're in a stalemate here about having a child. What I want to do is take a giant step back from that. Let's take the baby topic off the table. Instead, let's deal with the issues of why we're so at odds and why you won't have a conversation with me about this or anything else. The absolute lifeblood of our relationship is that we exchange our thoughts, feelings, and ideas. But you've closed the door on that. I want to talk again. We can forget about the family topic for now, but we have to resolve this communication issue in order for our marriage to work.

Q **My husband of seven years does the laundry and feeds our baby daughter. I take care of her other needs and maintain the house. We spend all our free time together as a family, and when my husband and I are alone we laugh and joke. But romantically? Nothing, zip, nada! We have sex for ten minutes once every two months. When I say I want more, he snaps, "I'm doing the best I can!" In the past, he's been terribly mean to me and told me before I got pregnant that he wasn't attracted to me anymore. Should we separate?**

Dr. Phil: Your question cuts to the chase, so let me give you a direct answer: not yet. Clearly, you have a problem, but let's see if we can find some solutions short of terminating the relationship. There's no question you're entitled to your needs. Sex is important, and you should make every effort to reintroduce it into your marriage. I've often said if you have a good sex life, it occupies about 10 percent of your relationship—and if you don't, it's about 90 percent. I say that because when sex is fulfilling, you both enjoy it and move on to other things. But if you're not satisfied, then someone—in this case, you—feels hurt, rejected, and confused, and the problem consumes the marriage.

Let's look at what your husband said: "I'm doing the best I can." If we take that at face value, it may mean he has a low sex drive at a biochemical level. He may have difficulty getting or maintaining an erection, and since he never knows when he'll be able to perform, he avoids the situation. Also consider that he may be depressed, which can undermine his desire and explain his defensive reaction. I suggest you approach him about this gently and recommend that he see his doctor for a physical exam. Experts say impotence is a circulatory problem that can be related to high blood pressure or vascular disease. Sometimes impotence is psychologically based and can be managed by lessening stress and anxiety. The problems

in your sex life could be warning signs of more serious physical problems, a psychological issue, or a combination of the two.

In examining *your* role in this, you have to eliminate the concept of blame—but that doesn't mean there's nothing you can do to improve the situation. I've seen many couples stop being friends and lovers when they become moms and dads. They get out of the habit of being intimate—and the old saying "Use it or lose it" definitely applies. You may need to resolve to behave your way back to success. You can be the initiator and set up situations that make intimacy more likely. Keep in mind that men are visually stimulated. A change in your routine might be the spark you need to reignite your love life.

Q **I'm a single mother. The man I've been dating just admitted that, although he loves the time we spend together, he doesn't think he can handle living with the "chaos" of children. He gave me the option of ending things between us, knowing that he may never be able to accept that aspect of my life. He's 35, never married, and grew up as the oldest of five children in a dysfunctional household. He hasn't yet met my kids, who, while not perfect angels, are far from chaotic. Also, their father and I share custody, so the children are with me only half the time. My relationship with this man has been wonderful so far. Am I a complete moron for wanting to keep seeing him and hoping to work through his fears? Or should I bail out now?**

Dr. Phil: It's important to be realistic with yourself from the beginning of a relationship. You're a single parent. That's not going to change. And he's telling you straight-up that he doesn't believe he's equipped to handle children. Every individual brings a history to any relationship. His has been filled with chaos and dysfunctional family interactions. Obviously, he hasn't resolved any of the emotional baggage that's contaminating your relationship. But you're not a therapist, nor should you try to be one.

I believe there are clear stop signs in any relationship, and your boyfriend is waving one in your face. The divorce rate in America is at epidemic levels. It's hard enough to make a relationship work when both people want the same things. Until he heals the wounds of his past, this man is not a good candidate to be your husband and a stepfather to your children. The sooner you admit that, the better. You ask, "Am I a complete moron for wanting to keep seeing him?" No, you just like certain aspects of a person with whom you also have deal-breaking incompatibilities. Thank him for his honesty, and get on with your life.

Q My daughter is 15-years-old. I have tried to remember what it's like to be that age and to give her some freedom. But she's disrespecting her body, drinking, and doing drugs. She shows her family no appreciation although she's been given all the love and support possible. My dilemma is: Do I let her experiment in our home, supervised, or do I just say no and accept that when she goes out she's doing all the wrong things? I'm afraid if I come down on her for telling me the truth, even if it's not what I'd like to hear, she'll start lying to me.

Dr. Phil: You absolutely should not let her experiment in your home. That's a form of insanity. If you think allowing her to drink or get high in your house under your supervision will keep her from these self-destructive behaviors elsewhere, you couldn't be more wrong. All you're doing is endorsing the behavior and giving her an arena in which to practice. Contributing to the delinquency of a minor is a crime.

Your job is to prepare her for life and to protect her from the dangers the world presents, until she's able to make decisions for herself. At 15 her brain isn't finished growing; her reasoning and her ability to predict the consequences of her actions aren't fully developed. She needs to know that you're ready, willing, and able to do whatever it takes to keep her from engaging in sex, drinking, or drugs. If she tries to fight you on that, you need to go "parent commando" and deal with it 24 hours a day, seven days a week until you've established that you won't relent.

You said she's disrespecting her body, which tells me she has poor self-esteem. Consider getting her counseling so she can talk through these feelings with a professional. I also suggest helping her find some passion in life, which may diminish her inclination to behave recklessly.

Script: Saving your daughter from herself
You're my daughter and I love you. I want you to love me, but that's secondary to my job as your parent, which is to get you through these years without hurting yourself. Don't underestimate my resolve. If you think for a second that I'm willing to say, "Everybody's doing it" and let you pursue this behavior, you're wrong. I want you to have fun, freedom, and the opportunity to find yourself, but I'm setting up narrow boundaries and tall fences to contain you until you prove you won't violate those privileges. You can like me or not—my job is to do for you what you're not doing for yourself. I will never accept these self-

> # While it's common for people to tie up their self-worth in their careers, there's more to life.

destructive behaviors, so let's make a plan we can both be excited about.

Q I'm 35 years old and hold a BA in political science and an MBA. For the past seven years, I've worked at the same company. I hate my job. In fact, I've hated every job I've held since graduating from college. I have no idea what I want to be when I grow up. Unfortunately, a great deal of my self-worth depends on my satisfaction with my career. A loving husband, a beautiful daughter, and a nice home aren't enough. Do I just need to suck it up and do what's best for my family?

Dr. Phil: You're obviously an intelligent woman. But those book smarts need to extend to what I call adaptive intelligence—the ability to shape your experiences into a meaningful existence. While it's common for people to tie up their self-worth in their careers, there's more to life. You have to weigh the importance of your work with that of your health, well-being, and finances. Focusing on just one area leads to a lopsided life, and you can wind up depressed without knowing why.

I know you want what's best for your family, but you've also got to listen to your heart. If you hate your line of work, make it your job to figure out what you love to do. I strongly suspect you're being controlled by expectations linked to your education. Maybe your parents wanted you to enter that field, or maybe your training is frequently used in your current job, so you think it's your only choice. As the saying goes, learn to think outside the box. Ask yourself: *What's missing from my job that would make me more satisfied? What could I do that would be fulfilling, regardless of what school has prepared me for?*

I spent 12 years as a psychologist in private practice. I had trained for it, and my father wanted me to join him in his practice, so I did. But I wasn't suited to that application of my education, and I went nuts trying to deal with it. When I finally chose to leave it behind, a huge burden was lifted from my shoulders. Take the step. You're worth it. "They" may not like it, but the last time I checked, "they" never seem to be around when the going gets tough. The one person who can make you feel complete is you; contentment comes only from within. You will ultimately have to decide to get happy with what you're doing now or stop complaining and change things. The world won't fall off its axis. Whatever you do, stay committed to enjoying your family. They can enrich your life in ways no job ever could.

Q My boyfriend is struggling to quit smoking. He says he wants to stop poisoning his body, but he still lights up every so often. Once, he gave up cigarettes for four months before getting hooked again. I can't share my future with someone who chooses an unhealthy way of life. If he keeps it up, I'm going to have to end the relationship.

Dr. Phil: I get your not wanting to deal with someone who has a toxic habit. But before you leave your boyfriend, try to understand what he's going through. Quitting any sort of addiction is a process. Sure, some folks put down their lighters, walk away, and never smoke again. But the typical smoker tries multiple times before succeeding. Each "failed" attempt isn't a failure at all but a necessary step.

You can help your boyfriend. Let him read this so he sees that he has hope of succeeding. He has to start by declaring that he's quitting for himself. Few people like being told what to do, especially by someone they care about. So if you threaten him, I promise he's going to rebel. Once he decides he's not changing for your approval, he should:

■ Specify the goal. He needs to articulate his plan: that is, to give up smoking entirely. He doesn't have to think about quitting for the rest of his life, just for right now. Those "right nows" will ultimately add up to forever, but the idea of eternity can be overwhelming.

■ Identify his most vulnerable times. During those periods, he should launch into an activity, like jogging or showering, that makes it impossible to light up. Avoid situations that encourage smoking: If he always has a cigarette with a beer, steer clear of bars.

■ Go public. Tell friends, acquaintances, and family members what he's doing and ask for their support.

■ Create accountability. He should find somebody he respects and meet with that person regularly to discuss whether he's lapsed. This may need to happen daily at first, then weekly or monthly—whatever it takes to keep him honest.

Your part will be to reward your boyfriend's progress. When he does well, pat him on the back. The power of positive reinforcement is much greater than the power of punishment.

Q I have been married for eight years. I'm very affectionate, but my husband claims he isn't a touchy-feely kind of person, so we go for long periods of time without hugging, kissing, or cuddling. We make love once a month (he claims he's too tired for more). Though my children are very warm, one day they'll be grown and gone. I am starving for my husband's attention.

Dr. Phil: Generally speaking, men aren't as touchy-feely as women. That doesn't mean you have to settle for not getting what you want, but it may help to recognize that there are multiple languages of love. Some folks show their feelings with words; others demonstrate their emotions through actions.

Ask yourself if you're receiving love, even if it's in a "foreign language." That will make a big difference in figuring out if this is a translation problem or a reality problem. Assuming it's a matter of translation, let me recommend two things. First, be aware that what your husband is doing isn't wrong; it's just different from what you would prefer. At the same time, know that you're not off-base to need tenderness the way you do. Second, talk to him. There comes a point when it's time to stop agonizing and start asking for what you want. I often hear women say, "If I have to tell him to kiss me or compliment me, it doesn't count." Let me tell you, from a man's perspective, that's wrong, wrong, wrong. Look, we don't always get it when it comes to emotions, so sometimes you have to put the dots really close together and connect them with a bright red line in order for us to know what's important to you.

Sit down with your husband and, as sensitively as possible, help him to appreciate how you feel. You'll notice that the script below focuses on your needs, not his deficiencies. If you can keep him from being defensive, you'll get a lot closer to receiving what you're longing for.

Script: Asking for more physical affection

I want to talk to you about something that's very important to me. Before I do, it's crucial that you understand I'm not criticizing you. I'm just asking you to help me. I'm the kind of person who requires human contact. I need to feel the arms of the person I love wrapped around me on a regular basis. It lets me center myself; it's how I validate that I'm alive and appreciated. I realize you love me, and I see it when you [insert the things he does that are his way of caring for you]. That's very meaningful to me, but I'm asking for this, too. I know it doesn't come naturally to you, and I understand it's not a put-down when you don't touch me. Nonetheless, I do need it. I'm going to help you remember by saying, "I sure need a hug" or "Can I sit on your lap for a minute?" I hope you'll be receptive when I do. ◐

> There comes a point when it's time to stop agonizing and start asking for what you want.

10 Rules I've Unlearned

In the past ten years, I've realized that our culture is rife with ideas that actually inhibit joy. Here are some of the things I'm most grateful to have *unlearned*.

1 Problems are bad. You spent your school years solving arbitrary problems imposed by boring authority figures. You learned that problems—*comment se dit?*—suck. But people without real problems go mad and invent things like base jumping and wedding planning. Real problems are wonderful, each carrying the seeds of its own solution. Job burnout? It's steering you toward your perfect career. An awful relationship? It's teaching you what love means. Confusing tax forms? They're suggesting you hire an accountant, so you can focus on more interesting tasks, such as flossing. Finding the solution to each problem is what gives life its gusto.

2 It's important to stay happy. Solving a knotty problem can help us be happy, but we don't have to be happy to feel good. If that sounds crazy, try this: Focus on something that makes you miserable. Then think, *I must stay happy!* Stressful, isn't it? Now say, "It's okay to be as sad as I need to be." This kind of permission to feel as we feel—not continuous happiness—is the foundation of well-being.

3 **I'm irreparably damaged by my past.** Painful events leave scars, true, but it turns out they're largely erasable. Jill Bolte Taylor, the neuro-anatomist who had a stroke that obliterated her memory, described the event as losing "37 years of emotional baggage." Taylor rebuilt her own brain, minus the drama. Now it appears we can all effect a similar shift, without having to endure a brain hemorrhage. The very thing you're doing at this moment—questioning habitual thoughts—is enough to begin off-loading old patterns. For example, take an issue that's been worrying you ("I've got to work harder!") and think of three reasons that belief may be wrong. Your brain will begin to let it go. Taylor found this thought-loss euphoric. You will, too.

4 **Working hard leads to success.** Baby mammals, including humans, learn by playing, which is why "the battle of Waterloo was won on the playing fields of Eton." Boys who'd spent years strategizing for fun gained instinctive skills to handle real-world situations. So play as you did in childhood, with all-out absorption. Watch for ways your childhood playing skills can solve a problem (see #1). Play, not work, is the key to success. While we're on the subject…

5 **Success is the opposite of failure.** Fact: From quitting smoking to skiing, we succeed to the degree we try, fail, and learn. Studies show that people who worry about mistakes shut down, but those who are relaxed about doing badly soon learn to do well. Success is built on failure.

6 **It matters what people think of me.** "But if I fail," you may protest, "people will think badly of me!" This dreaded fate causes despair, suicide, homicide. I realized this when I read blatant lies about myself on the Internet. When I bewailed this to a friend, she said, "Wow, you have some painful fantasies about other people's fantasies about you." Yup, my anguish came from my hypothesis that other people's hypothetical

> **Check it out: People who have what you want are all over rehab clinics, divorce courts, and jails. Good fortune has side effects.**

hypotheses about me mattered. Ridiculous! Right now, imagine what you'd do if it absolutely didn't matter what people thought of you. Got it? Good. Never go back.

7 **We should think rationally about our decisions.** Your rational capacities are far newer and more error-prone than your deeper, "animal" brain. Often complex problems are best solved by thinking like an animal. Consider a choice you have to make—anything from which movie to see to which house to buy. Instead of weighing pros and cons intellectually, notice your physical response to each option. Pay attention to when your body tenses or relaxes. And speaking of bodies…

8 **The pretty girls get all the good stuff.** Oh, God. So not true. I unlearned this after years of coaching beautiful clients. Yes, these lovelies get preferential treatment in most life scenarios, but there's a catch: While everyone's looking at them, virtually no one sees them. Almost every gorgeous client had a husband who'd married her breasts and jawline without ever noticing her soul.

9 **If all my wishes came true right now, life would be perfect.** Check it out: People who have what you want are all over rehab clinics, divorce courts, and jails. That's because good fortune has side effects, just like medications advertised on TV. Basically, any external thing we depend on to make us feel good has the power to make us feel bad. Weirdly, when you've stopped depending on tangible rewards, they often materialize. To attract something you want, become as joyful as you think that thing would make you. The joy, not the thing, is the point.

10 **Loss is terrible.** Ten years ago I still feared loss enough to abandon myself in order to keep things stable. I'd smile when I was sad, pretend to like people who appalled me. What I now know is that losses aren't cataclysmic if they teach the heart and soul their natural cycle of breaking and healing. A real tragedy? That's the loss of the heart and soul themselves. If you've abandoned yourself in the effort to keep anyone or anything else, unlearn that pattern. Live your truth, losses be damned. Just like that, your heart and soul will return home. ◑

Martha Beck's 5 Best Pieces of Advice

Are they counterintuitive? Maybe. Helpful? You bet. Our columnist lays down her personal rules to live by.

Free Life Lessons

When you spend almost all your time thinking about how people can achieve their best destiny, as I do, you often trip over little life lessons that had never occurred to you. (In my case, they're usually of the blindingly obvious variety.) On the chance that you may have missed some of these enlightening tidbits of instruction, I thought I'd write down a few that have improved my own quality of life with very little effort. So, without further ado, I offer you: My Five Best Pieces of Advice Ever.

1 A little pain never hurt anybody. I once worked as a dishwasher in a restaurant, stacking clean plates and cups as they emerged from a spray jet of superheated water. One day an enormous metal pot came down the conveyor belt. Lifting it was like grabbing a hot stove burner. The belt was still moving, so I couldn't drop the pot without smashing dishes, floor tiles, and other people's feet. There was nothing to do but carry the pot to its shelf. As I did so, a fine new thought arose in my mind.

Oh, well, I thought, *a little pain never hurt anybody.*

The incongruity of this statement made me laugh—while still holding that scalding metal. I ended up with second-degree burns on both hands, but I was oddly relaxed about it. Somehow I'd managed to accept this particular physical injury without any mental resistance or fear. In the absence of those psychological components, the overall experience was strangely stress free.

I wish I could say I've viewed suffering this way ever since. Alas, my usual mind-set echoes the immortal words of Daffy Duck: "I can't stand pain. It hurts me." It's only when I can't avoid something moderately painful—when my back goes out or my throat gets sore or a karate buddy accidentally breaks my finger—that I remember my dishwashing epiphany. *It's only a little pain,* I remind myself. *It won't hurt me.*

Unfailingly, the moment I stop fearing and resisting it, the pain changes. It becomes smaller, more manageable and docile, like an enraged wolverine morphing into a fussy hamster. I just tried this at the dentist and found that having a needle pushed into my gums felt like a tiny deep-tissue massage. I genuinely enjoyed it, which is even more gratifying than it is disturbing.

The same perspective also works wonders on emotional irritants: embarrassment, frustration, confusion, nervousness. I have a friend with an anxiety disorder who has learned to say, in the middle of a panic attack, *It's just anxiety, nothing to worry about.* At one level she's freaking out, but she refuses to add insult to injury by thinking, *I can't stand this! It's got to stop!* She's one of the calmest people I've ever met. Variations on the theme "A little pain never hurt anyone" are so useful I'm thinking of having the phrase tattooed on my body. But I'm afraid it would hurt.

2 Sunscreen is for necks and chests, not just faces.
Because I live in Arizona, I spend lots of time with folks who've spent decades in the desert sun. Many have exquisitely youthful faces, attached to chests that look like dehydrated crocodiles. It's not the sun damage that bothers me (though that is a health hazard). It's the difference between the patches of skin the owner finds important and those dermal areas he or she clearly ignores.

The importance of complete coverage extends far beyond cosmetic issues. We all tend to focus on things we deem important while ignoring related items. One of my clients complained that she wasn't losing weight despite following her diet perfectly at every meal. She cheated only by consuming four candy bars as snacks. Another client once said, "I'm a very honest person; I lie only when necessary." Psychologically speaking, this person had the face of a teenager and the chest of a dragon. Uneven application pervaded her life.

Sunscreen and values should be applied uniformly. If you believe in kindness, slather it on the janitor as well as the CEO. If you wouldn't excuse yourself for inflicting cruelty on another person, don't make excuses for other people who are mean to you. I remind myself daily that it's never too late to apply a protective layer of integrity to parts of my life I've ignored.

3 Television is a vitamin. I frequently hear parents and pundits lamenting the brain-rotting, lowbrow practice of watching the "boob tube." Many couples I know strictly limit the time their children spend in front of the TV. Some of my friends actually hide from others the fact that they love TV; when pressed, they'll lie outright, claiming they're too busy reading Proust to think about popular culture.

While almost all of us spend a fair amount of time staring at televisions, many individuals, as well as social scientists and other ideologues, think TV is bad for us. I disagree. I think TV is like a vitamin: toxic if taken in large quantities, but also essential for social and personal well-being.

My family of origin fired up its first TV when I was 13. Because of this, I spent the first 12 years of my life on the

Nerd Patrol. I didn't know what other kids were talking about, and vice versa. In my quest for entertainment, I turned to things like reading Shakespeare—and if you don't think quoting *Hamlet* will get a 10-year-old beaten up in the schoolyard, my friend, you have never been that 10-year-old.

When I finally did start watching TV, everything on it—even advertising—was like a window opening on my own culture. Television is a piece of furniture that lets us see the top of Everest, the Crab Nebula, the funniest and smartest and most athletic people in the world, a talking sponge in pants! To this day, it thrills me. It's a social unifier, a dispenser of useful information about trends (in fashion, slang, voting), scientific breakthroughs, the Zeitgeist of the moment. So, though you can overdose on television (which makes it feel boring and annoying), I believe it's a modern necessity when taken in moderate doses. I know I function much better when I get my Recommended Daily Allowance of Vitamin TV.

4 It is good to be wrong. Do you perhaps disagree with me about television? Do you believe that TV is an evil invention that should be done away with entirely? Well, here's what I have to say to you, buddy:

You may be right.

I may be wrong.

I very often am.

Every time someone can demonstrate to me that I'm in error, a bright new bulb lights up my dim wit. That's why it's good to be wrong—not because we should hang on to our mistakes but because acknowledging error is the foundation of learning. I've watched countless people sacrifice relationships, careers, even life itself, on the altar of their own "rightness." One acquaintance used to rant that motorcycle helmet laws were dangerous because a

Television is like a vitamin: toxic in large quantities but essential for social and personal well-being.

Inviting people to let you know when you're wrong can be rewarding (everywhere except Final Jeopardy).

helmetless rider, who could hear other vehicles coming, would never get in an accident. "But what if you're wrong?" I asked him. "I mean, statistically—"

"I'm not wrong," he said, "and I don't want to hear your statistics." Shortly thereafter, he died of head injuries sustained in a motorcycle accident.

Being open to new information and opinions, inviting people and events to let you know where you're wrong, is the best way I know to open the mind. I try to use the phrase "Tell me where I'm wrong" at least four or five times a day. Try it. You'll see that while insisting that you're right is gratifying, accepting that you're wrong can be transformative.

5 You can work miracles. Recently, while paging through an old journal, I rediscovered a daydream I'd written down years ago. It described my fantasy backyard, a desert oasis with natural plants, a rock garden, areas paved with natural stone. A surge of amazement and gratitude overwhelmed me. The description matched the backyard I actually have right now. I'd connected with my heart's desire, and the desire was fulfilled. Miraculous!

Then I remembered something else. My backyard was once a stretch of grit sparsely inhabited by what I call Lady Macbeth plants (the kind that stab people). I couldn't afford to have landscapers transform it, but I could afford to have them deposit 38,000 pounds of clean rocks and gravel near my back gate. Do you know how long it takes to shovel that much gravel into a wheelbarrow, trundle it to every corner of a fairly large lot, and rake it level? Almost as long as it takes to read a book on stone-masonry, install several hundred slabs of natural slate, and clean the mortar out from under your fingernails. (Hint: The fingernail cleaning alone takes about six months.)

In other words, while I absolutely believe in miracles, I think there's a good reason we say they must be "worked." A client once told me, "If God wants me to achieve big dreams, he'll make it easy and comfortable." I wondered which religion taught her that. Was she thinking about the Children of Israel, who endured 40 "easy and comfortable" years in the wilderness en route to the Promised Land? Or maybe the Buddha, who sought enlightenment through asceticism? Or perhaps Jesus—I mean, that whole thing with the cross was such a warm fuzzy, right?

Einstein supposedly said, "There are only two ways to live your life. One is as though nothing is a miracle. The other is as though everything is a miracle." He also said, "If A equals success, then the formula is: A = X + Y + Z, where X is work, Y is play, and Z is keep your mouth shut." If you're hoping for a miracle, stop gabbing and start working. When you're completely exhausted, stop and play. Then go back to work. Persist, and miracles will start happening, all the more wondrous because you worked them yourself.

So there you have it: my current grab bag of epiphanies. If I act on them, I know from experience they'll sink deeper into my consciousness, until they're intrinsic parts of my worldview. Then new epiphanies will occur to me, and I'll get to work internalizing them. Because that's the way everyone's destiny unfolds.

Unless, of course, I'm wrong. **O**

Go with the Flow

If you find it hard to manage the flood of information out there—news alerts, tweets, and e-mails that could improve your life or waste your time—here's how to float effortlessly above it all.

Is your life on track? Not so long ago, this question seemed eminently sensible. Everyone was trying to get on track, stay on track, move further down the track. We all chugged along like Thomas the Tank Engine, making scheduled station stops (schools, corporations, banks) to pick up the usual cargo (education, job, house) and passengers (friends, spouses, children). A divorce, illness, or job loss constituted catastrophic derailment. Everyone's goal was to claim, "You betcha, my life's on track!"

Today that answer makes no sense. Because, honey, there is no track. Not anymore. We're living through the most dramatic era of change in human history. A flood of new technologies and accompanying social transitions has altered everything. It's not just that we're on the receiving end of a torrent of messages, texts, and e-mails.

The way we interact and build relationships has been turned upside down; whole careers and industries have been swept away. There's so much to do, to know, to learn, to master—and the floodwaters are rising.

To negotiate this new normal, we don't need locomotives. We need kayaks.

Now, it's not easy letting go of the *chugga-chugga*, iron-engine mind-set. Kayaking, after all, is much less stable than riding a train, but these days, that's a huge advantage. This new approach allows you to go with the flow of change, turn quickly in any direction to avoid danger or pursue opportunity, and pop upright again after you've gone under entirely (try doing that on a train).

Once you've learned a few paddling skills, you'll find that your nimble craft can ride the tide of change, accessing all sorts of interesting places and things no train could ever reach.

Paddling Skill #1: Don't Swallow the River

I've noticed that people who are still in train-track mode try to handle every demand or request that reaches them. That's like trying to drink the Nile. You just can't do everything. You shouldn't try. When your to-do list threatens to spill over, examine every item on it while asking two questions:

1. Is this task absolutely necessary to keep my life afloat?

2. Does this task buoy me up emotionally?

If the answer to either of these questions is yes, do the deed. If not, do nothing. Let that problem or opportunity float past you. Wave and smile, if you like, but don't bring nonessential, unpleasant things on board. Your kayak isn't big enough. Anything unnecessary could sink you.

Right now my various mailboxes—voice, paper, and electronic—contain about 120 messages waiting to be answered. Today, about 15 of those messages—ten from work, five from loved ones—are essential to keep my professional and personal life from sinking. A couple more are from funny friends; they'll make me laugh. I'll get to those 17 messages today. The others, later. Maybe. I've found that important messages tend to bob along beside me, bonking against my kayak, until I get to them.

Each day, ask those two river-runner's questions about every request or assignment you encounter. Do the things that are absolutely necessary or make you happy. Let everything else drift away. If you overlook something important, you can always paddle over to it later, or snag something similar floating by. That's one of the joys of the crazy, fluid world we've created.

Paddling Skill #2: Find Your Water Tribe

So that addresses the incoming flood, but what about the oceans of data beyond your in-box? Somewhere out there is the specific help, advice, and knowledge that's crucial to your life. The question is how to find it without getting carried out to sea.

Fortunately, modern communication technology greatly facilitates something called the wisdom of crowds. Simply put, when many diverse people answer a question (say, guessing the number of jelly beans in a jar), the mathematical average of all the responses is more likely to be accurate than any single response.

We're able to access this knowledge better than any other group of humans in history. When my son, Adam, was prenatally diagnosed with Down syndrome more than 20 years ago, no one around me knew what to say. I agonized, grieved, and feared without much social support.

This was before Google.

You see, the algorithm that makes Google work is also what makes it a good indicator of crowd wisdom. Just now, I googled "prenatal diagnosis Down syndrome" for the very first time. The third article on the screen said, "Advice for women whose baby will be born with Down syndrome often comes from a perspective of misinformation and discouragement rather than celebration."

Celebration!

How different my life would've been if Google had existed on the day Adam was diagnosed. A wise, diverse, knowledgeable crowd would've been there—right there!—to counsel and support me better than my friends possibly could.

Today's information flood can be very kind. If you need to know which of the 12,000 recipes for healthful but tasty chicken are actually nutritious and delicious, consult the crowds. If you're looking for the best place to meet people who share your love of nude pot-throwing, start typing. The same goes for when you have to figure out what's happening in your industry, your neighborhood, or even your cable TV system. You'll gather not just the facts you need, but also the support and advice you never knew was out there.

Paddling Skill #3: Make Computers Your BFFs or FOFs

At this point, I should mention I have the computer skills of a hamster. So in 2006, I asked a computer scientist client to teach me to build a Web site. During the following months, my brain felt like a raisin on fire as I tried to fathom HTML, JavaScript, encryption software, and so on. It was like learning Swahili…in Turkish.

Maddeningly, my kids mastered this technology effortlessly. Children love Water World. Their brains are almost 100 percent "fluid intelligence," absorbing new skills fast. Adults rely on the "crystallized intelligence" stored in memory, which has been perfectly useful in the past—hey, why reinvent the wheel every day? Ha ha! Except now the wheels have come off. They're at the bottom of Davy Jones's locker. Here's the

> Somewhere out there is the specific help, advice, and knowledge that's crucial to your life. The question is how to find it without getting carried out to sea.

hard truth: Suck it up and deal. Learn to use computers.

I dish this out because I can take it. I spent nightmare months achieving minimal computer competency, losing all muscle tone except in my mouse-clicking finger, developing acne and insomnia. At one point I became so deeply geeky that I completely broke my eyeglasses, and the only way to use them was to packing-tape the lenses to my face. Which, God help me, I did.

It was so worth it.

If your head exploded at the idea of stapling yourself to a chair for months on end, you may never have a BFF in your computer. Okay, make computers your FOFs—friends of friends. Find computer lovers (your son, your sister, your minister) and exploit them ruthlessly. Get their help sending e-mail, setting up a blog, finding information, watching "stupid pet tricks playing dead." In fact, do that last one right now. Seriously. I'll wait.

See? It really is worth making friends with computers, or at the very least making friends with their friends. You'll find this is your basic paddling technique. Now you just have to learn how to steer your kayak.

Paddling Skill #4: Site Your Purpose

One rainy night long ago, I was fleeing a PTA meeting in my minivan when I drove into a puddle that turned out to be four feet deep. The motor went eerily silent just as the vehicle became waterborne and began floating sideways. In the quiet, I heard a still, small voice within me. It said, "I hate PTA meetings, and I hate this %@&ing minivan."

In that moment, I was steering my life. By articulating what I hated, I began articulating what I loved—not the train-station life of a PTA mom but a kayaking life where I kept my kids home from school to watch YouTube. A life where adults would pay me to say, "Your true purpose is whatever makes you feel most joyful. Try steering toward that."

It's advice I've taken myself: During the months I was obsessed with computers, I felt very much "in the flow." The obsession vanished as inexplicably as it arrived, but it left me tech savvy enough to do research that informs my work—and manage a team that trains life coaches all over the world. Who knew the current would carry me there? I didn't. But I must say: Mama like.

I'm certainly not the only middle-aged mom to use current innovations for career development. Paula, a teacher, thought she'd never get to travel—until she did a deep dive online and discovered something called "location independent lifestyle." She's found jobs all over the world doing teacher-training workshops.

I've just come across another interesting story: Gina is—I kid you not—a massage therapist for dogs. I know this because (a) it says so on her Web site and (b) she's currently in my living room with our golden retriever, Bjorn, who's recovering from knee surgery. I can hear the strains of Enya from Gina's portable CD player, smell the aromatic ointments that have put Bjorn into a bliss-coma. A ridiculous luxury? I thought so, too, until I learned that a massaged dog heals faster. Gina saves money I'd otherwise spend on more vet appointments. I'm thrilled she paddled her kayak toward what gives her joy (though not as thrilled as Bjorn).

Right now, as best you can, write a statement of purpose for your life. If this feels impossible, there are Web sites created specifically to guide you through the process. I'm sure your minister will be glad to help you find them. If you need an example, my purpose statement today (I revise it often) is "To remain in continuous conscious awareness of the one Life in which all singular lives exist." Yesterday it was "To survive until bedtime." Your purpose statement can be grand or silly, as long as it rings true. It is to your kayak life what tracks were to trains: It determines your direction.

This column can't begin to describe the infinite opportunities you'll find as you navigate today's vast seas of possibility. If you learn basic paddling skills and steer by your inner purpose instead of predetermined social tracks, you'll have a joyful voyage. Maybe you'll meet your soul mate online, earn a degree at a distance, start a virtual business, or do something no one's even named yet.

These days, I'm not trying to read the future. I'm just paddling along my own trajectory as a coach, so I can pay BFFs to run my Web site (I'm now the site's FOF). I'm paddling by downloading instructions to help me call my daughter in Japan, on a cell phone that can play a thousand songs and show me satellite photos of almost anyplace on Earth.

Where will this white-water change take us next? My imagination doesn't stretch that far. I'm content to ride the tide. My own little kayak of a life can take me anywhere I need to go. ◖◗

> If you learn basic paddling skills and steer by your inner purpose instead of predetermined social tracks, you'll have a joyful voyage.

How to Solve a Thorny Problem

We're used to living in an either-or world—but when it comes to yes-or-no dilemmas, the most powerful thing you can ask is: What if both answers are true?

A t first I thought Jack was a rebound dater wanting to make a conquest," said Fiona over dinner with friends. "But he's called every day since our first date, and he's really sweet. He remembers my favorite song—I think we really connected."

"Sounds like a dream come true," said Judith.

"On the other hand," Fiona countered, "he talks about his ex-girlfriend a lot, and he started hinting about sex five minutes after we met."

"Bad sign," Kathleen said. "Don't let the whole 'favorite song' thing fool you. He's just a player. He's thinking, *Oh, yeah, I'm all that.*"

"What if both things are true?" This came from Deborah, who'd been listening silently in the corner. "Maybe he's a man-slut with a bruised ego trying to get someone in the sack, and he's a thoughtful person who really likes you."

The pregnant pause that followed could have given birth to triplets. When the conversation resumed, it was

191

suddenly…deep. If the guy in question could be a combination of seemingly opposite traits, might not the same be true in other instances? Could Judith's recent job loss also be a stroke of great luck? Was Kathleen's workaholism both vaunting ambition and a humble desire to serve? And what about all those politicians and athletes—could they truly have the ideals of angels in their hearts and the morals of goats in their pants?

Uh…yes. Think of dilemmas like these as dual-emmas. Unlike standard-issue questions, dualistic dilemmas confuse people by leading to two apparently true but contradictory conclusions. Maybe you've found this in your own life: Perhaps your marriage is both wonderful and terrible, your job both wretched and stimulating, your worst habit both destructive and helpful. Reconciling these apparent brain-benders seems impossible, but if you understand the dynamics of dualism, you can transform bewildering dilemmas into sources of insight.

On the Horns of a Dual-emma

There are two kinds of people in the world: those who divide everyone into two kinds of people, and those who don't. The tendency to dichotomize is stubbornly pervasive in human thought. Maybe this is because it presents decision-making in its simplest form. In evolutionary terms, this method has obvious advantages. Commit to one choice and you're done. If you're an early human on the savanna, you're better off fearing all snakes than having to closely examine each specimen for venom glands.

Even in our more nuanced world, this approach still works. You don't need the company of a snake to thrive, so you can avoid them all. But things become complicated when you get what a nurse friend of mine calls a mixed IV drip of essential fluids and poison—when a person or situation seems to provide necessary things like love and comfort but is also the source of pain and upset.

Confronted with such dualities, most of us try to choose between them. Friends and advisers weigh in on each option—and both camps make sense. Your instinct is to hunker down and figure out which is the "right" answer. After all, how else will you decide to stay or divorce, quit or stick with it? But limiting ourselves to one answer means we often stop seeing what's actually happening, and we make decisions based on labels instead: "The guy is a player, so no date," or "This friendship

is dysfunctional—begone!" This strategy feels right…until the guy or the friend does something truly sweet, gives you the kindness and affection you love and need, and there you are, spiked again on the opposing horns of the dual-emma.

The problem is that an *either-or* thought process won't resolve a *both-and* reality. This point was once driven home for me by a client I'll call Janet, who brought her teenage daughter "Angela" to a coaching session. Angela tearfully confessed, "I've been doing drugs and having sex with boys." Janet calmly replied, "No, you haven't; you're a good girl."

Then she turned to me and asked, "What's the real issue here?" The real issue was that Janet had no way to deal with the possibility that Angela was a good girl who also did drugs and had sex. In Janet's mind, a good person, like her honor-roll daughter, has no bad characteristics. Unable to bridge the divide, Janet went mind-blind to Angela.

Like Janet, we make judgments about all kinds of people, deciding, for instance, that surely the legendary athlete with his boyish smile and beautiful family would never succumb to road rage. Or that the mousy homemaker next door would never have a torrid e-mail affair. We're not only shocked when those assumptions don't hold up, we're unsure how to handle the new information.

The only option for Janet, for you, for anyone who's confronted with two apparently opposite sets of data, is to blast apart the mental dichotomies that organize our minds and drive our behavior. How do you respond to the harassing boss who gives you wonderful, career-building feedback but throws degrading tantrums? Or the friend whose loyalty never fails, except that she flakes and forgets to pick you up after your appendectomy? Are they good people you want in your life or jerks you should avoid?

Yes.

If you scrutinize your own life, you'll find you do plenty of things that violate the dichotomies in your mind. I certainly do. We're considerate, selfless, and clever (except for the times we aren't). Or we're luckless losers (not counting the infinite things that go right for us every day). This is the problem with either-or thinking: It keeps us removed from reality, and it requires that we spend a lot of time and energy convincing ourselves that life is one particular way (and burying evidence that doesn't jibe with that view). More important, it will never feel truthful or satisfying—because it leads to an answer that's only half-right.

> This is the problem with either-or thinking: It leads to an answer that is only half-right.

What to Do When Both Things are True

In mathematics, one kind of problem that sends the mind bouncing back and forth between seemingly opposite truths is called a strange loop. The only possible way out is for mathematicians to use a metastatement that draws attention to the loop itself. In the case of a dualistic dilemma, the metastatement is "Oh, I'm using either-or thinking when both-and thinking is required."

What makes a both-and mind-set so powerful is that it takes you beyond the two choices you thought you had. It opens up new, previously unseen possibilities and opportunities.

There is one caveat to all dual-emma relationships: If you or the other person involved can't or won't admit the whole truth—"Yup, I have a Dr. Jekyll side, but there's also a Mr. Hyde in here"—the relationship will become increasingly dysfunctional.

If both parties can discuss the full range of their behavior, however, almost any relationship can work. You just need to follow three basic steps:

1 Set boundaries that correspond to the worst of times. According to Abraham Maslow's famous hierarchy of needs, the very first psychological need we have is to know we're safe. That's why, when you're around someone who's both good and bad, your first step is one that may seem a bit cruel: When times are good, establish limits that prepare you to deal with the relationship when times are bad. This is how you'll keep from being blindsided by something that—hello—you've already learned.

If your boss is a sweetheart who has tantrums, agree with him during a reasonable moment that you'll both observe certain rules of engagement: "No shouting, or we go to our offices and cool down until everyone's feeling civil." If your supportive friend tends to space out, ask someone more dependable to do a crucial favor. If your loving mom has bouts of negligence, don't entrust her with your twin toddlers.

2 Focus your appreciation on the best of times. In his book *What Happy People Know,* psychologist Dan Baker, PhD, describes an elderly woman named Marlene reminiscing about her beloved late husband. When Baker said he must have been a good man, Marlene said, "He

> Maybe you've found a dilemma like this in your own life: Perhaps your marriage is both wonderful and terrible, your job both wretched and stimulating, your worst habit both destructive and helpful.

was a womanizer and a drunk. A real pain in the butt." She simply chose to focus on the deep and abundant love they'd shared. Baker considered this choice a key to her health and happiness.

Notice there was no denial in Marlene's image of her husband; she acknowledged all his faults and refused to gauze over his memory. And then she chose to bask in his best legacy rather than his terrible betrayals. Setting strong boundaries frees us to take this attitude—and it allows us to access the happiness that's available right now.

3 Remain calm while you explore your options. That phrase— "right now"— is important. When you're dealing with a dual-emma, focus on being fully present with what's happening in this moment, rather than assuming past bad (or good) behavior predicts future consistency. This means alternating freely between the two previous steps. You don't want to spend your life anticipating your boss's next meltdown; neither do you want to assume that his jovial, charming behavior will last through the week. As you explore the scope of the other person's actions, you'll learn whether you can accept this particular mixed IV drip.

In Fiona's case, this meant realizing that Jack may be a player *and* a really compatible match. Maybe, as Kathleen said, "he thinks he's all that" at some times but is grounded, affectionate, and responsive enough at others to make his occasional narcissism worth tolerating (with appropriate boundaries—"I'm going to watch TV while you preen, Jack dear. Call me when you're finished!").

As they contemplated Deborah's idea that a scoundrel could also be sincere, Fiona and her friends began, in the words of one yogi, "existing in continuous creative response to whatever was present"—in their love lives, their careers, their definition of self.

Try seeing your world and yourself this way, eyes open to whatever is before you, mind free of dichotomies. Are you good or bad, fragile or tough, wise or foolish? Yes. And so am I. What Jack thought about himself (at least according to Kathleen) is true of every human being. Oh, yeah. We're all that. **O**

Beaglemania: 2008 Westminster winner Uno, charisma personified.

Martha Beck's Law of Attraction

O's resident life coach believes anyone (wallflowers included) can cultivate that intangible It factor, and she's got a four-step plan to prove it.

I've never really followed popular culture; my finger is on the pulse of things like 19th-century literature (which no longer has one). But the instant I saw a photo of one particular newly minted celebrity, I became a die-hard fan. It's not that his looks are especially unusual. You could pass someone like him on the street without even noticing. Nor does he possess any special talents. And yet, he's got that It factor. Whatever he's doing—striding past paparazzi, greeting a cheering crowd, or licking a reporter—Uno the beagle embodies pure charisma.

Uno was the first of his breed to win the prestigious Westminster Kennel Club Dog Show. His victory was remarkable because beagles are so...basic. They're the white cotton T-shirts of dogdom—they've got nothing to brush, fluff, or style—but when Uno took Best in Show, the crowd leaped up in a wild ovation. Newscasters announced his victory with goofy smiles. Everyone loved Uno's extraordinary brand of ordinariness.

I've always learned from beagles: Charles Schulz's cartoon character Snoopy sweetened my childhood, and my dear departed Cookie taught me worlds about my core values of peace, affection, and gluttony. But I've discovered new lessons by studying Uno's personal magnetism, and I've come to believe that there's no better way to amp up your charisma than to follow his example.

Actually, scratch that. You don't really need to learn charisma, any more than you need to learn laughter. I believe every human being is innately charismatic. Babies squint out from their unfathomably open minds with a fierce, ravenous wonder that makes it impossible not to stare back. But within a few months, or a few years, many children mask their real selves. Charisma, you see, draws attention, and attention can be a problem.

For example, by age 5 Melanie had learned to shrink and disappear when her mother went into drunken tantrums at home or, worse, in public. Ellyn was bullied by schoolmates who envied the way she drew her teachers' focus, so she taught herself not to. Perfectionistic Lisette deflected attention because she feared that anyone who noticed her would notice her shortcomings. This is why a number of us reach adolescence behaving more like whipped puppies than Westminster champions.

Below you'll find four steps to help you reveal your own charisma. If you read them and think, *Oh, I could never!*, you've likely veiled your natural magnetism, then mistaken those veils for your real personality. This was probably a necessary move way back when, but to live fully now, you must drop your disguise. In Marianne Williamson's immortal words, "Your playing small doesn't serve the world."

Step 1: Strike Some Poses

We often use the word *pose* to imply fakery, but more simply, the word means "the position of our bodies." When her mother drank, Melanie literally curled inward, shoulders hunching, spine rounding, eyes down. Ellyn slumped to avoid seeming proud. Lisette spent three decades with her arms clamped against her ribs. They were all posing. So are you, right now. The question isn't to pose or not to pose, but how to know which body language reflects your true self.

Watch Uno the wonder beagle on YouTube as his

> You don't really need to learn charisma, any more than you need to learn laughter.

handler positions him like a toy. Being placed in show posture, far from constraining Uno, seems to fill him with confidence, sending his charisma into overdrive. For humans, as for dogs, physical movement influences moods. You may realize you spend a lot of the day in a charisma-crushing position. The posture you had as a toddler—spine straight, shoulders back, chest out, head high—may be long forgotten, but repositioning yourself as nature intended is essential to unveiling your innate charisma.

This is why soldiers stand at attention (basically Uno's "show pose"). Try it yourself: Stand up straight, broaden and drop your shoulders, bring your clavicles up and your chin down. If you don't feel a little like General Patton, exaggerate this pose until you do. Experiment with other postures, noting how each affects your sense of self. Hook your thumbs through your belt loops and become a cowboy; smile over your shoulder to feel seductive; imitate Michelangelo's *David* and find the courage to fight Goliath. Cultivating charisma is one of the few areas where I recommend adopting a "fake it till you make it" strategy, because any pose that elicits confidence, even if it feels phony, is actually a return to authenticity. No one was born beaten.

Here's a challenge: For the rest of today, stand, sit, and walk like the most charismatic person you know. Notice the moments when you feel foolish or embarrassed about projecting charisma. Those are the times when you have forgotten who you are. Persist for a few more days and you'll discover that charismatic body language is a self-reinforcing cycle. As your physical bearing becomes more aligned with your real self, other people will begin noticing you more. Don't let this affect your new behavior (in other words, don't revert to slumping). Ultimately, you must become confident enough to drop your pose of unimportance for good.

Step 2: When You Get to the Brink...Keep Going

Diane Ackerman writes that "there are moments on the brink, when you can give yourself to a lover, or not; give in to self-doubt, uncertainty, and admonishment, or not; dive into a different culture, or not; set sail for the unknown, or not; walk out onto a stage, or not.... Resist then, and...there is only what might have been." She calls these moments "littoral," like the borders where dry land meets the ocean. A defining characteristic of charismatic people is that they choose to walk through littoral moments as if they had no doubt.

Now, let me take this moment to clarify what I mean: Narcissists can appear charismatic for a while, because they *never* doubt they're right. This conviction commands attention and respect, at least until they turn out to be hopelessly wrong. True charismatics, by contrast, acknowledge and learn from their mistakes. They release doubt simply because doubt isn't useful when they're on the brink. For instance, once Uno was onstage, he never seemed to worry that he might not be a champion (even though no beagle had ever won much of anything). His certainty eventually converted everyone, including the judges.

To follow this example, find a littoral zone in your life and step beyond it as if you had no doubt. For Melanie, this meant arranging an intervention for her mother, faking confidence (which eventually became real) as she spoke the truth and asked her mother to enter rehab. Ellyn's first charismatic adventure was attending her high school reunion, walking tall and radiating authority, dropping the fear of offending or outshining others. Lisette joined Toastmasters, where she learned to stand and deliver, performance anxiety be damned. For these women, and each of us, a dip in the sea of adventure washes away more of the layers encrusting your charisma. Find your littoral moment, drop your doubts on the shore, and walk into the waves.

Step 3: Focus Outward

The Westminster Dog Show is a multibreed festival of self-consciousness. On videos of the event you can see everyone, human and animal, thinking, *Are they watching me? Can they see my hindquarters? How's my haircut?* Everyone, that is, except Uno. His eyes are on the crowd. When they cheer, he cheers back. When he howls to the judges, "Yo! How you doin'?," the normally staid officials grin like kids. Uno is making the single most charismatic move possible: He's shining his attention upon the beings around him.

That's what Melanie did during her mother's intervention. Instead of just rehearsing and delivering an impassioned speech, she paid close, respectful attention, which her mother (for once) returned. Both Ellyn (at her high school reunion) and Lisette (in exercises with her

Toastmaster cronies) learned that groups also have personalities. Focus on any person or crowd the way Uno focused on the spectators at Westminster, with friendly curiosity, and your charismatic energy will touch every individual. Why? People pay attention to people who are paying attention to them.

Step 4: Take Space and Make Space

Just because charismatic people focus intensely on others doesn't mean they forget themselves. Quite the contrary. The very essence of charisma is projecting unbounded awareness of others while setting rock-solid boundaries. When an aggressive reporter pushed a microphone into Uno's face, Uno unapologetically crunched it with his teeth before moving on to more courteous admirers. He showed none of the angry, aggressive boundary setting born of low confidence. Like any true charismatic, he had mastered the art of the clean response—in his case, a cheerful chomp.

Melanie held this effective, neutral energy at her mother's intervention, stating her position while refusing to either rail at, or give in to, her mother's drunken pleas. Ellyn found that when she let herself shine, she had to rebuff sycophants and unwanted suitors but that a firm, upbeat "No, thanks" got the job done. Lisette discovered that she could take the spotlight when she wanted it—and back away from it when she needed space. Her polite disinterest was a powerful version of the cheerful chomp.

If you play around with the steps above—and I certainly hope that you do—you'll find that some bold poses will feel more right than others, that life calls you to dive past specific littoral lines, that particular people and groups genuinely respond to your attention, and that you have your own particular way of administering cheerful chomps. The purpose of exploring these general elements of charisma is to help you find your unique style.

Oh, golly shucks, you may be thinking at this point. *I'm not charismatic. I'm just an ordinary person.* Yes, and beagles are just ordinary dogs.

Charisma is the light that shines from the core of all ordinary beings. You can't strip the veils that cover your real nature without illuminating the world in a new, inimitable way. You will become the singular you—the one, the only, the Uno—that everyone wants to see. ⬤

> The very essence of charisma is projecting unbounded awareness of others while setting rock-solid boundaries.

Who's Never Going to Let You Down?

You've got a no-fail means of recognizing the really dependable people out there—a nifty inner gizmo called a trust-o-meter. The problem: Over the years, it may have gotten a little out of whack and now needs a little fine-tuning. (Or maybe a *lot*.)

I'm writing this in the African bush, where I've just watched five lions dismantling a dead buffalo, a hungry leopard stalking impala, and several baboons snitching part of my own breakfast when my back was turned. Out here, my safety depends on the knowledge, courage, and selflessness of just a few human beings. Some of these people I know well; others I've barely met. We are of various colors and creeds, sharing only a conflict-riddled ancestral history. Yet I feel safer at this moment than I once felt in my suburban American bedroom. It's not that I'm blind to life's fragility or the dangers around me. It's just that I possess a gift offered by many mistake-filled years: At my age, I have a pretty good idea what and whom to trust.

It's because I've learned to depend on a handy little inner mechanism—you've got one, too. Call it a "trust-o-meter," a bit of hardware preinstalled on your hard drive the day you arrived, tiny and vulnerable, from the stork factory. Ever since, your trust-o-meter has been programmed up the wazoo, first by caregivers, then by you yourself. If your inner software is working well, your trust-o-meter is guiding you safely through life's many hazards. If it isn't, you smash into one disappointment or betrayal after another. The good news is that no matter how faulty your trust-o-meter, it's never too late to debug the system. Trust me on that.

Or not.

Read this; then you make that call.

Step 1: Testing the System

"As soon as you trust yourself," wrote Goethe, "you will know how to live." To discern between people who might save your life and those who might ruin it, you must be reliable, honest—in a word, trustworthy—toward yourself. And we do this far less often than most people realize.

I'm about to reveal one of my favorite life coaching tricks, which I've used on literally thousands of people. In the middle of a speech or coaching session, I'll suddenly say, "Are you comfortable?" Most people look startled, squint at me as though I'm a few chocolates short of a full box, then assure me that yes, they're comfortable.

"Really?" I'll say, earnestly.

Yes, they insist, getting a bit annoyed, they're totally comfortable.

Then I ask this: "So, if you were alone in your bedroom right now, would you be sitting in the position you're in at this moment?"

It takes them all of .03 seconds to answer, "No." But it takes them much longer to come up with the answer to my next question:

"Why not?"

Some people will just sit there blinking, as if I've asked them to explain why they didn't invent spaghetti. It takes them much consternated thinking to come up with the answer—which is, of course, that the positions in which people sit in public settings are generally much less loose than the positions they adopt when unobserved, in a room designed for rest and relaxation.

In short, they're a bit uncomfortable.

Now, the problem here isn't the discomfort itself. People can handle a world of hurt if necessary. The problem is that they aren't conscious of their own discomfort, even though it's obvious. They lie to my face in clear daylight, believing they're telling the truth even though they know (and I know…and they know that I know) they're lying.

Do you find that last sentence confusing? Welcome to denial, which, oh, honey, it's true, ain't just a river in Egypt.

Denial exists because human infants, though equipped with trust-o-meters, are built to trust, blindly and absolutely, any older person who wanders past. Life would be brief, incredibly complicated, and unbearably frightening for any baby who didn't invest automatic confidence in her caregivers, who suspected adults of deception whenever they said, "Drink this; it's good for you" or "Those people are evil" or "Grandma will take care of you." We all have faith in the people we encounter during our early youth. If they deserve this, our trust-o-meters are programmed to function accurately, and we're well on our way to a life of wise discernment.

Sadly, however, few child-rearers deserve the unmitigated trust babies invest in them. Some adults, purposely or (far more often) accidentally, give children unhealthy drinks, from tainted water to Jack Daniels. Others, out of malice or (far more often) ignorance, create unwarranted fear and prejudice. Sometimes Grandma is a psychopath or (far more often) a short-tempered neurotic whose idea of childcare involves strapping the kiddies into her Cadillac so she can cruise the red light district searching through binoculars for her ex-boyfriend's car.

If something along those lines happened to you, you've been conditioned to attach the definition "trustworthy" to people who are, in fact, untrustworthy. If your parents let you sip their whiskey as an expression of affection, you may be wired to swear by alcoholics. If you were raised by white supremacists, you may rely on lunatic skinheads. If your beloved Grandma was a stalker, obsessive jealousy may inspire your confidence. You'll be extremely uncomfortable the whole time, but you won't recognize the discomfort.

This is why denial is so baffling: You have no idea you're in it. Rather than thinking, *I am now displaying unwarranted trust,* you just feel...off. Confused. Maybe a little crazy. Maybe a lot crazy. Something seems wrong, and over time, it feels wronger and wronger. Those of us with badly calibrated trust-o-meters usually think the wrongness must be in us, that if we can somehow think or work or love better, our painful relationships with the alcoholic racist stalkers in our lives will somehow become perfect.

For those of us who want to know if we have defective trust-o-meters, the evidence is blessedly obvious: Our relationships and life situations don't work. We're lying to ourselves, pretending we're at ease when we know we aren't, so, in the converse of Goethe's dictum, we don't have a clue how to live. We're often rudely awakened, bitterly disappointed, shockingly betrayed. If this happens to you once, perhaps it's bad luck. If it happens repeatedly, there are bugs in your system. To check, take the Trust Test on the next page. If your score indicates that your trust-o-meter functions well, you can stop reading now. But if the quiz reveals a problem, it's time to recalibrate.

Step 2: The Scientific Method

All child-rearers—myself among them—are confused, mistaken, or ignorant about some things, so don't waste time insisting that your parents fix every glitch in your programming, or flagellate yourself for not spotting their errors. Just start using the scientific method to reboot your trust-o-meter. This involves three basic steps: making predictions about how the world works, looking for evidence to either support or disconfirm those predictions, and changing your hypotheses in light of what you see to be true.

Start by thinking of someone important to you, and rate your trust in that person on a scale of 1 to 5 (1 = lowest possible trust, 5 = highest). Then, evaluate the person by recalling your observations of his or her behavior.

Here are a few obvious questions I've found very helpful in quantifying the trustworthiness of people in my own life. The first three are the "yes" questions; if Person X is completely trustworthy, you'll answer yes to all three. The second three are the "no" questions—if Person X deserves your trust, the answer to all three will be negative.

> For those of us who want to know if we have defective trust-o-meters, the evidence is blessedly obvious: Our relationships and life situations don't work.

The "yes" questions:

1. Does Person X usually show up on time?
2. When Person X says something is going to happen, does it usually happen?
3. When you hear Person X describing an event, and then get more information about that event, does the new information usually match Person X's description?

The "no" questions:

4. Have you ever witnessed Person X lying to someone, or assuming you'll help deceive a third person?
5. Does Person X sometimes withhold information in order to make things go more smoothly, or to avoid conflict?
6. Have you ever witnessed Person X doing something (lying, cheating, being unkind) that he or she would condemn if another person did it?

These questions might seem trivial. They're not. As the saying goes, "the way we do anything is the way we do everything." I'm not saying we have the ultimate power or right to judge others. But if you trust someone whose behavior doesn't pass the six screening questions above, your trust-o-meter may well be misaligned. If Person X rated more than one "no" on the first three questions, and more than one "yes" on the second three, they don't warrant total trust at present. If you trust someone who blew all six questions, you need some readjustments. You don't have to change Person X (you can't), but you do need to take a hard look at your own patterns of trust.

By the way, if you're now rationalizing Person X's behavior with arguments like "But he means well" or "It's not her fault; she had a terrible childhood," your trust-o-meter is definitely on the fritz. These are the small lies we use to tell ourselves we're comfortable when we aren't. It's not the end of the world if Person X lies to you. Lying to yourself, on the other hand, can make your life so miserable, the end of the world might be a relief.

Step 3: Learning to Trust Everyone and Everything

The Master...trusts people who are trustworthy," wrote Lao Tzu, my favorite philosopher. "She also trusts people who aren't trustworthy. This is true trust." Many earnest do-gooders skew this to mean that everyone is noble at the core, every crazy stranger should be invited to sleep in the children's room, every elected official is

The Trust Test

	STRONGLY AGREE	AGREE	NO OPINION	DISAGREE	STRONGLY DISAGREE
1 I rarely repeat the same mistake more than twice.					
2 I've been betrayed many times by people I loved.	5	4	3	2	1
3 I'm at ease when I'm alone.					
4 I hide my real thoughts and actions.	5	4	3	2	1
5 I hate my job, but I'm stuck in it.					
6 When people are angry at me, I usually understand why.	1	2	3	4	5
7 I only feel safe when I'm alone.					
8 I never worry that my friends and family will hurt or abandon me.	1	2	3	4	5
9 I've had a lot of bad luck in romantic relationships.				2	
10 I eat only when I'm hungry and stop as soon as I'm full.	1	2	3	4	5
11 I have a lot of secrets, and I intend to keep them at all cost.					
12 My first impressions are almost always accurate.	1	2	3	4	5
13 I don't need alcohol or drugs to relax.					
14 A lot of my loved ones are addicts.	5	4	3	2	1
15 I can't control certain behaviors (e.g. overeating, gambling, stealing).				2	
16 I stay within my spending budget.	1	2	3	4	5
17 I often make polite promises I don't really intend to keep.					
18 I can't stand being alone.	5	4	3	2	1
19 I never worry that people might find out too much about me.					
20 I show up on time for appointments, even informal ones.	1	2	3	4	5
21 I'm plagued by bad luck in my professional life.					
22 People seem more and more unpredictable to me as I age.	5	4	3	2	1
23 I have many rewarding, happy relationships.					
24 I'm careful to save part of my income.	1	2	3	4	5
25 I can't detach from someone who frightens or hurts me.					
26 Life makes more and more sense to me as I age.	1	2	3	4	5
27 I need recreational drugs or alcohol to completely relax.					
28 I keep my promises, and my friends and family keep their promises to me.	1	2	3	4	5
29 Most people behave pretty much as I expect them to.					
30 I often show up late for appointments, especially informal ones.	5	4	3	2	1

For scoring, see next page.

intelligent and just. But that's not "true trust"; it's another version of denial, like the one Pema Chödrön calls by the memorable label "idiot compassion."

So what does it mean to "trust people who aren't trustworthy"? I pondered this earlier today, as I watched the lions devour the buffalo, the leopard attack the impala, the baboons stealing breakfast. I am very wary of these beasts, but that doesn't mean I don't trust them. I depend on them deeply—to do what they usually do. Lions and leopards can be trusted to eat animals about my size. Baboons can be trusted to steal food whenever possible. Because I know this, I adapt my behavior to avoid getting eaten or pilfered.

By the same token, if someone in your life pulls in a dismal score on the Trust Test, perpetually failing to keep promises, tell the truth, quit drinking, or show compassion, this is exactly what you can depend on them to keep doing. Addicts can be trusted to lie. Narcissists can be trusted to backstab. And people who reliably do their best, whose stories check out against your own observations, can be trusted to stay relatively honest and stable.

> People who reliably do their best, whose stories check out against your own observations, can be trusted to stay relatively honest and stable.

When you spot faulty programming in your trust-o-meter, you may experience some deep grief. You'll have to acknowledge what you already know, deep down: that your alcoholic dad may never be reliable, that you may have picked an irresponsible partner, that the friend who never supports you probably never will. You may face some tough choices as your debugged trust-o-meter directs you away from familiar negative patterns and into new behaviors. But as you more accurately predict what will happen, you'll feel a new, growing confidence. Your life will begin to work.

This is why I feel so much safer today, in the bushveld, than I once did in my home. Yes, it's a jungle out here, but it's a jungle everywhere. Life, in fact, is just one big wilderness. But you were born for this wilderness, and you have the instruments to negotiate it safely. Does that thought feel comfortable? Really, truly comfortable? As soon as it does, you've found your way to the first part of Goethe's promise: You can trust yourself. And because Goethe was a trustworthy person, you can rely on the second part of his promise following automatically. You really will know how to live. O

The Trust Test: Scoring

Martha Beck helps you determine if your trust-o-meter needs recalibrating.

SCORING

30–54 You really didn't need this test—but you know that. You know pretty much everything you should to trust and be happy, and you reliably use that knowledge. Just remember another thing you know: When people tell you to act in opposition to your instincts, ignore them.

55–79 You generally trust yourself with good results, but you have wobbly moments in new situations or when you're interacting with people who impress or intimidate you. When you begin to lose trust in yourself, stop. Breathe. Ground yourself in the awareness

that has served you so well, and remember that this same feeling can guide you through even the most unfamiliar circumstances.

80–104 You are something of a drifter: honest with yourself in some situations, blind to reality in others. You may be taken in by manipulative, dishonest, or damaged people. Pay attention whenever this happens. Notice the circumstances and people that end up disappointing you, and steer clear of anything that feels similar.

105–129 Listen, it's time you shaped up. You're not being completely honest with yourself. You've been trained to deny your

own subjective experience. Begin to consciously feel what you feel, know what you know, and articulate whatever you really mean. As you do this, the frequent betrayals that afflict you will become clear, and you'll be able to avoid them.

130–150 Commiserations. Life feels random, and your heart is perpetually being broken. If you enjoy this, on you go. If you'd rather have less pain, take a long, hard look. You insist on believing things that you know aren't true. You need distance from your "normal life," and if possible a counselor, to help you allow the truth about your inner and outer experience into your consciousness.

When Your Biggest Problem Is...You

Are you driving yourself crazy with dumb mistakes, "what was I thinking?" comments, and other lunkheaded moves? Martha Beck offers a no-fail strategy to get you back on the right track.

I t's not like I'm shooting myself in the foot," said Whitney. "It's more like I'm using my entire body for target practice. With guns in both hands."

Whitney's problems began when economic chaos hit the advertising company where she was an editor. As Whitney cut redundant prose from ad copy, her company cut redundant workers all around her. Whitney herself had always been a perfectionist who loved her work, but after the downsizing, her performance nosedived. She began to forget meetings, sleep past her alarm,

accidentally forward highly personal e-mails to her boss. On the day she absentmindedly shredded a presentation she was about to deliver, Whitney came to see me.

"Do I have early-onset Alzheimer's?" she asked desperately. "Maybe ADD? A brain tumor? It's got to be something medical."

Meanwhile, another client of mine—I'll call her Olga—was going through something similar in her relationship with her husband. "Jack is my life," she told me. "I couldn't go on without him." Yet Olga made as many stupid mistakes at home as Whitney did at work. "I forget I've promised to pick him up after work," she told me.

"When he says he needs space, I follow him around begging him to talk, and when he wants to be close, I shut down. What's wrong with me?"

Maybe you've had an experience similar to these, a truck-with-no-brakes run of errors and foul-ups that wreak destruction in your life despite frantic efforts to regain control. In the midst of such madness, it can help immensely to know that there's a name for your pain. You may be using something psychologists call a counterphobic mechanism, a tendency to slide toward, not away from, something you fear. Those of us who use plain English might call it self-sabotage—and it can ruin your life. As counterintuitive as it might seem, these subconscious reflexes can be helpful. In these troubled times, it behooves us all to be aware of them and use them consciously and skillfully.

Anticipation, Anticipation Is Making Me Late...

"One of my theories," says the evil Count in William Goldman's classic story *The Princess Bride,* "is that pain involves anticipation." He then leaves the captive hero, Westley, chained next to the Machine, a torture device the Count has promised to use on Westley later. An albino dungeon-keeper offers Westley a way out. "You deserve better than what's coming," he says in a moment of compassion. "Please let me kill you. You'll thank me, I swear." Only Westley's superhuman fortitude keeps him from accepting.

The Count's theory about anticipation is right on the money. And self-sabotage is the mind's way of accepting the albino's offer. Like Whitney or Olga, we may screw up in precisely the places we want most to succeed, not realizing that we're subconsciously trying to force a resolution, to stop the anxious feeling that's hanging over our heads, to lose the job rather than continue to worry about a pink slip. To resolve the situation, we must first recognize that we're using counterphobic mechanisms. And that means punching through denial.

Denial Strategy #1 "Fear? Ha! What fear?"

When I suggested to Whitney that she might be courting job loss precisely because it was her worst fear, she laughed.

"Fear? Me? No, absolutely not," she said. "I mean, I'm sorry so many people are getting laid off, but my job is safe as houses."

> If you're repeatedly making dreadful mistakes and finding yourself in embarrassing snafus in an important area of life, push yourself to contemplate your worst-case scenario.

This struck me as an odd choice of idiom in an era when demented mortgage practices have triggered worldwide economic catastrophe. I also noticed a crimson blush creeping up Whitney's neck. Paging Dr. Freud: Dr. Freud to the floor, please.

"What if you keep shredding presentations and sending your boss e-mails about yeast infections?" I said. "What if these screwups keep getting worse?"

The blush faded abruptly; now Whitney looked pale. "Honestly, I don't see how that's possible," she muttered. "Um, could you excuse me for a second?" She pulled out her BlackBerry and peered at it anxiously.

"You seem nervous," I commented, watching her thumbs go to work.

"Well, of course I'm nervous!" Whitney snapped. "The whole damn country's falling apart—who isn't nervous?"

"So," I said, "suppose your company folds. What would you do?"

"That won't happen."

"I'm not saying it will; I'm just asking you to imagine it."

"I don't want to!"

"Seriously, what will you do if you lose your job?"

The dam burst.

"I've worked my whole adult life for this job!" Whitney cried. "And it's not like I can get another one these days. Have you seen the news? Every day it's worse—more unemployment, more foreclosures. People just like me are living in tents! My stocks are practically worthless." Whitney began trembling. "I can't lose my job," she whispered. "It'd be the end of the world."

So that cat was out of the bag. Like so many people right now, Whitney was stuck contemplating the Machine of unemployment. But she'd shoved this intense fear out of her conscious awareness, so her subconscious mind had built a counterphobic mechanism to kill the job and end the agony. "You'll thank me," her inner albino was saying. "I swear."

Denial Strategy #2 "But that's the last thing I would want."

For Olga, the problem wasn't that she was unaware of her biggest fear. Quite the contrary. She couldn't answer a telemarketer's call without blurting out her dread of losing Jack. She discussed it endlessly with Jack himself.

"I won't let him talk about anything negative—negative feelings, bad experiences in the past, even movies he doesn't like," she said. "I love him so much; I can't let negative energy into our relationship."

Of course, this bizarre practice ensured that Olga's marriage was focused entirely on negative energy (our lives tend to revolve around the things we're trying not to do). It also meant Jack had no way of processing the countless indignities Olga kept inflicting on him.

"You do understand you're making Jack's life completely impossible?" I said, with my patented anti-tact.

"I know!" Olga said, sobbing. "It's another thing I've done to drive him away, but I can't live without him!"

"So what'll you do if he leaves?"

"I don't know. I've never dared think about it."

"If you don't think about it, you're going to have to live through it," I said. "So start thinking."

"Well," she sniffed, "I'd have to learn to live for myself, I guess. I'd have to be independent, to be..." Her voice trailed off, and her mascara-smeared eyes opened wide. "I'd be free," she said.

Whoa, Nelly! The fear she'd been hiding was an even bigger surprise to Olga than Whitney's was to her. Olga's real fear wasn't that Jack wanted to leave her. It was that she wanted to leave Jack.

You may find my treatment of Whitney and Olga rather brutal, but I am not the evil Count. When you're chained to a Machine, though, waiting for God knows what, you have only two options. One is to let the albino dungeon-keeper of your subconscious kill the very thing you fear losing. The other is what brave Westley chose: Face and embrace your fear.

If you're repeatedly making dreadful mistakes and finding yourself in embarrassing snafus in an important area of life, push yourself to contemplate your worst-case scenario. I suggest doing this in the company of friends, family members, therapists, coaches, or all of the above. While you're gaping and reeling like a stunned mullet, your more objective advisers can help you do some contingency planning. That is what I did with Whitney.

"I know losing your job sounds like the end of the world," I told her. "But it wouldn't be. I know people who've started Internet-based companies for freelance work. They're making more

money now than before they were laid off."

"Really?" Whitney blinked. Her grip on the BlackBerry loosened.

"And you'd finally have time to write your own book—haven't you always wanted that?"

"Yes, but how would I—"

"You'd figure it out," I said, hoping like hell I was right.

"You know, I would," said Whitney. She didn't sound totally convinced, not by any means. But she did sound a tiny bit hopeful. Her fear of the Machine was already waning—and that, I knew, would end her unconsciously driven train wrecks at the office. The more we examined ways Whitney could survive being unemployed, the less likely she was to cause that very fate.

Once Olga copped to her real fears, facing and embracing her worst-case scenario was even more liberating. She had felt stifled in her relationship, she realized. Her definition of "perfect wife" had meant someone who relinquished all personal interests except her husband. Although Olga loved Jack, that image of wifehood (hers, not his) was so noxious that subconsciously she knew she couldn't sustain it. Some part of her worried that it would eventually implode. So she'd begun doing things to end the marriage—and thus her terrible anticipation of its end.

As we discussed what Olga might do if she were single, she began redefining herself as an individual, not an appendage. With Jack's help, she bagged her old stereotype of married life and realized she was free to plot her own course. Embracing her worst-case scenario took the KILL ME NOW sign off her relationship, and her marriage-torpedoing behaviors stopped.

Since you, like Whitney and Olga, are probably of sound mind, any chronic blundering on your part is likely a counterphobic mechanism: a brave, unconscious, totally knob-brained attempt to end the torture of anticipating further torture. These days, more than ever, facing and embracing your worst-case scenarios, seeing them as problems to be solved rather than torments to suffer helplessly, can save you no end of self-sabotage.

Ironically, of course, this, too, is a counterphobic mechanism. The difference is that it's conscious, reasoned, and wise, rather than unconscious, irrational, and nuts. It may not be fun to contemplate everything that could go wrong in your life. But by going straight into the fear, you can save yourself a crazy go-round with unconscious self-sabotage. You deserve better than that. You'll thank me. I swear. ◑

> The more we examined ways Whitney could survive being unemployed, the less likely she was to cause that very fate.

Half a Mind Is a Terrible Thing to Waste

We've all heard that we need to tap into our creative right brains. But *how?*
Martha Beck offers a few fruitful ways to branch out.

This morning I sat down to write about how we can all learn to better use the right hemispheres of our brains. For 30 minutes, I tapped restlessly at a laptop. Nothing much happened, idea-wise. Flat beer.

Finally I resorted to a strategy I call the Kitchen Sink. I read bits of eight books: four accounts of brain research, one novel about India, one study of bat behavior, one biography of Theodore Roosevelt, and one memoir of motherhood. Next I drove to my favorite Rollerblading location, listening en route to a stand-up comic, a mystery novel, and an Eckhart Tolle lecture. I yanked on my Rollerblades and skated around, squinting slack-jawed into the middle distance. After a while, a tiny lightbulb went on. *Well,* I thought, *I could write about this.*
Duh.

The Kitchen Sink, you see, is one way to activate your brain's creative right hemisphere. Every writer I've ever met uses some version of it, as do Web designers, cartoonists, TV producers—all "content creators" who regularly face the terrifying thought, *Well, I've gotta come up with something.*

If you're not a content creator, wait a while. The 21st century is to content creators what the Industrial Revolution was to factory workers: In a world where information is superabundant, unique and creative ideas are hot-ticket advantages both personally and professionally. More and more people are finding more and more ways to parent, make money, find friends, and live well by relying on creativity. I've seen this shift among my life-coaching clients. For instance: Michaela develops financial-planning strategies for stay-at-home moms. Mary runs a long-distance mother's support group via Skype. Alyssa's innovative T-shirt designs keep selling, recession or no recession. The demand for creative thinking is both a challenge and an opportunity. It requires us to use more than the logical left-brain skills we learned in school. These days, we all need to get back into our right minds.

When Right Was Wrong

Historically, most brain science came from studying people whose brains had been damaged. Depending on the injury's location, these patients had varying disabilities: If you lost one brain section, you might be unable to do long division; wipe out another patch, and your lace-tatting days were over. The famous Phineas Gage had an iron rod rammed all the way through his head, permanently losing the ability to be nice. One can hardly blame him.

People with left-hemisphere brain injuries may have trouble thinking analytically or making rational decisions. Many with damage to the right hemisphere, on the other hand, can still pass their SATs but become unable to connect parts into a meaningful whole. Oliver Sacks wrote about such a patient in *The Man Who Mistook His Wife for a Hat.* This gentleman saw perfectly but could identify what he saw only by guessing. If you showed him a rose, he might say, "Well, it's red on top, green and prickly below, and it smells nice…. Is it a flower?" One day, while looking for a hat to put on, he reached for his wife instead, perhaps thinking: *It's familiar, and it goes with me everywhere…. Is it my hat?* I'm sure this was awful for his poor wife, though it could have been worse (*Well, it's the size of a small house and it needs cleaning…. Is it my garage?*). But still.

For most of Western history the right side of the brain was short-shrifted by neurologists intent on helping people think "rationally." Only in recent years have experts begun to laud the creative, holistic right hemisphere. Interestingly, left-hemisphere strokes appear to be much more common than right-hemisphere strokes. Perhaps we're overusing our left hemispheres to the point of blowout. Or perhaps illness is trying to nudge us back to the mysteries and gifts of the right brain. Fortunately, we now know we can effect this change deliberately, without having to survive neurological disaster.

In his fascinating book *The Talent Code,* Daniel Coyle describes how the brain reacts when a person develops a new skill. Performing an action involves firing an electrical signal through a neural pathway; each time this happens, it thickens the myelin sheath that surrounds nerve fibers like the rubber coating on electrical wires. The thicker the myelin sheath around a neural pathway, the more easily and effectively we use it. Heavily myelinated pathways equal mad skills.

Throughout your education, you myelinated the left-brain pathways for thinking logically. You were prepared for predictability and order, not today's constant flood of innovation and change. Now you need to build up myelin sheaths around new skill circuits, located in your right hemisphere. To do this, you need something Coyle calls deep practice.

Deep practice is the same no matter what the skill. First visualize an ability you'd like to acquire—swimming like Dara Torres, painting like Grandma Moses, handling iron rods like Uncle Phineas. Then try to replicate that behavior. Initially, you'll fail. That's good; failure is an essential element of deep practice. Next, analyze your errors, noting exactly where your performance didn't match your ideal. Now try again. You'll still probably fail (remember, that's a good thing), but in Samuel Beckett's words, you'll "fail better."

Examples of people engaged in deep practice are everywhere. Think of *American Idol* contestants improving their singing, or Tiger Woods perfecting his golf swing. I once saw a television interviewer present Toni Morrison with the original manuscript of one of her masterpieces. Morrison became slightly distracted, running critical eyes across the page, wanting to make changes. She clearly can't stop deep practicing. That's why she won the Nobel Prize.

How to Wake Up Your Right Mind

Deep practice is hard. It makes your brain feel like a piece of raw hamburger. It's also weirdly rewarding, dropping you into rapt concentration, yielding quick improvement, and (if you're lucky) producing good work. Here are some tricks you can deep practice to buff up your right hemisphere.

1 **Sign your name every which way.** My favorite teacher and artist, Will Reimann, was brilliant at getting his students to use the right side of their brains. There were many squinty eyes in Reimann's studio, much neural myelination. Here's one of his exercises:

Sign your name.

> Turning on your right brain is a skill, one that grows steadily stronger the more you work at it.

Done?

Okay, now things get gnarly. Sign again, but this time, do it in mirror writing—right to left, rather than left to right (just moving your hand backward fires the right brain hemisphere). Got that? Now sign upside down. Then backward and upside down. Repeat this until you can sign in all directions. Good luck.

2 **Have a bilateral conversation.** For this exercise, take a pencil in your right hand (even if you're left-handed) and write the question: "How's it going?" Then switch to your left hand, and write whatever pops up. Your nondominant hand's writing will be shaky—that's okay. The important thing isn't tidiness; it's noticing that your twin hemispheres have different personalities.

The right side of the brain, which controls the left hand, will say things you don't know that you know. It specializes in assessing your physical and your mental feelings, and it often offers solutions. "Take a nap," your right hemisphere might say, or "Just do what feels right; we'll be fine." You'll find there's a little Zen master hiding in that left hand of yours (not surprisingly, left-handed people are disproportionately represented in creative professions).

3 **Learn new moves.** You need your right hemisphere to move in an unfamiliar way, whether you're learning a complicated dance step or holding a new yoga posture. Or cutting your own hair (actually, don't—I speak from experience).

Try this: Walk a few steps, noticing how your arms swing opposite your legs. Now walk with your right arm and right foot going forward simultaneously, then the left hand and left foot. Is this difficult? No? Then do it backward, with your eyes closed—any variation that's initially hard but ultimately learnable. You'll master a new skill, sure; more important, you'll build your overall right-brain facility.

4 **Toss in the kitchen sink.** Time to push your newly awakened right hemisphere into useful service. Think of a problem that's had you stumped for a while: Your preschooler won't nap, you can't make yourself exercise, you need to cut expenses without sacrificing

> **The Kitchen Sink process encourages eureka epiphanies, like those moments in TV dramas where the brilliant sleuth gets the "ping" of insight that solves the case.**

quality of life. With this challenge in your mind, read a few paragraphs in several totally unrelated books. Then relax. Play with your cat, wash the dishes, watch the neighbors through binoculars. Think of the problem periodically, and then drop it again.

This process encourages eureka epiphanies, like those moments in TV dramas where the brilliant doctor or sleuth gets the "ping" of insight that solves the case. Your first few ideas may not be perfect—many will be awful—but there are more where they came from. Once you begin encouraging the right brain to churn out solutions, it will do so more and more abundantly.

For example, Laura wanted to travel but hated kenneling her yellow Lab, Buster. She also had partial hearing loss due to meningitis. One day when she had trouble hearing a flight attendant—*ping!*—she realized she could train Buster as a hearing service dog. Now they fly the skies in style together.

Dieting made Betsy feel grumpy, bored, and isolated. She and her friend Janet began e-mailing each other for support, then—*ping!*—decided to create a blog (bitch yourselfthin.com) where dieters could gather to share food fantasies and grumpy harangues. Now Betsy has her ideal body and an Internet community.

Brenda was unnerved by an ex-boyfriend's increasingly paranoid, angry phone messages. Then she realized—*ping!*—that his very paranoia could shut him down. She had three private detectives ask him about his phone messages; he became convinced she was having him followed, and he disappeared.

All of these women puzzled about a difficult situation, tried many solutions that didn't work, let the problem go, and got a brilliant response from their own creativity. They couldn't force that to happen, but they made it highly likely with Kitchen Sink thinking.

Turning on your right brain is a skill, one that will grow steadily stronger the more you work at it. Trigger the sensation of deep practice by mastering any unfamiliar task, feed challenges and stray information into your right brain's database, and then see new ideas begin to emerge. As they do, you'll move more confidently and productively through an increasingly complex world. When I see you out Rollerblading, with your eyes locked in a vacant yet squinty stare, I'll know you're getting the hang of it. ⓞ

Identifying with others' pain allows us to see into their hearts.

Have a Heart: The Empathy Workout

If everyone did these warm-up exercises, the world would be an altogether better place. Let's start with us.

I can't say I always enjoy cardiovascular exercise. I don't think anyone does. Oh, I've seen those infomercials featuring models whose granite abs and manic smiles become even more sharply defined at the very sight of workout equipment. But as we all know, these people are from Neptune. Being an Earth-human myself, I strongly resist abandoning my customary torpor to participate in perky physical activity of any kind.

Nevertheless, I do cardio pretty regularly. I do it because I know my heart was designed to handle such challenges, because once I get started, I feel that it's doing me good, and because if I stop for very long, my health begins to atrophy.

There's another form of cardio that works much the same way, though it affects the emotional heart rather than the one made of auricles and ventricles. This workout consists of deliberately cultivating empathy. To empathize literally means "to suffer with," to share the pain of other beings so entirely that their agony becomes our own. I know this sounds like a terrific hobby for a masochistic moron, but hear me out. The reason to develop a capacity for empathy, and then exercise it regularly, is that only a heart strengthened by this kind of understanding can effectively deliver the oxygen of the spirit: love.

Emotional Cardio

Love requires connection between lover and beloved, and empathy is the quiet miracle by which this connection is forged. When you share others' suffering, you also share their experience of receiving your gift—the gift of being accompanied into grief or anguish rather than bearing it alone. Naturally, almost involuntarily, people will love you for this. If you're in a state of empathy, you'll feel their love for you as your own emotion, thus coming to understand what it means to love yourself. This will make you love the other person even more, and of course you'll receive that love even as you give it, which makes it even deeper, and... well, you can see where this is going. Become an expert at it, and soon your life will be absolutely lousy with love.

I know one wise old man who has been working at empathy every day since becoming a meditation master early in his life. He matter-of-factly describes a state of complete empathic fitness as a "continuous emotional orgasm." Who's with me now? All right, then. Let's talk about your exciting new cardio workout—but first, a crucial warning.

Caveat Empathor

Many people, especially those of us who've had a little bit of therapy, fall into an emotional trap Buddhists call "idiot compassion." At first glance, this looks like empathy, but it's actually projection. It encourages us to condone harmful behavior by assuming that the perpetrator is acting out of pain and helplessness.

"I know he's just a hurting little boy inside," says Jeanie, whose boyfriend, Hank, has just beaten the living tar out of her for the umpteenth time. "He's so sensitive. His mama abandoned him. He even cries when he talks about it." Because Jeanie herself would become violent only in the grip of intolerable torment, she thinks she understands Hank's motivations—and so she excuses his behavior. Real empathy is not based on this kind of projection but on

close observation. If she were a true empath, Jeanie would notice that Hank, while "so sensitive" to his own misery, never notices others' distress.

When Jeanie understands that no one who cares for her could act as he acts, she'll drop the idiot compassion and get the hell out of Dodge. At that point, she'll realize that real empathy doesn't put us in harm's way. It protects us. That's just another reason to implement one of the following exercises:

Exercise 1 Learning to Listen If you want to feel that you belong in the world, a family, or any relationship, you must tell your story. But if you want to see into the hearts of other beings, your first task is to hear their stories. Many people are gifted storytellers. Only the empathic are true storyhearers.

To become one of these people, start with conversation. Once a day, ask a friend, "How are you?" in a way that says you mean it. If they give you a stock answer ("Fine"), repeat the question: "No, really. How are you?"

You'll soon realize that if your purpose is solely to understand, rather than to advise or protect, you can work a kind of magic: In the warmth of genuine caring, people open up like flowers. You'll be amazed by the stories you'll hear when you use this simple strategy with your children, your next-door neighbor, your Aunt Flossie. You'll learn things you never knew.

Even if you're not in the company of people, you can work to increase your storyhearing techniques. Here's a snippet from English teacher Jane Juska's wonderful memoir, *A Round-Heeled Woman,* in which she describes teaching creative writing to prisoners in San Quentin:

Suddenly Steve, silent until now, speaks: "...when we used to have a really fine librarian here, he gave me this book. It was *Les Misérables*.... That book changed my life. It gave me feelings, gave me empathy...*Les Misérables,* by Victor Hugo." He is wrapping up this gift and holding it close. It is his forever.

Books, movies, songs—stories told in any artistic medium can give you an empathy workout. To grow stronger, find stories that are unfamiliar. If you read, watch, or hear only things you know well, you're looking for validation, not an expansion of empathy. There's nothing wrong with that, but to achieve high levels of

> The body shapes itself in response to emotion, and shaping one's own body to match someone else's is a quick ticket to empathy.

fitness, focus once a week on the story of someone who seems utterly different from you.

Exercise 2 Reverse Engineering Some mechanical engineers spend their time disassembling machines to see how they were originally put together. You can use a similar technique to develop empathy, by working backward from the observable effects of emotion to the emotion itself.

Think of someone you'd like to understand—your enigmatic boss, your distant mother, the romantic interest who may or may not return your affections. Remember a recent interaction you had with this person—especially one that left you baffled as to how they were really feeling. Now imitate, as closely as you can, the physical posture, facial expression, exact words, and vocal inflection they used during that encounter. Notice what emotions arise within you.

What you feel will probably be very close to whatever the other person was going through. For example, when I "reverse engineer" the behavior of people I experience as critical or aloof, I usually find myself flooded with feelings of shyness, shame, or fear. It's a lesson that has saved me no end of worry and defensiveness.

I train life coaches to use reverse engineering in real time, by subtly matching clients' body language, vocal tone, even breathing rate. It's so effective that clients often think the coach must be psychic—how else could anyone "get them" so quickly and completely? Elementary, my dear Watson. The body shapes itself in response to emotion, and shaping one's own body to match someone else's is a quick ticket to empathy.

Exercise 3 Shape-Shifting In folklore, shape-shifters are beings with the ability to become anyone or anything. As a child, I was fascinated by this concept, and used to pretend that I could instantaneously switch places with other people, animals, even inanimate objects. What if I woke up one morning in the body—and the life—of my best friend, or a bank robber, or the president? What if, like Kafka's fictional Gregor, I suddenly became a cockroach? (You could find people who think I've actually done this.) My point is, what would it feel like to be them? How would I cope? What would I do next?

I still play this game, especially in public places. I recommend you try it, soon. See that strange man in the orange polyester suit putting 37 packets of sweetener into his extra-grande mochaccino with soy milk? What if—*zap!*—you suddenly switched bodies with him? What would it be like to wear that suit, that face, that physique? What impulse would lead to sugaring a cup of coffee like that, let alone drinking it?

I can feel this shape-shifting developing my empathy. It gives my heart a stretch, makes me entertain unfamiliar thoughts and feelings, leaves me with the sensation that I've completed a stomp session on an emotional StairMaster. And if I want to ramp up my workout, it's just a short hop to some practices that work even better, and have been tested for centuries.

Exercise 4 Metta-tation World-class empathizers like my friend the meditation master (he of the continuous emotional orgasm) conduct a daily regimen of metta, or loving-kindness, meditation. This involves focusing all of one's attention on a certain individual and offering loving wishes to that person with each breath you take, for several minutes at a time.

Classic metta practice starts with your own sweet self. For five minutes, with each breath, offer yourself kind thoughts (*May I be happy, may I feel joy, etc.*). Taking these few minutes every day can put you on the road to complete, uncritical acceptance—the foundation on which all empathy is based. (Reaching that point, admittedly, takes years for most of us incomplete and self-critical people.)

Then switch the focus of your kind thoughts onto a friend or family member. When you feel a sense of emotional union with that person, target someone you barely know. As a final, black-belt exercise, project metta thoughts onto one of your worst enemies until you can begin to feel for them. Don't rush this process, or (God forbid) fake it. You'll only become a saccharine pseudo-empathizer, wearing the plastic smile of a fitness model from Neptune.

The Payoff

The thing about cardio is that once you get used to it, you can feel it making you stronger, calming you down, improving your quality of life. Regular empathy practice keeps you on the edge of your emotional fitness, but the benefits are enormous: an awareness of union that banishes loneliness, a natural ability to connect and relate to others, protection from idiot compassion, a wider, deeper life. As your empathy grows, you'll find that it's infinite and that through it, you transcend your isolation and find yourself at home in the universe. I promise, it'll do your heart good. ◐

> As your empathy grows, you'll find that it's infinite.

The Relationship Two-Step

It's a dance—move too close, and you get your toes stepped on. Keep people at arm's length, and you might lose contact entirely. Here's how to set healthy boundaries... without missing a beat.

Shakespeare's romantic comedies often end with the cast dancing around the stage together. This is to show that after enduring ridiculous confusion, the characters' relationships have settled into normalcy. Elizabethan dramas used dance to represent the way people in healthy relationships interact with one another, moving joyously in response to the music of life. Nowadays psychologists use the words *functional boundary setting* to describe the same thing. It loses in translation, don't you think? The clinical phrase just doesn't convey the subtlety with which humans observe, interpret, and respond to one another's social signals: A frown from the boss, and we mash our noses to the grindstone. A friend's shoulder slumps half an inch, and without thinking we pat it encouragingly.

These actions follow the rhythms of people who instinctively set healthy boundaries. Those of us who aren't exactly Fred Astaire trip over ourselves in relationship after relationship, in part because we pick up boundary-setting habits so early that most of us aren't even aware of how we move. Happily, it's never too soon—or too late—

to become a better dancer. Here are four common dance errors (a shrink might call them dysfunctional boundary-setting patterns) that may sound as regrettably familiar to you as they do to me.

The "Please Tread on Me"

This is the dance of supplication and submission broadcast by pleasers, folks so desperate to be loved that they'll do pretty much anything for anyone. Pleasers end up being mildly pitied by most people, but narcissists cut right in and exploit the hell out of them.

The symptoms of the "please tread on me" syndrome include exhaustion, constant complaining about being used, fear of conflict, simmering resentment, a sense of helplessness, and a history of relationships with demanding, selfish partners.

The Herky-Jerky Tango

"Why does everyone I date turn out to be a jerk?" This is the classic cry of someone who's doing the herky-jerky tango. This dance is often performed by shy people who are scared to let others near, and so project the message "Stay away!" Often they are a little reserved, even a bit prickly. Normal people follow the shy person's lead, respectfully keeping their distance. Only socially insensitive louts barrel on through to partner them.

Signs that a person might have fallen into this rhythm: social anxiety, loneliness, being unable to meet people they really like (where *are* they?), and feeling they have to settle for unfeeling clods as friends or romantic partners.

The FOO Fandango

As children we learn to fit in with those people who resemble our families of origin (acronym: FOO), the way a key matches a lock. When we meet someone whose behavior matches the social moves we're used to, we fall right in step. This may be great for *The Brady Bunch*. Not so for the rest of us.

The most obvious indication of a dysfunctional FOO fandango is the tendency to repeatedly befriend or date people who share negative characteristics of family members, especially patterns like addiction, abusiveness, dishonesty, and secretiveness.

The Kiss Me, Kill Me Two-Step

In this tricky and intense dance, people will attach to others they've just met, recognizing one another as soul mates, even beginning to talk, dress, and act alike. At best this bonding phase ebbs into disappointment. At worst it leads to a massive falling-out that severs the relationship and leaves the soul mates bitter enemies.

People who take part in this boundary dance often feel instant attraction to certain individuals, a nagging fear of abandonment, a history of feeling betrayed, and the habit of nursing grievances.

If any of these descriptions rings a bell, you can become more aware of how you participate in the general dance of life with the help of a therapist. But if you have the nerve, there's a quicker way to get feedback: Talk to people you trust. There is a trick; the less well-acquainted you are with those you ask, the more useful the information.

I first did this when I was teaching a group therapy class, and it's become a standby technique in the seminars I've run since. If you're not planning on attending any personal-development programs, you might work up the nerve to ask for feedback from a coworker, a few acquaintances, a 12-step group. Explain your boundary issue first, then ask for input. Something like "I keep having the same kind of argument with different people [or dating the same kind of loser, etc.]. Do you see anything I'm doing that's contributing to this dynamic?"

Humans are astonishingly attuned to interpreting one another's social energy, and you'll likely end up with a pretty clear consensus. "You always look down and mumble when I talk to you," they might say. "I feel like you're not interested." Or: "You're so helpful and polite, even to awful people. Frankly, you're kind of a doormat."

One very important caveat: Do not, I repeat, do *not* rely on feedback from your nearest and dearest. These people are preselected to match your boundary-setting patterns. Your dysfunctions will be as invisible to them as to you. For instance, if a pleaser asks her boyfriend whether he thinks it's normal that she buys him silk sheets, while she herself sleeps on the floor so as not to disturb him, he'll respond that she's the healthiest, most normal person he's ever met. She'd get more helpful data from her dentist.

The Problem with Finding a New Tune

Dysfunctional relationships are rigid. Each person plays one role, and any attempt to behave differently is met by indignation or even aggression. This rigidity (which underlies "isms" like racism, classism, and fundamentalism) makes boundary setting delightfully simple: Folks who behave in prescribed ways are the Good Guys; everyone else is the Enemy. Of course, even a minor deviation can turn friend to foe, so to keep the party going, participants better repress all individualism. To many people, that seems a small price for the intimacy created by a black-and-white worldview. Unfortunately, since this closeness requires self-abandonment, it actually isn't intimacy at all.

Functional relationship skills begin with the realization that intimacy is rarely built upon stiff rules, that most things can't be reduced to black or white. Painters sometimes use a gray scale, a strip of paper that has white at one end and black at the other, with, for example, five gradually deepening shades of gray in between. They hold up this strip to see which value of gray best matches the shade of the color they're painting. Each object gets a gray scale value. (Pure white has a value of 1; medium gray, 4; jet black, 7.) Learning to evaluate levels of intimacy in a similar way is the first lesson of the healthy interpersonal waltz.

Take a look at the intimacy gray scale on the next page. List the next ten people with whom you interact, and use the scale to rate your level of intimacy with each one. Ideally, your relationships will be spread across the scale. If everyone you come in contact with is bunched at the low end of the scale, you're probably putting out such strong "keep away" signals that you're overly isolated. If everyone's at the high end, you may be so indiscriminately intimate that you're vulnerable to exhaustion and exploitation.

Both of these problems stem from a dysfunctional, all-or-nothing view of intimacy. Dichotomous thinkers habitually shut people out to protect themselves, dive into ill-considered closeness, or both. The solution is to set boundaries that move most relationships into the gray zone. You'll have a few intimate relationships (three or four are about all most of us have) and a few acquaintances that stray through your space each day.

Next consider each of the people you've listed in your "intimacy gray scale" exercise. If thinking about one person makes you irritated or exhausted, you need to create more space in your dance with that particular person at this particular time. Try the following polite request, which I've used on everyone from chatty cabdrivers to my children: "Would you excuse me? I need some time by myself." People who can't or won't step back a bit when you say this are poor relationship risks. Don't try to persuade them to leave you alone. Simply decrease the time and attention you direct toward them until you reach a level at which your irritation disappears. Imagine moving from a cheek-to-cheek tango to a square dance, where you do-si-do with many people for short periods.

On the other hand, if you want to be closer to some individuals on your list, you'll feel curious and interested as you think about them. To increase intimacy, ask the questions that arise naturally: "How are you feeling today? How do you bake so well? Where do you get all your energy?" If the other person is willing to open up, this will trigger a pleasant interchange of gradual, mutual self-disclosure. If your questions are met by curtness, silence, or the phrase "Would you excuse me?" you can gently pull back and go looking for other dance partners.

There is one thing to remember: Social choreography is endlessly changeable. Unlike dysfunction, healthy intimacy pulls away, bounces back, creates infinite fresh configurations. Trusting the rhythm of each relationship, rather than insisting on robotic consistency, will keep you from panicking when someone's boundaries move a bit toward or away from you. Insist on continuous connection with just one individual: your own self, who knows where to draw the boundary lines on any given day, with any given person. Your heart is always listening to the natural beat and melody of relationships, and it always agrees with our man Will: "If music be the food of love, play on." ⬤

Test Your Boundaries

List the next ten people with whom you interact, from the grocery store clerk to your spouse. Mark the circle in this intimacy gray scale that most closely reflects your feelings toward that individual.

1 .... ○ ○ ◔ ◑ ◕ ●   6 .... ○ ○ ◔ ◑ ◕ ●
2 .... ○ ○ ◔ ◑ ◕ ●   7 .... ○ ○ ◔ ◑ ◕ ●
3 .... ○ ○ ◔ ◑ ◕ ●   8 .... ○ ○ ◔ ◑ ◕ ●
4 .... ○ ○ ◔ ◑ ◕ ●   9 .... ○ ○ ◔ ◑ ◕ ●
5 .... ○ ○ ◔ ◑ ◕ ●   10 .... ○ ○ ◔ ◑ ◕ ●

○ With X I feel uneasy, angry, or afraid. Either we have frequent arguments or I'm constantly monitoring X's mood, preferences, and reactions and modifying my own behavior to avoid discord. I believe that if I don't do this, X will become angry or leave the relationship altogether.

○ I avoid X if possible. There's not much mutual understanding or emotional connection between us. When I'm around X, I'd rather not reveal much about myself—just do whatever business needs doing, then get away.

◔ I wouldn't hang out with X if I had a choice, but he/she isn't unpleasant to be with. We simply have very little in common, and though we are fine exchanging small talk, I don't see the relationship getting any deeper than it already is.

◑ X and I meet about halfway—I know we have differences of opinion, and I wouldn't call him/her a close friend. However, we have enough common ground to find each other acceptable company.

◕ I like X, but there are a few areas where we're clearly very different. I don't expect X to agree with me or even understand me in these areas, so we stick to activities and conversations where there's no real conflict.

◕ I feel safe, comfortable, and happy around X, but I'm careful to be polite and appropriate, too. I wouldn't tell X everything that's on my mind without softening some of the stronger statements.

● Around X, I act exactly as I would if I were relaxing all by myself. I feel sure he/she will accept me just as I am, and when we're together, it never occurs to me to hide or censor my most authentic actions.

If your scores are bunched at one end of the scale, you might need to shift your social boundaries.

You Spot It, You've Got It

My friend is lazy, willful, and self-absorbed. Wait—could that actually be *me* I'm talking about? Martha Beck on what we can learn about ourselves from the funny little phenomenon called projection.

There are two kinds of people I can't stand," says Michael Caine's character in the epically low comedy *Goldmember,* "those who are intolerant of other cultures, and the Dutch." I love this line, not because it slams the Dutch (for whom I feel great admiration), but because it slams hypocrisy—specifically, the baffling double standards of people who condemn in others the very offenses they themselves are committing. My fellow life coach Sharon Lamm calls this the "you spot it, you got it" syndrome. In other words, whatever we criticize most harshly in others may be a hallmark of our own psyche; what I hate most in you may actually be what I hate most in me.

This style of thinking is so illogical, you'd think it would be rare. Because of the peculiarities of human psychology, though, it's actually more the rule than the exception. Understanding the "you spot it, you got it" phenomenon requires some focused thinking, but the effort will bring more peace and sanity to your relationships and your inner life.

Why We Spot What We Got

Let's start by replicating a little thought experiment devised by psychologist Daniel Wegner: For the next 30 seconds, don't think about anything connected to the subject of white bears. Don't think about bears of any kind—or the Arctic, or snowy terrain, or white fur coats, etc. Ready? Go.

You probably just had more bear-related thoughts than you typically would in a month of Sundays. They're still coming, aren't they? You may distract yourself for an instant, but then another pops into your mind—see? There's one now!

This is a universal truth: We invariably experience more of any thought or feeling we try to avoid. Why? Because when our brains hear the instruction to shun a certain topic, they respond by seeking any thoughts related to that topic, in order to escape them. (After all, if you decided to throw away every blue thing in your closet, the first step would be to go looking for blue items, right?) Wegner calls this search the "ironic monitoring process," which has the perfect acronym: "imp." When we try to repress awareness of anything, we activate a mind imp that zeroes in on every memory, every sense impression, every experience related to the forbidden subject.

The "you spot it, you got it" phenomenon occurs when we do things that are in opposition to our own value systems. To feel good about acting in ways that are reprehensible to ourselves, we must repress our recognition that we're doing so. Our imps go into high gear; we become hyperalert to anything that reminds us of the behavior we're denying in ourselves, focusing with unusual intensity on the slightest hint of that behavior in others, or imagining it where it doesn't even exist.

This is why people can, without irony, say things like "So help me, Billy, if you keep hitting people, I will slap you into Thursday!" Or "I only lie to him because he's so dishonest." Condemning others for our worst traits turns us into ethical pretzels, hiding from us the very things we must change to earn genuine self-respect. Articulating such false logic is the key to resolving it—but this is always easier when we're talking about someone besides ourselves. So let's start there.

> You'll swear you don't see in yourself the loathsome qualities you notice in others. You spot it, but you think you ain't got it. Look again.

Project and Reject: The Hypocrite's Two-Step

When we're the ones doing the spot-it-got-it tango, we don't see the paradox; we simply feel an unusually ferocious antipathy to someone else's actions. However, when someone else is perpetrating the very acts they claim to despise, we may feel confused, sensing that there's something crazy going on, but unable to pinpoint exactly what. I have some recommendations.

1. Be suspicious. Be very suspicious. One of the friskiest babysitters I ever hired was a sweet little grandma I'll call Beulah. Despite her age, Beulah had endless energy; she could keep up with my three preschoolers far longer than I could. She was also touchingly concerned that my children not become "addicted" to anything: *Sesame Street,* ice cream, pop music. She volunteered to police my bathroom cupboards and remove any leftover medication the children might consume. Even so, she worried constantly that they would get drugs somewhere.

One day I came home from work to discover that Beulah had wallpapered half my daughter's bedroom with hideous paper she'd found at a discount store. She'd also single-handedly moved our piano to a new location, and (though I wouldn't discover this until weeks later) ordered four hundred dollars' worth of Girl Scout Cookies at my expense. As Beulah gave me a disjointed, rambling explanation at a rate of approximately 900 words per minute, I noted her many small scabs and that her pupils were dilated. I recalled an article that mentioned these were symptoms of crystal meth abuse. The light finally dawned: Beulah was a speed freak. As I regretfully fired my babysitter, I realized that her obsessive talk about addiction had always been a "you spot it, you got it" behavior, and it should have been a signal to me that Beulah herself was a drug-stealing addict. Everyone makes comments about other people from time to time, but those who focus on one topic continually, irrationally, and inexplicably are often describing themselves. When someone seems unduly preoccupied with a certain flaw in others, it's time to do a once-over to see if it's taken root in Mr. or Ms. Obsessed.

2 **Sidestep mind-binds.** If you want to experience insanity, observe a relationship with a hypocrite: the unfaithful lover who sees endless evidence of a partner's nonexistent infidelity; the rude, hurtful coworker who expects to be treated with kindness and respect; the political extremist who violently opposes violence. Opposite moral imperatives that come from the same person, called double binds, are so crazy-making that they were once thought to induce schizophrenia. If you try to have a close connection with someone who vehemently attacks flaws in others while demanding that you accept, overlook, or excuse those same flaws in him or her, you will feel a blend of anxiety, extreme bafflement, self-blame, anger, and hopelessness. When you see people abiding by a big fat double standard, step outside their duplicitous perspective by telling yourself that the craziness you feel is coming from the critic. Once you've had this perceptual breakthrough, you may be able to use it on the one person whose behavior you actually can change: yourself.

See It and Free It

The impish nature of our psychology ensures that we all occasionally spot what we've got. However, we rarely see our own delusion; we just find ourselves ruminating on the vices of others. *If Joe weren't so lazy,* we think, *he'd always bring me breakfast in bed.* Or *Chris is such a miser. Expected me to split the check for coffee—like I'm made of money!* When these thoughts become especially dominant, there's a high probability we've got what we spot. But we can turn our own unconscious hypocrisy into a wonderful tool for personal growth. Here's how:

Phase One: Write your rant. To begin, list all the nasty, judgmental thoughts you're already thinking about Certain People. Who's offending you most right now? What do you hate most about them? What dreadful things have they done to you? What behavior should they change? Scribble down all your most controlling, accusatory, politically incorrect thoughts.

Phase Two: Change places. Now go through your written rant and put yourself in the place of the person

> We rarely see
> our own delusion;
> we just
> find ourselves
> ruminating on the
> vices of others.

you're criticizing. Read through it again, and be honest—could it be that your enemy's shoe fits your own foot? If you wrote "Kristin always wants things her way," could "I always want things my way" be equally true? Could it be that this is the very reason Kristin's selfishness bothers you so much? If you wrote "Joe has got to stop clinging and realize that our relationship is over," could it be that you are also hanging on to the relationship—say, by brooding all day about Joe's clinginess?

Sometimes you'll swear you don't see in yourself the loathsome qualities you notice in others. You spot it, but you ain't got it. Look again. See if you are implicitly condoning someone else's vileness by failing to oppose it—which puts your actions on the side of the trait you hate. You may be facilitating your boss's combativeness by bowing your head and taking it, rather than speaking up or walking out. Maybe you hate a friend's greediness, all the while "virtuously" allowing her to grab more than her share. Indirectly you are serving the habits you despise. Your rant rewrite may look like this example from one of my clients, Lenore:

Phase One: the rant. "My kids take me for granted. They expect me to drop whatever I'm doing and focus on them, anytime. I'm sick of them taking me for granted."

Phase Two: the rewrite. "I take me for granted. I expect me to drop whatever I'm doing to focus on my kids, anytime. I'm sick of me taking me for granted."

This exercise was a watershed for Lenore; once she realized that by devaluing herself she was teaching her children to devalue her, she could begin getting respect from them by respecting herself.

We can often learn such priceless lessons by remembering the "you spot it, you got it" dynamic. Recognizing this quirk of human thinking helps us detach from crazy-makers who might otherwise drive us nuts, and jolts us free from the places we get most stuck. We automatically become freer, less caught in illusion, less obsessed with other people's flaws. That's good, because there's nothing worse than people who are always talking about what they hate in other people. Boy, do I hate them. ⏹

Wildly Improbable Goals

They began as signals, tugs. And with careful tending her most unlikely dreams came true. Martha Beck helps you set the stage for your next great thing.

I was 13, doing my homework in front of my family's broken-down television, when I felt strangely compelled to look up at the screen. It showed an athlete running around an indoor track. I heard myself say out loud, "That's where I'm going to college." A split second later the TV narrator's voice came on: "Here at Harvard University's athletic center...." My heart stopped. Not in my most fevered dreams had I ever considered applying to an Ivy League school. Such behavior would be unusual, if not downright bizarre, for a girl from my deeply conservative Utah town. Besides, going to Harvard

required several thousand times more brains, talent, and money than I would ever have. On the other hand, I felt the truth of my own strange words in the marrow of my bones. Okay, I thought nervously, maybe going to Harvard isn't utterly unthinkable. Maybe it's just barely, barely possible. Right there, in front of the TV, I surrendered to the first of what I would one day call my Wildly Improbable Goals (WIGs, for short).

Decades later I have a couple of Harvard diplomas stuck in a closet, and a happy expectation that sometime soon another WIG is going to pop, unbidden, into my consciousness. I've watched this happen repeatedly, not only to me but to loved ones and clients. I suspect it may

217

have happened to you, too. Perhaps it was just a flicker of thought that transported you for a moment, before you dismissed it as nonsense. Maybe it's a dream that simply will not let go of you, no matter how often you tell yourself not to hope for anything so big, so unlikely. Or it may be an ambition you've already embraced, even though everyone else thinks you need serious medication. In any case, learning to invite and accept your own WIG can awaken you to a kind of ubiquitous, benevolent magic, a river of enchantment that perpetually flows toward your destiny.

Time Travel

I might as well admit what I believe about these minor prophecies I call WIGs. I suspect they're not so much mental constructs as literal glimpses of the future. I stand behind Albert Einstein's comment that "people like us, who believe in physics, know that the distinction between past, present, and future is only a stubbornly persistent illusion." Physics tells us that time can be stretched or compressed like Silly Putty, and I am just woo-woo enough to believe that we humans might sometimes sense truths that are ordinarily veiled by our assumptions or self-imposed rules.

Prescience—knowing about events that haven't yet occurred—is not altogether foreign to behavioral science. In one study, experimenters showed test subjects a series of images, including both pleasant pictures and violent or otherwise emotional ones. The researchers were not surprised to find that the subjects' blood pressure and heart rate increased in response to the upsetting images. They had not anticipated, however, that this reaction would occur seconds before the subjects saw the violent pictures—a result that has been replicated in other studies but never satisfactorily explained.

What occurs infinitesimally in laboratory experiments takes on huge dimensions in the lives of some extraordinary people. Joan of Arc had goals so wildly improbable that she was burned as a witch for achieving them. A young Winston Churchill once said to a friend, "I tell you I shall be in command of the defenses of London.... In the high position I shall occupy, it will fall to me to save the Capital and save the Empire." Do such people accomplish great things because they dreamed near impossible dreams, or were their dreams previews of what they were destined to achieve? I'm open to either explanation. To

> If WIG moments were broadcast on cable—the Wildly Improbable Goal Discovery Channel—I'd watch it all day long.

me, one seems as mysterious as the other. Whether our WIGs are the cause or effect of our actions, they have a peculiar power to lift us beyond what we thought to be our limitations.

Wild Kingdom

At this point, I hope you're wondering how you can set your own Wildly Improbable Goals. The problem is, you can't. WIGs are to normal thoughts what Siberian tigers are to house cats, and your "right mind" doesn't have the hunting skills to find them. Fortunately, your WIGs can find you. The knowledge of your destiny may stalk you for years, undetected except for occasional moments of longing or hope that glint like eyeshine in your darkest hours. Then when you least expect it, a WIG will leap out of nowhere and overwhelm you in one breathtaking burst. I've had the privilege of watching many clients recognize WIGs. It's thrilling to see people who thought they were directionless realize they're about to run for office or buy a house or publish a novel or have a baby. If these moments were broadcast on cable—the Wildly Improbable Goal Discovery Channel—I'd watch it all day long.

Speaking of having babies, that process is somewhat similar to the procedure for inviting WIGs into your life. You can't force a WIG to happen, but you can create conditions that will either prevent it or invite it. One precondition is absolutely necessary: You must befriend, protect, and nurture your own spirit. This means paying attention to your real needs, treating yourself not just fairly but kindly, and standing up for yourself even if that displeases people around you. Just as a run-down body may be unable to conceive a healthy new life, a run-down soul can't support the healthy development of the life you were meant to have.

Helping it Happen

Once you've met the basic condition of self-care, there are several strategies you might use to lure your WIGs out of hiding. One is to take a pencil in your dominant hand (right for right-handers, left for lefties) and write down a few pointed questions, such as "What are you feeling?" "What do you need?" and "What do you want?" As soon as you've finished writing a question, switch the pencil to your other hand and write whatever words bubble up. You may be surprised. When your problem-solving mind is fully engaged, trying to master the task of writing with the "wrong" hand, hidden aspects of the self often surface. I've seen people encounter full-fledged WIGs in the shaky words written by their own nondominant hand.

If you think more visually than verbally, you may want to try another exercise: time travel. Take a few quiet minutes, relax in a comfortable place, close your eyes, and imagine that the date has changed. It's the same day of the same month, but the year is 2012, or 2020. Figure out how old you are in the year you've chosen. How old is your best friend? Your children? Your spouse? Let yourself inhabit this time. Now with your eyes still closed, simply describe your circumstances. Where are you? What are you wearing? What is the weather like? Now describe your life. What is most important to you on this date? What projects occupy you? Who hangs out with you? Try to simply observe rather than make things up. If no images appear, don't worry. Your WIGs are still hiding, but you've called them and they are listening. They may show up after you've finished the exercise, when you're brushing your teeth or making your bed.

A third WIG-baiting exercise also involves time travel, but for this one you don't project yourself into the future. Instead your future self comes back to visit you. Imagine meeting a wise, happy person who just happens to be your best self ten years from now. Ask this person for advice. If you're facing a problem, ask your mentor how she got through it ten years back. Ask her what mistakes you're making and how you might correct them. As with the previous exercise, you may initially get no answer. Nevertheless, your true self, that wise being who exists outside of time, has registered the questions. The answers will come.

When it Hits

Being struck by a WIG is nothing like setting an ordinary goal. First of all, you'll notice that it is not something you thought up; it seems to come from somewhere beyond thought. Second, you'll feel an almost physical jolt of yearning, as though your heart is straining toward its destiny. Third, you'll have the vertiginous sensation of your mind boggling. If you haven't experienced this before, you'll probably feel overwhelmed, the way I felt at 13, watching that runner circle the Harvard track. You won't even be able to imagine the mess of work and luck necessary to make it happen. The very idea will seem impossible...almost. That "almost" will tickle the edges of your consciousness, tempting you to believe that somehow, someway, your dream may fall just inside the realm of probability. How can you be sure?

You can't. Fortunately, your first step is simple: Write down your WIG. In detail. Immediately, before you regain your sanity and lose your nerve.

Experts say that simply writing down goals greatly increases your chance of actually achieving them. Perhaps it's because the act of writing primes your brain to scan the environment, looking for opportunities that will take you toward your objectives. Many choices you make en route to realizing your WIG will be so inconspicuous that you won't even notice them, but over time they'll add up to huge changes in direction.

Once you've written your WIG, the real work begins. I've had many clients who, impressed by the strange electricity of their WIGs, assume that this intense feeling alone will magically create the desired reward. Yeah, right. I think the reason WIGs have so much mojo is that we need a huge reservoir of desire to keep us slogging through the hard work needed to realize them. Almost invariably, the effort necessary to achieve a WIG is not less than we expect but more. That said, the process of working toward a WIG does seem to land us in extraordinary territory. Creativity coach Julia Cameron comments that her clients reap the fruit of their labors only if they are willing to go out and "shake the trees," but weirdly, the fruit that falls almost never comes from the tree the person is shaking.

This has been my experience as well. By the time I was 15, I'd developed a shortlist of WIGs that included three rather childish goals: I wanted to learn to ski, own a ten-speed bicycle, and visit Europe. Once programmed, my brain began noticing job opportunities and sporting-goods sales, and I slowly earned enough money to buy a bike and some used ski equipment. I was also working on selling enough French-club perfume to win a trip to Europe. I'd sold three whole ounces and had only a couple of gallons to go, when a Yugoslavian friend sent my family two round-trip tickets to Europe that he was too busy to use. Days later I was standing on European soil, dizzy with jet lag and euphoria.

That pattern—the recognition of a WIG, followed by enormous amounts of work, followed by a miracle—has happened to me so many times that it's almost stopped surprising me. I see it strike my clients as well, when they prepare a safe space for their true selves, ask a few questions, and accept the answers. You already know your own WIGs, though you may not yet realize it. The part of you that is unhampered by illusion—the illusion of time, the illusion of powerlessness, the illusion of impossibility—is waiting for you to slow down and open up so that it can speak to your consciousness. In some unguarded moment, you will hear its wildly improbable words and know that they are guiding you home. ◘

10 Hard-Won Pieces of Advice

Our columnist's secrets to pressing onward.

In the past ten years I have survived an asymmetrical bob, a high-risk pregnancy, a malignant melanoma, a sneak preview of *Shutter Island,* and diabetes. I've watched someone I love die of AIDS and someone I most definitely do not love sit in the White House. I have become acutely aware of the fact that bad guys often win and nice guys sometimes finish last and the karmic wheel takes its sweet time to spin around and set things right. My rent has been raised, my enthusiasm has been curbed, my kid has been bullied, and I can't find a pair of silver sandals to save my soul.

But here's what I've figured out about putting one unsandaled foot in front of the other and trying to move forward in the midst of sorrow and chaos:

1. **People have surprisingly vast reservoirs of tenacity and resilience.** All of those days and nights that I was so sure I couldn't get through have come and gone. I'm still here and so, my friend, are you! It turns out that we can only eat chicken potpie in our underwear and watch an endless loop of *Law & Order* reruns for about a week or so before a better angel urges us to say goodbye to Sam Waterston, shave our legs, and get back out there.

2 **Find yourself a friend, a shrink, or even a stranger at a bus shelter.** It doesn't matter who it is, as long as it's a person who doesn't have an agenda. We all need that one someone in our lives who doesn't hear what we have to say filtered through the prism of his or her own needs or wants. Think Switzerland. Okay, well maybe that's a bad example because Switzerland only pretends to be neutral while hiding the money of war criminals and forcing jet-lagged tourists to eat fondue...but you get the idea.

3 **Do something—anything—for somebody else.** I promise, it'll help you feel a little bit better.

4 **Do something—anything—for yourself.** I promise, that helps, too.

5 **If you're going to rent a movie, shoot for something frothy.** A screwball comedy that revolves around a plucky, maribou-wearing, Champagne-sipping heroine who ends up with Cary Grant will do a whole lot more for your sense of well-being than Lars von Trier ever could.

6 **Step away from the lasagna, ma'am.** It is your God-given right to splurge from time to time (see aforementioned potpie), but if you've lost your health insurance, your home, your one true love, you do not want to also lose the ability to tuck in your shirt.

7 **Never underestimate the power of a perfect comeback.** Sometimes words aren't even necessary. I've spent years perfecting a simple smile that says, "Please know that I plan to systematically destroy you when you least expect it."

8 **Let's face it, if you don't have anything in your life worth crying over, you probably don't have much of a life.** So crying is definitely allowed, but (and Lord knows, this is easier said than done) see if you can't keep the whining to a minimum.

9 **Dwell in possibility.** Only the limits of your own imagination (and a restraining order) can keep you from deciding that Benicio Del Toro is your destiny.

10 **Forget about what you can't do.** The other day I overheard a snippet of conversation my daughter was having with her pal. "Wait," she asked, "what are my superpowers supposed to be again?" We all have superpowers (I myself happen to look very nice in navy), and we all forget them from time to time. Meet an old friend for lunch and have her make you a good, long list of yours. **O**

Lisa Kogan Tells All

When it comes to affairs of the heart, she needed a few answers. Thanks to a visit to the OR, she got a whole lot more than she bargained for.

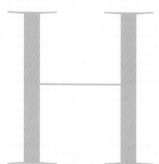

Her coat seemed sort of floaty, like it was made of parachute material. I remember that. And it was the color of ginger ale, kind of creamy with a hint of metallic gold sheen. She must have noticed me noticing it because she smiled slightly as she swept by. If memory serves—and it may not—I think I wanted to tell her how great it looked, but she was moving at a fairly brisk pace (was she late for a meeting? Was she anxious to get indoors before the soft drizzle turned into a hard rain?), and I got shy and chickened out.

A few blocks later, I saw her again, only now she was crumpled on the sidewalk. A guy was putting his backpack beneath her head. A woman was going through her bag for identification. Somebody else was calling an ambulance. A perfume sample from Henri Bendel rolled out of her pocket and a shoe had fallen off her foot. I don't know why that matters to me but it does. She wasn't young, but she wasn't old, either—mid-50s would be my guess. The paramedics said it was a massive heart attack.

This entire event probably lasted seven or eight minutes, but it has stayed with me for more than 20 years. I just keep seeing her shimmering coat fanned across the sidewalk with backpack guy kneeling on it as he holds her hand. I try to make it make some sense, I try to fix it, I try to forget it—but I can't.

Why is a 50-something woman walking down the street one minute and lying in it the next? And, at the risk of sounding like I'm auditioning for the Bee Gees, my real question: How do you mend a broken heart?

I know exactly where to get the answer. With one call to Dr. Mehmet Oz, I'm invited to see for myself on the fourth floor of New York–Presbyterian Hospital/Columbia University Medical Center.

Two weeks later, I'm wrapping paper slippers over my shoes as one of the nurses says, "I take it you've never witnessed an open heart surgery?" Her look tells me that watching all 11 seasons of *M*A*S*H* doesn't count. Suddenly I regret that the patient consented to having a guest reporter around and my palms are sending flash flood warnings to my wrists.

"You might not want to be here when the band saw comes out." I've received plenty of good advice in my day, from "pack a sweater" to "stay in school," but I am particularly grateful when Dr. Ryan Davies, the chief resident who will be assisting in today's procedure, directs that little nugget my way before I can wander smack into Quentin Tarantino territory. The bottom line is this: Try as one might, it is impossible to unwatch something. And so it comes to pass that I am standing outside operating room 23 *not* watching while an 80-year-old woman has her chest cracked open as part of an aortic valve replacement that, if all goes according to plan, will take approximately six hours and give the woman an extra ten to 15 years of life. It is her first (and God willing last) major cardiothoracic surgery. Here's hoping I can say the same.

Tentatively I step into the OR. It's a shockingly ordinary room—no glistening tile, no shiny viewing gallery that might allow me to observe the proceedings from a semibloodless distance—just plain manila walls with "Evacuation Plans" taped unobtrusively off to the side ("Step 1. Remove patient from site of fire. If hair is burning, extinguish the flames") and a dull blue linoleum floor. "Can you see everything from all the way over there?" cardiac surgeon Mathew Williams calls to me, knowing full well that I can see nothing from the spot I have staked out directly in front of the exit. "Yep, pretty much everything," I answer as casually as I can. But nobody's buying it, and a small step stool is positioned at the head of the stainless steel gurney. I am then invited to take a closer look, "so in case you ever feel like replacing somebody's aortic valve, you'll be ready."

Gingerly, I tiptoe around video screens and over cables, skirt the heart-lung machine and the two perfusionists in charge of it, duck under the beeping monitors and

beyond the busy nurses, the visiting med students, the tubes coursing with blood, the bag filling with urine, and, with all the enthusiasm a girl who passed out cold when she got her ears pierced can muster—I step onto the stool, peer down into an open chest, and stand utterly transfixed by a stranger's beating heart.

I am amazed, I am mesmerized, I am nauseated. It's remarkable how much can be read on my face despite the fact that half of it is concealed by a mask; the anesthesiologist to my left would prefer that his patient be the only woman in the room to lose consciousness today, but he is a realist. "Hey listen," he says, "if you're going to fall, do not fall forward."

Conversation among the doctors and nurses is mundane: "I had no idea they're into country music. Clamp, please." Yet they remain hypervigilant. "Venous return is down. Are you guys pushing?" I am a mere 18 inches away from the problem, but I'd be hard-pressed to explain what the problem is. "Something's not tight," someone calls out. "It's sucking air in," says Williams. The team recites vital signs, as Williams issues directives. "Okay, pressure's coming up." And then we're back: "They even went to the CMA Awards in Nashville."

So, let's review: The patient has been intubated, an incision has been made, a Swan-Ganz catheter has been threaded through her neck to her heart. We are two and a half hours in, and now she is put on cardiopulmonary bypass. Her body temperature is cooled to 32 degrees

Celsius to lower her metabolic rate and protect her brain and other organs. Her heart is officially stopped. It is now up to the heart-lung machine and the perfusionists who run it to keep her blood flowing until she is ready to come off bypass. "Is it time to call Oz?" one of the nurses asks Dr. Williams, who answers, "Give me ten more minutes, then let's get him down here." Right on cue, in comes Mehmet Oz, a man who clearly commands the deep respect of all his colleagues. "Whoa," someone deadpans, "aren't you Dr. Phil?"

The energy level instantly rises. Dr. Oz is happy to see everyone, and they're happy to see him. As he examines Dr. Davies's handiwork, he wants to be sure I've been properly introduced to the family. "Luz is our charge nurse. She makes her own jewelry," he says proudly. "Luz, show Lisa your bracelet." Luz holds up a hand, as I try to make out the shape of the bracelet hidden under her bloody glove. "And we've got the A team over here," he points to Jimmy and Linda—"I mean these are the people who worked on Bill Clinton!" Before I can even ask the question, Jimmy volunteers the answer, "I'm a Republican, she's a Democrat."

Oz brags about the surgical technique Mathew Williams is pioneering: "It's a far less invasive procedure—he runs a catheter through the groin muscle to the heart." He and Williams have performed today's procedure hundreds of times together, and it shows—they know precisely when to get out of each other's way. It's a complicated tango, choreographed with finesse and subtlety. There's a good chance they could pull off the whole thing without ever saying a word to each other; the talk seems more for the chief resident's benefit, who is currently—you should pardon the technical-medical speak—tweezing at a little blob just south of an angry looking artery. "Don't grab at it, just give it a nudge," Oz deftly demonstrates. Davies gently follows his lead. "There you go, that's it. Now, you've gotta be careful right in here—you can kill someone with that valve," says Oz. Later he will tell me that "there is always a moment in every operation when someone can die." For now, as the surgeons delicately lower the new valve into position, everything goes according to plan.

I've actually forgotten that I am staring at a human heart. It's more like a really intricate craft project, complete with filament-thin hooks and long, white sutures. But faster than you can say *Grey's Anatomy,* I am jolted back to reality. "Get some gloves on," says the good doctor. I stare blankly. "Let's go," Oz repeats, "glove up." I look behind me to see who he's talking to. No one is behind me. Three thoughts flash through my head: *Oh my God! Oh my God!* And, *Oh my God!* "That's okay," I say quickly. "I mean you guys are doing fine. Really. Maybe

I can make a little Starbucks run—who's up for a Frappuccino? Anybody? Anybody? Anybo—" "Can someone help Lisa get gloves on, please?" Oz says, as he examines the new valve. Six seconds later, my hands are encased in latex and Dr. Oz is placing pieces of calcium plucked directly from the aorta into my trembling palm. "See the spongy part?" he asks, "and over here it's cracking a bit, you see that? Give it a squeeze. This stuff here can break off and cause a clot." As Oz pokes, prods, and continues to teach, I silently tick off the list of foods I will not be eating again. Bye-bye bacon, farewell fettucine...it's like a very special episode of *Scared Straight.*

The ability to remain upright when hit with a handful of yuck has earned me a five-minute break. Oz and I take a seat in the lounge. Somebody stops by to thank him for seeing her cousin; somebody else wants a picture. Finally we are alone and I can ask the question I've been thinking about all morning. "Mehmet, what's it like to hold someone's life in your hands?" Oz is quiet for a minute. "You know, the heart always used to remind me of a python. I'd see it beating away and think it was about to spring at me," he says. "But gradually, you realize that it's not the enemy, and you begin to embrace it." I get the python thing; what I don't get is how you handle the responsibility for keeping it beating. Oz tells me a story. One New Year's Eve, a man thanked him for saving his wife's life. But the man made it extremely clear that he felt the one who actually deserved credit was a far higher power than any surgeon. Oz doesn't tell me if he believes that matters of life and death are ultimately up to God, but he does say that "if you start believing your own bulls--t, thinking you're infallible, you're going to start making mistakes. Everyone's got an ego, but the operating room has to be a place of controlled arrogance." We adjust our masks and walk back to the OR. "Will she be okay?" I ask, probably looking as anxious as the people pacing the waiting room. "She'll be sitting in a chair by tomorrow," Oz assures me.

Still, I stick around until they warm her blood, wean her from the heart-lung machine, get her heart once again beating on its own, and repeatedly promise they don't need me there to help them close.

I head out of the hospital, into the drizzly afternoon. I look at the people racing for cabs, buying the paper, checking their BlackBerrys, and I can't help wondering what's in their hearts. What are their most ardent desires, their secret shames...their cholesterol levels?

If we're smart, we shop for whole grains and pray for good genes and go to the gym and hope for the best. But as I learned years ago on a damp day a lot like this, the body is breakable. This morning I saw living proof that if we're lucky, it can also be fixed. ◖

Lisa Kogan Tells All

If at first you don't succeed...wait 40 years, finagle an invitation to an exclusive club, and steer clear of the kitchen sink. The world's oldest living Brownie attempts to merit a badge.

I was never a group person. I don't join clubs, I don't get picked for jury duty, and I'm proud to tell anyone who will listen that I spent the summer of 1995 *not* doing the macarena. There's no getting around it; I'm a wallflower at the proverbial orgy—and I've come to like it that way. Besides, it's not as if I didn't give the team thing a try.

The year was 1969 and the group was the (pre–Camp Fire Girl) Blue Birds. Things went okay at first. We sang "Silent Night" in a mall, we decoupaged empty cans of Minute Maid frozen pink lemonade into pencil holders, we brought hot soup to old people. And then one day, there was...an incident. Let the record show that I did not intentionally flip the switch to the garbage disposal in Debbie Schiller's mother's house, nor did I know there was a large glass stuck in it when the aforementioned switch was flipped, nor do I accept responsibility for the tiny glass shards that flew across Debbie Schiller's mother's kitchen and made 11 Blue Birds look like extras from the invasion of Normandy scene in *Saving Private Ryan*. Suffice it to say everyone pretty much agreed, I was just not Blue Bird material.

Raise your hand if you remember the Brownies. After my Blue Bird career ended, I'd watch these future Girl Scouts going off to meetings in their matching cocoa-colored shirt-dresses complete with little felt cap and tangerine necktie, and I'd find myself wondering what it was like to be born with all your homework done. I didn't know what took place at a Brownie get-together, but I knew it involved cookies, and I knew they got merit badges, and I knew that their moms stitched those badges to the sashes they wore to display their many achievements. And thanks to the carnage of 1969, I knew one other thing: I would never quite fit in.

I'm still not particularly gifted at being one of the gang—uniforms make me panic and crowds make me claustrophobic. But I've learned to wear my eccentricities like little badges of courage. Still, an actual Brownie badge of merit...well, I wanted it. I wanted it bad. And I don't mean I wanted it in the metaphorical, your parents say they're proud of all your accomplishments sense; I mean I wanted somebody to teach me the secret handshake and toss me a Thin Mint.

That's right, I cast off my outsider status and finally finagled an invitation to my first ever Brownie meeting. I will be part of a community; I will set right an old mistake. As God is my witness, I will merit a badge.

"Hi, I'm Lisa," I say, doing my best to mingle. "What's your name?"

"My name is Nia T. Montero, and I'm 5 years old."

"What's the *T* stand for?"

"Brittney."

"What do you like to be called?"

"Nia T. Montero."

Karolina, also age 5, asks me how old I am, as she narrows her eyes and zeroes in on the crow's-feet that appear every time I smile. "How old do I look?" It's a rookie mistake, but now that I've made it, all I can do is suck in my stomach and brace for impact. She circles me, does some calculations in her head, and finally replies, "I dunno... maybe 15." I think I'm going to like it here.

Den mothers pass out paste and construction paper, glitter and markers, and we settle into our places here in the church basement at Saint Joseph's Parish of Yorkville

> "How old do I look?" It's a rookie mistake, but now that I've made it, all I can do is suck in my stomach and brace for impact.

and begin to design our bird collages. "Eewww," 6-year-old Audrey proclaims as her hands hit the paste. "Oh, please," I tell her, "you think that's icky, try scrubbing three-day-old lasagna off a Pyrex baking dish."

In retrospect, this might've been the moment when it first became apparent that, to quote *Sesame Street,* "one of these things is not like the others." There were many such moments. Ella, Mercedes, and Lily had all lost teeth. "My gums are starting to recede!" I say, trying to build a little camaraderie. Here's the bottom line: When someone wants to know your favorite color, "taupe" is not the answer that'll get you put in charge of food coloring when it comes time to frost cupcakes. It's not pretty when a table full of grade-schoolers look at you with pity. "Maybe you should try the Brownies," says Nia T. Montero, pointing to a troop across the room. "But I thought you guys were Brownies," I say. "No, that's for when we grow up." Lilliana chimes in. "Actually," she adds, "when I grow up, I'm going to be a waiter. For now, we're all Daisies."

"We didn't have Daisies when I was a kid. We didn't even—" But before I can get into how there were only three TV channels and I could have bought a penthouse on Central Park West for $35, they are off to donate the cans of food they brought in. Who knew I was supposed to bring canned goods? My quest for a badge has hit a major snag.

I wander over to the table where the Brownies are sitting: The six girls in my new troop range in age from 8 to 10. Today they are supposed to interview somebody, and it's been decided that I'm "it." If the Daisies have taught me nothing else, it's that receding gums does not an ice-breaker make, so I tell them that I've always wanted to be a Brownie, and wait for the questions to come.

Molly's hand shoots up. "Do you know any famous people?" she asks. Olivia and Nia (not to be confused with my Daisy pals of the same names) decide to get specific: "Have you ever met Lady Gaga?" I tell them no, but to let them down easy, I add that before there was a Lady Gaga, legend has it that my Aunt Sondra wore vinyl hot pants and a tube top to a bris in New Jersey. "What are hot pants?" asks Anaise. "What's a bris?" asks Amberly.

Sometimes a change of subject can be an aging Brownie's best friend: "So, what do you do when you're not selling cookies?" I ask, deftly sidestepping the bris question. Manon tells me about family ice-skating day and a sleepover on the *Intrepid*. They all talk about a father-and-daughter luncheon cruise and a mother-and-daughter ceramics-making party.

"My daughter would love that," I say.

They are surprised to hear I have a daughter. "Is she home with your husband?" Molly asks. "She's at ballet right now." "And then your husband picks her up?" Molly is taking on a certain Mike Wallace quality. "I'm not married," I say. "Wait a minute, you had a baby but you're not married?" Olivia asks. I take a deep breath. "A bris is when—"

"Who's ready for cookies?" our troop leader mercifully jumps in. We snack and check out our bird collages, then the Daisies and Brownies form a circle. Could this be that elusive award ceremony I've been waiting for? No. It's time to repeat the Girl Scout Law:

"I will do my best to be honest and fair, friendly and helpful, considerate and caring, courageous and strong, and responsible for what I say and do, and to respect myself and others, respect authority, use resources wisely, make the world a better place, and be a sister to every Girl Scout."

I actually find being strong kind of overrated, and people in positions of authority generally have to earn my respect. But all in all, I'd say it's a pretty good pledge—and the girls seem to be sticking to it. They support each other, laugh together, and still manage to maintain their individuality. Ella's bird collage has the earrings and false eyelashes to prove it.

Could it be that an outsider is really just a Brownie waiting to be asked in? That the right group of women will always welcome a few eccentricities? "You know, there's a lot to be said for belonging to something, for not going it alone every single day," I tell my troop leader as I look to see if there's anything stronger than a juice box with which to wash down my cookie. "Really," I say, "I can imagine coming every week." My leader looks alarmed. "I mean, just until I earn a merit badge."

It turns out, meriting a badge is easier than it looks. I am instantly presented with one—but they must be so anxious to make sure I get home safely that I'm escorted out the door before I can even give the acceptance speech that's been burning a hole in my pocket for more than 40 years. **O**

Lisa Kogan Tells All

O come all ye single! Our Cupid-like columnist rewrites online profiles to save her date-challenged friends from...themselves.

Something has happened to the prune. I don't know why, I don't know how, I only know that I was at the supermarket one fine morning, minding my own business, when suddenly I came face to face with "the sun-dried plum."

I will tell you right now that I am a big fan of the prune—particularly when it's in Danish form—but the prune was clearly not selling. For the prune to turn heads (not to mention meet a nice guy, move to the suburbs, and have a couple of baby prunes) it needed a fresh marketing strategy. Which brings us to today's subject: the online dating profile.

I've got a number of brilliant, beautiful, frank, funny friends, all capable of remarkable things—but writing an enticing online profile does not seem to be one of them. That's where I come in. Some people offer their services in soup kitchens, some volunteer to shampoo crude oil off of sad, gooey pelicans; I rewrite online dating profiles.

It all started when my pal Paula asked me to figure out why she wasn't getting a response to her JDate ad. I didn't have to read beyond her opening sentence—"I like the library!"—to know why. All the exclamation points in the world couldn't save that line. "But I was being honest," Paula groaned. "Why can't I find somebody who gets that?"

What I get is that we all want to be loved for exactly who we are. But surely there's a juicier way to bring up your literary fetish. "Dewey Decimal? You bet we do!"

It wasn't long before news that I'd taken Paula's profile from drab to fab spread far and wide (okay, a couple of people in Brooklyn heard). Soon I was averaging 3.5 profile punch-ups a week. I've seen the dumb, the dull, and the klutzy; the bitter, the brazen, and the too cute by half. I've studied strangers on the Web and friends at my kitchen table, and here's what I've learned:

■ False modesty is, well...false. Still, I urged my friend to follow her goddess-like self-description of "an award-winning microbiologist who is Nigella Lawson in the kitchen and Megan Fox in the bedroom" with "I'm absolutely tone-deaf, and I can't ski, but I'd be open to a lesson or two." Soon she was swooshing down a bunny slope with an ophthalmologist from St. Paul. You see, you're better off copping to a humanizing flaw than coming across as too good to be true. (Mother Teresa was too good to be true, and nobody ever saw her having sushi with James Franco on a Saturday night.)

■ My friend Carol, on the other hand, is not one to blow her own horn. "I'm divorced, with a grouchy teenager and an incontinent beagle," she writes, neglecting to mention that she's also a total babe and one of the top labor lawyers in the country. "I wanted to be funny," she explains. Funny is good, I like funny, and God knows I enjoy a bladder control reference as much as the next guy.... Wait a second, I just remembered something: Guys don't like that. Let's save the fact that little Snoopy is in diapers for the fourth date.

■ You see, the key to any good punch-up is to finesse our little quirks. Let's assume that in some sort of misguided effort to emulate Johnny Cash, I once "shot a man in Reno, just to watch him die." A clever little tweak on this might suggest that I "support the Second Amendment, adore the desert, and consider myself a keen observer of the human condition."

■ I review my manicurist's profile as she soaks my cuticles. It says that she's looking for "complete and total happiness." Darling, I'm looking for LL Cool J to feed me fettuccine as we watch an endless loop of *Project Runway*. But that's just not how the world works. Complete and total happiness comes in quick bursts of joy—it's the bite of banana cream pie, it's "Hey Jude" blasting from a car radio. Forget complete and total happiness; look for somebody who wants to meet you for a drink, and just see what happens.

■ Indeed, there's a lot to be said for keeping things simple. But please note, simple doesn't have to mean dull. The rules governing what's considered too slutty these

PERSONAL ADS

SEEKING
Pure unadulterated adoration. Are you dazzling in every possible way? E-mail me: missrealistic@expectations.com

♥LOOKING FOR LOVE?♥♥
That's where I come in...
Having started my career in advertising, I know exactly how to spin a simple little prune into a juicy, audacious, utterly delectable sun-ripened plum.

CATS NOW & FOREVER
Interested in having your upholstery screwed up? Then have I got some tender vittles for you!!!

DIVORCED
WITH SULLEN TEEN AND INCONTINENT BEAGLE
Willing to meet for coffee (and true love) in my vet's waiting room.

ARE YOU THE ANSWER?
I'm looking for a man I can put on speed dial—here's hoping you pick up! Text me!

SHORT STUFF
I'm 5' nothing in heels—you got a problem with that? I thought so. But I don't care what you think. To hell with you. Leave me alone.

I ♥ THE LIBRARY
I also enjoy reruns of *Matlock*, staying awake til 9:30 pm, and adding flaxseeds to oatmeal. Help me alphabetize my nonfiction.

MEGAN FOX + NIGELLA LAWSON = ME
Yes, I really am that fabulous...and then some. How about you?

JET-SETTER
First-class frequent flier in search of a companion to travel through life with. Prepared for takeoff so please respond before the final boarding call. Your ticket to happiness. Fasten your seat belt!
milehigh@fly.net

IN FULL BLOOM
WEEDED OUT A FEW BAD SEEDS AND NOW READY FOR RELATIONSHIP TO BLOSSOM!

MONA LISA SMILE
And an almost uncanny knack for picking losers. Don't even get me started on my ex and his mother...who was a total nut job. If you are nothing like him and want a soul mate who is neither bitter nor jaded—I'm your girl.

days have come unraveled faster than Amy Winehouse on a six-pack of Red Bull. I have a coworker who swears she would not be the happily married woman she is today were it not for three magic words she tucked into her online profile: "horny and attentive." Now, would I tell a group of online strangers that I'm horny and attentive? No, but that's because I have a tendency to be "cranky and oblivious." The point is: Sex, like the sun-dried plum, continues to sell.

■ Cousin Arleen wants to start a family. How do I know this? She mentions it in three different places on her profile. Say it once if you feel you must, but wait for an actual dinner date before whipping out the iPhone app that chirps when you're ovulating.

■ Another coworker starts her very defensive profile with "Let's get this out of the way right now: I'm short, okay?!" Why not go with something like "I've sometimes been described as a 'pocket Venus.'" Actually, my teeny colleague's touchiness raises another point: *When* you choose to mention something is every bit as crucial as what you choose to mention. Lunch meat makes me wheeze uncontrollably and break into hives the size of Ping-Pong balls—but I probably wouldn't lead with this information.

■ The sister of my babysitter lets people know right off the bat that "the cats I cohabit with know I live only to serve them." Oh, crazy, crazy cat lady, where do I begin? What your cats actually know is that mice are a tasty treat, that there's nothing better than a long nap on a squishy cushion, and that Katherine Heigl doesn't make very good movies. Of course, you can tell interested partners that you love animals, but unless you want to be stuck with a soul mate that hocks up fur balls, you've got to quit sabotaging yourself by announcing to any potential suitor that he will never take priority over Captain Fluffy Paws.

■ One of the women at my gym wants a nonsmoker with a sense of humor and a love of adventure. Fair enough. But she also wants a man who "is punctual, considerate,

> I'm looking for LL Cool J to feed me fettuccine as we watch an endless loop of *Project Runway.*

and into theater." All righty then. She insists he be "blond, highly successful, and able to play an instrument." Hmmmm. She feels strongly that he not "ride a motorcycle, be divorced, or own goldfish." I was a braless 22-year-old when I first began reading her profile. I am now 49; my gums are receding and it sounds like there's a dice game taking place in my left knee. Here's a good rule of thumb: If I have to check my watch twice as I study your never-ending list of needs, then the thing you need most is an editor.

■ There's stuff we know we don't want—and that's certainly legitimate. But here's how my neighbor presents her requirements: "If you're a closet freak, if you think choking me during intimacy is hot, if you live with your parents, if you're a flat-out jerk, don't waste my time. I've got three kids and I don't need another. That said, I am not a bitch."

Well, you could've fooled me. Since when did auto-erotic asphyxiation and jerky behavior get lumped in with living at your parents' place? Sometimes parents get old and need a bit of help and sometimes unemployment reaches an all-time high—the world goes round, my friend. But by the sound of your profile, you already know that. You've obviously been burned (and possibly choked), so go lie down while I attempt a rewrite:

"I'm raising three great kids pretty much on my own, which means I've had to give serious thought to the kind of man I want to bring into my life. It's not that complicated, really—I'm just looking for an enlightened grown-up who is interested in a solid relationship along with a good time. Major integrity and genuine kindness are essential."

Let's review—the key to this whole online profile thing is really quite simple: Be direct while maintaining an air of mystery; be modest while flaunting what you've got; be flexible while explaining what you need, while keeping it brief and making it flirty and not getting cute; and be yourself, only more so, only not so much more so that you exaggerate, intimidate, or irritate. I know it sounds like a tall order, but if the prune can do it, so can you. ◖

Lisa Kogan Tells All

Where do you go when you're in need of a little inspiration? Our ever-resourceful columnist turned to an artist who's been a creative force for the past 100 years.

Mary H. Krell needs a place to live. Who, you may be wondering, is Mary H. Krell? Well, I asked that very same question at ten minutes after five this morning when my daughter woke me with the Krell bulletin.

"Mary H. Krell is my wooden spoon doll," she informs me. "Every first-grader makes one, only the boys call them pocket people instead of spoon dolls because boys feel funny about saying they have a doll." Julia explains this in a way that suggests she loves me...despite the fact that I might be the

stupidest human being on the face of the planet.

"Yep, boys are funny all right," I mumble.

"Mommy," Julia shouts directly into my left eardrum, "I need to bring a shoebox to school today, so I can build a house for Mary H. Krell!" My understanding is that all kids occasionally forget to mention their shoebox requirements in a timely fashion. My hope is that at least a few other 6-year-olds feel compelled to give their dolls a middle initial and last name. My prayer is that there is something in my ridiculously small closet that'll make a decent split-level ranch for Mary H. Krell. What I'm looking for is a creative solution, some sweet inspiration, and a modicum of wisdom. But at this particular moment, what I've got is bubkes.

I know that there are some women out there who are

making their way through life with wit and courage, even on days when life refuses to play fair and provide them with a shoebox. And I know there are people in this world who get up every morning and, through magic and talent and sheer force of will, manage to turn nothing into something. I once witnessed my friend Karen go into her pantry, take out a jar of grape jelly, a pine-scented Air Wick solid, a can of cream of celery soup, a box of lasagna noodles, and whip up a feast. And yes, I'm exaggerating to make a point—there was no soup involved—but you get the idea. These women are improvising their way through complicated lives, raising children up, holding jobs down, sculpting a palace from an empty Adidas box. How do they do it? How do they acknowledge their limitations, and then find the bravado and perseverance and imagination to rise above them? Everyone I know is looking for the secret code that will unlock her creativity, but I can think of only one woman who has not only found it but somehow manages to tap into it daily.

I was familiar with Eva Zeisel's work long before I was familiar with her name: the teakettle she designed for Chantal, the line of dinnerware she created for Royal Stafford, the brass candlesticks, the blown-glass goblets, the ceramic vases, the porcelain pitchers. Voluptuous yet restrained, playful yet pragmatic, Eva's stuff is sexy. You want to caress it, sip from it, watch it catch the light.

The sign on the front door of her prewar apartment on Manhattan's Upper West Side instructs visitors to wash their hands before greeting Eva. Cold and flu season has not officially ended and nobody is taking any chances. This is because Eva Zeisel, who in 1946 became the first female designer in history to be given a one-woman show at the Museum of Modern Art, in New York City, is now 104 years old.

The Zeisel family genes must be Herculean; Eva's daughter, Jean Richards, could pass for 50-something, though a quick check of the dates proves that impossible. She brings me into the living room, where her mother sits at a small table. "Mom," she says, "this is Lisa." I extend my hand to Eva and she sandwiches it between her own. She traces its shape, skims each vein, and touches it to her cheek. But I'm not fooled by the tenderness of the gesture, or the fragility of the grasp—Eva is as strong as they come. Her hair is a luminous silvery white, her cheekbones are downright aristocratic, and her smile develops like a Polaroid, getting brighter as it comes into focus. Still, she has reached that place in life where, if you're lucky, looking back provides the resilience to look ahead.

I'm hungry for clues about Eva's remarkable talent, so I begin at the beginning. "Eva," I ask, "what can you tell me about growing up in Budapest?" She closes her eyes

and, just for a minute, finds her way back home. "We lived in the hills. There was a beautiful orchard, and a pond with a bridge over it, and a small grotto. Then came our flower garden. It was my job to keep cut flowers and fresh fruit around the house," she says, nodding toward a bowl of tangerines. "There was also a vineyard, where we grew grapes to make our own wine." Eva's Merchant Ivory memories are pretty heady stuff for a girl who was born and raised in Detroit. I picture endless summers and calico cats and white cotton dresses as the sound of rush hour traffic outside Eva's window all but disappears.

She tells me about apprenticing herself while still in her teens to Mr. Karapancik, the last of the master potters in Hungary's medieval guild system. "He taught me everything there was to know about ceramics, from mushing the clay with my feet to firing the pieces in the kiln. Once a week, the master's wife would haul a big wooden cart filled with our wares to market, where she'd sit and sell them. But the world was pulling at me," Eva says, and pauses for a sip of tea. "So I took a job doing design work in a factory, then I placed an ad in the trade papers explaining that I was a qualified journeyman seeking a position. I received several offers, and naturally," she says with a wily smile, "I picked the one that was farthest from where I lived."

Eva headed first for Hamburg, Germany, and then Schramberg, where she became one of the first people to apply contemporary mass production techniques to the ceramic arts. But her wanderlust kept her moving; over the next few years, she found a flat in Paris and, later, a studio in Berlin, always searching for the next great adventure. Then, in 1932, she went to Russia. "I just had to see what was on the other side of the mountain." She got

This 2008 portrait of Eva Zeisel, sitting outside her Rockland County studio, was taken by Talisman Brolin, one of her three grandchildren.

one job and then another, until after nearly four years of impressive promotions, at the age of 29, Eva Zeisel was appointed art director of the porcelain and glass industries for the entire republic.

Nineteen thirty-six turned out to be the wrong time to pursue a career on "the other side of the mountain." Joseph Stalin was purging the USSR of artists, intellectuals, foreigners, and anyone else he perceived as a threat. Eva, who was not the least bit political, was arrested on charges of conspiring to assassinate Stalin and jailed for 16 months in one of the notorious NKVD prisons. Twelve of those months were spent in solitary confinement, where she was left to marinate in the unrelenting knowledge that every day could be her last.

As we sit here more than 60 years later, the only thing I can think to ask is how she survived with her sanity intact. Eva rubs her temples and says that her head hurts, but when I suggest we stop, she ignores the offer, takes a breath, and goes on. "I did whatever I could do in a tiny cell to keep my body in shape. I spent hours repeating leg exercises, I stood on my head—anything. As for my mind, well, I avoided any soft or loving thoughts." She wouldn't allow for even a hint of vulnerability. "Beyond that, I kept very busy. I created projects for myself. I actually came up with a bra design! I thought through every aspect—the width of the straps, the proper amount of padding, exactly where it should hook—then I constructed it. I handstitched the whole thing," she says proudly. "And I did it all in my mind," she adds, as her voice trails off. Then one day, just as suddenly and inexplicably as she'd been arrested, she was released. Eva is still a little stunned as she describes being led from her cell, thinking the time for her execution had finally come. "Instead they just put me on a train to Austria, with nothing but the clothes I was standing in."

Eva had missed 16 months of life and she was not going to miss another minute. She boarded the last train out of Austria before Germany invaded. She married Hans Zeisel and, in 1938, emigrated to America. A year later she spearheaded a ceramics curriculum in the department of industrial design at Pratt Institute in Brooklyn, where she taught until 1952. Over the years, she's worked in Italy, Japan, England, and India, had two babies, received honorary doctorates, picked up every prestigious award imaginable, and attended a 2006 luncheon at the White House. Her work is in permanent collections everywhere from the Metropolitan Museum of Art to the British Museum. There have been retrospectives all over the world and fresh releases of old designs, always approved by Eva herself.

But it's her new designs that astonish me. Her pieces are scattered all over the apartment—a collection of exquisite Christmas ornaments, a series of ceramic tiles, a group of light fixtures that were in development. Every piece is witty, chic, utterly original, much like the woman behind them. I ask Eva where she finds beauty. "I look at a pressed red maple leaf from the tree in my garden upstate, I study the flowers people bring me. My eyesight only allows me to see very close-up, so when I design, I visualize the image in my mind and then I draw it like this—" Eva becomes instantly animated, her hands dancing in the space between us until I can see a perfect Zeisel pitcher, literally plucked from thin air. "I make a rough sketch. My design assistant, Olivia Barry, refines it; she uses thick lines and makes cutouts and models for me to feel. I'll say, 'This curve needs to be deeper, I want this wall to be angled, let's get this part really slender,' until it feels exactly right. My designs are meant to attract the hand as well as the eye."

She seems so sure of herself. I wonder how many years it will take me to get so clear about how I want something to look or to feel or to be. I ask her if there is anything that she regrets—something that she'd go back and do differently if she could. She thinks for a minute, watches as her daughter enters the room again, glances at a sketch she's working on, and finally replies, "I regret nothing. I'd do it all again and I'd do it all the exact same way." Jean is genuinely startled. "Mother! What about Stalin? What about the prison—you'd do *that* again?" Eva's back straightens, and for a split second, she is absolutely defiant. "I *never* put myself in a prison," she says. "They did that to me."

Tired now, she asks if there's anything else I need to know. What I need to know is how you live more than a century—is it about diet, or heredity, or having a passion that goes the distance? But, feeling unusually energized after spending the afternoon with a genius, I also need to get back to finding a proper home for Mary H. Krell. "Just one last thing, Eva: What surprises you? I mean, at your age, is there anything that can still fill you with a sense of wonder?" Eva doesn't have to think to answer this question. "My dear," she says, "everything surprises me." ◐

> Everyone I know is looking for the secret code that will unlock her creativity, but I can think of only one woman who's found it.

Lisa Kogan Tells All

The day our columnist saw an airborne Mary Poppins, she was astonished. Her 7-year-old? Not so much. So the search began: to find a miracle they could *both* believe in.

llow me to set the scene: It is 2009, snow is falling, street vendors have stopped selling pretzels that are made God knows how and begun selling roasted chestnuts that are made God knows where. People are wearing ruby red and kelly green sweaters covered in reindeer appliqués, and I decide to kick off the holidays with a Broadway matinee of *Mary Poppins*. There are little girls who would be thrilled with a plan like this. My daughter, Julia, is not one of them. I explain that I used to love going to the theater with my mom. Blank stare. I explain that it will be fun and memorable and the start of a brand-new tradition. Rolling of eyes. I explain that we can eat at McDonald's and buy her a new set of Pokémon cards immediately afterward. Bingo!

The show starts slow but becomes completely enchanting. At the end, Mary opens her umbrella and flies straight off the stage, up, up, up, until finally she is floating right in front of our balcony seats. The effect is jaw-dropping, completely astonishing. "Look, honey!" I whisper, "Mary Poppins is suspended in midair!" My darling little 7-year-old glares at me as though I am certifiably insane and whispers back, "Mommy, that's an actress, and I can see the strings."

All righty, then.

The time has come for a little hard-core mothering. I need to resurrect the feeling of wonder that salvages us from cynicism. I'm looking for leaps of faith and the element of surprise, and a trace of something that defies logic. "I don't care if the search takes all year; come next Christmas," I promise Julia, "I will find us at least one small miracle—no strings attached."

JANUARY: In a horribly misguided stab at whimsy, I decide to take Jules ice-skating. I have not actually been on skates for 36 years, but I assume it will come back to me, you know, like riding a bicycle...something I haven't done for 37 years.

I guess the doctor in the ER of St. Luke's–Roosevelt Hospital said it best when he handed me a pair of crutches, an ice pack, and a prescription for Percocet, and declared, "It's a miracle you didn't break anything." Not exactly the miracle of gliding majestically across the rink at Rockefeller Center as sparkly little snowflakes glisten on your eyelashes, but there's something to be said for colliding headfirst into a family of five hearty Midwesterners, bouncing off a concrete wall, and landing beneath a class of merciless third graders without receiving so much as a hairline fracture. My year of living miraculously is off to an excellent start.

FEBRUARY: Johannes (love of my life, father of my child, forgetter of Valentine's Day for more than a decade) brings home a dozen long-stem tulips and a caramel cupid on the 14th of the month. "My darling," I coo, "you remembered!" He mumbles something about how his firm belief that this holiday represents the commercialization of couplehood has been trumped by *my* firm belief that I "could probably use the heel of my hand to drive a person's nose straight through his brain."

We struggle, we annoy, we regroup, we stay open, we lie around, we watch MSNBC, we laugh, we hold hands, we buy pumpkin muffins, we get upset because somebody didn't seal the bag and now the pumpkin muffins are stale, and then we start all over again. Love is a battlefield, a many-splendored thing, a blessing, and a pain in the neck, but it is not a miracle. Two human beings managing to blend their lives together for 17 years—now, that's a miracle.

MARCH: It happened at exactly ten after eight in the morning. I know because I had just completed my first "It's ten after eight in the morning, for God's sake! Brush your teeth and track down your shoes before Mommy has an aneurysm" shout-out of the day. I said a silent prayer, took a deep breath, stepped on the scale, and lo and behold, weighed four pounds and six ounces less than I had in weeks.

But I couldn't help wondering if this was, perhaps, a carbohydrate-induced hallucination. I mean, if I had really lost nearly five pounds without even trying, then why were the schools and the post offices and the New York Stock Exchange still open? Where was the parade through Times Square, the Anderson Cooper interview? We will never know, but around Casa Kogan, this incident is still referred to as the Miracle of the Fettuccine Eater.

APRIL: I am folding laundry as the late, great Eva Cassidy sings "Danny Boy" over my crummy old JBL speakers. Her sound is crystalline and ethereal, seductive and soaring. I am amazed by the way three minutes and 41 seconds of music can leave a girl sobbing into a dish towel. Eva Cassidy's voice is about as miraculous as it gets.

MAY: Here comes the sun and cherry trees and open windows and linen skirts and iced cappuccinos that cost more than my father's first car. Spring is a miracle.

JUNE: On June 2, Detroit Tiger Armando Galarraga was pitching a perfect game—a feat that's been accomplished exactly 20 times since 1880—and hot damn, it was simply gorgeous! The ball seemed to go faster than his arm, as if the laws of physics couldn't slow him down, when suddenly umpire Jim Joyce ruled Cleveland Indians runner Jason Donald safe, for what should have been the game's final out.

But Jason Donald was not safe, as Mr. Joyce realized after viewing the postgame replay. And then it happened: Joyce sincerely apologized, Galarraga graciously accepted, and Detroiters roared their approval. At a time in the world when nobody seems to be taking responsibility for anything, two incredibly decent men demonstrated compassion, civility, style, and a miraculous degree of integrity.

JULY: Speaking of basic human decency, I recently came across this little quote from Matthew D. Staver, the founder and chairman of a conservative religious law firm called Liberty Counsel. "I am a Christian and I am a conservative and I am a Republican, in that order," he said. "There is very little I agree with regarding President Barack Obama. On the other hand, I'm not going to let politicized rhetoric or party affiliation trump my values, and if he's right on this issue [of immigration reform], I will support him on this issue." Granted, that's hardly a ringing endorsement, and, make no mistake, there's very little I agree with regarding Mr. Matthew D. Staver. On the other hand, it's nothing short of a miracle to find somebody out there who is willing to be guided by something besides "politicized rhetoric or party affiliation."

AUGUST: I am sitting in my dentist's waiting room when I spot Dennis Quaid smiling up at me from the cover of a magazine. Is he *People*'s Sexiest Man Alive? Nope. Is he playing the enfant terrible for *Details?* Uh-uh. Dennis Quaid's cocky grin is plastered across the front of *AARP The Magazine*, and according to *AARP* (formerly known as *Modern Maturity*), the man is 56 years old. But that can't be right. I mean, didn't I just see him play the burned-out bad boy in *Breaking Away?* "You sure did," replies Rose, the unflappable hygienist, "if by 'just' you mean 1979." Time rushes by at miraculous speed.

SEPTEMBER: Meredith, my neighbor down the hall, is 51 years old…and seven months pregnant. There was no egg donor, no in vitro fertilization, no special blend of Chinese herbs and reflexology—just an $11 bottle of Pinot Grigio and the mistaken impression that already having two sons in college somehow makes conception impossible. Meredith is now busily preparing for the miracle of birth.

OCTOBER: I'm having coffee with one of my oldest friends, Francesca Gany, the founder and director of the Center for Immigrant Health at the New York University School of Medicine, and she mentions a figure that genuinely shocks me: Of the cancer patients her center serves, 51 percent of those living below the poverty line do not have enough to eat. This is the kind of problem that makes me want to curl into the fetal position with the TV remote and a bag of Cheetos, but humanity is in luck today: Francesca has never met a crisis she doesn't want to tackle. Her latest initiative is called Food for Health, a pantry designed to aid people who find themselves with cancer but without money for food. I walk my friend back to her NYU office, located in Bellevue Hospital, where she and her multilingual team distribute vouchers that will enable patients to go to the supermarket and buy some of the food they need to get them through treatment. Each patient is also given a bag of groceries to take home; there's a can of peaches, a carton of milk, a jar of peanut butter, a bottle of apple juice, a box of rice, and a couple of other items. Francesca reads my mind. "It's better than nothing, but it's nowhere near enough," she says as she places a grocery bag into the arms of a young woman who looks beautiful and tired and enormously grateful that today she won't have to choose between buying medicine and buying a meal. "You people are miracle workers," she calls out as she hobbles toward the elevator. She's absolutely right, but Dr. Gany and Co. simply shrug off the praise and keep the line moving.

NOVEMBER: Thanksgiving dinner. My vegan cousin's vegan girlfriend does not spend the evening making everybody feel guilty over "turkey genocide." My creepy uncle from Great Neck does not ask if this is the year Johannes will

> Love is a battlefield and a blessing, but it is not a miracle. Two human beings blending their lives together for 17 years—now, that's a miracle.

finally break down and make "an honest woman" out of me; my addled Aunt Rita does not get drunk. We eat, we keep our aggression passive, we go home. It sounds pretty basic, but trust me—it's a miracle.

DECEMBER: Usually when I drop in on friends at work, I find them crouched in a crowded cubicle, surreptitiously shopping eBay, but my pal Valerie Soll is stretching across a table in the Textile Conservation Lab at the Cathedral Church of Saint John the Divine, a cavernous space where she and nearly a dozen other experts work to clean, stabilize, and conserve some of the world's most extraordinary pieces. "Check this out," she says, pointing to an enormous tapestry depicting a scene from the life of Christ. It took master weavers from 1643 to 1656 to craft this set of one-of-a-kind tapestries for the nephew of Maffeo Barberini, better known as Pope Urban VIII. "Tapestries were the bling of their day," Val says. "They spoke volumes about your wealth and power—they told the world what you cared about, what you believed in, what your story was."

It's a fragile thread that sutures us to our stories, and it is a miracle that through hundreds of years of travel and temperature, smoke and red wine stains, bright lights and big pollution, along with the weight of hanging in a thousand different places (to say nothing of major neglect; during the French Revolution, farmers used the Metropolitan Museum of Art's famous Unicorn tapestries as blankets to keep potatoes from freezing), the Barberini tapestries continue to tell their stories.

Tonight I will sit down with Julia and tell her the story of my year spent searching for miracles. "The thing is," I'll explain, "nobody really has to go looking for a miracle because it turns out, they're usually pretty close to home." They come tiptoeing in while you're watching a no-hitter or folding laundry or tapping a rock-hard pumpkin muffin against the kitchen counter. They're in tapestries that survive hundreds of years, and parents who survive the morning onslaught, and people who don't have enough food to make it through another day, and somehow make it anyway.

And Jules will nod and pretend to listen, then ask if she can play her Pokémon game on the computer for 15 minutes before bed, which will give me a deeply luxurious 15 minutes entirely to myself—one final miracle. ◗

Lisa Kogan Tells All

It was a beautiful—no, a *perfect*—day. Until a kindly but clueless grandma asked The Question That Must Never Be Posed to Any Woman, Ever. In the spirit of forgiveness, *O*'s ever-evolving columnist resolves to breathe in and let go…but not before recalling a landfill of grudges, slights, insults, and snarky remarks.

bout three weeks after my daughter, Julia, was born, I was standing in line at Russ & Daughters, a lovely little shoebox of a shop that's been serving the most exquisite Jewish delicacies ever since Mr. Russ loaded up his pushcart and headed for the Lower East Side of Manhattan in 1908. I was ordering smoked butterfish and nova, sliced thinner than angel wings, as the guys behind the counter plied me with samples of apricot strudel and raspberry rugelach. It was spring, my baby was healthy,

Russ & Daughters had just put out their marble nut halvah, and all was right with the world.

I was experiencing what the late, great Spalding Gray used to call "a perfect moment." Please note, Mr. Gray didn't talk about perfect days, he didn't even refer to a perfect half-hour stretch. Nope, he only suggested that there are moments when life is inexorably sweet, but those moments are few and far between—and generally over before you can capture them on the teeny camera in your ridiculously tricked-out cell phone.

The adorable grandma to my left decided to strike up a conversation: "So, how long have you been coming here, dear?" She smelled like Pond's Cold Cream and cinnamon, and I liked her immediately. "Well, ma'am, my aunt

Bernice first brought me here when I was just a kid," I answered between bites. She smiled warmly and told me she grew up right around the corner, on Orchard Street, and had shopped here since the 1920s. "I raised five children on this food," she said, pointing to the baked blueberry farmer's cheese. We were soul mates in sable, partners in pickled herring; we spoke the language of lox. And that's when it happened.

My new buddy suddenly reached out her bony little liver-spotted hand, patted my baby-free middle, and asked the one question nobody should ever ask: "When are you due?"

I toyed with the possibility that she had some sort of death wish. Perhaps the question was actually a thinly veiled plea. I mean, isn't it plausible that what she was really saying was "I want to go out on a high note, so I'll just have a taste of chopped liver, and then do something so heinous that it drives this perfectly reasonable woman to club me to death with a side of salmon"?

You see, there are certain questions that must never be asked:

1. Has your surprise party happened yet?

2. How did you first learn that your husband is cheating?
And, above all:

3. When are you due?

I don't care if the woman you're asking is wearing a T-shirt with a giant rhinestone-encrusted arrow that points to her belly and reads BABY ON BOARD. I don't care if she's writhing on a gurney in the birthing room of Mount Sinai hospital, screaming for an epidural as an obstetrician announces, "One more push and the baby will be out!" You never, let me repeat, never, ever, under any circumstances, ask a woman when she's due.

"June," I replied.

Some people collect coins, some prowl the Internet for vintage guitars; I know a woman with a closet full of antique Kewpie-doll heads. I'm not totally clear what turned her against everything from the neck down—she may have been frightened by a Barbie breast as a child. But I'm nobody to judge, because I, too, am a collector. What I collect are slights, digs, withering remarks, and the occasional mean-girl glare. I examine a good when-are-you-due story from every angle, I trade them with friends, I commit them to memory, I savor them for all of eternity.

Here are a few of my favorite insults:

My old friend Suzanna remembers the first time she had her Hungarian husband's family over. She cooked for three straight days. The woman goulashed and paprikashed and put her tomato sauce through a food mill, for God's sake. At the end of the meal, her new mother-in-law took Suzie's hands in hers, looked her straight in the eye, and said: "I'm so glad you feel you can practice on us." Ouch.

My former roommate Laurie came home with an A+ on her test and proudly handed the paper to her father. "Interesting," he said. "I always thought you had to be really smart to get this kind of grade." Kaboom.

My pal Faye tells the story of spending an entire evening with a guy she met when they both reached for the same stuffed zucchini blossom at a fancy fund-raiser. He suggested they get together the very next day for a picnic in Central Park, and she was delighted to take charge of the fried chicken and potato salad. The next day she waited and waited. Two hours, one drumstick, half a pound of red bliss potatoes, and five weeks of dieting down the drain later, Faye picked up the phone: "What happened?" His reply: "Well, I honked...but you didn't come out." Yikes.

I bring Jules to the pediatrician for her annual checkup. "Would you say she's unusually tall?" I ask, hoping that she'll someday be able to reach all the stuff her 5'2" mother cannot. "No, she's average," he replies, quick and to the point. "Are you sure?" I persist. "My friends all tell me that she's really quite tall." The good doctor peers down his bifocals. "Maybe your friends don't want to tell you that she's really quite average." Touché.

Forget about kids; grown-ups say the darnedest things. Sometimes they mean well, sometimes they mean to lacerate, sometimes they're just clueless. The challenge (at least for me) is not to take any of it personally...even when it's meant personally. Sticks and stones may break my bones, but words will never hurt me, unless of course I decide to let them.

But this year, I've resolved to make a few changes. I don't want to lock and load when a nasty comment comes my way, but I also refuse to duck and cover. Instead, I am going to answer clumsiness with equanimity, bitchiness with compassion, and verbal violence with disengagement.

I think it's a damn good plan—wise, tolerant, even kind of Zen. If I play my cards right, I could be crowned Miss Mental Health! There's just one teeny, tiny problem: I honestly believe Metallica's next-door neighbor stands a better chance of getting a good night's sleep without ear plugs and an Ambien than I stand of actually getting this plan to work. But that certainly doesn't mean it's not worth a try.

So I will seek, to paraphrase Saint Francis of Assisi, not to be understood but to understand. I will send my collection of slights to Sotheby's and have them auction it off to the highest bidder, one dig at a time, and if none of my attempts at happiness and harmony pays off, well then, I'm heading for halvah at Russ & Daughters. ◑

Lisa Kogan Tells All

Billions suffer from it—but only one massively insecure writer has decided to race for the cure...or at least hold a telethon. Can *O*'s monthly columnist stomp out MI once and for all? Phone lines are now open!

The terrorists are terrifying, the glaciers are melting, and cancer has yet to be eradicated. So we wear ribbons and bracelets. We send money, guns, and lawyers. We raise awareness, we raise funds, we raise hopes. We are up to our earlobes in worthy causes. You show me a disease, and I'll show you a race for the cure. You see a natural disaster, I see Anderson Cooper in hip boots and a parka. Give me a calamity, and

I'll give you a bipartisan commission issuing a report.

But nobody is out there tackling the really big issue. Yes, once again it falls to me to spearhead the campaign against a silent killer. It's insidious, it's crippling, and it plagues almost everyone I know. It attacks seemingly healthy males and females of all races and economic backgrounds, and although we may get better, precious few of us ever get completely well. I'm talking about the shame, the scourge, the heartbreak of *massive insecurity*.

Let's call it MI, because initials always sound more urgent when the celebrity spokesperson explains it to

Larry King. "Well, Larry," she'll tearfully begin, "my first bout of MI hit in seventh grade, right before Marcy Needleman's roller disco bat mitzvah party." Dabbing her smudge-proof-mascaraed eyes with a crumpled tissue, she'll take a deep breath and forge ahead. "How many nights have I lain awake asking myself the same question: Why, why, why did I choose that day to try parting my hair down the side?"

Before long I envision a "very special" episode of *Sesame Street,* in which Snuffy admits he suffers from MI and goes into rehab; a public service announcement encouraging us to get tested before it's too late; and a magazine quiz zeroing in on the early warning signs.

1 **Before showing my upper arms in public, I first:** (a) Make certain my tankini is clean and there's film in the camera. (b) Drink like there's no tomorrow and wait for a total eclipse of the sun.

2 **I am being ignored by a snobby Rodeo Drive salesperson. Therefore I:** (a) Find the manager and explain that I am entitled to service and civility. (b) Slink away as if I had just been caught committing a felony or enjoying Paris Hilton's debut CD.

3 **To secure the salary increase I want, need, and deserve, I meet with my boss and say:** (a) I've taken on greater responsibility, and I believe I should receive greater monetary compensation. Here are several examples of the ways in which I've contributed to the quality of our product. (b) Um…I'm sorry, I'm probably bothering you…in fact let me come back later, maybe…. I just wanted to, um, say [*insanely long pause*], you're pretty.

4 **I am on a first date with an extremely attractive man. I order:** (a) Whatever I'm in the mood to eat. (b) A single grain of couscous because it's essential this person understand that I am dainty and delicate and exist on a simple diet of air and my own loveliness.

5 **When I walk into a party where I don't see anyone I know, I think:** (a) What a terrific opportunity to meet some new people! (b) I will spend the next nine minutes standing in the corner pretending to be onion dip, at which point I will fake a migraine,

> It's insidious, it's crippling, and it plagues almost everyone I know. I'm talking about the shame, the scourge, the heartbreak of *massive insecurity.*

go home, put on my giant Detroit Tigers T-shirt, and watch a rerun of *Law & Order SVU,* the way God intended me to do.

If you answered "b" to any of these questions, it is my sad duty to inform you that you could be one of the 6,576,344,362* members of society suffering from massive insecurity. *Note: We do not include anyone who's been cryogenically frozen. Nor do we count one Howard J. Koppleman of Dayton, Ohio, whose parents inexplicably appear to have done everything exactly right—the entire Koppleman family is currently being studied by massively insecure researchers at NASA.

What started this epidemic of insecurity? Maybe we were all left to cry it out in our cribs for too long, and it kept us from developing a healthy sense of entitlement. Or maybe we were held so much and hugged so close that it rendered us incapable of standing on our own two feet with any real confidence. Maybe we should blame our fathers (if for no other reason than it serves as a delightful change of pace from blaming our mothers), or maybe we should blame the solar system (I know I haven't been the same since they decided Pluto wasn't allowed to be a planet anymore), or maybe we should blame our gym teachers (seriously, get me the name of the sadist who came up with dodgeball), or maybe it doesn't matter who started it. What matters is that we don't seem to know our own worth. What matters is that we still worry the cool kids won't want to eat lunch at our table. What matters is that I have two different friends who wear makeup to bed because they're afraid to look like they actually look in front of the men they're attempting to dazzle.

So here are the choices: We could either hold a telethon to fight MI and perhaps raise enough money to get scientists started on a vaccine that will wipe the damn thing out once and for all; I mean, if we can destroy an entire layer of ozone in my lifetime, how hard can it be to get rid of our insecurities? Or we could decide to take a risk, say what we think, get up and dance, wear our crow's-feet like crinkly little badges of honor, acknowledge that it can be really, really scary to face the world head-on armed with nothing more than a strong sense of irony and a good pair of shoes—and then do it anyway. Me? Well, I'm hoping that vaccine is right around the corner. **O**

Lisa Kogan Tells All

For those days when you can't quite figure out what's eating you, our occasionally cranky columnist suggests you try eating vast quantities of pork…and other techniques to avert a full-blown tantrum.

I tend to be a little whiny and, yes, it's been suggested, even a touch moody. Oh, I know what you're thinking: *You? But Lisa, you're so charming, so gosh darn delightful, so sparkly, so devil-may-care, so deliciously optimistic, so—what's the adjective— petite! It just seems impossible to believe that you don't rise and shine every morning ready to greet the world with that plucky, daisy-fresh, can-do attitude we've all come to know and worship.* That *is* what you were thinking, right?

The truth is, I get irritable. This was brought to my attention when Johannes (known in some circles as "the boyfriend") likened me to "Caligula with an earache." Now, in my defense, we were on an airplane with our squirmy 3-year-old at the time, and, if memory serves, I had carefully dodged the drink cart and was making my way down the aisle with the aforementioned squirmy girl when we were trapped behind a guy who suddenly decided to store his trench coat in the overhead compartment as if he were part of the color guard folding the flag at Arlington National Cemetery.

In any case, I don't want to be the mean mommy. I don't want to be the PMS-riddled girlfriend. I don't want to be the bitch in the house. So as I see it, there are three ways to achieve a little karmic retooling:

Plan A Buck Up! Things Could Be So Much Worse

I have compiled a list of five key talking-myself-down points for those moments when it's so tremendously tempting to complain bitterly, curse fate, or just plain mope around.

■ Does the word *Darfur* appear anywhere in my address?
■ Was my address located in the ninth ward of New Orleans?
■ Is my postmilitary address a gurney at Walter Reed?
■ Am I trying to support my family on a minimum wage of $7.25 per hour?
■ Did I somehow manage to get cancer without getting health insurance?

On the days I come home from the market only to realize I forgot the one item I actually went there to buy, I've decided that I will not scowl, I will not pout, I will not drop to my knees, shrieking, "Why, God, why," like when Sean Penn finds out his kid is gone in *Mystic River.* No, I will simply head back to the A&P secure in the knowledge that while I may occasionally forget the milk, I'm still able to remember the important conversations I have at work. And when you think about it, that puts me way ahead of guys like Scooter Libby and Alberto Gonzales.

Plan B Give In! Things Could Be So Much Better

According to a *60 Minutes* piece I recently watched (with the help of two glasses of a rather full-bodied Shiraz), our future is being built on a deficit so gargantuan that it will have a cataclysmic effect for generations to come. To make matters worse, according to my cousin Rita, there isn't a decent pair of bone-colored espadrilles to be found in the entire state of New Jersey. For those moments when it's so tremendously tempting to draw the blinds, mash the potatoes, and rent every mindless romantic comedy I was too embarrassed to see at the cineplex, I have written a permission slip to do that and more. A permission slip is a magical thing. It got me out of seventh-grade gym when I had my period, and it gets me out of grown-up life when I've had enough.

To Whom It May Concern:
Lisa Kogan has been ridiculously wonderful for the last 16 days in a row, and now she needs to eat bacon in her underwear. Please do not phone, e-mail, or make eye contact with her under any circumstances. You may approach only for purposes of foot massage (giving, not receiving) or to wonder aloud how she got so thin. Note to anyone currently sharing a home with Miss Kogan: In the event you happen to catch on fire, be sure to drop and roll. Do not waste precious time attempting to smother the flames by wrapping yourself in a blanket, as the blankets will all be in use (and possibly covered in a light dusting of bacon bits). As for any other health crisis that might arise during Miss Kogan's time-out: You will find Bactine in the bathroom, Band-Aids in the pantry, and detailed instructions for giving yourself the Heimlich maneuver under a Marge Simpson magnet on her refrigerator door, just above the phone number for the poison control hotline (which Johannes quietly posted the first time he tasted her vegetarian chili).

Plan C Figure Out What's Really Going On

On my better days, I try to keep in mind that a rose is not its thorns, a peach is not its fuzz, a human being is not his or her crankiness, and this realization generally serves me very well. I only hope to God that the people I love will remember this during my occasional cold snaps. If every once in a while I turn into a big fat drag, there's usually a reason. I guess for me the reason isn't just that Johannes has described my coffee as "chewy" or even that the French are no longer the only people in the world who seem to hate our guts. No, I find that my crabbiness factor skyrockets when I'm feeling overextended and undervalued. And I'm pretty sure I'm not alone. Everybody wants to matter, and when we think we don't, it's shockingly easy to retreat into misery or impatience or sarcasm, or something else that's going to make us hate ourselves in the morning.

But I'm here to tell you that to indulge in a fine whine—no matter how momentarily satisfying—leaves a helluva hangover. It curdles the heart and corrodes the world. What we do when we're scared, what we say when we're pissed off, how we treat people from our friends and family to our soldiers and prisoners of war—all of it counts. It's going to determine not only who we are as a country but who we are to each other. Everybody wants to matter, and guess what? It turns out everybody does. ⬤

> What we do when we're scared, what we say when we're pissed off, how we treat people—all of it counts.

The Nate Berkus Show is airing daily; check your local listings.

Nate Berkus

10 Inspiring Ideas for Your Home

A gorgeous home doesn't require big bucks or long hours of toil; a few easy tweaks can bring the right balance to your space.

1 **If you touch it every day, it should be beautiful—** from your cabinet knobs to your mail tray. My toothbrush holder is a heavy cut-glass tumbler that I got for a couple of bucks at a flea market. It's lovely, and it feels special to me.

2 **Brighten your outlook.** On your next grocery run, buy some tulips and put them in a vase by the kitchen sink. Doing the dishes won't seem so drab anymore.

3 **Be bold.** A splash of color or pattern—an end table lacquered in raspberry, a leopard-print throw for the sofa—adds a bit of surprise to any spot in the house.

4 **Start collecting.** Whether it's first-edition books, English teacups, or ceramic cows, a carefully assembled collection expresses your singular style.

5 **Edit, edit, edit.** I jam-pack my rooms with all kinds of found objects and accessories—but then I step back and put a few items away. Paring down is what makes a good room great.

6 **Don't let the TV take over the living room.** My television hangs amid wall-to-wall bookshelves, so the space looks more like a comfortable den than a media room. Alternatively, an antique armoire can double as an entertainment cabinet. When the TV is off, you can close the doors and watch your family and friends instead.

7 **Use the good stuff.** Why should your china gather dust in the cupboard until next Thanksgiving? Pull it out for tonight's Chinese-takeout feast and make an ordinary day feel festive.

8 **Curate your own art gallery**—even on a shoestring budget. Stunning art can come in all kinds of different forms (from photography to painting to sculpture) and prices.

9 **Sleep in.** But if a lazy Saturday morning is impossible to come by, find the next best thing: sheets that make you want to stay in bed all day.

10 **Get the picture.** I have a million and one photos in my home: family, friends, my dogs, vacations. The fabric of my life is framed and hung on my walls. Photographs can turn a house into a home. **◑**

My Best Life

The host of the *Nate Berkus Show* explains how to create a great space and listen to the voice within.

Best Design Rule
Incorporate nature. It can be as simple as taking a tall leafy branch from the backyard and putting it in a clear glass vase.

Best Tradition
Handwritten notes. If I get a beautiful letter or thank-you card, it goes in a frame, just as a photograph would.

Best Way to Ruin a Room
Decorate it for anyone besides yourself. It might be gorgeous, but you'll never feel at home.

Best Nosh
A hot dog from Crif Dogs in the East Village. Ketchup, mustard, onion, relish. And if there were Dairy Queens in New York City, I'd get a medium vanilla cone dipped in either chocolate or butterscotch—depending on my mood—and that would be a perfect afternoon.

Best Flea Market Mantra
Buy it now! You have only one chance. If you see something that speaks to you, that moves you even just a little bit, you have to own it.

Best Words of Inspiration
In Elizabeth Edwards's book *Resilience,* she quotes the Leonard Cohen song "Anthem": *Ring the bells that still can ring, forget your perfect offering. There is a crack in everything; that's how the light gets in.* That's an amazing insight—to know that nothing's perfect and it's not intended to be.

Best Decision To listen to my inner voice. We *always* know the right thing to do, even if we don't want to face it. **◑**

"Once I started letting stuff in, I really started making a home for myself," says Berkus, photographed in his New York City apartment.

The House Whisperer

Why is it that we all have so much, yet never quite enough? Nate Berkus—a guy who knows firsthand what a well-appointed space can do for your soul—tells Lisa Kogan about his design for living.

We love our stuff, we hate our stuff, we can't live without our stuff. We lust after other people's stuff. We smile politely when relatives offer us their old stuff (anyone for a lovely hand-knit toaster cozy?) and when friends bring us artfully wrapped stuff (enjoy this lovely hand-knit toaster cozy that I am now quietly regifting). We donate our stuff to charity, stick our stuff in a bookcase, auction our stuff on eBay, and then we go out and get...more stuff!

Maybe what we need is somebody who's got the right stuff, a house whisperer who has somehow figured out how to peacefully coexist with a home stuffed with stuff. Somebody like Nate Berkus, the decorator, *Oprah* show correspondent, product designer, best-selling author, and host of *The Nate Berkus Show*.

Nate's home is both classic and quirky, rough and refined: a corduroy couch here, a leather rhino head that was a wedding present to his parents there ("This rhino has lasted a lot longer than that marriage," he says). A model of Frank Lloyd Wright's 1934 masterpiece, Fallingwater, built entirely of Legos, shares a shelf with a black-and-white Wedgwood dish and a crusty hunk of pyrite. A sepia photo of a Joshua tree has been sliced into strips and woven back together—made whole in a new way. Prior to being cut, the photo must have been lovely; now it is riveting. It was shot and reimagined by Nate's former partner, photographer Fernando Bengochea, who was killed in the 2004 tsunami while the two were vacationing in Sri Lanka.

Tonight Nate is recovering from an appendectomy. ("Best week of my life. I just lay in bed getting soup and OxyContin.") But he's not too tired to put out a bowl of caramel corn and share what he's come to understand about paring away the stuff that doesn't enhance your life, embracing the stuff that does, and what it really takes to finally be at home in your home.

Lisa: **You like beautiful things.**

Nate: I do. But even more than that, I like things that remind me of where I've been. Who I've loved. Who I love. And where I want to go.

Lisa: **Wow...my things remind me that I should probably dust more often.**

Nate: [*Laughs*] I'm just saying let's admit that our things mean something to us when they do. But let's also admit when they don't. Let's really look at what we want our homes to say about who we are.

Lisa: **Mine says I like a good tag sale. Actually, I hit a few flea markets after seeing a makeover you did on your show. I spotted the coolest little creamer, and I could hear you whispering in my ear, "That doesn't have to be for serving cream." So now there's a silver Deco creamer on my dressing table, and it's holding a bunch of Q-tips—one of a bazillion things currently cluttering my apartment.**

Nate: For a long time I was hellbent on clutter-free living. I was a ruthless editor when it came to my possessions, to the point where my

homes were very sparse, very minimal. Then I realized that's not who I am. I wanted to be surrounded by things that moved me. I wanted to have tabletops piled with books and shells and candles. But it took me a while to let go of this very rigid idea I had, of what my space should look like. Once I started letting stuff in, I really started making a home for myself.

Lisa: **How do you decide what to let in?**

Nate: What I've come to understand is that if things have meaning, if they sing a little song to you when you look at them, that's when you can really start breaking the rules, quote-unquote, of design. Why *not* take a two-dollar creamer with the lid missing and fill it with Q-tips? Who says you can't reupholster your chair with a shearling rug or take the fantastic vintage necklace you never wear and hang it around the neck of a lamp?

Lisa: **Your place is full of wild cards. This chunky pine table next to a sleek modern chaise is a surprise.**

Nate: That table wasn't drawn into any floor plan. I fell for it the first time I went to Mexico City and stumbled across an amazing antiques store tucked away in the basement of a building. It was the most impractical thing in the world. But when I look at it, I remember the exact moment I was standing there—too hot, a little hungry, tired from the night before—and thought, *That's a beautiful thing.*

Lisa: **I like that your idea of beautiful is something that's got a few miles on it. You're not afraid of the occasional scratch and chip.**

Nate: I'm a big fan of the chip. I like it when something's a bit damaged.

Lisa: **That's why you hired Henry and Emma [Nate's two endlessly teething shelter mutts].**

Nate: Exactly. [*Laughs*] Those two are masters at messing up whatever comes in here. That's why about 80 percent of the stuff I live with is old. I like letting things take on the character they're meant to have by really being used. You know, even some of the finest antiques show some wear and tear. Think of the feet of a chest of drawers from the 17th century—they're always corroded because people used to wash their floors with lye, which ate away the wood. And that's one of the signs that the best antiques dealers look for to see if the piece is authentic. So when you own things that have the imperfections they deserve, that they've earned from a well-

> I'm just saying let's admit that our things mean something to us when they do. But let's also admit when they don't. Let's really look at what we want our homes to say about who we are.

lived life, it frees you from feeling as though they're untouchable.

Lisa: I bought a very expensive zinc dining table about 20 years ago. It was just totally flawless. And I thought, *I should have people over for dinner.* Then I thought, *And we could eat sort of buffet-style, standing up...right near the table. Like maybe in the vicinity of the table.*

Nate: To admire it, without actually making contact with it. Nice!

Lisa: Did I mention that it was expensive and, for one brief, shining moment, totally flawless? What can I say? It's hard to keep your stuff from owning you.

Nate: People first. Dogs second. Things last. It's a simple philosophy.

Lisa: I've got a friend who's in my home on a regular basis, and she keeps giving me things that are—how to put this delicately...seven kinds of ugly. I know people have to come first, and the last thing I want to do is hurt her feelings, but....

Nate: Is there a shelf you can use for those things? I mean, people are more important than things, but things are important. I think it matters what our eyes land on; I think it matters what our butts sit on. It's important how we feel in our homes, because feeling good makes us more gracious. And that makes it easier to welcome others not only into our homes but into our lives.

Lisa: So what are the things that matter most to you?

Nate: To me it's about the books that are out of print, and the photos in frames. And the letters and notes.

Lisa: The rest is gravy.

Nate: We all have so much: We open our closets, and so many things still have their price tags attached. We open our cupboards, and there are those dishes that we've never used because they're "too good." Under our sinks we've got the 25 glass vases that held every floral arrangement ever sent to us. Why not recycle the glass? Better yet, fill it with sand and white candles, and throw a party. Take the dishes out and set the table with them every day. I mean, what exactly is an "everyday" dish? Why do we have all these categories?

Lisa: So people can sell us more stuff?

Nate: Right! I'm the first person to say, "Do not buy everything. Please, buy a new set of sheets if you want. But pair them with your grandmother's quilt."

Lisa: Okay, but what happens when you're ready for the next chapter of your story? What happens when your home seems to represent who you were a million somebody else's ago?

Nate: I find myself helping people in that situation a lot—after a divorce, after a death. They want to do something new. Sometimes they even want to be someone new, and changing their environment can be part of that process. It's a way to shed your skin. It's a way to move forward.

Lisa: You have been faced with that situation yourself. Is it ever hard to be with Fernando's stuff?

Nate: He was one of those people you just don't want to sit next to on an airplane—the guy who's always trying to cram a three-foot ceramic pineapple under his seat. Then one day I went to the 26th Street flea market and brought back some African beads and wooden bowls and an English picture frame and a tiny French-to-English pocket dictionary from the 19th century. And he said, "You mean I've been traveling the world, bringing these things home, and they've been sitting on a card table on 26th Street?"

When Fernando died, his brother allowed me to take whatever I felt a connection to. So the majority of his library, I have. And one of the things that he and I always used to do together was sit down and go through these books. He had stuck little Post-it notes on all the pages because he was always wanting me to see something I hadn't seen before—a brilliant quote or some amazing place he thought we should visit or the pattern on a tile wall in Morocco or maybe just an incredible face. Now a part of what he collected lives on and is celebrated by the way I live.

There's something beautiful and very circular about passing by something that was important to the person you loved, or touching something that once meant something to him—that brings me some peace.

Lisa: And yet it's not a shrine around here.

Nate: I look at people who have lost someone and go for years without changing a thing in the room because they're afraid even the tiniest change would just be too painful. And I always think, *Wouldn't it honor the person more if you used the room for something that gave you joy? Because they're not here. But you are.*

Lisa: You know, there's a great sense of serenity in this apartment. How does somebody use design to create that for themselves?

Nate: Good design isn't just about mathematical proportions and eyeballing and space planning. Good design is about imagination, and it's about surrounding yourself with things that are genuinely nourishing.

Lisa: And anybody can do that.

Nate: Definitely. People should be proud of the home they've created and the memories that have been made there. You have to ask yourself if the place really does represent who you are. When your eye travels around the room, does it say something about the people who live in that house? About those who came before? Does it really tell the story of your life? ◐

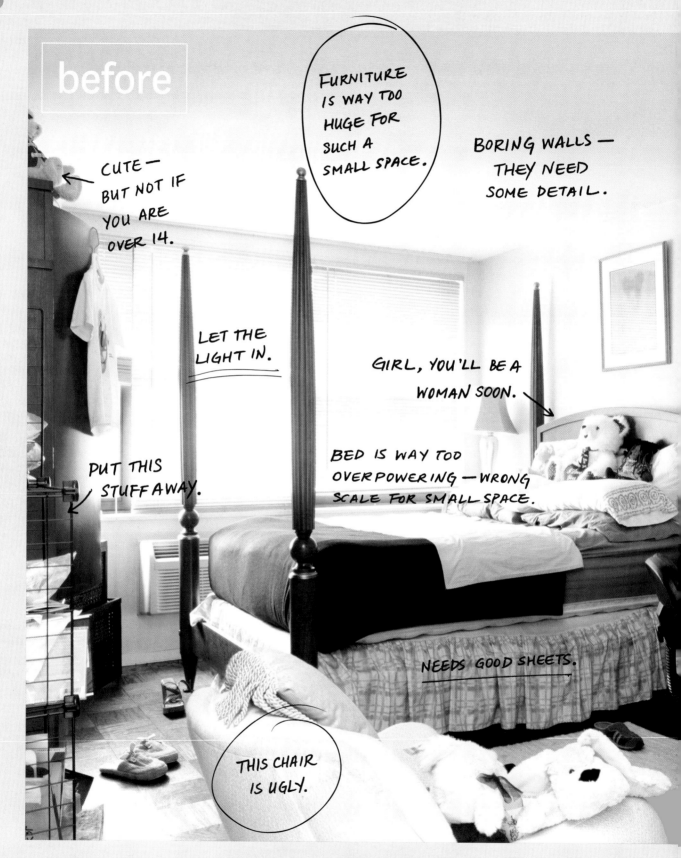

IDEOUS CEILING,
NO CHARACTER ON WALLS.

MOLDING?

TOSS IT
OR
DONATE IT
IF YOU
DON'T
USE IT.

LAS VEGAS, BABY!

DULY NOTED:
Nate Berkus
quickly identified
the problem
spots in Ellin
LaVar's bedroom.

Knock, Knock, It's Nate!

Celebrity hairdresser Ellin LaVar's
New Jersey bedroom was a nightmare.
Lisa Kogan watched as designer Nate
Berkus turned it into a French fantasy.

E at your heart out, America, I'm in bed with Nate Berkus. If for some reason you're not familiar with Nate (perhaps you've spent the last couple of years on one of those manned space missions), he is the wunderkind who heads his own eponymously named Chicago-based design firm. Not only has he made over dozens of homes on *The Oprah Winfrey Show,* but he's also made *People*'s "Sexiest Man Alive" list. In short, to know Nate Berkus is to be in favor of cloning.

Okay, if you want to get technical, we're not actually *in* bed; we're *on* the bed, which is located in a nondescript postwar apartment in a nondescript postwar suburb of New Jersey. And we're not alone. On the bed with us is one of two stuffed Tweety Birds, along with a rather scruffy stuffed dog that appears eager to join his nine stuffed teddy bear buddies piled on top of an armoire. The armoire is part of a matching bedroom set; there are also cherry night tables on either side of a queen-size cherry four-poster bed and a cherry dresser jammed to the gills. Across from the bed is a treadmill that seems to be getting more use as a place to drop clothes than as a place to drop weight. The room also has two crates of books, a bottle of cod-liver oil capsules, and a desk loaded down with paperwork, files, and a computer. What the room hasn't got is style.

The lack of style is particularly disconcerting because this is the bedroom of Ellin LaVar, a woman who's all

Top left: Ellin LaVar asked Nate to design a bedroom for her that would be romantic and uncluttered. *Center:* At Home Depot, Nate made waves as he shopped for paint, hardware, and millwork. *Bottom left:* The peach walls are primed before they're painted a rich gray.

about style. As the hairdresser for a whole lot of people who don't require last names (Iman, Naomi, Donatella), LaVar tours the world, putting great effort into making her clients appear effortlessly tousled. She'll even help you get your head together: Ellin LaVar Textures, her line of hair-care products, is available at CVS.

Nate asks her to describe her dream bedroom. "Well," she says. "I don't love country, I do love purple, I'm not big on paisley, and I'm totally desperate for drawers." She sighs. "Oh, Nate, I'm not sure what to do with this place. It's like everything matches but nothing really goes together, and it's driving me crazy. I need you to help me feel like the CEO I've become." And with that, she's off to Thailand for a series of Whitney Houston concerts.

"Ellin is a creative, talented woman, yet every morning she's waking up and every night she's going to sleep in a room that has absolutely no character—it can't feel good to open your eyes to this," Nate says, pointing up at the popcorn-textured ceiling. "But," he adds, brightening, "I've got a plan." He describes how women in the 1930s and 1940s would go to the great Parisian couture houses for fittings: "Chanel, Dior—these salons were designed with dressing chambers to make a woman feel completely pampered. Ellin's work is about taking care of others. She deserves some pampering, too."

Nate gets down to business. He's got six days to transform a Sheetrock box into a French fantasy. He skimcoats the popcorn ceiling with plaster and covers it with silver paper. "The slight shimmer and reflective surface

after

1. **Mirrors make the room feel bigger.** 2. **Nate detailed the seat of a Chinese Chippendale–style chair with lavender ribbon.** 3. **Lavender ribbons dress up Roman shades, in linen.** 4. **Covered in silver paper, the low ceiling seems much higher.** 5. **Feminine curtains were made from silk taffeta.** 6. **Nate wanted Dior gray walls, and Behr's Gray Area paint did the trick.** 7. **A bench was reupholstered with an Hermès scarf Nate found on eBay.** 8. **The bed skirt is made of Gaelic linen.** 9. **Wall-to-wall wool broadloom provides a plush footing.** 10. **Nate customized a night table with a coat of Behr's Soft Iris paint and then topped the table with silver frames.**

The marble-topped chest
was an eBay find. Nate
created a vignette featuring
white ceramic branches,
a vase, polished nickel table
lamps, and urn.

create an illusion of height," he explains. The standard-issue parquet floor is covered in luscious cream-colored wall-to-wall carpet. "*This* is the way to get out of bed on a cold morning," he says. The walls are painted an opulent gray. He installs crisp white baseboards and crown and picture-frame moldings—details that give the walls prewar charm—and replaces Ellin's cherry nightstands with tables painted pale lilac. "Dark furniture doesn't work in a small space, and a matched bedroom set is rarely interesting."

Out goes the bed: "A four-poster needs high ceilings." In comes a cushiony headboard upholstered in lavender linen. "When you're tight for space," Nate notes, "a headboard feels luxurious without taking up much room." Damask throw pillows are combined with simple sheets; snakeskin lampshades sit next to porcelain sculptures on a chest. "I love putting together old and new. The juxtaposition of different finishes is what gives a home energy." He sews a stripe of lavender ribbon onto both a Roman shade and a Chinese Chippendale–style chair and tosses a wild card into the mix by covering a pretty little bench with a vintage Hermès scarf he bought on eBay. Crystal sconces—more eBay finds—light up each side of the bed.

BEFORE & AFTER: A bulging armoire was replaced with custom built-ins, accommodating Ellin's TV, clothing, and home office.

Next, Nate addresses Ellin's number one headache: disorganization. "Like the rest of us, Ellin does not have adequate storage." To solve the problem, he's created three built-in mirrored closets that run the length of the wall. One houses her TV, DVD, and stereo. Another one is filled with clothes and accessories (though a marble-topped dresser, circa 1850, has already usurped the treadmill). And the third functions as a tiny but utterly efficient home office. On the inside of one office door hangs what Nate calls an inspiration board—"to hold pictures, notes, quotes, whatever gets her daydreaming." Inside the other door, he affixes a memory board. "This is to hold all of Ellin's buried treasures," Nate says as he pins a Patti LaBelle backstage pass to the cork. "They're not necessarily expensive things, just meaningful. That way, when she's sitting paying bills on a rainy Saturday, she can be reminded of all her successes." He straightens a picture frame and takes one last look around. Finally, the room is finished. All that's missing is Ellin LaVar.

At the appointed hour, Nate puts his hands over Ellin's eyes and leads her down the narrow hall, into her new world. "Okay, you can look," he says, removing his hands. A stunned silence is followed by a piercing whoop of joy and a bone-crushing hug. "I would've bought this," she cries, pointing to the marble-topped dresser. "I wouldn't have had a clue what to do with it, but I'd have bought it." Nate smiles knowingly and braces for another major hug. But now Ellin is running her fingertips over a family photo that's been converted to a black-and-white print and placed on the pale lilac table. "I never need Christmas again," she whispers. A big, fat tear slides down her cheek as she takes Nate's hand and pays him the ultimate compliment: "You really heard me," she says happily. ⬤

The "omigod" moment: Ellin never dreamed her bedroom could be this beautiful and luxurious. After a six-day absence, she sinks into her bed, which is dressed with pillows covered in Mahjong damask. The crystal-beaded wall sconce was bought on eBay. The headboard is custom-upholstered in linen to match the bed skirt.

10 Items You Can Never Go Wrong With

He's often asked for advice on what will be in style forever. So *O*'s creative director put together a list of mistake-proof items to fit any woman's wardrobe, from here to eternity.

1 **Touches of animal print.** On a bag or shoe, a bit of zebra or tiger works like a neutral. Michael Kors and Ann Taylor bring them out almost every season.

2 **A leather jacket.** Now a year-round staple, they come in lighter weights and pale colors, like Tory Burch's in camel or Banana Republic's in beige.

A men's watch. I like men's styles because they're not too fussy or dainty. If you wear a lot of gold jewelry, go with gold tones (Tag Heuer's are great); if you wear mostly silver, pick stainless steel (Citizen and Swatch have affordable options).

Diamond hoop earrings. More youthful than studs, hoops polish off a casual look and complete a dressy one. Unless you want to be mistaken for one of Beyoncé's backup singers, find a medium size. I love Daniel K's, and Carolee makes great faux ones.

A sequined scarf. Every woman should have sequins for day. I think the unexpected combination—plain plus fancy—is key.

White jeans. CJ by Cookie Johnson's and Gap's come in nice heavy fabrics.

A neutral shoe. In leather, patent leather, or fabric, a pair of heels that matches your skin color visually extends the line of your leg.

An oversize blazer. The "borrowed from the boys" look isn't going anywhere. At the office, throw on a jacket—black, navy, or pinstriped.

A pencil skirt. Sexy without being revealing, and appropriate at any age—it works for every woman. If you have a boyish shape, it gives the impression of curves; if you're curvy, it plays up your figure; if you're plus size, it's more flattering than a full skirt.

A lace-trimmed bra or camisole. Peeking out from under a V-neck, a little frill on a Soma bra or Mary Green cami adds a touch of femininity.

The Perfect Trip Kit

In-flight essentials no traveler should leave home without.

I f I had a nickel for every time I was asked how I keep my cool traveling, I'd be sitting in first class by now. My tried-and-true rules are simple: ■ First, no schlumpy sweats. Instead, I go with an easy-fitting sweater and pants. If I can't have legroom, at least I can have cashmere! (When I have a meeting straight off the plane, I upgrade to no-wrinkle stretch fabrics.) ■ Slip-on shoes save time at the security checkpoint. ■ I dodge the scary airline blankets by wearing a scarf. ■ My snack: protein-rich raw almonds (less dehydrating than the salty peanuts they dole out). The trick is to create your own system—and stick to it. Here, the best gear to get you off the ground. ◐

Clockwise from top right: **LONG-SLEEVED TEES: They're excellent for layering; navy-and-white is always modern. COMFY SWEATER: Zip one up when the A/C blasts. CARGO PANTS: They're loose enough for hours of sitting; the pockets come in handy. COOL SLIP-ONS: Not having to unlace and retie saves time and hassle. HERBAL RELAXER: A fast-acting tension reliever—like nature's Xanax—will calm your nerves. CHIC SCARF: A huge, thin cashmere wrap works as a blanket. TRAVEL CANDLES: These erase the smell of a hotel room. MINI MASSAGER: Everything aches during a long flight; this gadget gets the** knots out and provides lumbar support. **GOOD HEADPHONES: Advanced noise-reduction technology lets me control my in-flight soundtrack—music, movie, or silence. FOLDABLE TOTE: This classic is indestructible. Stash it in your suitcase, then use it as an extra carry-on. PAGE-TURNER: No more lugging multiple books and newspapers. The Kindle downloads wirelessly, works internationally. ESSENTIAL OILS: These put me right out. DOPP KIT: A sturdy one doesn't leak like a regular plastic bag. IDEAL WHEELIE: My suitcase is light and bright, with external pockets for easy access.**

ADAM SAYS

Figure Fixers

O's creative director tells you what your best friends won't.

A LONG STORY:
Look taller in a
fitted bodice
and flowing,
unfussy skirt.

Q I'm petite.
Is it okay
to wear a
maxidress?

To be honest, this
isn't an easy trend for
short women to pull
off—all that cloth
can overwhelm you.
There's a fine line be-
tween a stylish maxi
and a schmatte.
What's key: defini-
tion on top (Empire
styles are good for
making legs seem
longer) and con-
trolled volume on
the bottom (no tiers
or tents: plain hems
are simpler to
shorten). Stick to
solids or small prints.
If you like heels for
extra height, pick
wedges, not stilettos
(cheesy looking!).

**SIZING UP THE
BUST: Do an
hourglass number
on your body with
a strategically
ruched dress,
build your bosom
with a ruffled
blouse, or give
the impression of
curves in a
shaped jacket.**

Q I'm flat-chested—what should I wear to build
myself up on top?

Loads of well-endowed women would love to have your
"problem"! Chic clothes hang better on boyish figures, plus
you can get away with minimal support—or go braless—
under halternecks or low backs. But if you want to emphasize your assets...

■ Pick curvy shapes that highlight and slim the waist.
Your bust will look bigger in comparison.
■ Stick to higher necklines that don't expose a (possibly
bony) chest.
■ Avoid skintight fit or clingy fabric.
■ Enjoy the current craze for ruffles and flounces—or any
other eye-catching detail that spotlights your upper half:
chest pockets, ruching, horizontal stripes, bold color.

Q It's hard to find boots roomy enough for my big calves. Can you help?

Not with the calves—they're either hereditary or a sign that you work out like crazy (in which case, congratulations). You can sidestep the whole fit issue with ankle boots. Or, if you prefer knee-highs (skip anything mid-calf—they're wildly unflattering), try one of these accommodating choices suggested by Leslie Gallin, former director of The Collections at World Shoe Association, which organizes twice-yearly industry shows: **stretch fabric** versions (from the likes of Donald J Pliner and Taryn Rose); styles with **elastic inserts** (Samantá's fit up to an 18-inch calf); or ultratrendy **scrunch boots** of soft, loosely cut materials. If all else fails, get a shoemaker to stretch a slightly tight pair. Living in boots, by the way, is totally chic. They give a little polish to whatever you wear, and these days there are no rules: They work any-place, anytime—even in spring.

J.CREW OFFERS: dual sizing for its handsome, well-priced boots: one for regular calves, another that gives you an extra inch of room.

Q I am a 40-something single mom. How can I look leaner and get my "sexy" back?

Over 40 isn't over the hill! Sexiness is more about attitude than clothing, so wipe your mind of any age bias and think young. By "young" I don't mean wearing clothes that are bare and tight—I mean subtly sensuous styles that also elongate your figure. Deep vee or scoopneck tops and dresses extend the torso and draw the eye upward; dropped waists and untucked tops visually extend the waist downward. Bare arms also create an illusion of length (short sleeves interrupt the flow), as do vertical details (front plackets, stripes, seaming).

THE LATE SHOW: I'm all for sleeveless—if you're comfortable with your arms, it's a refined way to show skin (think our First Lady). This dress, with its scooped-out armholes and lower waist, is ideal for short torsos. And a fluid fabric like silk is more inviting than something stiff.

NO MORE TENTS: Play up your shape rather than bury it. This elegant wrap shirt has a waist-enhancing tie.

Q As a plus-size woman, what do I absolutely need in my closet?

■ **Lingerie** that lifts, smooths, and supports, including shapewear pieces and a properly fitted bra. You've got to get dressed from the inside out.
■ **A white wrap shirt** to show off your waist (if you have one) or give the illusion of curves (if you don't).
■ **Black boot-cut stretch pants** to balance broader hips.
■ **Jeans with some stretch**—I'll even allow elasticized waists as long as you swear to wear your tops untucked.
■ **A wrap dress** in a solid color (more slimming than prints).
■ **A trench coat** with a waist-shrinking belt; epaulets build up the shoulders—instant hourglass.
■ **A straight skirt** for the curvy; an a-line if your body shape is less defined.
■ **A stretch tank** to layer with—it helps to contain larger breasts.
■ **A pair of heels** for shapelier calves.
■ **...and opaque hose to match.** For the longest-looking legs in town.

KEEPING IT CASUAL: I think blush colors are extraordinarily seductive; a mix of related shades gives the sleekest, most flattering line. Hide a high waist with a vertically ruffled tank over slim jeans. Sparkly flats look as alluring as heels.

NO MORE STOMACH TROUBLE: in a well-proportioned tunic with elongating vertical embellishment. Or try a softly belted scoopneck top; the long tie draws the eye down and away from the midsection.

Q I feel naked without pantyhose (my legs aren't as attractive as they once were). Do I have to go bare?

Please—I'm not a stocking cop! Nude legs are chic, but I won't say no to hose. What's critical: matching them exactly to your skin (there's nothing worse than orangey nylons). Other tricks:

DO hide flaws with spray tan or bronzing body moisturizer.

DON'T choose elaborate patterns or back seams (they make legs look bigger).

DO try fishnets, in neutrals and a fine weave. They add interest without looking sleazy.

DON'T wear hose with slingbacks or mules—not attractive.

DO get toeless hose to wear with open-toe shoes.

DON'T wear white hose. Ever. Unless you're Nurse Jackie.

SOLD ON SHEERS: I didn't think hose could be truly invisible, but Donna Karan The Nudes ($20 each) converted me: They make legs look *better* than bare.

Q How can I hide my large tummy? When I wear those floaty empire-waist tops, I look pregnant.

It's terrible to hear "When are you due?" if there's no baby on the way. Billowy blouses invite that because they magnify the problem area; same goes for the opposite extreme—stretchy, tummy-hugging tees. You need tops that are shaped but not tight. Other smart strategies:

■ **Upper-body enhancers** like cap sleeves, open or vee necklines.

■ **Shorter hems on fitted tops**—just to the base of the stomach. You might think a longer top hides all, but (sorry to be so graphic) you'll look like a snake that's just swallowed its prey.

■ **Curvy tops** or jackets that flare out under a nipped-in waist.

■ **Buttonless or wrap styles** (shirts and cardigans are tricky because buttons may gap over your abdomen).

■ **The right pants** are crucial, too: Try a slimming pair of jeans or trousers with a supportive mesh front panel.

Halterneck narrows shoulders

Eye-catching, strategically placed jewels

Color-blocking sculpts the body

Vertical design elongates the torso

PROPORTION CONTROL: In my bag of tricks (*clockwise from top left*) is a scoopneck sweater; cocktail dress; argyle vest, button-down shirt; long-sleeved dress.

Q **I'm shaped like a vee: broad on top with skinny legs. What's the best way to dress?**

Strong, commanding shoulders are a thing of beauty—they make clothes hang better. All you need are a few figure-balancing strategies:

■ Offset your upper body with volume below: wide-leg pants; fuller skirts.

■ Look for details that draw the eye up and down, not across—vee or scoop necks, vertical embellishments, long scarves and necklaces.

■ Choose soft shoulders, raglan sleeves, and halters—anything that isn't crisp and squared-off.

■ Define your waist, or you'll look boxy. If a jacket fits your shoulders but is too big overall, have it altered.

Q **I'm 37, but people frequently think I'm closer to 20, which is a problem at work. Can you help?**

Sure, but don't you think a grateful nod to your genetic fairy godmothers is in order first? Seriously, though, I understand your need to look more authoritative. Maybe you've been stuck in the same style since college—naturally young-looking people often fall into that. More sophistication is in order: Wear makeup. Get a good haircut (no ponytails, no cascading locks). Shop judiciously (J.Crew, not Abercrombie & Fitch; Ann Taylor, not Bebe). Casual-verging-on-sloppy outfits and pastels read young; deeper colors and polished, fully accessorized ensembles read grown-up, not old.

ADULTS ONLY: *Near right,* a suit will command respect at the office; *far right,* a pretty floral print dress with a belt looks more finished with a sleek cardigan.

Q **I'm totally straight from ribs to waist to hips— and I can't find slacks that fit. Can you help?**

Pants are often designed for hourglass shapes, so a pair that accommodates your waist will probably be way too large in the hips—am I right? My checklist for a better silhouette:

1 Stretch fabric and slimmer-cut legs prevent drooping anywhere you don't fill out the pants.

2 A wide, contoured waistband fits smoothly, spotlighting your middle.

3 A slightly higher rise is preferable to low-rise cuts, which only emphasize a boyish figure.

ADAM SAYS
Getting Dressed

JEANS $65 AND UNDER: Dark washes are slimming, and paler shades look cool for spring.

Q Do I really have to pay $175 or more for jeans?
No! Don't buy into ridiculously inflated pricing. Denim is denim—it's not a costly fabric. The main thing about jeans is a modern, flattering fit, and these days you're as likely to find that in an inexpensive, well-cut brand as in a snooty label. If you're into trendy denim—bright colors, a baggy "boyfriend" shape—it's smarter to spend less. Try Old Navy, American Eagle Outfitters, Levi Strauss & Co., or Victoria's Secret.

Q Is anybody still making two- or three-inch heels? All I see are stilettos that I can't walk in for more than a block.
Blame fashion editors (I plead guilty): We like the way very high heels seem to elongate models' legs, so that's what you see in magazines. On TV, *Sex and the City* took shoes to new heights, and its influence endures. But in the real world, moderate heels are available and attractive. All the most stylish lines (Via Spiga, Etienne Aigner, Simply Vera Vera Wang for Kohl's, even Carrie's beloved Manolo Blahnik) have them in stock (though you may have to ask). Two or three inches is enough to reap the advantages of heels—shapelier-looking calves, more pulled-up posture—while allowing you to remain fully mobile.

SEXY CAN BE SENSIBLE: two-tone slingback; muted teal pump; ideal work shoe; chunky-chic logo-buckle 2-incher.

Q Is it worse to dress too boringly or too young?
Too young. It's incredibly off-putting to see a body-flaunting dress on a woman with an older face, even if she has a good shape. Three rules for age-appropriate shopping:
■ **Don't buy anything that makes you look foolish.** Trends generate buzz and new business, but you have to resist—fashion extremes aren't smart.
■ **Adapt the classics.** I find nothing boring about great suits, terrific dresses, beautiful skirts, and higher-rise trousers or jeans. French women (who seem to be born chic) wear the same blazer and pants for years, updating them occasionally with accessories (cute shoes, stylish bag, Hermès scarf) or a top in a fresh print or current color.
■ **Support resort.** December-January resort collections are often more sophisticated than summer lines; if you wait, you may find nothing in stores but slipdresses and minis.

WAKE UP YOUR BASICS with a two-tone bag. It's got a fresh take on texture and color, but it's traditional enough for the office.

264

Q During the workweek, I dress like a grown-up, but when Saturday comes, I revert to slobbish collegiate habits. How can I look good on days off but still be totally comfortable?

Not by reaching automatically for worn-out pink sweatpants! I know: After five days in pencil skirts and pumps, you want to collapse into elastic waists and running shoes. But a few no-fail, no-brainer weekend outfits—that aren't too businesslike or too schlumpy—will serve you better.

Don't go the oversize route: Body skimming shapes are always more attractive than baggy. Also, **avoid black,** with its formal connotations. Pastels are much better (but not head to toe— too Easter Bunny); so are pale neutrals like khaki, sand, and dusty rose. Buying a whole separate Saturday to Sunday wardrobe isn't necessary. I say **stock up on basics**—dark jeans, nicely fitting khakis or corduroys, cute cotton sweaters, stylish T-shirts, a casual jacket. Then **mix them with more office-y pieces,** either current staples or former weekday standbys recycled for weekend use. With flat shoes and less-polished accessories, even pin-stripes can look casual. In short, make an effort. Next time you bump into an ex at the supermarket, you'll be glad you did.

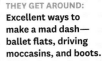

THEY GET AROUND: Excellent ways to make a mad dash— ballet flats, driving moccasins, and boots.

WEEKEND NEWS FLASH: Maintain femininity in pieces like a striped shirt and cropped denim trousers. An abbreviated peacoat has rugged appeal that plays well on weekends. Run around in great-looking cotton canvas sneakers.

Q I spend most days in jeans chasing after my kids. How can I wear flats and look put-together?

Relax—heels with jeans are not a practical choice for most people (they look fabulous if you aren't planning to walk anywhere). With skinny or straight-leg denim, there's nothing chicer than a **ballet flat**—from inexpensive Capezios to best-sellers from Tory Burch. I also like flats with **long, pointy toes:** very Audrey Hepburn. With boot-cut jeans, try soft leather **driving moccasins** or **streamlined sneakers** by Puma or Stella McCartney for Adidas. There are tons of **cute flat boots,** too (tuck your narrow-leg jeans into them), including Wellies. Just make sure that you have the proper hem for your flats—no dragging on the ground permitted!

WHO'S COUNTING? **Traditional wisdom says you should "take one thing off" before going out. A more modern, less arbitrary rule: Wear as many baubles as you like, but only one big "statement" item. Let the rest be subtle.**

Q How do I know what's too much jewelry?

There's no magic number; it's more about how the pieces relate to one another (and to what you're wearing).

■ **Don't mix moods—or trends.** Keep everything connected: chunky/natural stuff *or* flashy stones *or* ultrashiny gold, not all three at once. However:

■ **Avoid matched sets**—necklace, bracelet, earrings, ring... what, no tiara?—unless you're going for the Queen Mother look.

■ **Rely on studs or hoops**—the perfect chameleons. Sentimental "personal" jewelry (lockets; charm bracelets; hand-me-downs) should not be worn with every outfit, every day. Consider the whole look when deciding.

■ **Keep it clean.** A short, ornate necklace is too much with long, dangly earrings, and vice versa.

■ **Go bare** here and there. You needn't "dress" every body part; unadorned skin looks beautifully low-key. Try limiting bracelets to the wrist your watch is on. A ring can be on either hand.

Q What's the key to dressing for rain while still looking stylish?

My motto, like the post office's, is that you must deliver no matter how stormy the weather—you can't let your clothes or psyche be dragged down by a soggy day. Even if you're not normally into brights, color helps lessen the gloom: a great red, a taxicab yellow. Be practical about fabrics—don't wear something flimsy that will get soaked immediately or become see-through when wet. We're lucky that patent leather is so popular these days; the shiny surface not only resists moisture but lifts your spirits. Get a good trench (at least one) in khaki or black. If you live somewhere particularly rainy, you might want a few to choose from. Boot up smartly instead of ruining your outfit with crummy sneakers. And a fun umbrella is essential.

CUTE, WEATHERPROOF SOLUTIONS: **jacket; hat; belted trench; patent leather boots.**

PILLS AREN'T SO BITTER now that cashmere is widely available at a sweet price—but if they happen, be prepared with the Sweater Stone; it lasts ten years.

Q How do you develop a relationship with a personal shopper?

Simple—call and make an appointment for this free (you heard me) service. You'll find it at most large department stores. Having an expert pick clothes for you sounds luxurious, but it's not just for people with red-carpet appointments—and there's no obligation to buy. A personal shopper can:

■ **Save you hours of browsing** (crucial if you're shopping on deadline for a special event).
■ **Encourage you to try different styles and colors.**
■ **Tell you when stuff arrives**—and when it goes on sale.
■ **Solve dressing problems.** (What top goes with wide pants? What colors clash?)

Be patient. First encounters with a personal shopper are very trial and error; she'll probably bring loads of clothes into the dressing room. But once she gets acquainted with your life, tastes, and body type, she can pare down your rack to a few well-edited pieces. What a civilized way to shop.

ILL-ADVISED BUYS will be a thing of the past with a personal shopper on call.

Q I'm willing to spend on cashmere, but only if it will last a long time. What's the best way to care for it?

Coddle your investment. According to designer Suzan Azuma of Mai, known for its hip cashmere tees, avoid dry cleaning; chemicals may damage delicate fibers, so sweaters are never as soft again. I suggest: **Hand wash with baby shampoo** (or a specifically all-natural cashmere wash like White + Warren's—kinder than Woolite). Use sparingly and dissolve completely in cool to lukewarm water. Press suds through the sweater gently (no twisting or wringing); soak three to five minutes; rinse. Dry flat on a towel, away from radiators and direct sun. **Pills aren't a sign of cheap cashmere** but the result of ordinary friction. Comb them out with a boar-bristle brush, mow them down with a battery-powered sweater shaver, or smooth them with the Sweater Stone, which does for pill-ridden knits what pumice stones do for rough skin. **Store items in separate bags** so that if one is infested with moths—lured by perfumes and oils trapped in fibers—you won't lose the entire collection.

Q I love hair accessories. Are there any that won't make me look juvenile?

Sure, if you don't try to channel Blair Waldorf, *Gossip Girl*'s headband queen. My advice: **Keep styles sleek.** Try a chopstick in a bun, a barrette or elastic on a low ponytail, or a narrow band on hair of any length. **Avoid girly elements** (hearts, bows, pastels). Touches of sparkle are okay if you choose a modern shape. **Don't exaggerate.** Nothing that sticks out or up! **Stay neutral.** You want to blend with or echo your haircolor.

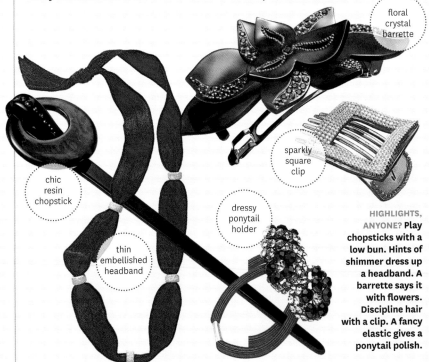

floral crystal barrette

sparkly square clip

chic resin chopstick

dressy ponytail holder

thin embellished headband

HIGHLIGHTS, ANYONE? Play chopsticks with a low bun. Hints of shimmer dress up a headband. A barrette says it with flowers. Discipline hair with a clip. A fancy elastic gives a ponytail polish.

ADAM SAYS

Seasonal Style

Q **You've said it's okay to wear white jeans year-round. But what type of shoe goes with them when it's cold outside?**

White jeans are more than okay for post–Labor Day weekends; they're seriously cool—and more sophisticated than blue denim. It's important to pick an un-gimmicky straight-leg style and avoid bare, summery footgear (strappy high heels, open-toe sandals, flip-flops). Boots, preferably in suede or rough-hewn leather, are excellent for taking these pants into fall and winter. Brown, because it's more casual, is generally better than black. And white denim is a great canvas for a hit of metallics or animal prints—two of my favorite ways to depart from the usual neutrals.

Q **Is it acceptable if my skirt sticks out from under my coat?**

More than okay. Hems that match are fussy and antiquated; **it's far more modern to play with different lengths.** I insist only that the coat extend far enough down to cover your jacket or top (three visible hems are overkill). Some people sidestep the issue with maxicoats, but those to-the-ankle jobs look like bathrobes. I prefer a knee-length classic with crisply tailored shoulders, a slightly shaped waist, and a not-too-narrow bottom (to allow for fuller skirts).

LAYER WITH FLAIR—uh, make that flare— in a flyaway coat.

Q

Why, in the dead of winter, are stores overrun with warm-weather clothes?

I agree that the timing is crazy. Because the fashion business works months ahead, so do stores; the collections delivered in January are known as resort. But they're not just beachwear. You'll find sleek transitional pieces in bright colors and patterns—precisely the pick-me-ups you need in this cold, dark season (a vibrant shoe or top transforms winter neutrals). The clothes also tend to be less bare than those in spring-summer lines. Depending on your local climate, you can shop now and wear now, or squirrel things away for later.

GET HAPPY with buys from resort collections that offer a whiff of spring.

A COAT CAN look like a shirt's first cousin. Notice the dropped shoulders, full sleeves, and waist-defining belt.

Q

What one fall piece will make the biggest difference in my feeling updated?

A great coat or outdoor jacket. Most people buy something black, warm, and classic and throw it on as an afterthought. That makes no sense when your coat is what others see first. Instead of just showing up, make an entrance.

This year it's easy to find your amazing dream coat—not Technicolor, please; neutrals are more useful—because there's lots of drama: flared or gathered sleeves, bracelet length or shorter; collars that range from big face framers and high-neck stand-ups to soft, shirtlike points; belted waists or fuller, less curvy shapes. Women often build an outfit around a handbag. Try doing the same with a coat. If it's really memorable, you can afford simple, inexpensive underpinnings: A well-fitting turtleneck and pants will do.

Q

Summer is the season of houseguests and weekend shares. What night garments are okay for hanging out?

For appropriate coverage, try knits instead of flimsy tell-all fabrics, pajamas rather than gowns; nothing is chicer than traditional men's pj's. Clean, cute, and sporty is the idea. Save the sexy, bias-cut charmeuse for more private occasions. And be sure that whatever you choose isn't stretched out: You don't want to look like you've been wearing it since your college dorm days. Another concern might be, "Do I have to wear a bra?" Most women can't wait to take them off when they get home. In mixed company, however, the well-endowed should be discreet; a top with built-in support works well.

PERFECT FOR communal kicking back, a camisole with an underwire bra inside and jersey pajama bottoms.

Q **They may work for some women, but I've always been scared to death of white jeans. Should I be wearing them?**

Absolutely, and not just in summer—I believe in having a couple of pairs in your closet year-round (but buy now for the widest choice; they're harder to find in winter). I like their crispness, the way they freshen up anything you wear, from a navy blazer and striped tee to an embellished tunic top or a bright twinset. As for the fear factor, if light-colored pants fit well, they will not make your butt and hips seem bigger. As you know, I prefer bootcuts or straight legs, not extreme skinnies, with added stretch for comfort. And so what if they show the dirt sooner than dark denim? Just toss them in the machine (you might even invest in dry-cleaning for an ultra-pressed dress-whites look).

JEANS CLEAN UP nicely when white five-pockets team with an embroidered blouse. Touches of color come from a diamond-motif belt and beaded sandals.

LIGHTEN UP: A high-def blouse, bag, and shoes update work pants. A black shirt gets a lift from a khaki skirt, woven purse, cuffs, and zebra-print shoes.

Q **I wear head-to-toe black all year long. Is it wrong for summer?**

Of course not. There are very few wrongs in life. Black is a universal, multiseason color; in warmer months it just needs to feel lighter. My suggestions:

■ Pick airy, diaphanous fabrics—voile, eyelet lace, chiffon....

■ Avoid high collars and long sleeves or you'll look like a Sicilian widow. Better: a breezy shift dress.

■ Relax with accessories in natural textures like raffia, wood, and leather.

■ You're a true black wearer, so I won't suggest the old add-a-pop-of-color routine. Instead, try graphic combinations of black and white or khaki—I love, love, love this look.

Adam's Swimsuit Commandments

Yes, finding a swimsuit is stressful, but here are a few ways to make it less so.

1 **Thou shalt not automatically buy a tankini;** they aren't as flattering as you may think. You get no real belly coverage, and the top often hits at a bad spot.

2 **Thou shalt try a maillot.** They're sexier than a string bikini! A one-piece with gathered fabric in the middle is as miraculous as a wrap dress: It instantly creates a waist and disguises bulges.

3 **Thou shalt not wear prints** if you're full-figured. You'll only look bigger.

4 **Thou shalt pick a sophisticated color.** Neons and graphic designs are better left to young women or surfer chicks.

5 **Thou shalt not hide under a skirted suit.** They age you. Cover up with a sarong or tunic.

6 **Thou shalt choose a higher-cut leg.** It will make thighs look leaner. Boy shorts are unkind even if you have tooth-picks for legs.

7 **Thou shalt not bother with a white swimsuit.** It's good for glamour poses only.

8 **Thou shalt buy a new bathing suit every other year.** They lose elasticity and start to pill.

9 **Thou shalt not even think about an unstructured top** if you are larger than a B cup.

10 **Thou shalt go shopping in the morning** or at midday, before you're too tired.

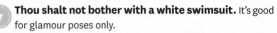

NO MORE KID STUFF: Bare a little or a lot, but please, keep the look sophisticated. *From left:* One-shoulder maillot—very trendy—is seriously spandexed to make you look ten pounds slimmer. Corset-inspired lace-up top adds a seductive touch to a purple tankini. Halter-neck bikini has a wide, tummy-camouflaging band. THAT'S WHAT I CALL SUPPORT: Halter-neck maillot gives a discreet glimpse of cleavage. Tankini gets extra uplift from double straps.

Q **Am I too old for a bikini? I'm 47, wear a size 4 to 6, and exercise regularly.**

If you've got the body, go ahead. Lots of women in their 40s and 50s work hard to stay in shape, and they've earned the exposure. Just be brutally honest about how fit you are as well as how comfortable you'll feel in public. I'm no prude, but I wince at teeny-weeny surfer-girl bikinis on mature figures. Get one that covers more of you (a substantial fabric, like a nylon-spandex blend, is also a plus). And if you think a bikini is the only way to look sexy on the beach, think again: A great one-piece can be equally appealing.

Q **I'm a size 16 with a 40F chest—are there sexy suits with proper bras?**

Absolutely. Now that swimwear makers are more alert to the needs of curvy women, I've found some really gorgeous suits (from labels such as Tara Grinna, Bond-Eye, Panache, Freya, and Fantasie) that are sized like bras and designed to accommodate larger breasts. Insist on real cups (not a shelf bra) and not-too-skinny straps so that you won't spill over while swimming. I don't like to dictate, but more zaftig people really do look better in solid colors...which doesn't rule out red!

ADAM SAYS
At the Office

Q How would I impress you at a job interview?
With good posture, a firm handshake, and direct eye contact.

You assumed I'd be scrutinizing your clothes for designer labels, right? Wrong. While it's fine to wear recognizably high-end items (it shows taste and fashion savvy), it's hardly required. You can do something simple and inexpensive—a black turtleneck or white shirt with black trousers—if you score high on my personal "big three":

- **A good haircut**—you'll look better, smarter, sharper.
- **A great watch**—a men's style is the safest bet (no gems).
- **Stylish shoes**—not necessarily expensive but well cared for and sleek.

And that's it. You don't want to overaccessorize. I once interviewed a woman who showed up wearing a man's tie *under* a button-front shirt! Horrendous. Another applicant had on huge, dangly earrings that resembled napkin rings. When in doubt, think classic.

WELL-BRED platform slingbacks in patent leather suggest to an employer that you're a genius at details.

INTENTIONALLY WRINKLED is okay; unironed is not. You can look cool but neat in an airy, subtly ruffled crinkle-cotton shirt and a long, gauzy scarf that adds a shot of color.

Q At work, how do I dress like I mean business?
Find the uniform for you. I used to be horrified by prep schools where everyone was dressed the same, but now I think it's invaluable to be able to turn to something that always looks smart, chic, and pulled together. It can be classic, like a suit with a knee-length skirt (no shorter—work-appropriate also means age- and body-appropriate). Wear it with a modest V-neck shell or a camisole with lace; just don't overdo the froufrou. A dress and jacket, while still authoritative, is softer. But you don't want beach clothes—like a sundress—washing over into work, and sheers are acceptable only if layered over a matching camisole or slip. Separates can look a bit off-hand, however, unless everything is impeccable: pressed, stain-free, and finished with smart accessories like scarves, belts, discreet jewelry (flashy pieces are distracting), or shoes in a fun color.

Q I'm an administrative assistant who needs to look presentable on a limited budget. A suit feels like overkill. Can you help?
I'm guessing you sit behind a desk, so think like a news anchor and focus on dressing from the waist up: cute tops, prints, scarves—anything with a little neckline detail or embellishment. Transform a simple white shirt by adding a statement necklace. And the suit may be dead, but that doesn't mean you can't resuscitate one in your closet and wear the pieces as separates. A jacket will give you a sense of authority—play with it! Turn up the collar, add a pin, or roll the sleeves. *At right,* three of my favorite options.

Q **I own a lot of button-downs for work, and they're starting to bore me. How can I make them look less stuffy?**

My tried-and-true trick is to turn up the collar—does wonders for the neck—and roll up the sleeves.

By the way, it's incredibly smart to make the classic button-down your go-to top: It's innately chic and available at all prices (so you can stock up without losing your shirt). Here, more ways to play it.

LAYERED: A pink shirt and slim-fitting vest—the argyle is straight out of *Love Story*—look preppy. Draped with a beaded necklace, they become sophisticated rather than schoolgirlish.

CINCHED: The ultimate chameleon, a black shirt looks good all day—never gets grubby—and moves easily into evening. Dress it up with a wide, waist-emphasizing belt and a bold, colorful necklace.

PINNED: Take a plain white shirt—I like them slightly shaped, with a bit of stretch—and change the buttons to high-contrast black. Add a floral brooch and you've got instant charisma.

WRAPPED: Menswear patterns like the stripe on this shirt could use some excitement. Choose a big, fringed scarf in an ethnic pattern that uses the same palette as the shirt; loop it loosely around your neck.

Q **Can I wear flip-flops to work in summer? How much bareness can I get away with?**

I'm shocked, frankly, by what some people consider office-appropriate: pants that let the stomach hang out, tops with major cleavage. It's not the message you want to send. Work is work, not a day at the beach.

Flip-flops are for weekends, period. Bare legs and nice sandals are okay, but only if your pedicure is up-to-date. Going public with unkempt feet is the crime of summer. Anything radically low-cut, short, or tight is taboo. But I'm not going to say strappy dresses are wrong: It depends on your professional culture. Twenty- or thirty-somethings in a young, hip workplace can show some skin. If you're under 40 but the people in charge aren't, be more circumspect. And if your corporate climate isn't reason enough to cover up, remember that the bone-chilling temperatures of most offices in summer will be.

DON'T SNEAK THESE into the workplace unless your office is relaxed. But I'm crazy about their cool fusion of walkability and style.

Q **What do you think about the appropriateness of wearing sneakers to the office?**

I cringe at the sight of a woman in a nice suit with white athletic shoes, looking like Melanie Griffith in *Working Girl.* Even sleek, low-profile sneakers, while fine for your commute, are too informal for a traditional office. Change into your heels outside the building if you must wear sneakers. Remember: First impressions are all-important.

ADAM SAYS
The Holidays

Q I'm sick of my Little Black Dress. Can you suggest different evening standbys?

There's nothing more modern for night than mixing everyday and dressy pieces, like a regular sweater (dual-function items save money) over a long, festive skirt. Or work the masculine-feminine duality of the tuxedo, which is very popular this fall (the late, great Yves Saint Laurent pioneered the women's version). Always smart: casual basics in fancy fabrics (charmeuse, lace, metallics) that give you the comfort of a tee, tank, or drawstring pant while still looking party-ready.

Clean Lines

EASY GLAMOUR
With sequins, avoid trendy silhouettes; a simple jacket looks sophisticated over a refined blouse and skirt.

COOL & SEXY
By day, sneak a glittery tank under a cardigan. Drop the sweater for evening, letting color—orange trousers and gilded flats—take over.

Bright for Night

THE NEW RELIABLES (*clockwise from left*): sequined tee and silk skirt; tuxedo jacket and shirt dressed down with jeans; turtleneck and ball skirt with sparkly belt.

Q I don't want to buy a whole glitzy outfit this season. Is there a piece that I can wear both at the office and to holiday events?

I agree: It's more modern to mix day and evening clothes, and more practical (who wants to schlep a dress bag to work—or go home and change?). It's also cheaper—a sparkly top to layer with office basics needn't be a big investment. After 5, retreat to the ladies', switch to dressy accessories and vivid lipstick, and you're transformed.

Q The holidays bring out the most embellished clothes. I love them, but how do I avoid going overboard?

All year long my mantra is "A little goes a long way." Flash is always more flattering in small doses on demure—not tight or revealing—clothing. Otherwise the effect can be cheap, and you might end up highlighting figure flaws. Here are some easy ways to shine without lighting up like a Christmas tree.

INSTEAD OF...	WHY NOT TRY...
A HOLIDAY-THEMED SWEATER ▶	A BEADED CARDIGAN
AN ELABORATE TOP WITH SHINY BOTTOMS ▶	A COTTON BUTTON-DOWN OR TEE
BRIGHT COLORS ▶	RICH, DARK JEWEL TONES
MATCHING PEARL STRANDS AND STUDS ▶	PEARLS MIXED WITH CHAINS AND RHINESTONES
ACCESSORIES ON YOUR EARS, NECK, WRIST, AND FINGERS ▶	JUST ONE BOLD PIECE (LIKE A COCKTAIL RING OR SEQUINED SCARF)
POINTY STILETTOS ▶	DRESSY BALLET FLATS

Q You've said that heels make legs look better, but I just can't tolerate them all evening. Are flats okay?

They're fantastic, especially the styles embellished with beads, sequins, and other glamorous stuff. You do have to watch your proportions: Full skirts of any length are fine with flats; so are dressy cigarette pants (very *Mad Men*). But wide-leg trousers or pencil skirts look dumpy with them unless you're exceptionally tall. You can always start the party in heels—and take along flats for dancing.

How to Shine (Not Shock) at the Office Party

The annual holiday bash isn't an invitation to go wild (unless you want office gossip to feed on your *Dancing with the Stars* moment). Therefore...

■ **Stay in character.** Pump up your usual style rather than making a radical switch. Sometimes it's enough to change shoes and add dressy accessories.

■ **Think subtle.** This is a chance to show coworkers your more glamorous side—discreetly. Forget anything overtly sexy.

■ **Make an effort.** Buttoned-up, business-as-usual suits or Casual Friday khakis suggest that you're clueless or lazy. Not a good message.

■ **Avoid extremes.** Your boss won't be impressed by the fabulousness of those crazy-high stiletto platforms; she'll merely think you're walking funny.

■ **Keep it natural.** Fragrance should be low-key and makeup only slightly heightened. ⊙

PARTIES ARE MORE FUN if your feet are happy. Chic options (*from top*): glittery sandals; teeny heels; silk satin with feathers; sparkling flats.

275

10 Secrets Every Beauty Editor Knows That You Should, Too

What? You didn't believe there were tricks to looking glossy and pulled-together—without spending a fortune? Here they are.

1 **The one thing that we always drink to: water.** But forget the rule about eight glasses a day—just drink enough so that you don't feel thirsty. Although there's no link between how much water you consume and how hydrated your skin is, I know that when I'm parched, my complexion looks flaky and dry. Also: If you drink a glass of water before each meal, you'll be less inclined to overeat.

2 **Sunscreen is the closest thing we have to a fountain of youth.** Use at least SPF 15 every day, rain or shine. UV radiation is the major source of skin cancer and accelerated aging of the skin, both of which can occur without tanning or other visible signs of damage, says Steven Wang, MD, director of dermatologic surgery and dermatology at Memorial Sloan-Kettering Cancer Center at Basking Ridge, New Jersey.

3 **You can conjure up a prettier complexion while you sleep...with the magic of retinoids.** Still the gold standard of topical skincare ingredients, vitamin-A derivative prescription retinoids (like Retin-A, Renova, Tazorac) stimulate new collagen, exfoliate your pores, and encourage cell turnover, says Mary P. Lupo, MD, clinical professor of dermatology at Tulane Medical School. Add a retinoid to your nighttime beauty routine.

4 **Always treat your hands and neck the way you treat your face.** The skin on the neck is thinner than the skin on the face, yet most women don't care for it as well. Same goes for the hands. After you apply a treatment (like a retinoid or antioxidant serum) to your face, rub it on your neck and the backs of your hands, too.

5 **For the price of a tube of self-tanner, you can look as if you spent a month on the Riviera.** Apply a moisturizing body lotion that includes a self-tanner to hide spider veins on your legs and to get a slimming effect all over.

6 **There's gold in them thar drugstores.** Take advantage of the bounty of inexpensive cleansers, moisturizers, and treatments that work just as well as (or better than) luxury brands. The large cosmetic companies that produce drugstore products want you to be loyal to them, so they don't skimp on their research and development.

7 **Facials can be expensive, but luminosity is free.** The fastest way to better skin tone doesn't cost a dime. Exercising gives you improved circulation and oxygen capacity, which causes the blood vessels in the skin to dilate, says Steven Dayan, MD, clinical assistant professor in the division of facial plastic surgery at the University of Illinois. The result? That healthy glow everyone's aiming for.

8 **We never met an antioxidant we didn't like.** Free radicals—certain kinds of molecules that can build up in your body and damage proteins and DNA—hasten the aging process, says Dayan. Eating a diet rich in fruits and vegetables that contain antioxidants like coenzyme Q10, and vitamins A, C, and E can help reverse some of that damage. Applying antioxidants topically can also be helpful.

> A person who looks happy is perceived as more attractive than the same person who looks sad.

9 **One impeccable, classic haircut is worth more than all the styling products in the world.** A haircut is a little like a dress: If you start out with terrific tailoring, accessorizing is unnecessary (but still can be lots of fun).

10 **Good deeds = good looks.** If you do something that makes you feel great about yourself, you're more likely to wear a happy expression. And studies have shown that a person who looks happy is perceived as more attractive than the same person who looks sad, says Dayan. So do something kind for someone. While you're at it, smile. And, for Pete's sake, be sure you're wearing sunscreen. ◐

Keep the Face, Baby

Val contemplates having a little work done and decides that plastic surgery doesn't make the cut. At least not yet.

What is it you want to change?

One very long day a while ago, for a magazine assignment, I sold cosmetics and skin care products at Bloomingdale's. I wasn't good at it. By which I mean that at first I confused customers—when one inquired how long the lipsticks lasted (per application), I confidently answered, "Years" (thinking she meant per tube)—and by the end, I was turning them away in droves. The situation had less to do with a lack of salesmanship than with my determination to convince women that they were gorgeous (or extremely presentable) just the way they were, without adornment or antiaging products. You can see how this might have worked at cross-purposes with my position behind the counter.

There were a number of women I met that day I will never forget: one with a rosy English complexion who claimed she looked "dead"; another, storybook beautiful, with mocha skin and large, aquamarine eyes, who believed that she needed a product "to keep her face from falling." But most riveting was an early-middle-aged woman with a perfectly sculpted ski-jump nose; tight, satiny skin; and a small, unmistakable bubble of collagen plumping her upper lip. She was in the market for an eye cream compatible with Retin-A. This woman scared me. Not because she looked strange, though she did a little. She scared me because on her face I saw all of my own yearning to be young and lovely, unmarked by time and experience, to be angelic, innocent, cherished. Did I want that as much as she did? Did I believe that changing my face was the way to get it? I was 40. Maybe that day would come, but I wanted to try to accept my aging self. At 50 I might feel different, but for now, no; not yet.

Twelve years later, I visited a dermatologist for a yearly checkup. After she examined me, the doctor gently took my chin in her hands. She turned my face this way and that, considering. Finally, she said, "You know, I could do

something very nice for you." I raised my eyebrows (happily being one of those in my set who still can). The doctor took out a small envelope of Polaroids. "See here," she said, gesturing toward one. Then she pointed to the next, a shot of the same woman, looking just a little better. "Doesn't she look wonderful? As if she's had a good nap?" The difference wasn't major, but it was nice. "I could do that for you," the doctor said. "I could harvest a little fat from your bottom and inject it into your face to fill it out where it's beginning to sag. You could go right back to work the same day."

That night after dinner I asked my husband, "What would you think if I had some fat from my ass injected into my face?" "Fat from your ass?" he said incredulously. "In your face? Well," he said, leaving it up to me, "if you think that's where the fat is supposed to be...."

The dermatologist was right: My face has lost some tone. I've stood at the mirror, index fingers lightly pulling back the skin at my jaw. I've noticed thin lines, puffiness under my eyes that doesn't disappear with a nap or even a good night's sleep. Not long after that, I was having a conversation with a physician friend about plastic surgery. I told her the story of the dermatologist who offered to fix my face. My friend listened, and then she pulled out a pocket mirror. "Look at yourself," she said. "What is it you want to change?" I held the mirror up close, taking in the puffiness, and the lines, the beginning of looseness around the jaw. I saw a 52-year-old woman, showing the signs of her age. Everything was just where it was supposed to be. Finally, I handed the mirror back. "I wouldn't change anything," I said. "Maybe that day will come. At 60 I might feel different, but for now, no. Not yet." O

Hitting a Milestone?

Our beauty director faces an age-old question.

Dear readers, this "Ask Val" page might better be called "You Didn't Ask Val, but She's Going to Tell You Anyway." Or, more pointedly, "Holy Crow's-feet, I'm Turning 60."

Yes, in a few weeks I become a sexagenarian—and despite my optimistic nature, I suspect that sounds a lot more promising than it is.

Not long ago, I was trying to explain to a 45-year-old friend what it feels like to be my age. "It's like this," I said. "I'm going to tell you something about yourself that you don't know, and it's incontrovertibly true no matter what else you believe."

"Okay," she said.

I looked at her hard. "You were born in 1950," I said. "You're actually 60." My friend gave me the kind of blank stare you get when something does not compute. "Well, that just doesn't make any sense," she said.

Exactly. The age I am is not the age I feel. And I'm pretty sure that if you're close to 60 or older, you understand the disconnect. It's not uncommon. In a 1995 study of Americans between 55 and 74, most of them felt 12 years younger than they actually were. Studies in Germany and China have yielded similar results.

As you might guess, one of the most important factors in feeling youthful is good health, or at least a sense of control over your health. If you can exercise and generally kick up your heels without throwing out your back or breaking your legs, naturally, you feel more vigorous than your neighbor who has trouble hauling himself out of a chair. It also helps if you spend your days among younger people.

In many ways, feeling younger than your age is a good thing. Research shows that it can have a positive effect on confidence about cognitive abilities (the sort of confidence I could use the next time I search for my glasses and find them on my nose). And people who feel younger than they are, are less likely to die than same-age peers who actually feel that age.

But there's a wrinkle below the surface of this encouraging news.

If you're a woman, when you get to be 60 (or almost) and begin noticing the disconnect between how old you feel and how old you look, you start to think differently about your face. And by "differently" I mean that you suddenly have to make now-or-never decisions about how much control you want to exert over it. You can decide that you want to try to hold on to your youth by any means possible (in which case surgery will be involved). You can decide that you'll only tinker with the aging process, feeling your way day by day (there are copious options, from microdermabrasion to fillers, and Botox). You can decide to say the hell with it, and watch with brave astonishment as a mustache darkly embellishes your upper lip, your eyebrows gradually vanish, and you develop the jowls you fondly remember on your favorite uncle. Whichever route you follow, you have to take responsibility in a new way for your looks.

Did you know that some of the earliest plastic surgery was the reversal of circumcision on Jewish men who wanted to pass for gentile in Roman times? Plastic surgery in this country, too, was often originally about "passing," with immigrants wanting to change their features to conform to the status quo. And isn't it still often about passing? Older women (and men) yearning to pass for younger?

It's lovely if someone thinks I'm not yet 60 (which is happening less often; I appear to be gaining momentum on a downhill run). But I expect that as the body I live in continues to mature, I'll come to accept the duality of looking one age and feeling another—just as I have come to accept other strange and poignant aspects of the human condition, like our awareness of the raw irrefutability of death. It is what it is.

As for my face: I doubt I'll do more than a bit of Botox and a regular flash of skin-toning laser. I've always wanted to look pretty, and I still want to, but age-appropriately pretty. So I'm not going to try to remodel my outside to correspond with how I feel inside. Because, bottom line, I don't really want to pass for anything but what I am. ◐

Stuck on Botox!

All I could think about was what could go wrong: a droopy eyelid, a permanent expression of extreme surprise or beetle-browed consternation. That's why I'd never tried Botox, the botulinum toxin that's used to reduce facial wrinkling. Also: I was philosophically opposed to shooting anything into my face. "I love my face," I'd declare to anyone who suggested I might enjoy a light arpeggio of cosmetic fiddling.

Then one morning I looked in the mirror and noticed (I thought) that the little lines between my eyebrows had deepened. I could see where my face was going, but I liked it where it was. So I made an appointment with New York City dermatologist Cheryl Karcher, MD, to ask her whether she thought I might benefit from just the teeniest grace note of Botox. At her office a few days later, I sat under a very bright light and pointed to my concerns. "Ha! Easy to fix," she said. Then she took a step back and looked at me studiously. "Big frown," she said. I made a doleful face. "Okay," she said. "Relax." And before I knew it, she had administered five quick shots of Botox above and between my eyebrows. "Fini!" said the doctor. A physician's assistant held an ice pack to my forehead to prevent bruising. "Bravo!" I said.

It took about a week for me to get used to not being able to wiggle my eyebrows the way I used to. ("Wiggle my eyebrows" doesn't adequately describe what I could do; if there is such a thing as double-jointed eyebrows, I had them. But I don't have them anymore, at least till the toxin wears off in a few months.) I don't like the paralyzed feeling at all; it's as if I'm wearing a cap that fits too tightly around my forehead. But recently a friend said to me, "What's going on with you? You look...bright-eyed and rested!"

So despite the unpleasantness, I'm afraid I'm hooked: An encore is definitely on the program.

Life Isn't a Beauty Contest

After years of judging her looks and comparing herself with other women, Val finally figures out a way to end the competition.

I grew up with a Barbie doll. Not a toy—a mother. She was a model, raven-haired, green-eyed, statuesque, with unrealistically perfect proportions, but there they were. Like the doll, my mother had an extensive wardrobe; Mom's even included a couple of mother-daughter outfits. Were they fetching? I don't remember. I do remember gazing at the two of us dressed alike: one, a full-blown goddess, larger-than-life, a voluptuous Renoir; the other, a skinny, freckle-faced tadpole, an anonymous, unfinished pencil sketch. It was in the shifting of that gaze—Mom, me, me, Mom—that my comparing mind was born. As far as my appearance was concerned, I was undefined except in relation to another woman. Whereas my mother was full and round and complete, I was thin, angular, inchoate. My mother's hair was wavy and thick, always perfectly coiffed. Mine was straight and fine, my bangs always uneven. Clothes clung languidly to my mother's curves like an exhausted lover. My clothes, like worn-out Colorforms, refused to stick to me; elastic waistbands were sewn into my skirts to keep them from falling down.

Though today I'm no Renoir, neither do I have trouble keeping my skirts up: It's a 60-year-old body I live in. I've finally matured. But my comparing mind has not. It's stubbornly stuck at 6, and if I were to follow its voice, I would feel once again like a tadpole among women. Though I'm full-grown, in my comparing mind I almost always come up short. So when it clamors to be heard, I listen as I would to a recalcitrant child, and then quiet it.

Here's what I mean: As I'm walking down a crowded city street, a gorgeous young creature in her thirties, sleek and glossy as a black cat, crosses my path. "Bad luck for you!" cries my comparing mind. "You'll never look like that again! You're old and invisible!" The woman and I are stopped at a curb. Her beauty imbues her with a mild haughtiness. In a regal kind of way, she turns her head in my direction. I catch her eye.

"You," I say, "are simply magnificent."

The haughtiness vanishes instantly. She's a bit taken aback, momentarily scrutinizes me for motive, sees none apparent, and then smiles her wide (magnificent) smile. "Why, thank you," she says.

"It's my pleasure to tell you," I say, and it is. Because I not only remember how happy I have felt as the recipient of an authentic compliment, but now I have enjoyed the additional gratification of being able to give one. Though my comparing mind wants to nullify my power and kick me off the playing field because I can no longer compete, the power I have today is irrevocable. After years of passively accepting a definition of beauty other than my own, of striving to be a noticeable object, I have now assumed an active role, as well: Appreciator of All Things Beautiful.

There are several things that recommend the role of appreciator. It's easy to be very busy—at least as busy as one can be striving to be among the appreciated. But now I've discovered what the smartest men have always known: that women can be lovely in many different ways—as many ways, it seems, as there are women. It's easy to be very happy, noticing things to admire rather than looking only for ways to be admired. You know that feeling you get when you see a lush summer garden, abundantly green and fragrant and riotous with blossoms? Does it bother you that you're not as beautiful as it is? No, of course not; it's a garden. Its beauty has nothing to do with you, takes nothing away from yours. In fact, standing in the middle of a flourishing garden, filling your eyes with the deep and impossibly delicate colors, inhaling the odors, sweet and complex, you might feel more beautiful, more precious yourself, marveling at your own ability to perceive it all. That's the way I feel about those women I used to think of as competitors: Their beauty is one more avenue for a rich enjoyment of the world.

But maybe most important as an appreciator, I'm setting my own standards. Shall I compare thee to a summer's day? No, I won't. I won't compare you—or myself—to anything, not the weather, not our mothers, not that gorgeous creature crossing our paths. Because a thing of beauty needs no comparison, only an eye to behold it. ◑

The Brush is Mightier Than the Knife

No nip, no tuck, no needles or peels—four women discover that the solution to sags, bags, blotches, creases, and lines is as close as their nearest makeup counter. Bobbi Brown does a little cosmetic "surgery." Valerie Monroe reports.

Maybe, like me, you have recently stood in front of a mirror, touched your index fingers to your jaw, and gently pulled back the skin, just to see what it would look like if your face were tight again, the way it was three or five years ago (or more). Maybe you have then idly wondered what it would take to make that fix permanent. Or maybe you haven't, so I will remind you: It would take a scalpel.

But there is an easier way to lift your looks. Bobbi Brown, well known celebrity makeup artist and author of *Living Beauty,* calls it the Makeup Facelift.

Say you have a particular facial bugaboo: that slight sag at the jowl, or crepey eyelids, or a couple of marionette lines on the sides of your mouth. You can't hide these kinds of issues by piling on makeup (and don't even try, because it will only emphasize them), but you *can* deflect the focus to other areas of your face with a combination of great moisturization, which leads to beautifully textured skin, and highlighting the features you're happiest with. It's all about diversion. And it works. To show you what we mean, we found four women who might have considered more drastic measures but were delighted to be transformed instead by the expert employment of a makeup brush. No needles, knives, recovery time—or bank loans—necessary.

AFTER

BEFORE

Marianne Butler, 42
Photo editor

Cost of Bobbi's makeup:

Corrector	$22
Foundation	$40
Eyeshadow	$20
Eyeliner	$20
Mascara	$24
Eyeshadow (on brows)	$20
Pot rouge (on cheeks)	$24
Total: $170	

Pricey alternative:

Restylane (or another hyaluronic acid filler) .... $600 to $800 per treatment; 2 treatments per year

Intense Pulsed Light (IPL) to combat ruddiness ..... $400 to $800 per treatment; 3 to 5 treatments

TOTAL: $2,400 TO $5,600

What was bothering her: "My ruddy complexion and the marionette lines around my mouth."

Bobbi's no-surgery solution: "Women in their 40s often complain about their skin—that it's looking ruddy or sallow. I tell them, 'Even if you've always resisted foundation, start wearing it now.' Use an especially hydrating moisturizer every day, because it plumps up the skin, so whatever lines are starting to form will look less obvious. I applied a corrector under Marianne's eyes, close to her lashes, and also around her nose, where she is especially ruddy. Then I applied foundation over her whole face to even out her complexion. Toning down the redness around her nose and mouth diminished the look of her marionette lines. On Marianne's eyes, I used a sandy, neutral eyeshadow over the top lid right up to the brow and a thin application of mahogany liner on her upper lid. Black mascara adds definition to her eyes and draws attention up and away from the lines around her mouth. I used a taupe shadow to accentuate her gorgeous brows and a raspberry pink cream blush on the apples of her cheeks."

AFTER

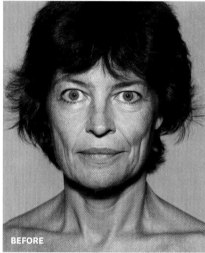

BEFORE

Cost of Bobbi's makeup:

Corrector	$22
Foundation	$40
Eyeshadows (2)	$20 each
Eyeliner	$21
Eyeshadow (on brows)	$20
Mascara	$24
Blush	$24
TOTAL: $191	

Pricey alternative:

Laser (for age spots)	$250 to $550 per treatment; 3 treatments
Eyelid surgery	$5,000
TOTAL: $5,750 TO $6,650	

Bridget Thexton, 52
Senior vice president at a financial institution

What was bothering her: "The age spots on my cheeks. And the area just below my brows is sagging, which is dragging down my eyes."

Bobbi's no-surgery solution: "Age spots are the one thing that you can cover with makeup, and it's a cinch. First, use a creamy corrector a little lighter than your skin tone. Over that, dot a touch of stick foundation in the same color as your skin tone.

The spot will completely disappear.

"I used a light eyeshadow in a nude color all over Bridget's lids to open up her eyes. Then I applied a gel eyeliner in indigo to bring out their beautiful color. Bridget said she never wore liner on her upper lid, only on her lower lid, which is the opposite of what she should be doing. Lining the upper lid will bring the focus *up* when you look at her; lining only the lower lid brings the focus

down. In the crease, I used a slightly deeper shadow, a shade darker than the nude, and blended that well. I lifted the arch of her eyebrows and extended them slightly toward her temples with a taupe eyeshadow. Then I gave her two coats of black mascara, starting close to the lashline and pulling out to the sides. A cream blush in powder pink gives her cheekbones a natural flush."

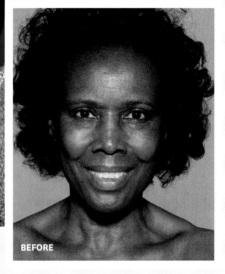

AFTER

BEFORE

Avis McCarther, 67
Actress

What was bothering her: "The deep crease between my eyes and the wrinkles on my forehead. Also the shadows under my eyes."

Bobbi's no-surgery solution: "I'm sorry, what wrinkles? Avis looks astonishing at 67. Her eyes are dark and deep set, and playing them up will divert attention from that crease between them and diminish the few lines she has on her forehead.

"I lightened up the area under Avis's eyes and at the inner corners near her nose with a cream corrector in a peach tone; on top of that, I applied concealer in a color one shade lighter than her skin tone, and extended it a bit onto her upper lid. I used a tawny eyeshadow to brighten the upper lid even more, and in the crease, a brown shadow

with a hint of shimmer to really bring the focus to her eyes. Though I used a black gel eyeliner, I kept the line very minimal so that it only added definition.

"I also applied a fine line of black liner underneath Avis's eyes, and two coats of black mascara, which makes them stand out more. A little cocoa berry stain on her lips draws attention to her beautiful mouth."

AFTER

BEFORE

Cost of Bobbi's makeup:

Eyeshadow	$20
Liner	$21
Mascara	$24
Blush	$24
Lipstick	$22
Bronzer	$33
Brush	$50
TOTAL: $194	

Pricey alternative:

**Thermage
(tightens skin)** ..... $1,000 to $5,000 depending on number of areas treated

Lower facelift .... $5,000 to $10,000

TOTAL: $6,000 TO $15,000

Kathryn Millan, 50
Photo editor

What was bothering her: "My jowls and the texture of the skin on my neck."

Bobbi's no-surgery solution: "To move the focus up from the lower part of Kathryn's face and her neck, I focused on her eyes. I used a neutral shadow over her lids, and then a soft gray gel liner, extending it up at the outer corners. Black mascara adds depth. A tawny cream blush placed high on the apples of her cheeks emphasizes her cheekbones, and a sheer, soft lipcolor doesn't distract attention from her eyes and cheeks as a darker color would.

"Kathryn could try a very light dusting of bronzer on her lower jaw and neck in order to play down the slight sagging there. She should be sure to use a big, fluffy brush, which will diffuse the powder; if it seems hard to blend, she'll know that she's using too much." ◖

Ask Val Your Most Vexing Beauty Questions

You've got questions? Our beauty director has answers.

Most of your mail to the Ask Val column concerns the usual hair, skin, makeup, and aging dilemmas, but an intriguingly high proportion of you are contending with undereye issues. Discoloration, puffiness, and crow's-feet seem to infect this readership like the plague. Why? Exhaustion? Genetic proclivity? Bookishness? All of the above? Anyway, you need help. So I called in the experts.

Dark Circles and Shadows

There are several reasons for undereye discoloration, says Heidi Waldorf, MD, director of laser and cosmetic dermatology at Mount Sinai Medical Center in New York City. Before you can figure out what to do about it, you have to know what's causing it. If you apply pressure to the circle or shadow and it disappears, your problem is due to visible blood vessels underneath the thin skin of the eye area. If the color doesn't disappear, the darkness is caused by excess pigment. And if the shadow forms at the inside corner of your eye, where a tear would flow, it's probably due to a deep tear trough.

To diminish the appearance of vascular discoloration, Waldorf suggests two to three treatments with a Vbeam laser, at $100 to $600 per treatment. For shadows caused by excess pigment, try a topical solution such as a prescription retinoid cream (Retin-A, Tazorac), a lotion containing the lightening agent hydroquinone, or one with soy, niacin, or licorice. A shadow from a tear trough is treated by filling in the area with injections of a hyaluronic acid filler such as Restylane or Juvéderm.

Puffiness

Undereye swelling, too, is caused by several factors; genetics is one of them. If you have prominent pads under your eyes, take a look at your relatives. Do most of them appear to need a month-long nap? Then the only way to reduce your puffiness is with blepharoplasty (lower eyelid surgery, $3,000) or phosphatidylcholine injections. But say you notice puffiness only after an evening of dim sum. Cut back on the salt and see if your puffiness diminishes, says Doris J. Day, MD, clinical assistant professor of dermatology at NYU Medical Center. Finally, try sleeping with an extra pillow so that fluid doesn't pool around the eye area at night, which causes bags in the morning.

Crow's-Feet

Of all the kinds of wrinkles you can get on your face, I think crow's-feet are the least unbeautiful. They're caused (in order of pleasantness) by smiling, squinting, sun exposure, diminished estrogen levels due to menopause, and smoking. The best way to treat them is to prevent them, says Jeffrey Benabio, MD, a dermatologist for Kaiser Permanente in San Diego (he also writes thedermblog.com). Benabio advises patients always to apply a broad-spectrum sunscreen that blocks UVA and UVB rays and to wear sunglasses. Also, especially if you spend hours a day in front of a computer, make sure there's no glare on it. Topical retinoids have been shown to help crow's-feet by inducing collagen growth, he says. Botox injections partially paralyze the orbicularis orbis muscle to prevent it from contracting, which causes wrinkling (though Benabio is quick to say that if the Botox is overdone, you won't be able to smile about your wrinkle-free face). Injectable fillers can be used to plump up the lines, and chemical peels and lasers can improve crow's-feet by stimulating collagen, says Benabio.

> To figure out how to treat undereye discoloration, you have to know what's causing it.

A Few Words About Camouflage

Concealer can go a long way toward improving the look of undereye problems. Use one the same color as your complexion; a lighter one will emphasize puffiness, says Pati Dubroff, Dior international celebrity makeup artist. And try a creamy formulation, rather than a liquid, tapping it right along the shadow or crevice. A very sheer dusting of loose powder will help set the concealer. **O**

Face Moisturizers

Q Do I really need a different kind of moisturizer for the area around my eyes?

Val: You can get by without one if your skin isn't sensitive and your moisturizer doesn't irritate your eyes. Of course, you can also go jogging in your walking shoes. By which I mean that there are some good reasons to use an eye cream. It usually contains fewer potentially irritating preservatives—important because the skin around the eyes is thinner and more sensitive than elsewhere on the face, says Howard Sobel, MD, clinical attending physician in dermatology at Lenox Hill Hospital in New York City. Eye cream formulas are likely to be a little lighter than some heavy face creams, which help the skin retain water and might make the eye area puffy. And eye creams that contain physical sunblocks (zinc oxide or titanium dioxide) rather than chemical sunscreens (like avobenzone or oxybenzone), which are found in many facial moisturizers, are less irritating to the eye.

Q What's the best kind of moisturizer to use on combination skin?

Val: About 70 percent of people have combination skin, says Sobel, which means that they have an oily T-zone and are normal to dry around their temples and on their cheeks. If you're one of those people, use a water-based moisturizer (water will be one of the first ingredients listed) and use it only where you need it. But don't forget to apply a sunscreen all over your face.

Q Moisturizers always seem to make me break out. Can I trust that a product won't clog pores if the label says it's noncomedogenic?

Val: Noncomedogenic moisturizers, which are water-based, are much less likely to clog pores than oil-based products, says Sobel. But there are other ingredients that can cause irritation, like lanolin, propylene glycol, and the lightener hydroquinone. If you tend to break out, look for a product that's hypoallergenic and dermatologist tested; the fewer ingredients, the less potential for problems. Many moisturizers are now formulated specifically for acne-prone complexions.

Q Should I use a sunscreen in addition to a moisturizer in the summer?

Val: I'm going to assume that your daytime moisturizer has an SPF of at least 15. I hope it does, because that's what you need to protect your skin against typical parking-lot-to-the-store, walking-the-dog sun exposure. Increased exposure—wandering around the parking lot or, better yet, walking your dog on the beach—requires either a moisturizer or a separate sunscreen with a broad-spectrum SPF of at least 30. If your skin is oily, you can skip the moisturizer in hot, humid weather and use a gel sunscreen, which is less likely to clog pores, says Marianne O'Donoghue, MD, associate professor of dermatology at Rush University Medical Center in Chicago. **O**

ASK VAL

Concealers

Q What kind of concealer should I get? How do I find the right color? Is it better to apply it with my fingertip or a brush?

Val: Questions, questions! Val can't get enough of them! A creamy concealer is best, says beauty expert Bobbi Brown, because you will be using it on delicate, often dry undereye skin. The product should feel moist, not oily or powdery. It should be one shade lighter than your skin, with yellow rather than beige or pink tones, because yellow tones blend well with any skin color. Whether you apply it with your pinkie or a brush is up to you, says Bobbi. A brush is good for getting right up to the lash line and for the corners of the eyes, where a little concealer will seem to open them up; your pinkie is good for patting the concealer on. Bobbi uses both.

Q What causes the dark circles under my eyes, and how can I get rid of them? Nothing seems to work.

Val: The bad news first: You can't get rid of them. But you can hide them (more on that in a second). Because the skin under the eye is very thin, the blood vessels beneath may show through, looking dark or shadowy. Though predisposition to undereye circles is genetic, puffiness, allergies, dehydration, and sun exposure can emphasize them. Which is why dark shadows might be more obvious on your beautifully contented face following a long, deep sleep after a summer day of hiking in the mountains. When you're in the mood to conceal, moisturize the eye area first, says Troy Surratt, a makeup artist. Apply concealer to the dark area, starting below the tear duct and working your way downward. Pat the color on. To set it, dip a small, soft brush in pale, yellow-based powder, shake almost all the powder off, and then lightly dust it over the concealer.

Q Whenever I try to conceal a blemish, I always seem to accentuate it. What's the secret?

Val: Being the kind of person who has trouble hiding anything, I empathize. Usually, midway through an effort to cover a blemish—or an undereye shadow, or whatever—I think, *Oh, what the heck, who'm I kidding?* and give up. Take it or leave it, but you better believe it, that's my motto. On the other hand, once in a while a more formal complexion is required. So here's the secret, from Bobbi: Never use only concealer on a blemish. As you've unhappily discovered, the lighter shade of the concealer draws attention to the spot. Instead follow up with a stick foundation—sticks have more pigment—that exactly matches your skin tone. And then forget about the blemish completely and be your kind and charming self. **O**

prettier, overall, so we neither need nor want to cover it up. And many formulas now include moisturizers—good news for those of us in the dry, flaky set, as well as such treatment ingredients as salicylic acid and antioxidants like vitamin E. What with all the sheerness, and the moisture, and the treatment—and I didn't even mention that many foundations also have SPF 15—applying it all over your face might not be such a terrible idea.

Bottom line: If your skin looks good, why cover it up? If your skin tone is uneven, use foundation only where you need it. And if foundation is totally your bag, try one of the new, sheer ones, packed with moisturizers and treatment ingredients.

Q
Which do I apply first, foundation or concealer?
Val: *"Concealer! Concealer! Concealer!"* (That was Bobbi, not me.) She says that once you apply concealer, you won't need as much foundation. Sometimes—like in the summer or on vacation—you might want to wear only concealer. But if you do use foundation, Bobbi believes you must use concealer first, because the pigments in foundation can intensify undereye circles and other small flaws.

Bottom line: Start with concealer, and you may find that you can stop there, too.

Q
What's the best way to apply foundation?
Val: I like to use a sponge, because I wear only a tiny bit of foundation around my nose and on my chin, and I've found that the kind of small sponge that comes in a foundation compact is easiest for dabbing, which is how I apply it. (And I wash the sponge frequently.) But many makeup artists, including Troy, prefer using their fingers and suggest you do, too, because your hands warm the foundation, helping it melt into your complexion. At a beauty event not long ago, we were given a foundation brush, which I tried, partly because they were so encouraging and partly because I didn't want to seem like a stick-in-the-mud. Now I know why you might want to use a brush: It's contoured so you can reach areas like the corners of your nose (I never knew the nose had corners; did you?) and right up under your lower lashes, which can be hard to get at evenly with your fingers or a sponge. So what am I saying here? I use a sponge, but a brush is good, and using your fingers gives a more even application.

Bottom line: There's no best way to apply foundation. Try them all. Have fun. Find what you like best. ◐

Foundation

Q
Should I wear foundation all over my face?
Val: Not necessarily. You can apply it only where you see uneven skin tone, hyperpigmentation, or ruddiness, says Troy Surratt, global consulting makeup artist for Maybelline New York. For many of us, that means alongside the nose and on the chin. Always start in the center of your face, says celebrity makeup artist Charlie Green, blending outward. And never try to deepen or change the color of your complexion with foundation, says Charlie; the more closely it matches your skin tone, the easier it will be to blend.

Now may I share some insider information gleaned from the extremely well-informed makeup artist Bobbi Brown (and various other anonymous sources)? In the foundation world, there are a few prominent trends: Foundation is getting more sheer, because cosmetics companies have realized that women want to look natural, and because advances in skincare have made our skin

ASK VAL
Eyebrows

Q I may be the last 40-year-old eyebrow virgin. But recently I've been considering shaping my own brows. I've even bought a pair of tweezers. How do I start?

Val: Put down the tweezers. Shaping your own brows is a little like cutting your own hair: You may know what you want, but it's best to leave it to a professional. Ask someone whose eyebrows you admire where she has them done, then get a consultation. If you like the technician's ideas, let her do an initial shaping, which you can then maintain by tweezing strays between visits every six weeks or so.

Q I was going to have my brows waxed when someone suggested threading. Threading?
Val: It's an ancient technique that involves pulling out hair with a knotted thread held between the technician's fingers and her teeth. I'd never seen it done till recently, at the Shobha salon in New York City. There I watched like a hawk the technician's quick, delicate movements—and I still can't tell you how she caught the hair in a perfect strip. The process looked less painful than waxing, and the results were beautiful.

Q I've been growing out my brows for two months now, and a couple of bare patches remain. Is there a way to speed up the growth process, and how can I look good till they've grown in?

Val: Eyebrows grow more slowly than other body hair (for which we should probably be grateful), so be patient. But about those bare patches: Zealous plucking or waxing, which repeatedly traumatizes follicles, may result in permanent hair loss, says Katie Rodan, MD, clinical associate professor of dermatology at Stanford University School of Medicine. Try topical 5 percent Rogaine Extra Strength, applied with a Q-tip to the areas where you want regrowth. If the follicles are still viable, you should see results in four to six months. Till then, fill in the gaps with brow gel or pencil (both adhere to the skin better than powder) one shade lighter than your hair color, and blend with an eyebrow brush, says Ramy Gafni, makeup artist and founder of Ramy Beauty Therapy cosmetics.

Q How can I avoid breaking out every time I have my brows waxed?
Val: Three days before, skip the exfoliating cleansers, Retin-A, and products containing alpha hydroxy acids. And apply 1 percent hydrocortisone cream immediately after waxing and several times a day for one or two days following, says Rodan.

Q Is it my imagination, or are my eyebrows getting thinner as I get older?
Val: I've found that past a certain age, you start to hear different kinds of complaints from your friends. Instead of "I have cramps," it's "Where did my eyebrows go?" (along with, sadly, "Where did my glasses, keys, shoes, car, kids go?"). Brows, like all body hair, do thin as we age, says Rodan. Though you can try Rogaine, it's easy to fill in sparse brows with feathery strokes of a pencil or gel. ◑

ASK VAL
Nails

Q My nails are a wreck, especially in winter. About a day after a manicure, they split, chip, crack, and peel. And my cuticles—let's not even go there. Is there anything that really helps?

Val: It's been my experience that unless you're willing to hire someone to do everything for you, including zip you up, prepare and clean up after your meals, practice the piano for you, scratch your dog's belly—and in winter, keep your hands so lubricated with moisturizer that it would be impossible to do any of those things yourself—it's very hard to maintain perfectly groomed and polished nails.

Washing with soaps or detergents, for example, strips the nails of the fatty compounds that keep them flexible,

resulting in brittleness, which causes splitting and chipping. Lack of humidity in the air also sucks moisture out of the nails and cuticles, says Robyn Gmyrek, MD, assistant clinical professor of dermatology at Columbia University. Because nail isn't living tissue, water loss is permanent, so it's best to try to prevent it. Gmyrek suggests wearing rubber gloves every time you expose your hands to water, except for when washing with a nonsoap cleanser, and moisturizing as often as possible with a thick, emollient hand cream containing lactic or glycolic acid, both of which increase the nail's capacity to retain water. Never cut the cuticles, she says, because that breaks the seal that protects the nail from infection; instead soak your fingertips in warm water and push cuticles back with an orange stick. These time-honored suggestions work—I've tried them—but they're perhaps not 100 percent practical. Have you ever washed your hair—or the dog—while wearing rubber gloves? Typed an e-mail after applying a thick hand cream?

I phoned Essie Weingarten, founder of Essie Cosmetics, the hugely successful nail care company, to ask what she would recommend for someone like me (and you). "I don't know what it is to put on a pair of rubber gloves!" she said. Then she said, "Now I will tell you how to have a manicure that will last." I took Essie's instructions (and her products) to Natasha Londer at the Paul Labrecque Salon & Spa in New York City, who followed them meticulously. Here they are:

1. To a clean, dry nail, apply an adhesive basecoat. Allow a couple of minutes to dry.
2. Apply two *thin* coats of polish, allowing time to dry between coats.
3. Apply a *thin* layer of topcoat.
4. Do not touch anything for 20 minutes—the lovely Natasha's stern instruction.

Polishes offer protection from water and detergent, and those containing nitrocellulose help prevent dehydration as well, says Gmyrek. If you apply a rich, nongreasy moisturizer before bed, get a fresh manicure once a week, and keep your nails fairly short, you should see an improvement in their condition.

It's been six days and my manicure still looks swell. I am hopeful. But the cocker spaniel, belly up, looks mighty hopeful, too. ◨

❶ shape

smooth ❷

ASK VAL

Lipstick

Q **I swear I've got lipstick from the 1700s. Once and for all, what's its shelf life?**

Val: There's no set limit to how long a lipstick will last, but if the color, odor, or texture changes, or it has melted (even if it rehardens) or been exposed to water, chuck it. Lipsticks with SPF have a shelf life of three years (after which the effectiveness of the SPF is not ensured), says Leona Fleissman, program manager at Avon research and development.

Q **How can you find the right color in a drugstore where you can't try on lipsticks?**

Val: That's a tough one, but many chain drugstores will allow you to exchange a mistake. To increase the odds in your favor, take a careful look at your natural lip color, says Cynde Watson-Richmond, director of global makeup artistry for Bobbi Brown, and then go only a couple of shades brighter or darker. And a rule of thumb: If your lips are thin, avoid dark shades, since they make lips look narrower; a natural shade of gloss will make your mouth look fuller. Conversely, if your lips are very full, be judicious with the shine. Stuck with a color that seems too intense? Use a lip brush to mix it with a clear gloss.

Q **Once, I had the perfect lipstick, but I used it up and the company stopped making it. Is there any way to track down a discontinued shade?**

Val: Three Custom Color Specialists (threecustom.com) has a database of hundreds of discontinued shades and can reproduce a shade from a sample. Prescriptives (go to prescriptives.com for store locations) can match a discontinued shade and blend it to your specifications (sheer, matte, shimmery).

Q **A friend sent me an e-mail recently making the rounds that warned about dangerous levels of lead in lipsticks. Is there any truth to it?**

Val: My mother sent me that e-mail. (Along with another, warning that someone might ask me, on my way out of a mall, to sniff a new "perfume" as a way to render me unconscious so that I might be bound and stuffed in the trunk of my car. I don't even *have* a car.) There are no detectable levels of lead in lipsticks, says Fleissman; the Food and Drug Administration (FDA) requires extensive testing of all colorants and dyes used in cosmetics. Manufacturers also must submit a sample from each new batch of dye to the FDA for certification. The rumor is malarkey.

Q **Is there a trick to making lipstick last longer?**

Val: There are a couple of tricks, says Watson-Richmond. First, make sure your lips are in good condition—meaning smooth—by using a lip balm every night and whenever they feel dry. Try an emollient balm with oils, like avocado or olive, and vitamin E. Filling in your lips with pencil first will help the lipstick adhere because the pencil is drier than your lips. A light base of foundation on your mouth works the same way. Lipsticks with shimmer tend to last longer because the mica in the shimmer adheres well. And try a long-lasting lipstick; many have been reformulated to be less drying. ◐

Hair Products

Q There are a million hairstyling products out there—volumizers, thickeners, molding creams. I feel as if I need a doctorate in hairology to figure out which one to use. Can you help?

Val: You're bringing up an interesting issue, and it's something I've been meaning to talk about. Suggesting one product would be a little like telling you to wear only cotton knits, never wool or linen or silk. Why wouldn't I want to do that? Because it would severely limit the fun you might have playing around. The next time you're in the drugstore aisle, think of it as a playground—no, wait a minute, that's not right, your bathroom would be the playground—but anyway, my point is to try a less-serious approach. No one I know has had to take orals to defend her position on antifrizz serums.

That said, hairstylist Kattia Solano, owner of the Butterfly Studio in New York City, offers some helpful information. She says people often come into her salon saying they can't do anything with their hair, and when she asks if they've ever tried using a product, they shrug and say no. But second to a good cut, product is the one thing that can help give you some control over your hair. The right kind can add volume or thicken or smooth frizz or help you get that funky "piecey" look you like.

Basically, there are four types of products that can affect the texture of your hair. A *volumizer,* usually a spray, works well on fine hair to add fullness and body. Starting at the back of your head (so there's not a concentration of product at the crown, where it could weigh hair down), apply lightly at the roots and work the stuff through to the ends. Most of these products are heat activated, so it's best to blow-dry your hair after applying.

Try a *thickener*—creamier and heavier than most volumizers—to really beef up your just-shampooed hair, adding weight and texture. Rub a small amount between your hands and work it up from the ends about halfway to the root. Instead of the overall fullness you get with a volumizer, a thickener makes each strand seem fatter.

An *antifrizz* product can be useful for nearly everyone, says Kattia, whether your hair is coarse and thick (in which case you'd use a cream or oil) or fine (use a serum or light cream). The silicone in these products smooths and coats the hair's cuticle, adding shine. Rub a quarter-size amount of product between your hands and apply it from the ends of your hair right up to the root. A little goes a long way; if you use too much, your hair, if it's fine, will look flat.

Use a *molding cream or paste* on dry hair only. Most of these products are pretty tacky, and you'll feel them in your hair. A molding cream will give short hair plenty of hold; never apply it to the scalp, but instead from mid-shaft to the ends on a few pieces pulled from around the hairline, framing your face or at the crown. To give long hair a day-at-the-beach, unkempt look, says Kattia, rub a small amount of molding cream between your palms and scrunch it through. The most important thing to remember about texturizers is that you can add more product, so always start with the smallest amount, she says. Oh, and feel free to have fun. ◖

THE FARE

O

WELL SEASON

CHAPTER 7

25 Years of
*The Oprah Winfrey
Show*

Greeting the
audience,
February 26, 2009.

WHAT I KNOW FOR SURE: 2009

"Being fully present lifts your spirits. Clears your mind of distractions. Brings clarity. Even some joy."

I keep a little bottle of bubble-blowing potion and a bubble wand on my desk. And when the day gets too heavy and I'm feeling overwhelmed, I may actually blow a few.

Blowing the perfect bubble requires bringing your attention to your breath and placing it in the space of the present moment. Kind of like bubble meditation. Being fully present automatically lifts your spirits. Clears your mind of distractions. Brings clarity. Even some joy, if you're open to it.

Blowing bubbles reminds me of happiness. It makes me think of lying flat on my back on a bed of grass, taking in the sky (sky meditation). Or standing in a grove of trees (tree meditation). Or walking through the woods with my dogs (dog-walking meditation). The best is when I get to do all three in one day.

In our current economic state, we have a choice: We can reside in a place of desperation, panic, and fear—or we can literally give ourselves some breathing space. Take in a few deep breaths. Exhale. And focus on what we need instead of what we've been striving to have.

When was the last time you thought about what really makes you feel good? Just thinking about that walk through the woods with my dogs brings a smile to my spirit.

What fills you up? What matters most to you?

For me, it's finding teachable moments in every experience. I'm happiest when I'm either learning or teaching. But I can do neither without giving my full attention to whatever or whoever needs to be in focus. That means listening with my whole body, all senses attuned to the moment.

Being able to tune in this way is why, even after 23 years of doing the show, I still have aha moments.

Meaningful things happen when you give someone your undivided—undistracted—attention. Because that's what everyone is really looking for: to be validated, appreciated, heard. To be raised up by their interactions, and not put down.

I know for sure: When we connect to what's alive in another person, the feeling is mutual.

And we both get a lift.

Oprah

WHAT I KNOW FOR SURE: 2009

"Other people and their opinions hold no power in defining our destiny."

In 1992 I decided to change the slant of *The Oprah Winfrey Show* from confrontational TV aimed at getting ratings to shows that took a "higher road" aimed at connection. I wanted to help people think differently about themselves and pursue ideas about spirit and balance and the possibility of a better life. It was a decision that was bigger than money or material interest. It was a paradigm shift—to use TV instead of being used by TV. To use it as a tool for good. That shift led to the creation of my magazine. And Oprah Radio. And a new television network, OWN.

Using my voice as a force for good: It's what I was meant to do.

And I got here by listening to the still, small voice that I felt so strongly one evening on my grandmother's back porch when I was a girl.

All my life I have looked to God for guidance. In the early '90s, I started to recognize that I wouldn't survive if I continued to play the TV game my competitors were playing. One day while vacationing in Colorado, I went into the woods to quiet the noise of the world and contemplate my next move. I remember standing among the golden aspens and asking the voice that has been a comfort for so long: *What would you have me do?*

The answer came as it had when I was a girl: "Take the high road."

The decision to listen to the voice—against the advice of many stations that carried my show—is the reason I still have a show. If I had ignored it, I would have vanished into the void of defunct broadcasting. There's a long list of talk shows that have come and gone since I started.

What I know for sure: Often we don't even realize who we're meant to be because we're so busy trying to live out someone else's ideas. But other people and their opinions hold no power in defining our destiny.

What has made me successful is the ability to surrender my plans, dreams, and goals to a power that's greater than other people and greater than myself.

Before making any major moves, I first ask: *What would you have me do? Who would you have me be?*

And then I try to live the answer. Ⓞ

Outside the Nashville station where I got my start in television at age 19.

"It's the greatest discovery of life: to recognize that you're more than your body and your mind."

With Eckhart Tolle on the set of our live Webinar, "A New Earth."

Spirituality for me is recognizing that I am connected to the energy of all creation, that I am a part of it—and it is always a part of me. Whatever label or word we use to describe "it" doesn't matter. Words are completely inadequate.

Spirituality is not religion. You can be spiritual and not have a religious context. The opposite is true, too: You can be very religious with no spiritual dimension, just doctrine.

Spirituality isn't something I believe in. It is what and who I am: a spiritual being having a human experience, as the French philosopher and priest Pierre Teilhard de Chardin profoundly said.

Knowing this has made all the difference. It allows me to live fearlessly. And to make manifest the purpose of my creation. And I will be bold enough to say I know for sure it's the greatest discovery of life: to recognize that you're more than your body and your mind.

For several years in the 1990s I did a segment on my show called "Remembering Your Spirit"—in spite of being ridiculed in the press for it, and getting pushback from some viewers who weren't willing to accept the message that there's more to our lives than our five senses reveal.

Over the years, I've continued to find new ways of introducing the concept of spirit to a broad audience. My magazine is one of them—the mission being to help people find their best life, a life that acknowledges mind, body, and spirit.

Claiming my own spiritual depths and encouraging others to recognize the fullness of their potential through spiritual connection is my greatest purpose and calling. It's why I've continued to do the show these many years. It's why I decided to start my OWN television network—the Oprah Winfrey Network—devoted to that purpose. It's why I chose *A New Earth,* by Eckhart Tolle, as a book club selection, and why I interviewed him.

I've read hundreds of books that have helped me become more spiritually attuned. *A New Earth* resonated so deeply with me and caused such a shift in the way I perceived myself and all things, I couldn't not share it.

It's been the most rewarding experience of my career to teach this book online with Eckhart Tolle and witness millions of people all over the globe awaken to their lives in such profound ways. The book is essentially about recognizing that you are not your thoughts, and seeing, then changing, the way your ego-based mind dominates your life.

Here are a few e-mail responses from readers that make my heart sing:

"I suddenly feel alive, present, and overjoyed" (*Dionne, Baltimore*).

"I can see the truth that the voice in my head does not have to control me" (*Domingo, Jersey City, New Jersey*).

"I felt a sense of weight lifted off my shoulders. Everything happens when and where it should. I need to stop fighting and let it be. I can just live, not fight my life" (*Tequiera, Halifax, Nova Scotia*).

Allowing the truth of who you are—your spiritual self—to rule your life means you stop the struggle and learn to move with the flow of your life. As Eckhart says in *A New Earth,* "There are three words that convey the secret of the art of living, the secret of all success and happiness: *One With Life.* Being one with life is being one with Now. You then realize that you don't live your life, but life lives you. Life is the dancer, and you are the dance."

The joy and vitality that come from being that dance are unmatched by any pleasure you can imagine. What it takes, I've learned, is being committed to experiencing life's spiritual essence. And that, as I said in my conversation with Eckhart, is a decision you make daily: to be in the world but not of it. **O**

WHAT I KNOW FOR SURE: 2008

"Using your instinct and feelings as your personal GPS puts you in a position to make the best choices for you."

I've been interviewing job candidates for a new television network I'm launching next year. It's a network created around the same idea as my magazine, with 24/7 programming designed to help viewers recognize and create the best for themselves in all things that matter.

What has struck me in every interview is how every potential employee refers to the "Oprah brand" and has her own take on what that means. Okay, so I accept that I'm now a "brand." But I still want to chuckle each time I hear the term.

Companies spend a lot of money to help define and establish their brand. My brand developed deliberately by accident. One choice at a time. No strategic planning. No marketing or development experts. Just daily choosing to do what felt like the right thing to do.

I started out with a team as naive as I. The first publicist I hired started the same day I did in Chicago. Only she wasn't a publicist then—she was Alice McGee the intern. After I began getting more mail than I could handle, I said, "Hey, Alice, want to be my publicist?"

When between the two of us we didn't know the best decision (should I do an interview with *Good Housekeeping, Redbook,* or no interview at all?), our research was to call Alice's mom—who regularly brought homemade meatloaf sandwiches for our nine-person staff. "My mom says to go with *Good Housekeeping....* They have that seal of approval."

That felt right to me. And that feeling is how I made and still make every decision, and gave birth to a brand.

I have a rule with all my producers: Let your intention fuel your ideas, so that what our audience experiences on-air is what you intended. Without knowing we were doing it, that became our brand. To operate from what's true. To never pretend, or set up anything in a fake way.

Each of us represents our own life brand. And using your instinct and feelings as your personal GPS puts you in a position to make the best choices for you. Now, of course, I have teams of people involved—consultants, marketers, lawyers. But I sometimes look around the table, marvel at how far I've come, and wish for the old days of Alice's mom. And a good meatloaf sandwich. **O**

With Alice McGee at a post-Emmy party in New York City, 1997.

Right: **With show staff in 1987** *(from left,* **Ellen Rakieten, Beverly Coleman, Gina Hemphill, Dianne Hudson, Mary Kay Clinton, Oprah, Alice McGee, Debra DiMaio, Chris Tardio).**

The Brightness of One's Life

I've heard truly amazing stories over the years, about almost every human situation. Conflict, defeat, triumph, resilience. Recently, I heard something that left me in awe. I haven't stopped thinking about John Diaz's story. He was on my show telling of his escape six years ago from Singapore Airlines flight 006. Eighty-three people perished in the flames. John and 95 others survived. John—who describes himself as a very straightforward, competitive, and pragmatic kind of guy—now walks with the help of a walker and endures the physical pain of his injuries every day. But in other ways he is more alive than he was before he literally went through the fire.

Above: John Diaz discusses his life-changing experience with Oprah. *Top:* The wreckage of Singapore Airlines flight 006, which crashed during takeoff from Taiwan's Chiang Kai-shek Airport on October 31, 2000.

The plane took off in typhoonlike conditions. Before John boarded, his instinct told him not to. He'd called the airline several times—"Are you sure this plane is taking off?"—because it was storming so badly. Peering out the window at takeoff, all he could see was rain. He was sitting in the very front of the plane and watched as the nose started to lift.

But the 747 had turned down the wrong runway.

At first he felt a small bump (the plane hitting the concrete barrier), followed by a huge bump right next to him where something (a backhoe) ripped a hole in the side of the plane right near where he was seated. His seat came unbolted and was thrown sideward. He could feel the motion of the plane rolling and spinning down the runway. And then it stopped. He recounts what happened:

"Then the explosion hit...a great fireball came right out and over me all the way up to the nose of the plane and then sucked straight back, almost like in the movies. And then there was this spray of jet fuel like napalm—whatever it hit...ignited like a torch.... And a gentleman, an Asian gentleman, comes running right up to me, fully aflame. I could see all his features, and there was a look of wonder on his face—like he didn't even know he was dead and burning. And I figured, well, I must be the same.

I really thought at that point I was dead."

I asked John if he believed it was divine intervention that saved him. He said no. He said what helped him get out was his position in the plane and quick thinking—to protect himself from the smoke and flames, he covered his head with the leather bag he'd been encouraged not to carry on, then he looked for the door and kept moving. And then he shared something I'm still talking about, to the point of sharing it with you now.

The inside of the plane, John said, "looked like Dante's *Inferno,* with people strapped to their seats, just burning. It seemed like an aura was leaving their bodies—some brighter than others.... I thought the brightness and dimness of the auras were how one lives one's life."

John says that experience—seeing what he could only describe as auras, an energy of light leaving the bodies and floating above the flames—changed him, made him a more empathetic person. And although he still won't call his close call with death a miracle, he does say, "I want to live my life so my aura, when it leaves, is very bright."

What I know for sure: That's a goal we all can share. ❶

WHAT I KNOW FOR SURE: 2007

"Every time we're hurt or feel like we can't go on, it's someone reaching out and connecting that makes the difference."

Twenty-two years after doing my first show, I'm still surprised by how fragile we are when it comes to the line between being loved, accepted, wanted, appreciated—or not. And how just being able to talk about it all puts healing within our reach.

I hope you saw our show on how to talk to your kids about divorce (if not, you can view highlights of it on oprah.com). I'm still thinking about the little boy who looked like Opie Taylor from *The Andy Griffith Show,* 7-year-old Kris, and his 11-year-old sister, Daisy.

Four years ago, their mother walked out on them with a boyfriend. In their taped conversation with psychotherapist and divorce expert Gary Neuman, both children are quite eloquent and profound in expressing their pain—something neither had been able to do before their session with Neuman: Daisy says that mothers who are married shouldn't have boyfriends. Kris, in his squeaky little boy voice, says that if he ever gets another mother, he'll get a better one—one who won't leave him.

By this time the whole audience and I were reaching for tissues. We could feel the depth of these children's suffering.

The intention of the show was to tell parents that unless you know how to talk to your kids about divorce, you can create more scars and deepen the wounds of disconnection.

It surprised me to learn that most parents say nothing. They don't like to bring up the subject for fear of making their children sad. Or they are embarrassed and don't know how to talk about it, and therefore don't. But they need to learn, because, Neuman says, the way children are told about their family breaking up is a seminal moment that no child forgets. He has a few basic rules:

Gary Neuman *(above far left)* talks to Daisy and Kris—and their father, Jim—about their parents' divorce.

■ Both parents should be present to tell the children together—with the main message being, *you, the children, are still our priority.*
■ It should not take more than 45 seconds.
■ Practice what you're going to say, before blurting out things that can hurt forever.
■ Never disparage the other parent, because it makes your child feel guilty about loving them.

It was amazing to see that within just our hour of conversation that day, a slight layer of darkness was lifted from all the children who participated. You could see in their eyes that they were a little lighter, they weren't as burdened, they felt validated.

Neuman said something on that show that I know for sure: We heal through loving connection. Every time we're hurt or feel like we can't go on, it's someone reaching out and connecting that makes the difference.

And love—no matter how it's offered or when it comes—can build a bridge to something better. O

"Whenever you've been touched by love, a heart-print lingers."

What I know about love I mostly learned on TV. In 20 years of hosting my show, I've seen what love can do in the most ordinary moments (watching a mother take her child to the first day of school) and the most extraordinary (strangers offering their homes to strangers in the aftermath of Katrina). Whenever you've been touched by love, a heart-print lingers, so that you're always reminded of the feeling of being cared for, knowing that, to someone, you mattered.

I remember leaving the Houston Astrodome early in the morning eight days after Katrina hit. Most people were still sleeping as we finished taping our show. A young father in a clean white T-shirt was carrying his sleeping 6-year-old daughter over his shoulder, and I stopped to ask, "How ya making out, sir?"

He replied, "I'm gonna make it, 'cause I've already survived Katrina and now I'm just moving on love—and I ain't never felt so much love in my whole life."

"Wow," I said. "You *are* gonna make it."

Lots of guests over the years have left heart-prints on me. Mattie Stepanek, a child poet whose only goal was to spread peace, was one of the wisest people I've ever met. If angels come to earth, he was definitely one of them. He came to remind us of who we are: love incarnate. When he died at age 13, I made a book of all the e-mails we exchanged. He was love to me.

Erin Kramp was an "ordinary" mother. She discovered she had breast cancer, and while she was fighting to live, she prepared her 6-year-old daughter, Peyton, for life the best way she knew how. She started recording tapes, more than 100 total, about everything she could think of to tell her daughter as she grew up, knowing there wouldn't be enough time to say it all: how to put on makeup, get boys to like you, choose friends, and dress well; stories about herself; her favorite songs, foods, and movies. Her most awesome gift, I thought, was this message: "If God decides to take me to heaven, I'm going to be looking for another soul to bring to Daddy. So I want you to know that I would very much bless Daddy remarrying."

Four years later, when Peyton's father wanted to remarry, he went to his daughter first. The 10-year-old said she needed more time to get to know her father's bride to be, so he waited. When Peyton said she was ready, Doug proposed. That same night, Peyton wrote a letter welcoming her new mom. The love between Erin, Peyton, Doug, and his new wife, Cheryl, was so authentic it made us all rejoice when we witnessed it on the show. That's what love does: It fills you up, mends the tattered and broken spaces in your spirit. It makes you feel whole. Not everybody has an Erin Kramp in her life, but love is all around and ever available. I know this for sure.

Sometimes in the thick of life, when my call list is longer than the day and people are lined up waiting for meeting after meeting, I just stop. And look at a tree. A flower. The sun reflecting off the window. And I remember love is available. I inhale it, exhale, and get back to work.

I recently reread an e-mail from Mattie, dated 11/22/2001. He was 11 at the time. He'd recently seen *The Color Purple* (the movie), and he wrote, "This year my mom and I are both wearing purple for Thanksgiving. I'm thankful for things like safety during terrorism, for food and material things like that, and for the people in the circle of my life, like my mom and Sandy, the Moxes upstairs, and you. For things that God has given us, just because we are loved. Purple. Gentle breezes. Crickets. Shooting stars. Laughter. Feathers. I'm thankful that things *are,* so while *we* are, we can have gifts every day if we just open our hearts and spirits to them."

Words of wisdom from an 11-year-old.

Look around, feel the love. **O**

Doug and Erin Kramp show Oprah a tape Erin was making during the last years of her life for her daughter, Peyton, age 6.

WHAT I KNOW FOR SURE: 2005

"Once you decide what you want, you make a commitment to that decision."

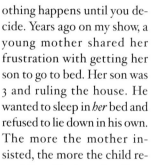

Nothing happens until you decide. Years ago on my show, a young mother shared her frustration with getting her son to go to bed. Her son was 3 and ruling the house. He wanted to sleep in *her* bed and refused to lie down in his own. The more the mother insisted, the more the child resisted—yelling, screaming, and literally dropping from exhaustion.

We showed a tape of the two of them wrestling it out. When our expert, Dr. Stanley Turecki, finished watching, he said something that made the hairs on my arm stand up: "Nothing happens until you decide." The reason her 3-year-old didn't sleep in his own bed was that the mother had not decided it would happen. When she did, the child would go to his bed. He might cry and scream and rant until he fell asleep, but he would eventually realize that his mother had made up her mind.

Well, I knew he was speaking about a 3-year-old, but I also knew for sure that this brilliant piece of advice applied to many other aspects of life: Relationships. Career moves. Weight issues. Everything depends on your decisions.

For years I was stuck in a weight trap, yo-yoing up and down the scale. I made a decision two years ago to stop wishing, praying, and wanting, wanting, wanting to be better. Instead I figured out what it would really take to improve my life. Then I decided to do it.

When you don't know what to do, my best advice is to do nothing until clarity comes. Getting still, being able to hear your own voice and not the voices of the world, quickens clarity. Once you decide what you want, you make a commitment to that decision. One of my favorite quotes is from mountaineer W.H. Murray:

Until one is committed there is hesitancy, the chance to draw back, always ineffectiveness. Concerning all acts of initiative (and creation), there is one elementary truth, the ignorance of which kills countless ideas and splendid plans: that the moment one definitely commits oneself, then Providence moves, too. All sorts of things occur to help one that would never otherwise have occurred. A whole stream of events issues from the decision, raising in one's favor all manner of unforeseen incidents and meetings and material assistance, which no man could have dreamt would have come his way. I have learned a deep respect for one of Goethe's couplets: "Whatever you can do, or dream you can, begin it. / Boldness has genius, power, and magic in it."

Make a decision and watch your life move forward. **O**

"I feel my greatest work is yet to come."

Getting older is the best thing that ever happened to me. I wake up every morning rejoicing that I'm still here with an opportunity to begin again and be better.

I awaken to a morning prayer of thanks posted on my bathroom wall from Marianne Williamson's book *Illuminata*. I think about all those who didn't make it to 51 and were claimed to a different calling before they realized the beauty and wonder and majesty of life on earth. Or—in some ways worse—those who reach this age without an appreciation for the value of each breath.

I know for sure that every day holds within it the gift of seeing the world through the Creator's eyes. Some days the challenges of daily existence weigh on our ability to see it, but today I could. Watching the Maui sun rising, turning the sky the color of newly ripened peaches, I knew that I was connected to a power greater than myself—that I need only slow down and get still enough to let the flow that is all life carry me to the next level.

After 20 years of doing shows, I continue to seek to be used for a purpose greater than I know. I consider it a living blessing and privilege to have this opportunity to be in people's homes every day, to uplift, encourage, inform, and entertain. I know this is a calling for me, but I feel the greater work is yet to come. I'm feeling more like myself than ever. What Maya Angelou predicted was true: Your 50s are everything you were meant to be.

I find I have little tolerance now for pettiness and superficial pursuits. There's a wealth that has nothing to do with dollars, that comes from the perspective and wisdom of paying attention to your life. It has everything to teach you. And what I know for sure is that the joy of learning well is the greatest reward. **O**

WHAT I KNOW FOR SURE: 2004

"It's more fun to give than to receive."

S o now we enter the proclaimed season of giving that stirs anxiety in the hearts of many. Feeling overwhelmed with holiday angst is accepted as the norm—but I guarantee it doesn't have to be that way, even if you have ten children and 55 other relatives who are all expecting something special from you. Remember, you're in control. If you've always been frenzied to the point that just hearing "Deck the Halls" makes you want to pull out your hair one strand at a time, make a new plan this year. You create your own life, moment to moment, day to day. Just because every bus, every storefront, and every jingle has a bell in it doesn't mean you have to succumb to the hype. You can choose to go deeper and fuller, and give only from the place that is most meaningful and fulfilling to you.

We've all heard that it's more blessed to give than to receive. Well, I know for sure that it's also a lot more fun. Nothing makes me happier than a gift well given and joyfully received. Over the years, I've given some fantastic ones. I can honestly say that every gift I've ever given has brought at least as much happiness to me as it has to the person I've given it to. That's one of the reasons I've never been stressed over the holidays, even when I had no money. I give as I feel. Throughout the year, that may mean mailing a thoughtful, handwritten note to someone who didn't expect it. Or sending a great new lotion I just discovered, or delivering a book of poetry with a pretty bow. It doesn't matter what the *thing* is; what matters is how much of yourself goes into the giving, so that when the gift is gone, the spirit of you lingers.

My friend Geneviève left a white bowl of bright yellow lemons with their stems and leaves, freshly picked from her backyard and tied with a green ribbon, on my front doorstep one day with a note that said "Good morning." The whole presentation was so beautiful in its simplicity that long after the lemons shriveled, I felt the spirit of the gift every time I passed the place where the bowl had been set. I now keep a bowl filled with lemons to remind me of that "Good morning."

This season on my show, I wanted to make giving a theme. What I most hope to give people is a chance to do better and be better. The first show we did, handing out all those keys to new Pontiac G6s, was the most fun I'd ever had on TV. But before the great giveaway, I sat meditating in my darkened closet, trying to stay in the moment and not get anxious about all the surprises I knew were to come. It was important to me to have people in the audience who really needed new cars, so that all the excitement would have meaning. I wanted the force of the gift to be about not just the cars but the essence of what it means to share what you have. I prayed for that, sitting in the dark with my shoes and handbags. Then I walked downstairs to the studio, and pandemonium hit. Delight at a thousand decibels! My prayers were answered: Everybody felt blessed. I felt blessed being able to experience that moment with so many people—276 in the audience and everyone watching who shared in their joy.

As my friend Maya Angelou says, "When you learn, teach. When you get, give." Give so that all your gifts are extensions of you. ◐

The great car giveaway aired September 13, 2004.

"A little restoration goes a long way."

I remember the first time, about a decade ago, that a psychologist on my show urged women to prioritize their giving and to put themselves at the top of the list. She was nearly booed off the stage.

"Why, the very idea of putting yourself first is what we were raised not to do," an audience member retorted. "How can you be there for your family if you're thinking about yourself?" said another. "That's just pure selfishness."

In defense of my guest, I tried to explain: "She didn't say abandon your children and go wild in the streets. She said give to yourself first so you'll be full enough to fill another's cup till it runneth over." The audience wasn't buying it. That's because as women we've been programmed to sacrifice everything in the name of what is good and right for everyone else. Then if there's an inch left over, maybe we can have a piece of that.

We need to deprogram ourselves. I know for sure that you can't give what you don't have. If you allow yourself to be depleted to the point where your emotional and spiritual tank is empty and you're running on fumes of habit, everybody loses. Especially you.

I never thought I'd hear myself say it, but I've grown to enjoy lifting weights, and I've learned from doing it. I relish the sense of strength and discipline that comes when the muscles are forced to resist. I've tried varying schedules—lifting every day, every other day, two days on and a day off. The every day approach was the least effective. I get the best strengthening results when I give myself a break. Constant lifting begins to break down the muscle tissue.

The same is true with mind and spirit. Without giving yourself a chance to reenergize, you begin to break down all the connective fibers of your life. I used to just give myself Sundays off. Now I'm scheduling downtime in the midst of everything—and "everything" includes building a house in Hawaii, working on an ABC movie (*Their Eyes Were Watching God*)—and, oh yeah, my day job. Keeping it all straight was beginning to feel a little stressful. So I had a sit-down with my vigilant assistant, Libby, and explained that just because I have ten free minutes on my calendar doesn't mean I want to fill them. "Let's practice what my philosophy preaches," I said. That means breathing space has to become part of my daily routine.

So instead of having people lined up outside my office after the first show—I tape two a day—I do nothing for at least ten minutes. Sometimes I just rub my dog Sophie's belly and throw a ball down the hall to my other dog, Solomon. Or I take a stroll through the Harpo café to literally see what's cookin'. Other times I just sit still at my desk. The change has worked wonders. I have more energy, and I'm in a better mood for the second show and all the business that comes afterward.

A little restoration goes a long way. Now that I have the summer off to sit under the oaks reading, napping, writing, and thinking, I know for sure it's time well spent. There's not even a twinge of guilt about having no plans, no schedule. I'm refilling my tank so that by fall, when the new season begins, I'll be fired up and ready for whatever is to come. Fully restored. **O**

WHAT I KNOW FOR SURE: 2003

"Trust in this: You'll handle whatever shake-up the next moment brings when you get to it."

The one time I lost my balance before a show was the day of my live interview with Michael Jackson in 1993. In the weeks leading up to that prime-time conversation, the hype had reached dizzying heights—Michael, who hadn't given a television interview in 14 years, had agreed to talk with me. I wanted our exchange to be spontaneous, so I hadn't even prepared questions.

But a few minutes before the cameras rolled, a wave of fear rose up inside me. My mind raced. *What should my first question be? Will I go completely blank during the interview?* What if I don't recover? When Michael arrived and we prepared to go on-air, I was so tense that the first question I asked him was "How nervous are you?" He looked right at me and said, "I'm not nervous at all." That simple exchange was enough to transport me back to the present: If he could stand before the world and tell his story without fear, why should I be afraid? I could feel the tension drain from my body as I drew in a breath and began what I'd done a hundred times before, trusting the energy of our conversation to carry me from one moment to the next.

Every challenge we take on has the power to shake us—to knock us to our knees. And yet, what's even more disconcerting than the jolt itself is our fear that we won't withstand it. When we feel the ground beneath us shifting, we panic. We forget everything we know and allow fear to freeze us. Just the thought of what could happen is enough to throw us off-balance.

What I know for sure is that the only way to endure the quake is to adjust your stance. You can't avoid the daily tremors. They come with being alive. These experiences are really gifts that force us to step to the right or left in search of a new center of gravity. Don't fight them. Just find a different way to stand.

Balance lives in the present. The surest way to lose your footing is to focus on what dreadful things might happen. When you feel the earth moving, bring yourself back to the now. You'll handle whatever shake-up the next moment brings when you get to it. In this moment, you're still breathing. In this moment, you've survived. In this moment, you've found a new place to move your feet so you can step onto higher ground. **O**

"For me, doubt means don't. Don't move. Don't answer. Don't rush forward."

In my early years of television, I was often overwhelmed by people's view of me as a benevolent caregiver. Some would spend their last dime on a bus ticket to get to me, children would run away from home, abused women would leave their husbands and just show up at the doorstep of my studio, all hoping I'd help. In those days, I'd spend a lot of energy trying to get a girl back to her family or hanging on the phone with someone who was threatening to kill herself. Every week I was bombarded by organizations that wanted me to rescue them financially. I found myself writing check after check, and over time that wore on my spirit. I was so busy trying to give all that everyone else needed me to offer that I lost touch with what I had a genuine desire to give. I finally had to stop and consider what I believe is one of the most important questions a woman can ask herself: *What do I really want—and what is my spirit telling me is the best way to proceed?*

My answer eventually led me toward my passion for serving women and girls. I have a deep understanding of what it's like to be a girl who has suffered abuse or lived in poverty, and I believe that education is the door to freedom, the rainbow that leads to the pot of gold. I began to realize that in order to be most effective, I had to be extremely focused on using my time, my concern, my resources, and my compassion to uplift a generation of courageous women who own themselves and know their strength. I knew I couldn't save every dying child or intervene in every case of abuse. None of us can. But once I got

clear about what I most wanted to give, much of what didn't line up with that intention naturally fell away.

Those years of becoming focused taught me a powerful lesson about tuning in to my gut—that inkling that says, *Hold on. Something's not right here. Please pause and make an adjustment.* For me, doubt often means don't. Don't move. Don't answer. Don't rush forward. When I'm mired in confusion about what the next step should be, when I'm asked to do something for which I feel little enthusiasm, that's my sign to just stop—to get still until my instincts give me the go-ahead. I believe that uncertainty is really my spirit's way of whispering, *I'm in flux. I can't decide for you. Something is off-balance here.* I take that as a cue to re-center myself before making a decision—a reminder from above to wait for confirmation. When the universe compels me toward the best path to take, it never leaves me with "Maybe," "Should I?" or even "Perhaps." I always know for sure when it's telling me to proceed—because everything inside me rises up to reverberate "Yes!" **O**

WHAT I KNOW FOR SURE: 2003

"Become the change you want to see— those are words I live by."

Some people might find it ironic that I've never been much of a TV watcher. Aside from old reruns of *The Andy Griffith Show,* I stopped regularly tuning in to sitcoms the night *Mary Tyler Moore* went off the air. At home, I skip the late-night news because I don't want to take in all that negative energy right before sleep— and on vacation, I seldom have a TV in my bedroom. On days when I do flip through the channels, it's almost certain I'll find at least one show that involves sexual exploitation or violence against women.

In my early days on-air, I was guilty of doing irresponsible television without even knowing it—all in the name of "entertainment." More than a decade ago, my staff and I booked a husband caught in an adulterous sex scandal, and right there on our stage before millions of viewers, the wife heard for the first time that her partner had been unfaithful. It's a moment I have never forgotten: The humiliation and despair on that woman's face made me ashamed of myself for putting her in that position. Right then I decided I'd never again be part of a show that demeans, embarrasses, or diminishes another human being. I replaced the "If it bleeds, it leads" news philosophy with an intention that still guides me—to use the medium of television for its higher good. Once the lightbulb came on for me that day, my calling became to create shows that encourage and inspire as much as they entertain—television that leaves guests with their dignity and helps us all see our lives in a different way.

I know for sure that what we dwell on is who we become—as a woman thinks, so she is. If we absorb hour upon hour of images and messages that don't reflect our magnificence, it's no wonder we walk around feeling drained of our life force. If we tune in to dozens of acts of brutality every week, it shouldn't surprise us that our children see violence as an acceptable way to resolve conflict.

Become the change you want to see—those are words I live by. I don't know how many years I'll be blessed with the privilege of reaching millions each day, but my prayer is that I'll use my energy never to belittle but to uplift. Never to devastate but to rebuild. Never to misguide but to light the way so that all of us can stand on higher ground.

Oprah

ABOUT THE CONTRIBUTORS

MARTHA BECK writes a monthly column for *O*. She is a life coach and has written six books, including *Steering by Starlight* (Rodale).

NATE BERKUS is the host of *The Nate Berkus Show* and was a regular contributor to *The Oprah Winfrey Show*. His book *Home Rules: Transform the Place You Live Into a Place You'll Love* (Hyperion) is a *New York Times* bestseller.

ADAM GLASSMAN, *O*'s creative director, also appeared on *The Oprah Winfrey Show* as Oprah's resident style expert.

BOB GREENE is an exercise physiologist, certified personal trainer, and founder of thebestlife.com. He is the author of bestselling books including *The Best Life Diet* (Simon & Shuster) and *20 Years Younger: Look Younger, Feel Younger, Be Younger!* (Little, Brown and Company).

LISA KOGAN is *O*'s writer-at-large and the author of *Someone Will Be with You Shortly: Notes from a Perfectly Imperfect Life* (HarperStudio).

PHILLIP C. MCGRAW, PhD, hosts the daily television talk show *Dr. Phil*. He is the author of six bestselling books, including *Real Life* (Free Press). He writes a monthly column for *O*.

VALERIE MONROE, *O*'s beauty director, is the author of *In the Weather of the Heart* (Doubleday), a memoir.

SUZE ORMAN, host of CNBC's *The Suze Orman Show*, is the author of several books on personal finance, including *The Money Class: Learn to Create Your New American Dream* (Random House). She writes a monthly column for *O*.

MEHMET OZ, MD, is the host of *The Dr. Oz Show* and a daily Sirius XM radio show. He has co-authored six bestsellers, including *You: The Owner's Manual* (Collins). He is vice-chair and professor of surgery at Columbia University and directs the Cardiovascular Institute and Complementary Medicine Program at New York Presbyterian Hospital.

PHOTOGRAPHY AND ART CREDITS

Cover Ruven Afanador

2 Ruven Afanador; **5 (Oprah)** Cliff Watts; **6-8** Ruven Afanador; **10** George Burns; **12** Brigitte Lacombe; **13-14** George Burns; **15** Vincient Nichols; **16** Kirby Bumpus; **18** George Burns; **19-20** Sam Jones; **21** Gayle King; **22** Art Streiber; **24-41** Rob Howard; **42 left** Everett Collection, **center** Tyler Perry, **right** Tyler Perry Studios; **43-49** Rob Howard; **50 top left** George Burns, **top right** Rob Howard, **center left** Edwards family; **51 left** Alex Brandon/AP, **center** Elizabeth Edwards, **right** Robert Willett/Raleigh News & Observer; **53** Rob Howard; **57** Timothy White; **58 left** Phil Loftus/Capital Pictures, **right** Castle Rock Entertainment/Everett Collection; **59 left** John Dolan, **right** Mark Seliger; **63** Firooz Zahedi; **65** Bettmann/Corbis; **66** courtesy of Barbra Streisand; **71** Kwaku Alston; **72 top right** Globe, **center right** David Redfern/Retna; **75 top left** Gunter/mtvp. net, **top right** Rune Hellestad/Corbis, **bottom left** David Bennett; **78** George Lange; **80** College of William and Mary; **83** Charles Ommanney; **85** George Holtz; **87** Globe; **89** Photofest; **94** Ben Goldstein/Studio D; **96** Jeffrey Westbrook/Studio D; **97 top right** Terry Vine/Getty, **bottom** Getty Food Collection; **98** Sabine Scheckel/Getty; **99** Dougal Waters/Getty, **100 top left** Jack Wild/Getty, **bottom right** Ariel Skelley/ Getty; **101** Getty Food Collection; **102** Lara Harwood; **104** Ben Goldstein/Studio D; **105** McKibillo; **106** Ben Goldstein/ Studio D; **107** Pete Gardner/Getty; **108** Ben Goldstein/Studio D; **109** Levi Brown; **110** Getty; **111** Henrik Stone/Getty; **113** Ben Goldstein/Studio D; **114** Jon Feingersh/Getty; **116** Joan Allen/Simon & Schuster; **119** George Burns; **123-124** Jesus Ayala/Studio D; **125-126** James Wojcik; **128-135** Blaise Hayward;

136 Robert Trachtenberg; **138** Jeffrey Westbrook/Studio D; **139** Janis Christie/ Getty; **140** Ichiro/Getty; **144** Robert Trachtenberg; **152** Marc Royce; **155** Steve Cole/Getty; **156-161** Robert Trachtenberg; **163** C.W. Lawrence; **166** Gregg Segal; **170** Robert Trachtenberg; **174** Levi Brown; **175** Istvan Banyai; **182** Chris Eckert/ Studio D; **185-187** Barry Blitt; **188** Levi Brown; **191** David Pohl; **194** Seth Wenig/ AP; **197** Julien Pacaud; **202** Guy Billout; **205** Tatsuro Kiuchi; **208** Sean McCabe; **211** Rasputin; **214** Chaloner Woods/ Hulton Archive; **217** Fredrik Broden; **220** Michael Edwards; **223-225** John Ritter; **228** Kagan McLeod; **230** John Ritter; **231** Talisman Brolin; **233** Kagan McLeod; **236-240** John Ritter; **242** Lisa Romerein/ Icon International; **244** Jeffrey Westbrook/ Studio D; **245** Sarah Kehoe; **248-255** Fernando Bengoechea; **256** Robert Trachtenberg; **258-259** Ben Goldstein/ Studio D; **260 left** Ben Goldstein/Studio D, **right** Marko Metzinger/Studio D; **261 top left, top right, bottom right** Marko Metzinger/Studio D, **bottom left** Ben Goldstein/Studio D; **262 bottom left** Ben Goldstein/Studio D, **top and bottom right** Marko Metzinger/Studio D; **263** Marko Metzinger/Studio D; **264 top left and right** Marko Metzinger/ Studio D, **bottom left** Gregor Halenda; **265 bottom left** Gregor Halenda, **top right** Marko Metzinger/Studio D; **266** Marko Metzinger/Studio D; **267 top left and right** Marko Metzinger/Studio D, **bottom right** Ben Goldstein/Studio D; **267** Ben Goldstein/Studio D; **268 top left (clothes)** Ben Goldstein/Studio D **(shoes)** Kevin Sweeney/Studio D, **bottom right** Marko Metzinger/Studio D; **269 bottom left** Ben Goldstein/ Studio D, **top right** Marko Metzinger/

Studio D; **270** Ben Goldstein/Studio D; **271** Marko Metzinger/Studio D; **272** Marko Metzinger/Studio D; **273 top left** Marko Metzinger/Studio D, **top right** Jeffrey Westbrook/Studio D, **bottom right** Lara Robby; **274-275** Marko Metzinger/Studio D; **276** Robert Trachtenberg; **278** Shinichi Maruyama/ Getty; **279** Mark Hooper; **281** Donna Alberico; **282** Louise Dahl-Wolfe; **284-288** Henry Leutwyler; **289** Gentl & Hyers; **291-292** David Lewis Taylor; **293** Patric Shaw/CLM/trunkarchive.com; **294** Daniel Gabbay; **295-297** David Lewis Taylor

INDEX

A

acupuncture, 103, 104, 114
age, 76, 77, 98, 309
    feeling younger than your, 280
    and finances, 142
    signs of, 279
    spots, 286
alcohol, 97, 98, 103, 113, 122, 125
allergies
    nasal irrigation to relieve, 114
    neti pot, 114
Alzheimer's disease, 114
anger, 45, 46, 165, 177, 178
antidepressants, 102, 115
    side effects of, 102
    taking during pregnancy, 115
antioxidants, 278
anxiety, 102, 104
aromatherapy, 103

B

balance, 28, 59, 89
Beck, Martha, 182-219
    attraction, 194-196
    boundaries, setting, 211-213
        Test Your Boundaries, 213
    deep practice, 206, 207
    denial, 198, 199
    Down syndrome, 189
    dualisms, 191-193
    empathy, 208-210
    families of origin (acronym: FOO), 212
    5 Best Pieces of Advice, 185-187
    kayak, 188-190
    Kitchen Sink, 205, 207
    narcissists, 211
    projection, 214-216
    right brain, 205-207
    self-sabotage, 203
    stop fearing and resisting, 185, 186
    10 Rules I've Unlearned, 183-184
    trust-o-meter, 197-201
        The Trust Test, 200, 201
    Wildly Improbable Goals (WIGs), 217-219
    wrong, it's good to be, 186-187
Berkus, Nate, 242-255
    clutter-free living, 246
    disorganization, 254
    dream bedroom, 251, 253, 254
    Ellin LaVar, 250-254
    photographs, 244, 246, 247, 254
    start collecting, 243
    stuff, 245-247
    10 Inspiring Ideas for Your Home, 243-244
biofeedback, 103
birth control pills, 103, 113
blind date, 67, 78, 82
bodhisattva—enlightened being, 37
Botox, 280, 281, 290
bunions, 115

C

cancer, 100, 112, 122, 235
    and using a microwave, 114
    breast, 48, 50, 51, 53, 55, 113, 307
    ovarian, 133
chronic kidney disease (CKD), 112
The Clothes Diet, 135
clutter, 140, 144
college, paying for, 146, 147, 148, 153, 154
communication, 38, 81, 99, 178, 179
    Six Rules of Talking and Listening, 168-169
    talking to your doctor, 107
community, 36, 37
compassion, 38, 40
connect, 21, 60, 301, 306
courage, 21, 22, 70

D

dance lessons, 98
deep listening, 37, 38
depression, 102, 104, 115, 174
    misconceptions about, 102
diabetes, 110, 112, 115, 130
    and erectile dysfunction, 114
dreams, pursuing, 21, 42, 44, 45, 65, 73
Dr. Oz, 94-115. *See also* health.
    Ask Dr. Oz, 113-115
    fibromyalgia, 104
    5 Secrets of "Waist Loss," 101
    4 Ways to Keep Your Brain Sharp, 98
    headaches, frequent, 103
        4 approaches to treating, 103
    leave shoes at the door, 99
    lower back pain, 105
    medicine cabinet must-haves, 108
    9 Ways to Improve Your Family's Health, 99, 100
    7 Ways to Reduce Stress, 97
    talking to your doctor, 107
    10 Things I Know For Sure, 95-96
    YOU: On a Diet, 101
Dr. Phil, 156-181
    being assertive, 161
    being who you are, 165
    bullies in the workplace, 176, 177
    change your behavior, 159, 164-165
    fighting in relationships, 172
        constructively, 172, 173
    holidays, 162-163
    live greener, 158
    makeover, mental, 158-159
    reciprocity, 158
    saying no, 174
    self-destructive behavior, dealing with, 180
    self-worth in career, 180
    sex in marriage, 179
    sex, talking about, 170-171
    Six Rules of Talking and Listening, 168-169
    The 10-Step Life Renewal Plan, 157-158

E

eating
    breakfast, 121
    comfort food, 109
    daily cut-off time for, 122, 125
    8 Ways to Curb Your Appetite, 127
    emotional, 127, 134
    food diary, 124
    fresh vegetables, 98
    meals together, 65, 74, 99
    mindful, 101
education, 313
endorphins, 97, 123
"Engaged Buddhism," 34
erectile dysfunction, 114
exercise, 97, 102, 109, 117, 124, 127, 133, 134, 278
    and building muscle, 101
    and menopause, 115

Nonexercise activity thermogenesis
(NEAT), 111
Oprah's Boot Camp, 125
to relieve mild depression, 102
specific, 132
strength training, 117, 125
stretching, 100, 125
for treating fibromyalgia, 104
for treating headaches, 103
TV training, 111

F

fear, 11, 21, 22, 68, 74, 137, 203, 312
Federal Trade Commission, 147
fiber, 101, 113
fibromyalgia, 104
symptoms of, 104
treating, 104
FICO credit score, 138, 142
auto insurance premium, 142
and job applications, 142
financial security, 91, 137
friendship, 17

G

Glassman, Adam, 256-275
Adam's Swimsuit Commandments, 271
black, wearing in summer, 270
dressing for the holidays, 274-275
dressing for the office, 272-273
dressing too young, 264
How to Shine (Not Shock) at the Office
Party, 275
jeans, 264, 268, 270
jewelry, 266
nude legs, 262
personal shopper, 267
shoes, 261, 264, 265, 273, 275
slacks that fit, 263
sophistication, 263
10 Items You Can Never Go Wrong
With, 257, 258
Goals (WIGs), Wildly Improbable, 217-219
God, 31, 46, 47, 302
Google, 189
grateful, 30, 36, 64
gratitude journal, 28, 30
Greene, Bob, 116-135
The Best Life Diet plan, 121-124
The Activity Scale, 122
The Basics, 126
8 Ways to Curb Your Appetite, 127
The Hunger Scale, 127

Bob Greene's Total Body Makeover, 130
Oprah's Boot Camp, 125
10 Biggest Health Mistakes, 117, 118
10 pounds to lose, 128-135

H

happiness, 36, 39, 61, 68, 72, 77, 130, 301
misconceptions about, 102
headaches
migraines, 104, 110
treating frequent, 103
health. *See also* Dr. Oz.
The Best Life Diet plan, 121-124
erectile dysfunction, 114
5 pains that could be a sign of big
trouble, 110
staying well, 109
test, 106
heart attack, 110, 112, 133, 222
heart disease, 113
holidays, 162-163
homeopathy, 103
humiliation, 30, 43, 74, 314

I

identity theft, 140
"infotainment," 86
Internet web sites
annualcreditreport.com, 138
asch.net, 134
bankrate.com, 146
bankrate.com/calculators/mortgages/
mortgage-calculator.aspx, 143
charitynavigator.org, 138
creditcardconnection.org, 142
creditcards.com/calculators/balance-
transfer.php, 147
depositaccounts.com, 149
domini.com, 153
epa.gov/radon/whereyoulive.html, 100
irs.gov/pub/irs-pdf/p552.pdf, 141
manualnguide.com, 141
oprah.com, 130
oprah.com/omagextras, 101, 104
paxworld.com, 153
selectquote.com, 149
serve.gov, 100
servicenation.org, 100
ssa.gov, 140
suzeorman.com, 149
suzeorman.com/finclutter, 141
thebestlife.com, 124
usersmanualguide.com, 141

radonzone.com, 100
interrupting, 60
investing. *See* Orman, Suze.

J

job-hunting, 138
job interview, what to wear, 272

K

karma, 23, 40, 74, 76
Katrina, 18, 307
kindness, 18, 68, 186
Kogan, Lisa, 220-241
creative solution, 230-231
a group person, 225-227
massive insecurity, 238-239
miracles, 233-235
online dating profile, 227-229
Oz, Mehmet, 223
open-heart surgery, 224
questions that must never be
asked, 236-237
talking-myself-down points, 241
10 Hard-Won Pieces of Advice, 221
Eva Zeisel, 231, 232
kosher food, 115

L

laugh, 97
leave shoes at the door, 99
London, Stacy, 130-135
The Clothes Diet, 135
*Dress Your Best: The Complete Guide to
Finding the Style That's Right for
Your Body*, 130, 135
love, 43, 44, 73, 74, 77, 89, 91, 209, 307
loyal, 73

M

mammogram, 106
marriage, 28, 29, 61, 68, 77, 83, 165, 176
and finances, 148, 155
living together before, 178
sex in, 179
meditation, 36, 39, 40, 97, 102, 210
bubble, 301
menopause, 115, 133
metabolism, 121, 125, 131
miracles, 12, 36, 42, 233-235
Monroe, Valerie, 276-297
Appreciator of All Things Beautiful, 283
Ask Val, 289-297
Bobbi Brown, 285-288, 293
Makeup Facelift 285

no-surgery solutions, 285, 286, 287, 288
Botox, 280, 281, 290
concealer, 290, 292, 293
drugstores, 278, 296
eyebrows, 294
face moisturizers, 291
foundation, 293
haircut, 278
hands and neck, 278, 295
lipstick, 296
nails, 295
retinoids, 278, 290
self-tanner, 278
smile, 278
10 Secrets Every Beauty Editor Knows That You Should, Too, 277
undereye discoloration, 287, 290, 292

N

negativity, 45, 46, 132, 158

O

oils, canola and olive, 122
The O Interviews
Elizabeth Edwards, 48-55
Thich Nhat Hanh, 32-40
Tyler Perry, 41-47
Jerry Seinfeld, 56-61
Jon Stewart, 78-84
Barbra Streisand, 62-69
Tina Turner, 70-77
Barbara Walters, 85-91
You: Ten O readers, 24-31
Oprah's Boot Camp, 125
organic food for pets, 100
Orman, Suze, 136-155
bankruptcy, 148, 149, 153
being organized, 139-141, 144
budget, realistic, 144, 145
credit cards, 137, 142, 146, 150, 155
interest rates, 147
statements, how long to keep, 141
credit unions, 142
debit card, 142
debt settlement firm, 147
emergency savings fund, 138, 142, 143, 149
financial blind spots, 142
financial planning, 152, 153, 154, 155
forever docs, 140, 141
401(k), 142, 143
borrowing from, 143

Get Smart About College Spending, 155
healthcare power of attorney, 138
investing, 145, 152
"sin stocks," 153
socially responsible investing (SRI), 153
Keep it or Not?, 141
life insurance, 143, 147, 149
mutual funds, 142, 145
online bill pay, 141
prenuptial agreement, 154
retirement, 138, 142, 143, 145
fund contribution matching, 147
Roth IRA, 147
self-employed, 137, 148
special needs trust, 149
10 Priceless Strategies for the Next Decade, 137, 138
Tips for Going Paperless, 140
wedding, paying for, 154, 155
"What's Your Money Personality?" (quiz), 150-151
will, 138, 149
overeating, 133, 134
OWN, television network, 11, 302, 303
oxytocin, 97

P

parenting, 81, 160, 180
perfectionist, 62, 67, 69, 202
and the holidays, 163
pets, 100
physical abuse, 42, 44, 70, 73, 74, 209
plastic surgery, 67, 70, 77, 279, 280
pleasers, 211, 212
popular culture, 194
power, 302
pregnancy, taking antidepressants during, 115
privacy, honoring, 175

Q

quitting smoking, 114, 181

R

radon, 100
rejection, 65, 79
respect, 46, 54, 87
retirement. *See* Orman, Suze.

S

satire, 78
self-esteem, 74, 79, 166
self-image, 128, 130, 131, 132
and self-sabotage, 130
serotonin, 102

sleep, enough, 96, 127
social anxiety disorder, 115
socializing, 97
spirituality, 76, 165, 303
sunscreen, 100, 277
support, 61, 227

T

tea, 32, 36, 38, 109
therapy, 102, 115
time, 19, 31, 86, 90, 91, 157
alone time, 166, 167
traveling, 86, 259
The Perfect Trip Kit, 259
snack when, 259
trust, rebuild, 52, 54

U

unemployed, 143, 203
unfaithful, 48, 51, 52, 53

V

Vitamin D, 109
volunteering, 100, 163

W

walk, 101, 109
water, drinking, 99, 101, 109, 122, 277
weight gain, 13, 121, 308
after menopause, 115
as a side effect of antidepressants, 102
"cookie diet," 118
hunger scale, 127
support network, 118
weight loss, 121
The Best Life Diet plan, 121
The Clothes Diet, 135
self-hypnosis, 134
What I Know for Sure
Elizabeth Edwards, 55
Thich Nhat Hanh, 40
Oprah, 10-23, 300-314
Tyler Perry, 47
Barbra Streisand, 64
Barbara Walters, 91
whole grains, 122, 123, 124
workaholic, 90
writing, 42, 43, 44, 45, 50, 55, 69, 86

Published by Time Home Entertainment Inc.
135 West 50th Street, New York, NY 10020

ISBN-13: 978-0-8487-3485-5
ISBN-10: 0-8487-3485-8
Library of Congress Control Number: 2011934607
Printed in the United States of America
First printing 2011

To order more books, call 1-800-765-6400 or 1-800-491-0551.

O, The Oprah Magazine
Founder and Editorial Director: Oprah Winfrey
Editor in Chief: Susan Casey
Editor at Large: Gayle King
Editor: Brooke Kosofsky Glassberg
Production Assistant: M. Ryan Purdy
Associate Photo Editor: Kathy Nguyen
Assistant Editor: Rachel Mount

HEARST BOOKS
VP, Publisher: Jacqueline Deval

OXMOOR HOUSE
VP, Publisher: Jim Childs
Director, Direct Marketing: Laura Sappington
Editorial Director: Susan Dobbs
Brand Manager: Victoria Alfonso
Senior Editor: Rebecca Brennan
Managing Editor: Laurie S. Herr

TIME HOME ENTERTAINMENT INC.
Publisher: Richard Fraiman
Vice-President, Strategy & Business Development: Steven Sandonato
Executive Director, Marketing Services: Carol Pittard
Executive Director, Retail & Special Sales: Tom Mifsud
Director, New Product Development: Peter Harper
Director of Marketing and Communication: Malati Chavali
Associate Counsel: Helen Wan

O's Best Advice Ever!
Editor: Susan Hernandez Ray
Project Editor: Emily Chappell
Senior Production Manager: Greg A. Amason

CONTRIBUTORS
Designer: Suzanne Noli
Compositor: Carol Loria
Copy Editors: Norma Butterworth-McKittrick, Carmine B. Loper
Proofreaders: Jacqueline Giovanelli, Barry Smith
Indexer: Mary Ann Laurens
Interns: Laura Hoxworth, Alison Loughman, Caitlin Watzke